The Unofficial Guide to the Art of Jack T. Chick

Jack T. Chick

Chick Tracts,
Crusader Comics,
and
Battle Cry
Newspapers

Kurt Kuersteiner

Schiffer Publishing Ltd

4880 Lower Valley Road, Atglen, PA 19310 USA

Dedication

In Memory of my brother, Boone
A crusader for the Rule of Law.

WARNING!

If you have no sense of humor about controversial matters, we urge you to avoid this book. Our intent is not to offend or pick on any particular group, but to discuss in an entertaining way issues that some people take *very seriously*. These issues include religion, sexual orientation, conspiracies, and much more. **This is not a politically correct book.** (Especially the *Reviews* chapters.) It's difficult to enjoy Chick's work if you get upset every time he makes you laugh at someone else's expense. We also have fun at Chick's expense. These are, after all, *comics*, and "funny books" are meant to be funny. So relax and enjoy yourself. If you're like many readers, the person you'll get upset with the most is yourself—for not collecting Chick tracts sooner!

"Chick tract" is a registered trademark of Chick Publications, Inc. Chick Publications did not authorize this book nor approve of any of the information contained herein. This book is derived from the author's independent research.

Published by Schiffer Publishing Ltd.
4880 Lower Valley Road
Atglen, PA 19310
Phone: (610) 593-1777; Fax: (610) 593-2002
E-mail: Info@schifferbooks.com

For the largest selection of fine reference books on this and related subjects, please visit our web site at **www.schifferbooks.com**
We are always looking for people to write books on new and related subjects. If you have an idea for a book please contact us at the above address.

This book may be purchased from the publisher.
Include $3.95 for shipping.
Please try your bookstore first.
You may write for a free catalog.

In Europe, Schiffer books are distributed by
Bushwood Books
6 Marksbury Ave.
Kew Gardens
Surrey TW9 4JF England
Phone: 44 (0) 20 8392-8585; Fax: 44 (0) 20 8392-9876
E-mail: info@bushwoodbooks.co.uk
Free postage in the U.K., Europe; air mail at cost.

Designed by Mark David Bowyer
Type set in Stymie Lt BT/Humanist 521 BT

ISBN: 0-7643-1892-6
Printed in China
1 2 3 4

Contents

It began in the early 1960s. While protesters pushed America to the Left, an unassuming artist used his lunch hour to draw right-wing Christian fundamentalist cartoons. And his target was *the world.*

His name is Jack T. Chick. Almost every American has seen his provocative tracts. They're the pocket-sized religious comics which mysteriously appear in bathrooms, airports, malls, and virtually everywhere else. He's been cranking them out for 40 years in 100 different languages, producing over half a *billion* copies and 170 titles. The eye-grabbing propaganda is distributed by an invisible army of religious crusaders out to convert the planet.

Chick tracts are an extraordinary part of American pop culture. They're enshrined in the Smithsonian Museum. They're the subject of countless parodies. They seem completely out of date in today's politically correct times, a throwback to Eisenhower era attitudes and the Religious Right. Some people hate what Chick tracts say. Supporters love them. Others find them amusing "camp."

Kurt Kuersteiner explores this intriguing artist and his colorful cast of contributors, including: John Todd, the ex-Satanist who revealed to Chick how the *Illuminati* operate the music industry for Satan; Dr. Alberto Rivera, the ex-Jesuit priest who claimed to have inside information of Vatican plots to restart the bloody Inquisitions; Dr. Rebecca Brown, a physician who suspected witches were running her hospital and murdering the patients. You'll also hear about alleged conspiracies by the Masons, Mormons, Muslims, Jehovah's Witnesses, role playing gamers, and many more! Plus, you'll get the inside scoop on Kuersteiner's fascinating visit to Chick Publications, his personal meeting with the reclusive Mr. Chick, and the surprising discoveries made inside Chick's giant archives vault.

Prepare yourself for an incredible journey into the demon-filled world of America's most outspoken cartoonist: Jack T. Chick—A man whose remarkable work has long been overlooked while hiding under our very noses.

Pre-Foreword

Chick tracts are one of the most remarkable collectibles around today. Almost everything about them is unusual. Their size, humor, controversial nature, conspiracy theories, the innovative way they are distributed, and the fact they are still being published in these politically correct times. Chicks are truly unique!

If you've ever picked up a Chick tract and wondered what it's all about, you're about to find out. And if you've considered collecting these little dandies, now is an excellent time to start while there's still a chance of obtaining rare titles without mortgaging your home. How much longer that will remain the case is uncertain. What *is* certain is that future generations will also find these tracts incredible pieces of Americana and will want to collect them as well.

Whether you're familiar with Chick's work or simply curious to find out what all the fuss is about, you're in for a treat. Chick is a one-of-a-kind artist who's still creating and selling some of his best work for less than two bits each. Let there be no doubt about it: Chick tracts are one of America's cheapest thrills!

My deepest appreciation to Rev. Rich Lee, a dear friend who not only contributed many reviews and comments included in this book, but has been a constant advocate for the enjoyment of Chick tracts. I'd also like to thank the following persons for their help in this undertaking:

All my English teachers for their inspiration and love of the language, especially Mrs. Betsy Sellers and Dr. Thomas Wright.

Ya Fang Wang for her support and assistance with this project.

Bob Fowler for his pioneering research on Chick.

Debbie Drake, Ray Ruenes, and Hal Robins for their proofreading help.

Michael Schmal for his older tract contributions.

Tina Skinner for getting the ball rolling on this project.

The friendly staff at Chick Publications.

Chaplain Dann for his homemade tracts and tales of passing them out.

Both my Catholic sisters, who didn't disown me for being a heretic and a Chick fan.

And the many contributors to www.chickcomics.com, whose remarks are generously sprinkled throughout this work.

—Kurt Kuersteiner

Foreword

Bob Fowler

Who collects Chick tracts? Surprising answer: many kinds of people. They are soul-winners, atheists, intellectuals, comic book collectors, even members of other religions. When did these people first encounter Chick tracts, what were their initial reactions, how were they affected, and what do they think about Chick tracts today? Answer: there are all kinds of Chick stories out there. You will read a few of the best in this book.

I have heard and read a number of stories about people who were first exposed to Chick tracts at a very young age. This is not always a pretty sight, as Chick himself would admit. Fortunately, I did not encounter Chick tracts until young adulthood, around 1970. I am particularly fond of two tracts rescued from the sidewalks of downtown Los Angeles. Though trampled and permanently scarred, both of these tracts are a proud part of my collection. If anyone had told me in 1970 "Bob, someday you'll be a tract peddler yourself," I would have laughed, "Haw Haw Haw!"

But damn if I didn't become a Chick tract collector, then an obsessive Chick researcher, and finally … a vulgar little tract peddler! Today, I promote Chick tract collecting and give free tracts to the people I meet who are genuinely interested in them. I also sell tracts to Chick collectors at comic book shows. Not your typical soul-winning Chick witness, but a tract peddler nonetheless.

But what about this Kurt Kuersteiner fellow, this Johnny-come-lately trying to muscle into The World of Chick? Kurt is a dedicated Chick collector, the webmaster of a comprehensive Chick collector's website, and a diplomat between Chick collectors and Chick Publications. He has made up for lost time, and appears determined to establish himself as the unassailable monarch of the Chick collectors' empire. Kurt and I have very different temperaments, but these differences benefit both of us because each does things that the other will not (or cannot) do. We share our results, each convinced that it was the other guy who did the hard part. I salute Kurt on his Chick book and hope that he will never hear those terrible words, "depart from me…".

Bob Fowler has been collecting and archiving Chick's endless variations for years. He is the author of *The World of Chick,* a detailed Chick reference book that is available worldwide via amazon.com.

Now was the time for God's awful judgment on Pharaoh and his army. God moved the pillar. They drove like mad into the valley in the water, trying to catch the Israelites. The chariot wheels snapped — horses fell. The entire army was bogged down between two great walls of water and then… the Lord Jesus commanded the waters to close. They did, and Egypt lost its king and its army in the churning sea.

Egypt was destroyed. The crops were gone, the economy was bankrupt because they had given the Israelites most of their gold and silver. All the firstborn were dead, (including their flocks and herds) and all the mighty men of Egypt were gone. The government no longer existed. It was total disaster for Egypt. It never recovered.

An Army of One

Loved and hated throughout the world, Jack Chick is one of America's most controversial artists, yet few people know who he is. Almost everyone has seen his tracts. They're the little 3 x 5 inch Christian comics left in bathrooms, bars, bus stations—almost any public place. They've been flown over communist Cuba and rained from the heavens by plane. They've been corked in bottles and floated to foreign seaboards. They've been translated into "wordless gospels" and given to primitive tribes who cannot read or write but understand the pictures. Peace Corps volunteers report African villages awash with them. Having printed over half a billion copies in over 100 different languages, Chick is one of the most widely read writers of our time. What's more remarkable is that his work is completely self-published. Such success is unheard of from any other artist *or* author.

Chick's work isn't available everywhere, however. Some governments confiscate his materials whenever they are found. The Soviet Union did so in the past, and various Islamic states do so today. Even democracies have censored his work. Progressive Canada and repressive South Africa both banned his comics in the 1980s because their anti-Vatican themes were considered too controversial. In spite of these restrictions (or maybe because of them), such countries received plenty of Chick materials via smugglers. It seems impossible to silence the gospel word of J.C. (Jack Chick).

Who is Jack Chick? He is the president and main artist for Chick Publications, a privately owned publishing company located outside Los Angeles. Distributorships can be found in England, Canada, Australia, South Africa, and Germany. One of the keys to Chick's success is the low cost of the finished product. His tracts retail at just 14 cents each. Missionaries and soul-winners give millions of them away every year. His profit per tract is microscopic, but the volume in which he does business has earned his company millions of dollars. Jack Chick is, in effect, the Henry Ford of publishing.

Like Ford, Chick has been accused of anti-Semitism. Chick is actually very pro-Israel, and believes Jews are God's chosen race. What really angers many critics is Chick's attempts to convert members of their religion to Christianity. How successful his tracts are in this regard is unknown, but no religion likes competition.

Another thing that earns Chick minus points is his prediction that all non-Christians go to hell. This belief is vividly portrayed in graphic (albeit cartoon) detail. Almost all his stories wind up with a sinner cowering before the Great White Throne of Judgment. The Faceless God checks the Book of Life for his name, and if it's missing, booms, "Depart from me, ye cursed, into everlasting fire!" The accused often begs for mercy, claiming never to have known about Jesus. The Faceless God thunders back that he's wrong, because God in his infinite love sent a soul-winner to hand deliver a gospel tract which the sinner unwisely ignored. The poor wretch is quickly dispatched to his hellish reward. After attempting to literally *scare the hell* out of the reader, Chick then offers a sinner's prayer to help new converts repent and become born again.

These recurring themes and offensive "in your face" messages have made Chick tracts stand out among a sea of free advertisements and propaganda. What makes them more special is the artwork. All of Chick's tracts are stuffed with black and white cartoon panels. Chick draws in a distinctive style that ranges from simplistic to highly detailed. Chick's second artist, a black minister named Fred Carter, is one of the finest comic artists ever. Carter's tracts feature beautiful line art. His full color *The Crusaders* comic books are stunning. Combined with Chick's storytelling skills and sensational plots, the two make quite a team.

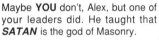

Conspiracies play a big part in many Chick tracts. In *The Curse of Baphomet*, the Masons are accused of links with witchcraft. (©1991 Jack T. Chick.)

Conspiracy theories are a major ingredient in Chick's writing. Railing about them throughout his tracts and comics have made Chick many enemies. They've also provided a devoted audience of true believers, as well as skeptics who find such views hilarious. The conspiracies run a wide range of secular to supernatural schemes.

In the 1970s, Chick published the accusations of John Todd, an ex-Satanist who claimed to have insider knowledge about a secret satanic organization, the *Illuminati*. He told Chick how the group controlled the record industry and cast spells on the music, which in turn, cursed the teenagers who listened to it. The books and comics that Chick published on this subject helped fuel a fad of record burnings by Christians throughout the country. Todd now has a record of his own—a criminal one. He was arrested for "statutory rape and transporting a minor across the state line." He was sent to prison for several months in 1976 for the incident (Metz 1979, 37).

Facing page: The ultimate splash page—Pharaoh's army is washed up by an angry God in *King of Kings* ©1980 Jack T. Chick. (Art by Fred Carter.)

In the 1980s, Chick publicized a bigger conspiracy, this time with the help of Dr. Alberto Rivera. Alberto claimed to be an ex-Jesuit priest who was assigned to infiltrate and destroy Protestant churches. He said he was only a small part of a larger worldwide network of Catholic saboteurs. The ultimate goal of the Vatican was to bring back the Inquisitions and install a one world government with Catholicism as the official religion. Alberto claimed he saw proof that the Catholic church was under Satan's influence while he was a Jesuit. He left it to become Protestant in 1967. He predicted that betrayed Jesuits would kill him. Rivera died in 1997 at age 61; his wife believes he was poisoned (Cicchese 1997).

A few years later, Chick blew open another conspiracy, this one revealed to him by Dr. Rebecca Brown. Rebecca was a physician who discovered her hospital had been taken over by witches. She claims all hell broke loose after she interfered with their efforts to kill her patients. She's been fighting demons as a deliverance minister ever since. She's currently making big bucks reprinting the books originally published through Chick's company, as well as writing additional ones with her new husband, Daniel Yoder, who claims his first wife was tortured to death by a Rabbinical Cabal (Fisher 1996).

And there's more. Much, *much more*. Chick uncovers demonic conspiracies by the Masons, Jehovah's Witnesses, Muslims, evolutionists, homosexuals, role-playing gamers, communists, Mormons, druids, et al. The list of Satan's puppets goes on and on; about the only thing the devil isn't accused of is being lazy. Some of these groups have launched boycotts and public pressure campaigns to put Chick Publications out of business, but what hasn't destroyed Chick has only made him stronger. As a result of the pressure to remove his product from Christian bookstores, Chick broke into the direct mail market and became a trail blazer in Internet sales. Now he's doing better than ever. Chick's two biggest nemeses, the Catholic and gay communities, continue to inspire new titles from the cartooning crusader. Chick's adversaries learned too late that anyone who tries to take out the king of underground comics had better succeed in the first attempt.

These ongoing feuds and inflammatory topics have only attracted a larger audience of Chick fans. Like kids gathering around a school yard brawl, everyone enjoys watching a good fight—unless they're dragged into it. More than a few Chick readers have found themselves featured in

Chick led the charge in attacking racism among conservative Christian publishers. *Operation Bucharest* (©1974 Jack T. Chick) was sometimes subtle—but often bold—in promoting equality.

his tracts in a less than flattering light. His very first tract, *Why No Revival,* criticized spiritually dead churches. It also featured the likenesses of several people in his own congregation, a detail that was not appreciated when he returned to church. Chick feels, with God on his side, he's obligated to expose sin wherever he sees it, even among his supporters.

Another example occurred in the early 1970s. Chick was among the first to use comics to criticize racism, especially among Christians. This was not just a fad either. He jumped into the cause with both feet, making one of his two regular *Crusader* heroes an African-American. He also went after the Masons, some of which were until then Chick customers. He releases a new tract every two months, the topic of which is kept a closely guarded secret until the day it is offered for sale. Who will be the next to be exposed as an ally of evil? Will it be *your* organization? One never knows until it's too late to stop the presses.

Surprisingly, Chick has never been successfully sued. He has the First Amendment to fall back on, but probably feels his greatest protection is from above. He has yet to go after the Scientologists, who are renowned for their determination to fight enemies with everything at their disposal, including the courts. Don't expect fear of reprisals to discourage Chick from exposing the truth as he sees it. If anything, the challenge only strengthens his resolve. He could be saving the best fight for last!

Jack Chick was born in 1924 (Ito 2003). He's been publishing tracts for over four decades. He's well past retirement age, but shows no sign of slowing down. As of this printing, he's still healthy, enthusiastic, and strong. Chick's artistic skill continues unabated, despite suffering a stroke in 1993. In fact, he's spent the last decade directing his magnum opus, an hour long movie featuring the first-class art of Fred Carter. This project will present the Bible in pictures with hundreds of intricately painted full color pictures. Chick's plan is to translate it in a variety of different languages so missionaries can project it on the sides of buildings throughout the world to aid in their presentation of the gospel. It's a bold new direction for a publisher of his age.

In 1998, Chick's wife of 50 years passed away. His invalid daughter died not long thereafter. He eventually remarried. The new Mrs. Chick is Chinese and about half her husband's age (Ito 2003). Chick treasures her and wants to stick around to share her company. Those hoping to outlast him may be in for a long wait. He's been quoted as saying he plans to retire at age 90, when he wants to tour the missionary field for three years (Cicchese 1997).

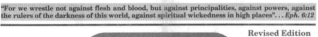

Chick is probably the only book publisher with his own newspaper, which he gives away for free. *Battle Cry* was eventually reduced to newsletter size, but it still covers current events from a very conservative religious viewpoint.

Many people throughout the world collect Chick's 170+ tracts, spurred on by curiosity, admiration, or outrage. His 20 different full color comics are also cherished collectibles, especially among fundamentalist Christians and/or conspiracy buffs. The most antagonistic of all of Chick's work, however, isn't disseminated in comic or tract form, but a newsletter called *Battle Cry*. This call to arms is sent free to his regular customers every couple of months along with his newest tract. It was originally issued as a full-sized newspaper in 1983 to fight the public pressure Catholics were organizing for boycotts. The paper has shrunk to newsletter size since then, but the content remains as explosive as ever. Recent headlines include, "Dr. Rivera's 15 Year Old Claims Verified by Current Events," "Homosexuals Parenting: Study Proves It's Dangerous For Kids," "More Proof That Roman Catholicism Isn't Christian," "Mormonism: It's Based On Myths," and "Muslims Using Hate Laws Stamp Out Religious Freedom in Canada." Chick obviously hasn't mellowed with age.

Chick's military experience continues to resurface in his tracts. *Holy Joe* ©1972 Jack T. Chick.

Since the 1960s, the rest of America has become more liberal. Not Chick. He continues to promote a conservative life-style and fundamentalist form of Christianity that hasn't been widely practiced since the Eisenhower era. While mainstream society embraces moral relativism, Chick is spurred on to greater action by his perception that humanity is fulfilling prophecies of the end times. The same determination is displayed by his employees as well. Various company catalogs have promised to rush orders out as fast as possible, since the future reader of the tracts could die at any moment and 24 hours could make the difference between salvation or eternal damnation.

The more politically correct society becomes, the more reactionary Chick's materials seem in comparison. There are other radical right-wing publishers besides Chick, but they are micropublishers. None of them crank out anywhere near the volume of zealous material that Chick does. A distant second runner up would probably be Tony Alamo, a Jewish convert to Christianity who utilizes the vast wealth he earned as a businessman to fuel his ministry and disseminate his own hard-core fundamentalist newsletter. Alamo and Chick have crossed paths several times, and the two have a mutual disdain for the *Great Whore of Babylon,* a derisive term from Revelation which they claim predicts the Pope.

Like Chick, Alamo maintains independence from "the system" which uses economic carrots and whips to discourage anyone from upsetting the *status quo.* Unlike Alamo or other religious big-shots, Chick was never a televangelist who garnered fame and fortune on TV or radio. On the contrary, Chick has remained hidden from the public eye, refusing interviews and dodging reporters. He has made it clear he doesn't want the limelight and doesn't trust the media. Reporters have ambushed him in the past and referred to his materials as hate lit, a description that makes Chick bristle (Chick 1999, 8).

The end result is a man who is probably the most famous "unknown" artist alive. To casual readers, even his name is unrecognizable. They only know the "J.T.C." initials he signs his work with. Acquiring a photograph of him is next to impossible. One of the few papers to publish his image had to resort to using his high school yearbook photo! Chick remembers what Alberto said about the Jesuits wanting him dead, and he doesn't intend to make their job any easier.

Many people have met Jack Chick in a checkout line, restaurant, or mall, but they never knew it. He often hands these strangers free tracts, the same way he suggests his customers should (Chick 2000, 8). They never suspect the man who actually wrote and drew the tract is the same man who handed it to them.

Chick definitely marches to the beat of his own drummer. He's unafraid to gamble everything if it's for something he believes in. As a teenager with a scholarship, he left acting school early to join the Army and fight in the Pacific during World War II. He feels lucky he wasn't killed fighting the Japanese, not because he feared death, but because he wasn't a Christian and it would have sent him to hell (Chick 2000).

Chick was discharged in 1946. It was 1948 before he was saved. Although no longer a soldier, Chick is still a fighter. He continues to sprinkle combat analogies in his diatribes, referring to his tracts as "ammunition" and calling his newsletter *Battle Cry*. The enemy is Satan, an invisible adversary that is so cunning that few believe he's a threat—that is, until they're dead. Chick continues to sound the alarm and hope that enough will heed his warning and respond before it's too late.

The irony is that Chick himself believes the end is nigh and doesn't expect to live through the upcoming tribulation. Long before the popular *Left Behind* series sold millions of books promoting the tale of the rapture, Chick popularized the concept in one of his early masterpieces, *The Beast*. This 48 page cartoon classic is packed full of gloomy predictions of the end times. Satan creates a one world government, which executes defiant Christians with roving motorcycle guillotines. Great plagues and pestilence torment the terrified population. World War erupts as the armies of *The Beast* attack Israel, killing two-thirds of the Jews. The Battle of Armageddon ensues and only then do the good guys win. Christ rules on Earth for a thousand years. Sinners, who until then have been patiently waiting in Hades for "The Final Judgement," are judged and sentenced to the Lake of Fire. Like much of Chick's work, it is very sensational.

Everybody wants to be loved. But by whom? Chick only cares about being loved by Jesus and the rest of the world be damned (despite his best efforts to save them). Even if the future is predetermined, Chick believes in fighting the forces of darkness no matter what the outcome. Surrendering to Satan is not an option. He tells readers, "When I go out, I want to go out with honor, and I want to take as many with me to Christ as I possibly can." (Chick 1984)

Chick is not a politician. He doesn't dodge tough questions or remain vague on divisive issues. Rather, he takes strong stands without regard for those he may alienate by doing so. In his audio tape, *Let's Make A Stand,* Chick states he is not out to please men. He quotes one of his favorite passages in Luke 6:26: "Woe unto you when all men should speak well of you, for so did their fathers to the false prophets." In other words, if everybody likes you, you must be doing something wrong. Such contempt for public approval is refreshing in an age where popularity and celebrity status have become highly treasured commodities. Unlike so many other rebels who went mainstream, there is absolutely no sign of Chick "going soft" or "selling out."

Chick has more than talent and marketing genius. He has guts. Whether you love him or hate him, it's difficult not to admire his strong determination to promote his beliefs at all costs.

The Chick phenomenon is a remarkable story that deserves telling. Those who are expecting a condemnation of his politically incorrect views will be disappointed. The goal of this book is not to judge the validity of Chick's claims or his religious beliefs. That's up to you (and the Faceless God above) to decide. The objective here is to examine a unique artist and his lifetime of intriguing work. It's a fascinating journey, so let's begin.

Some call him crazy, but Chick doesn't care. He carries on his task of saving the sinners in spite of their contempt. *The Beast* ©1966 Jack T. Chick.

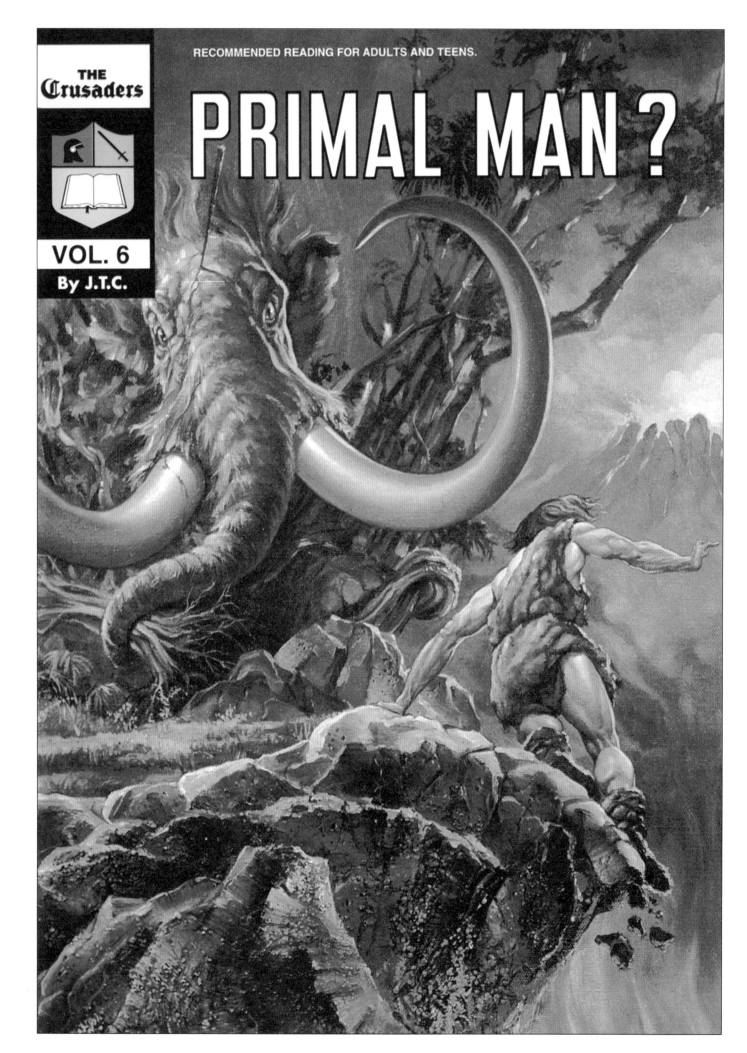

The Early Years

IN THE BEGINNING

①

Chick is rather quiet about his past. He doesn't have a PR agent sending out bios of his early years. A browse through Chick's website reveals a terse account of his roots. A more complete picture emerges after combining this information with articles published in the *Inland Valley Daily Bulletin* (12/21/97) and *Brill's Content* (Nov. 1999).

Jack Thomas Chick was born in the mid-1920s in Alhambra, California. His parents were Thomas and Pauline Chick and they lived in a simple middle class neighborhood. Chick had a fondness for doodling early on. He told the *Bulletin* that he flunked the first grade because he was drawing too much. The subject matter was supposedly airplane dog fights.

Chick's High School yearbook photo (circa 1942). One of only two known photos to surface publicly.

He went to Alhambra High School and became involved with acting. Some classmates recall him as being handsome, quiet, and a hard worker. Other classmates were less impressed with Chick. His Christian classmates later admitted that they avoided him and decided never to witness to him because of his bad language. They thought he was "the last guy on Earth who would ever except Jesus Christ." (Chick 2002)

THE RECLUSE:
The rediscovered 1948 Pasadena photo of Chick

Chick's Pasadena Playhouse photo (1948). The other known picture of Chick to be published.

He earned a two year scholarship at the Pasadena Playhouse School to study acting. He started in the fall of 1942 but his studies were interrupted after the Japanese attacked Pearl Harbor. He joined the Army in February 1943. He specialized in communications and rose to the rank of Sergeant. He spent three years in the Pacific. His overseas service included New Guinea, Australia, the Philippines, and five months in Japan after the surrender. He was discharged on January 28, 1946. Chick returned to the states wishing to finish his schooling. He graduated from the Pasadena Playhouse School in 1948. It was there that he also met his future wife, Lola Lynn Priddle. They married the same year he graduated (Cicchese 1997).

Facing page: *Primal Man?* ©1976 Jack T. Chick.
(Art by Fred Carter.)

In an open letter published in February 2002, Chick recalls how he first visited his Christian in-laws in 1948 while honeymooning with Lynn in Canada. "My vocabulary had a military flavor using words that everybody used. I didn't see anything wrong. I smoked like all the guys in the army did. I didn't notice that I was smelling up [their] home ... By the next morning my mother-in-law said to my wife, 'What in the world did you marry?'

"By Sunday morning I think she had had enough of me and insisted that I listen to a religious radio program called *The Old Fashioned Revival Hour.* The preacher was Charles E. Fuller. By 8:30 that Sunday night I hit the kitchen floor on my knees asking the Lord Jesus to save me. My life had changed."

Chick returned to California with a new set of values. He began to question his acting career goals. He told the *Bulletin,* "I went out to 20th Century Fox and saw how they treated women and I said me and my wife are not going to be part of this."

Chick's new bride had her own standards as well. Chick wanted to become a missionary, but she vetoed the idea. Her aunt had been a missionary in Africa. She was pregnant and being carried across a river in a stretcher when one of the natives carrying her lost his leg to a hungry crocodile (Chick 2002).

Chick ended up working a less adventurous job at his father's sign painting business. He eventually left that job to work as a graphic artist at the AstroScience Corporation in El Monte, California (Cicchese 1997). One of the welders at the aerospace firm gave Chick a copy of *Power From On High* by Charles Finney. "That book pushed my button," he explains on his company's site, "I went to church and saw all the deadness and hypocrisy, and I thought, 'That's why there's no revival.' So I started making these little sketches. My burden was so heavy to wake Christians up to pray for revival." (Chick 2002)

Those sketches evolved into the original version of *Why No Revival?,* but Chick couldn't find anyone who was willing to publish it. He finally borrowed $800 from the credit union and paid for the first printing himself in 1961. This was not a small tract, but an extra large size booklet about the dimensions of a regular magazine turned sideways.

Soon afterwards, Chick was driving down the road and saw a group of teens. He didn't care much for teenagers or their rebellion at the time, but he had a strong reaction when he saw them. The recollection from his site states, "All of a sudden, the power of God hit me and my heart broke and I was overcome with the realization that these teens were probably on their way to hell. With tears pouring down my face, I pulled my car off the road and wrote as fast as I could, as God poured the story into my mind." (Chick 2002)

Fifteen minutes later, the story to *A Demon's Nightmare* was complete. Chick went home and illustrated it. The funds to print the tract were provided by AstroScience's wealthy owner, a Christian named George Otis. Chick considers this his first *soul-winning* tract (©1962).

The revival lectures of Charles Finney inspired another Chick work, a 64 page book called *The Last Call* (©1963). This was also a horizontal format booklet, although most of it was text. Many classic Chick illustrations filled the pages, including an opening series of five panels predicting the outlawing of Christianity in America.

His second soul-winning tract would be his most famous. According to the December 1983 issue of *Battle Cry,* a pastor asked Chick to come with him to witness at Prison Camp 9 near Azusa, California. Chick assembled a large cartoon flip chart to show to the inmates. Those drawings later became *This Was Your Life* (©1964), Chick's bestselling tract. The results were promising from the start. Of the eleven inmates in attendance, nine of them accepted Christ when Chick was finished.

Chick indicates that his first art studio and office were little more than his kitchen table. He had great difficulty getting bookstores to carry his gospel cartoons. It was too radical of a concept. "We were having a tough time out there," he explains on his site, "A lot of bookstores were really outraged at some guy using these cartoons to present the gospel. They thought it was sacrilegious." Yet many of those who did carry them discovered that they sold.

All of these early tracts were oversized by today's standards. All four can be found "distributed by Rusthoi Publications" with early 1960s copyrights and measure slightly larger than 5 x 8 inches. That changed after Chick spoke with Bob Hammond, a missionary broadcaster at *The Voice of China and Asia.* He explained to Chick that the communists had great success spreading their propaganda by passing out mini-comic tracts to the ignorant masses (Chick 2002). Chick adopted the idea. As the size and cost of Chick's tracts shrank, the audience steadily increased.

Chick teamed up with George Collins, a fellow aerospace employee. Collins, who continues to serve as Vice President of Chick Publications and editor of *Battle Cry* to this day, manages the business side while Chick focuses on the creative side.

The demand for pocket-sized Christian tracts grew and so did Chick's company, yet the staff has always remained below a few dozen with little turnover. Chick continues to do what he does best: write mini-sermons and illustrate them in an eye-grabbing style. Along the way, his company has branched out into book and comic book production, all promoting a hard-hitting Christian message.

Chick has suffered more than his share of personal tragedies. He experienced a stroke in late 1995 that temporarily affected his drawing hand. About two years later, his beloved wife of 50 years passed away after a protracted illness. Then he lost his only child, Carol, after a lengthy illness. But Jack T. Chick is a survivor. He survived his mother's attempt to abort him, a fact he learned when he was 40. (It's a revelation he discusses frankly in a July 2000 open letter to customers.) He survived the war in the Pacific when many fellow soldiers did not. He survived his stroke and went on to draw new tracts. He survived the painful loss of his family and has since become happily remarried. His business has survived boycotts, changing social norms, economic feast and famine, and crossed over into the new millennium stronger than ever.

Of course, Chick cannot survive forever. But he's created an artistic and business legacy that has defied the popular trends and will likely continue long after he's gone.

The Pasadena Playhouse Memoirs, (probably) Chick's earliest published art.
Notice his bird-like signature. ©1947 Jack T. Chick.

This act takes place 8 times a year, in witches' covens throughout our country, that practice of human sacrifice during the black sabbaths.

*Upside down red cross… a symbol of human sacrifice.

**1 Corinthians 10:20-22

Conspiracies!

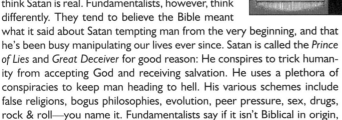

Do you believe in Satan? While all Christians believe in God, many of them doubt that the devil exists. A recent survey (Tiansay 2001) indicated that only 20 percent of mainline Church members think Satan is real. Fundamentalists, however, think differently. They tend to believe the Bible meant what it said about Satan tempting man from the very beginning, and that he's been busy manipulating our lives ever since. Satan is called the *Prince of Lies* and *Great Deceiver* for good reason: He conspires to trick humanity from accepting God and receiving salvation. He uses a plethora of conspiracies to keep man heading to hell. His various schemes include false religions, bogus philosophies, evolution, peer pressure, sex, drugs, rock & roll—you name it. Fundamentalists say if it isn't Biblical in origin, the chances are, it's Satanic.

Suspecting Satan of involvement in day to day schemes isn't far fetched, if one accepts the premise that Satan is real and actively involved with our lives. The possibilities are endless. Could he really be involved in sabotaging churches? If you were Satan, wouldn't you? Churches make a logical target. Could Satan be involved in service organizations to help the needy? Naturally! It's the perfect place to give potential Christians false hope that good works will get them to heaven without confessing their sins and accepting Christ. Could Satan be running the music industry? Of course! What better way to corrupt young minds and encourage sex and drugs?

Jack Chick believes Satan is continuously working to lead as many people to damnation as possible. Everything happens for a reason, the direct result from either the forces of good or evil. Even good Christians are under constant attack by demons who are determined to undermine their salvation and stop their ministry to others.

In an open letter dated May 15, 1997, Chick states,

"We can pretty well tell how effective a new tract will be by the intensity of the spiritual warfare that we go through while making it. From the very beginning, it was obvious that Satan didn't want **Gun Slinger** to be written. It was a fight to the very end. Every person involved in its production got hit from unexpected directions. That's just the cost that must be paid to create an effective soul-winning tract."

In other words, there is no such thing as coincidence. Humans are mere pawns in a worldwide chess game played out by God and Satan. God wants to save the pieces, Satan wants to smash them. The devil has a major advantage: Most of the pieces doubt the players really exist. All Satan has to do in most cases is maintain their doubt until the clock runs out. To accomplish this, he'll use every trick and scheme he can dream up. He'll infiltrate the schools, the churches, the popular culture, he'll even rewrite modern translations of the Bible to water down the Word of God. Conspiracies are everywhere because deception is Satan's forte.

Chick did not develop a conspiracy-ridden world view on his own. There is a Protestant tradition of conspiracy theories in general. Thanks in part to the persecution of the Inquisitions, many early Protestants viewed the Catholic Church as evil incarnate. Many of the Protestant "founding fathers" claimed the Vatican represented the Whore of Babylon. A few examples include Luther (who started Lutheranism), Calvin (who began Calvinism), and John Knox (who established Presbyterianism). While most

When Catholics organized boycotts against Chick publications, Chick saw it as proof that the allegations made by Alberto were true. *My Name? In the Vatican?* ©1980 Jack T. Chick.

mainstream churches have decided to "forgive and forget" their anti-Vatican roots, many of the fundamentalist groups have not. So Chick is hardly alone in that belief, he's just more vocal about it than others. And the more protest and pressure the Roman Catholics organize to stop him, the more certain Chick is that he's right.

But it was more than traditional Protestant paranoia that made Chick blame Satan for every misfortune. He received a lot of encouragement from other sources. In particular, there were three people who had profound influence on the conspiracy theories promulgated in Chick's tracts and comics. Those three individuals were John Todd, Alberto Rivera, and Rebecca Brown.

Each one of these people has a remarkable story, not only in the conspiracies they tell, but in their own personal lives as well. After all, once they revealed their conspiracies, Satan and his minions set out to destroy them, their ministry, and their credibility (according to their supporters). So any resulting firestorm of controversy would be expected as a form of spiritual counterattack. Exposés and dirty laundry are just Satan's ways of distracting readers from listening to *the message* Chick's "insiders" are trying to express. Chick has never renounced any of his conspiracy gurus, even when they contradicted one another or after embarrassing details about them surfaced. If they were in trouble with the media or the law, Chick stuck by them when everyone else didn't.

We're going to examine each one of these colorful characters in order of their appearance, as well as what they said, what they did, and how it transformed Chick's work.

John Wayne Todd, a.k.a. Lance Collins

Chick first met Todd in 1973 at a meeting of the *Amazing Prophecies* group with Evangelist Doug Clark (Plowman 1979). Clark was a quintessential televangelist from Trinity Broadcasting, complete with a silver tongue and a bouffant hairdo. Chick eventually went on a tour of the Holy Lands with Clark, but that was before Clark became an F.B.I. fugitive for embezzlement (Lee 2002).

Todd claimed to have been raised a witch, but was saved on September 1st, 1972 in San Antonio. He had just seen the movie *The Cross and the Switchblade*. As he stepped outside, someone handed him a copy of Chick's *Bewitched* tract. He became shook up by its contents, which seemed custom written for him. He entered an ex-burlesque club called *The Green Gate Club*. He met a Christian there named Claude Elmer who was working late on a Coke machine. The two got to talking and Elmer led him to Christ. (Hicks and Lewis, 64-65)

Within a year, Todd set out to expose the dirty secrets and evil plans that the witches, Satanists, and Illuminati had been working on for years. He would give speeches at churches and Christian groups warning them of the danger. Todd did all this despite an alleged contract on his life for leaving The Craft. As he said in his *Voice of Victory* tape (1978), "They that come out (of Witchcraft) — they start at $10 thousand bounty and go up to several hundred thousand." (Hicks and Lewis, 68)

Todd was especially important to silence, because he claimed he wasn't just *any* ex-witch. He was one of the top dogs and knew where all the bodies were buried. He usually started out his lectures by providing some sensational history about himself.

He said his family changed their name from Collins (as in *Dark Shadows*) before the Civil War, since the Collins reputation in witchcraft was too well known (Hicks and Lewis, 36). He was initiated a high priest at age 18. Todd describes his early adulthood in a written paper handed out at his meetings, called *The Christian During Riot and Revolution* (Hicks and Lewis, 38-40). It states:

"He requested permission to join the military so that he could establish witch covens at military bases. Permission was granted and he proceeded to establish witch covens at every military base where he was stationed. He was sent to Vietnam where he fought as a Green Beret.

"After finishing his duty in Vietnam he was sent to Germany. While there he got into an argument with an officer who had been over him in Vietnam. This led to a pistol fight in which the officer was killed.

"During the course of Todd's trial his lawyer tried to plea-bargain for a 35-year sentence, after which John would become eligible for parole. This was rejected. When John's cell mate was released, John asked him to get word to a certain individual in the United States who John knew to be a witch. Within days a United States senator and congressman showed up. Twenty-four hours later John received an honorable discharge with all information of the shooting incident purged from his record."

Satan uses a chain of command to get things done. The devil rules the demons, the demons instruct the Illuminati, and the Illuminati secretly orchestrate lesser evil organizations (especially Witch covens). *The Hunter* ©1987 Jack T. Chick.

Todd figured his mother, a big shot witch, had gotten together with other witches and they had cast a spell to get her son out. But there were more powerful forces at work. Unbeknownst to him at the time, Todd was being groomed for a top slot in an organization that secretly ran the witches and most of society in general: The Illuminati. He was flown back to the states, given money, and put on another plane to New York where he was trained by members of the Druid Council of Thirteen.

"On May 1, 1971, John was initiated to become a Grand Druid high priest. He was given a 13-state area to administer. He established his headquarters in San Antonio, Texas. He states that over 90 percent of the politicians in that 13-state area receive financial support from him and take orders regarding political decisions from him. He stated that these orders were passed down from a Rothschild Tribunal to the Grand Druid Council, and the Council passed them on to individuals and organizations under their authorities." (Hicks and Lewis, 42)

"John continued as a high priest for a year and four months. On August 1, 1972, he saw a chart giving the plan for a world takeover. "ILLUMINATI PLAN FOR WORLD TAKEOVER

Remove president and vice president:

Nixon had beat the Illuminati in the election when he beat George McGovern. Nixon defied the Illuminati when he made peace overtures to Red China.

Republican successor throws election to Democrat—Jimmy Carter. Democrat president gets following laws enacted:

1. New gun law to take guns away from citizens.
2. The removal of tax exemption from churches
3. Genocide Act.
4. Presidential martial law powers.
5. The anti-hoarding act.

"WORLD WAR III

Caused by Israel battling over petrol, farm lands, and chemicals.

"PLAN FOR AMERICA

Make every person a total dependent on the Rothschilds by:

1. Creating a pseudo fuel shortage.
2. Confiscating all guns.
3. Calling for 'helter skelter.'
4. Declaring martial law—suspend Congress. Activate National Guard to keep order. One policemen for every five people.
5. With anti-hoarding act outlaw all food and medical supplies from being stored.
6. Issue a security card to govern all buying and selling.
7. Destroy monetary system.
8. Issue new currency.
9. Destroy all crop land."
(Hicks and Lewis, 43-44)

The plot culminates with Rothschild sending everyone against Israel (except America) for oil. Neutron bombs are used to destroy the people but save the buildings and resources. Once the war is over, the victor rules the world from Jerusalem.

It's easy to understand how this conspiracy must have clicked with Chick and others who believed in the Great Tribulation. Most fundamentalists interpret Revelation as predicting the Antichrist will attack Israel and rule the world from Jerusalem in the end times. The mid-1970s certainly *seemed* like the end times to those looking for signs. There was tension with the Soviets, inflation, strikes, recession, a falling dollar, rampant crime, drugs, promiscuous sex, and the unprecedented removal of a President. All societal norms were being challenged. Then President Carter came along and campaigned as a good-old Southern Christian, but once in office, his policies were anything but conservative. John Todd shows up and explains it all part of a master plan to deliberately cause chaos and anarchy. Even Carter is implicated in the plot.

Again, from *The Christian During Riot and Revolution* (Hicks and Lewis, 45).

"In the middle of August 1972, John said he received a letter from the Rothschilds on Rothschild stationary that stated, 'We have found a man who is willing to become world ruler and remain obedient to the Illuminati. His name is Jimmy Carter'."

According to Chick, many of today's seemingly senseless crimes are actually organized by witches to please their evil master down below. *The Trick* ©1986 Jack T. Chick.

Not all this conspiracy theory was expressed by Todd when he first met Chick in 1973. It developed over time as Todd gave many public speeches, and the daily news deteriorated further. But Chick accepted Todd's basic premise that witchcraft was behind many of the horrible crimes being committed, as well as subverting Churches and promoting sex, drugs, and rock and roll. It all made sense, because the witches were run by the Illuminati (which meant "enlightened ones") and they were in turn controlled by Lucifer (the "angel of light").

Witches may deny they believe in Satan, but Todd and Chick saw them as stooges, serving Satan whether they knew it or not. Chick incorporated many of Todd's claims in the second of his new state-of-the-art Christian comic book series, *The Crusaders*.

The 1974 title was *The Broken Cross,* and it begins with the solemn statement, "My deepest appreciation to Johnnie Todd (Lance)- EX-Grand Druid over 5,000 witches' covens, for the authenticity of the occult information used in this story. JTC."

The comic tells the story of a girl kidnapped and murdered by witches/Satanists. The small rural town is run by them, including the sheriff and the local (liberal) pastor. There's plenty of cloaks and daggers throughout the tale, especially at sacrifice time. It is considered a favorite among readers to this day.

The Illuminati show up in the 1978 release of *Crusaders* called *Angel of Light*. The introduction recognizes Dr. Lloyd Anderson, Dr. Ray Batema, Rev. Alexander Hislop, Wally Tope, and John Todd for supplying documentation for the book. Once again, a woman is kidnapped for the purposes of Pagan sacrifice, but the Crusaders are on the scene and stop it. They then spend the rest of the comic converting the girl and her boyfriend by explaining the history of Druids, witches, the Illuminati, and Satanism in general.

Page 26 states, "Satan's attack through politics and finances comes through a well organized undercover group called The Insiders or The Illuminati (the enlightened ones who follow the Angel of Light, Lucifer). It's been reported that this international group is controlled by the House of Rothschild." After Todd's predictions failed to pan out and Chick hooked up with Alberto, he replaced the last sentence with the statement, "It's been reported by Dr. A.R. Rivera (ex-Jesuit priest) that this international group is controlled by the Vatican."

There shall not be found among you anyone…that useth divination…or a witch; …or a consulter with familiar spirits, or a wizard….For all that do these things are an abomination unto the Lord. Deut. 18:10-12

A speaker who looks similar to Todd leads a church in a friendly burning of Dungeons & Dragons™ merchandise. *Dark Dungeons* ©1984 Jack T. Chick.

Crusaders #10 also credits John Todd in the introduction, then goes further and gives him a starring role in the story under his witch name of Lance Collins. He does the same thing in the comic that he was doing in real life. He goes around to churches and lectures about how the record industry is run by witches who curse the music and attach demons to each recording (*Spellbound?* 1978, 19-25). For exposing their methods, the witches set out to murder Collins. The Crusaders foil the attempt, and Collins succeeds in leading the Church in a burning session of rock records and occult items. This comic is considered by many to have influenced similar record and book burnings around the country during the same time frame.

The year 1978 was also the height of John Todd's influence. His reputation as a former witch with insider info on the end times had spread like wild fire among Fundamentalists, helped by the comics and public speeches, but also by Todd's massive cassette tape ministry (Hicks and Lewis, 14-15). Listeners bought the tapes and often passed them on to friends or made copies and mailed them across the country. Todd possessed (no pun intended) charisma and his elaborate eyewitness tales of secret plots captivated audiences.

But new and old scandals were converging on Todd. It began in January 1974, when he was confronted at Melodyland Christian Center in Anaheim, California, for promoting witchcraft on the side and having sex with the girls in his ministry. One of the girls turned to drugs and overdosed at age 16. Doug Clark publicly exposed Todd and would no longer endorse him. This is the same Clark who first featured Todd on TV, and who, according to Todd's ex-wife Sharon, "kept John on the gory, grizzly details [because] the kids especially liked it ... It was all sensational, all went to his head. It was the first time he had ever had bodyguards and all at the meetings. Doug really played on it to get attention." So despite having tutored Todd in the art of sensationalism, Clark deserves credit for being one of the earliest to sound the alarm about his problems. (Hicks and Lewis, 74-76)

Chick knew about the scandal, but thought Todd had been set up by the dark forces he was exposing. Chick continued to call Todd and encourage him to return to Christ. An open letter from Chick, dated June 1978, reveals fascinating details about everything that was going on behind the scenes.

CHICK PUBLICATIONS June 16, 1978
PO Box 662
Chino, California 91710

To Whom It May Concern:

This letter is in regard to my association with John Todd.

I first met John in 1973. I found his information on the occult fascinating. We worked together on a Crusaders story entitled, "The Broken Cross." Since its publication I know of witches coming to Christ through this story. A police captain visited a friend of mine and told him the book was the most factual he had ever read on the subject.

John Todd began winning young people out of the occult. His ministry started growing. When John took these young people to a church called "Melodyland" in Southern California, I was told they announced from the platform that no witch could be saved. That was disaster to John's ministry. He was involved with churches and Full Gospel Businessmen and all of them were of the charismatic persuasion. John was promised support that never came.

When attempts were made on John's life, the Christians shied away from him. In those years witchcraft was avoided like the plague. Everything turned sour. No Christian would touch John, so he went back to the only thing he knew, the occult. He and his wife, Sheila, opened up an occult bookstore.

I kept calling John, telling him he was saved, but he believed the Armenian doctrine that once he went back to sin he was lost forever. I kept at him. He pushed the occult religion at me, but I wouldn't give up and I told him he still belonged to Jesus. I called him my brother and he

told me to stop calling him that. When I almost gave up, John called me and told me that he and Sheila had come back to Christ.

John remembered when he was training for the position of a Grand Druid priest that a huge sum of money supposedly was passed from the Illuminati to the organization called "Melodyland," and John believes that is why his ministry was hit.

Since coming back into Christian work, John has had many attempts on his life, verified by his wife. John is exposing Masonry which has infiltrated our churches. It's an unseen enemy. John has given me valuable information on 2 new publications, "Angel of Light" and "Spellbound". The latter on rock music will have a devastating effect on Christian rock music. I thank God John is risking his neck to warn us of the dangers and techniques used by the Illuminati.

John was attending Faith Baptist Church in Canoga Park, California. On my word, Pastor Roland Rasmusson helped John get speaking engagements. John has made mistakes from the platform. It's understandable. He is in a new line of work. Both John and his wife have used extensive drugs and are still suffering from the effects. Some of the mistakes were deliberately fed to John to make him look bad. I can verify that through his wife, Sheila.

Pastor Rasmusson was caught in a hard place when John quoted the wrong input from the platform. Then, one of his church members was given an old tape to re-use. On it was a message John had made while instructing classes in the occult when he had backslidden. The tape was played to the deacons, and I believe pressure was put on Dr. Rasmusson to disassociate himself from John. They knew John had been backslidden because he told them that. I got the same material from John on the phone when I was trying to win him back to Christ.

I was assured the tape would only be played to the deacons, but since then, copies have fallen into various hands, and this is now being used as a club. Pastor Rasmusson still calls John his brother and he told me he believes John is saved. When John preaches, pastors tell me of revival and the most difficult to reach came to Christ, including Masons.

My question is: Who is behind John's attackers? I know the Masons are delighted. So is the Illuminati. Are the ones attacking John winning souls? Why is it aired publicly? If John goes down because of the pressures from Christians, it will be a day of rejoicing for the occult.

I back John up 100% with all his faults. I know this brother is doing his best to advance the kingdom of God. We must keep one fact in mind. John is not a minister, but a Christian layman sharing what he knows about a very explosive subject. We should be eager to know about what is going on in the enemy's camp, and to my knowledge, John Todd is the only one qualified to give us that information. I encourage you to stand with him in the face of this onslaught.

JACK T. CHICK, PRESIDENT, Chick Publications, Inc.

Chick issued a second open letter days before Halloween 1978. In it, Chick talks about a recent attempt on Todd's life and responds to more dirty laundry that was being circulated about Todd's past. It reads like a script to *Dallas*, except the famous soap opera drama was never as surreal as the stories told by John Wayne Todd.

CHICK PUBLICATIONS October 26, 1978
PO Box 662
Chino, California 91710

To Whom it May Concern in the Lord:

This letter should be a warning to us on how subtle the enemy can be as an angel of light. I consider John Todd a friend and a brother in Christ.

On Sunday evening, October 22nd, I received a phone call that gunfire had hit John's house. My wife and I drove to his place at about 9 PM. There were five squad cars in front of his house.

John's face was gray. Someone had fired a shotgun through the baby's window aiming at John reading in the front room. It missed the children sleeping in the front bedroom and sprayed through the hall, hitting John's arm and breaking part of the front window. John jumped up, ran to the back of the house, and as the man went over the back wall, he responded to John's command to halt by firing his shotgun at John. Todd fired two shots. Eight neighbors saw the man going over the wall. No one could say this attempt on John's life was self-inflicted as they claim the others were. I saw the blasted window, the torn curtains, and the pellet wound in John's arm. The oldest girl, age 6, told me when the shooting started she put the babies on the floor to protect them. What a price to pay for exposing the occult!

New disturbing material has arrived in the mail with letters and newspaper clippings covering a period of time when John Todd had pulled away from the Lord, from July 1975 until March 1976 and beyond. In John's defense, I would like to give the other side of the story.

As some of you know, when John and Sheila backslid, I called them many times trying to get them to come back to the Lord, so I'm familiar with much of what happened during this time. The pressures John Todd faced after working with me on "The Broken Cross" in 1974 contributed to his backsliding. When the occult put the heat on John, Christians didn't want to become involved. His support vanished. The incident that broke the camel's back took place in the Midwest.

A pastor asked John to refurbish an old building which belonged to his church, telling John he would use it as a retreat for ex-witches and for drug rehabilitation. John and Shiela put in 18 hours a day plus $2,000.00 of their own funds as well as their furniture into this place. The night it was finished John said the pastor changed his mind and wanted someone else to run it. An argument took place. The pastor pushed Shiela and she had a miscarriage that night.

Everything was gone. They headed for Ohio in a Greyhound bus with only two suitcases and three boxes of clothing. They were broke and hungry when they reached Shiela's folks. Because of their past history with the occult in that area of Dayton they were not welcomed in the churches. By now they were very bitter.

The occult world would never forgive John Todd for writing "The Broken Cross." He was branded a traitor. Too many witches got saved reading that book. John's Catholic Landlord, Mr. James Seifer, wanted to invest his money either in an adult or an occult bookstore. He decided on an occult store and offered John and Shiela 50% if they'd run it. They agreed. This was September 9, 1975. They had gone back into the world. The Illuminati was outraged. It was like some cheap hood trying to set up a prostitution ring in an area controlled by the Mafia. John Todd, the outcast, had moved into their territory. He had to be destroyed. I used to call the occult store and tell them I loved them and that Jesus loved them and wanted them to come back to Him.

Now we come to the insidious plot to wipe out John Todd as I believe it happened. Most of the people involved were directly tied to the Illuminati via the pope of the occult called Gavin Frost. I've been told the enforcer, who wants the Christians destroyed, is Isaac Bonewits who heads up the Aquarian Anti-Defamation League. These were some of the heavyweights John was facing. The others were high priests and priestesses in local covens as well as Masons. Now understand, no legitimate witch was allowed in John's store. It had been boycotted.

John was surprised when two real witches came into his store bringing a 16-year-old runaway named Karen Schnipper. She had been beaten by her father. Immediately John felt sorry for her. He had been a beaten child. They asked for John's help. Here's where it gets interesting.

The two witches were Bob and Julie Pritchet (not sure of spelling). They were known as "Terror" and "Albarros" (not sure of that spelling either) which means the Black One, or Undergod, or the devil. These two were leaders in the local Church of Wicca, under the control of Gavin Frost, the pope of the occult. The girl, Karen, was a witch from Chicago. John estimated her to be a second level witch. She had a history of incest and heavy drugs. She offered John $200.00 to drive her to Chicago to get away from her brutal father. He had a broken hand from hitting Karen. John agreed to take her.

Before he got to Chicago, John stopped and called Shiela. She told him there was an all-points bulletin on him for kidnapping. The police were waiting for John in Chicago, the father had made the charge. I believe the witches plotted the whole setup. The police offered John immunity if he'd bring the girl back. The deal was made through John's boss. All charges were dropped. John admits he and Shiela were deep into sin. They were away from the Lord and miserable.

In January 1976, a 13-year-old girl was missing from a children's home in Dayton called "Shawen Acres," located about a block from the occult store. A police officer by the name of Robert Keen who handled hundreds of cases singled out this girl. He accused John of killing her. According to police reports, John says this 13-year-old girl was a habitual runaway because her father raped her at age 10 and she had become a member of the motorcycle gang called "The Outlaws." She was a known prostitute.

Officer Keen searched John's house and pushed one of the employees around, breathing threats of a murder charge against John Todd. This officer claimed to be a Christian. I called John on the phone that day and he told me about some of this man's actions. He was bitter. I said, "John, from what you're telling me, he isn't a Christian." There was no love. After a while the case was dropped.

In February of 1976 John was arrested for the Karen Schnipper kidnap case again. It was a shock. He applied for bail. At the same time he was hit with a warrant for his arrest in Carlsbad, New Mexico, for forgery. Bail was denied. The warrants for his arrest from New Mexico turned out to be phony. John was not wanted. They finally gave him bail.

Now the Illuminati made a deal with him. On February 21, 1976 at 7 pm John and Shiela were invited to a dinner with Gavin Frost, the pope of the occult and his associate Isaac Bonewits. They warned John to never mention the Illuminati again. John refused. They were furious. The next day in a Unitarian church, Gavin Frost denounced John. A "wanted" poster was to be issued for John raising the price on his head by the organization.

An interesting meeting took place. Gavin Frost, the pope of the occult who despises Christianity, and Isaac Bonewits, his enforcer who seethes with hate for the believers in Christ, met with the Christian police officer as friends. Isn't that strange? The other man was Wes Hill, the man who reported all the stories on John Todd and for some reason always misquoted him. It looks like they all had something in common.

In March 1976, I got a surprise call from John. He called me "Brother." I praise the Lord because John and Sheila had come back to Christ. They closed the occult store and burned its contents. He was still on bail. The trial was coming up. Unknown to John, his lawyers were Masons. They told John if he agreed to say he was guilty of driving Karen across the state line he would be released. John agreed. For some reason a visiting judge from Tennessee presided. He also was a Mason. He gave John the maximum sentence of 6 months with no probation.

The first night in the institution, the nurse insisted that John get a shot of Phenobarbital and Valium, claiming his records showed at one time he had been an epileptic. They pumped so many drugs into John that by the end of three months he was in critical condition, moving him from the Veterans' Hospital to the General, and back again. They were also hitting him with 6 shots a day. He was being over-dosed purposely. A specialist was only allowed to see John once. He took a blood sample and said John was critical and in a toxic state, poisoned by Dilantin in his body. John didn't recognize Sheila. He was having 10 to 12 seizures a day.

Sheila got on the phone and begged me to help her. I told her to get a lawyer. She did. The Lord was with her. The lawyer contacted a Judge Shields and said that John Todd through the lawyer would file a suit in inhumane punishment against this court. The judge ordered John released. John's life was saved. The Illuminati lost that round. God had answered our prayers.

Interesting note: While John was in jail that little 13-year-old runaway that John was accused of murdering by Officer Keen called up her mother to say she was out of the state of Ohio and that she was alive.

John was released on December 23, 1976. After the first of the year Judge Shields gave John permission to go to Phoenix, Arizona, for a job. Later, John moved to Alabama and called his probation officer to see if it was all right. The officer said it was fine.

John and Sheila told me they would try to warn the churches one more time what the Illuminati is doing to our churches and what they have planned for us. It takes guts to tell what's coming. John makes mistakes on certain statements and he'll admit it. He is a Christian layman, not a minister.

Part of the material being circulated includes letters from ex-police officer Keen and part of the news clippings from that area. All this was when John was backslidden. John points out the letters ex-Officer Keen sent were secret within the occult organization. Only witches or Masons could possibly get their hands on them. The last people on earth I would believe would be Galvin Frost, the pope of the occult

and his enforcer, Isaac Bonewits, who I've been told commit animal sacrifices and who knows what else to the prince of darkness. These men are not my brothers in Christ. They hate the ground we walk on. God help us when we have to rely on witches for information.

At least John has given us the warning. He is being blasted by witches and Christians alike. As far as I'm concerned, his past is under the blood. John has confessed all this to the Lord Jesus.

It would be easy to compromise and give in to these pressures, but I won't. I believe and love both John and Sheila. They are fighting for survival, never knowing where the next shotgun blast will come from.

I know that as a result of his messages revival is breaking out. Pastors have called me by phone and told me that the kids are burning their rock music and getting saved.

I believe the dear brothers in the Lord who are sending out this material have made a mistake in not knowing who they are lining up with. I pray these attacks cease and that we may all be in much prayer about this. John and Sheila need our support as they face an unbelievable powerful force who would stop at nothing to destroy them. They are counting on Christians to help them silence John. If I thought for one minute John was a phony, I would not hesitate for a second to expose him. I've prayed and sought God about this matter and I believe John is a true brother in Christ who has been given a very difficult ministry.

JACK CHICK, President, Chick Publications, Inc.

Chick continued to stick up for Todd, but at the same time, tried not to become an *enabler* for Todd's sexual escapades. It would wind up being an impossible task. Why did Chick try so hard to stand by such a flawed individual? One likely reason is because Chick knew what it was like to be abandoned by fellow Christians the moment controversy hit. He remembered how few defended him after he published the antihomosexual tract, *The Gay Blade,* in 1972. He openly complained about how everyone abandoned Anita Bryant for similar reasons in *Let's Make A Stand.*

However, there was another motive Chick stuck by Todd ... compassion. In a January 4th, 1979 interview (Hicks and Lewis, 80) with David Lewis, Todd's ex-wife Sharon explains:

"While John and Sheila were in New Mexico, Jack Chick called me. Told me where they were. Said I should 'really blow the whistle on them.' Jack knew what was going on. He loves John like the father John never had. Jack sees the emotional need and can't turn away from him, although he's tried several times. Jack never hurt anyone, he's the most godly man I have ever known."

Even church leaders can be part of Satan's scheme, especially if they are liberals who don't use the King James version of *The Bible*. *The Broken Cross* ©1974 Jack T. Chick.

But Chick's defense wasn't enough to fend off the ever growing list of Todd critics. Todd didn't help matters by announcing a long list of Christian leaders who were secretly working for the Illuminati. They included Chuck Smith, founder of Calvary Chapel and *Maranatha! Music*, whom he accused of taking millions in Illuminati payoffs (Hicks and Lewis, 106). He claimed Ralph Wilkerson of Melodyland was, "the Illuminati's top infiltrator, he is the man who must appear before the Council of 13. I was there when Wilkerson opened several briefcases containing $10 million in cash" (Hicks and Lewis, 98). He said the president's sister, Ruth Carter Stapleton, was, "the most powerful witch in the world" (Hicks and Lewis, 121). Todd also alleged that Jerry Falwell was working for Illuminati boss John R. Rice and accepted $50 million in payoffs (Hicks and Lewis, 127). He asserted that "A Cherokee medium told [Oral Roberts] to lay on hands, and he used to attend her séances regularly" (Hicks and Lewis, 128). Todd also claimed that Debby Boone's song, *You Light Up My Life*, was really a praise to Lucifer (Hicks and Lewis, 128). He said Billy Graham's foundation "supports Illuminati projects and they are channeling money into it" (Hicks and Lewis, 129). He described the popular writer C.S. Lewis as, "A top occult church member and writer for the Illuminati, never saved" (Hicks and Lewis, 68). He remarked of Kathryn Kuhlman, "When I was a witch, she was one of us" (Hicks and Lewis, 129). What about Christian programs like the PTL Club? Todd said, "they talk in tongues. I came from witchcraft and witches talk in tongues" (Hicks and Lewis, 117). The 700 Club? "I heard on the 700 Club that God has gone

to a new dispensation" (Hicks and Lewis, 117). He said the Southern Baptists in general were "taken over with Masons and the Illuminati" (Hicks and Lewis, 129). Even the ultraconservative Assemblies of God wasn't safe from Todd's accusations: "There are a lot of Masons" (Hicks and Lewis, 119). And the Charismatics? "We gave $35 million to Charismatics in two years" (Hicks and Lewis, 113).

Jimmy Carter was not the only famous politician that Todd made surprising accusations about. Todd said he saw George McGovern plunge a dagger into the heart of a girl during a Satanic sacrifice (Hicks and Lewis, 73). On *The Gap* TV program, Todd boasted he used to be the personal occult advisor to the Kennedys. "John F. Kennedy was not really killed. I just came back from a visit with him on his yacht!" (Hicks and Lewis, 76)

Critics say Todd dropped from sight in 1979 because the lies became too outlandish while the exposes became too convincing, including several 1979 articles in *Christianity Today* and *Cornerstone*. There was also a 160 page book called *The Todd Phenomenon* (1979) which didn't leave much room for sympathy. The book included a foreword by Mike Warnke, who warned, "We as Christians have to be careful of those who take the name of the Lord in vain." Warnke himself would be exposed as a phony ex-Satanist in 1992 (Lee 2002).

The Todds provided a different explanation for their withdrawal. They claimed they isolated themselves in preparation for the big economic collapse and impending Illuminati worldwide takeover. It was all supposed to happen sometime around 1980. For all the juicy details, check out the 1979 open letter from Todd's wife, Sheila, to their supporters.

P.O. Box 115
Florence, Montana 59833
January, 1979

Dear Brothers and Sisters:

Greetings in the name of the Lord Jesus Christ.

I want to start this newsletter by apologizing for it being late. The reason for the delay is that we have just moved. We are now in the general area of our retreat. Praise the Lord for His glory! We are praying for the soon return of Jesus as it can only make us happier than anything we have ever known.

We have received a lot of letters asking about the things John said on the tape, "Helter Skelter," and if anything has changed. On the contrary. The riots have started in California like John said they would. This timetable is right on schedule, and October 14 or 15 is still the date they have planned to change the money over. Of course, they could try to do it to us sooner. John still believes that all Christians should try to get out of the cities and store food and some type of defense.

We also feel that we should store Bibles and tracts. We personally feel that the Chick Publications tracts are the best because you can just place one in somebody's hand without out a lot of explaining...

John is feeling completely well. He is no longer booking any meetings as it is so close and his life is in so much danger. We feel that we can do much more by sending out a newsletter and our tapes.

We want to thank you who have sent offerings. It is only your support that keeps this newsletter going out. Thank you for your prayers and help. Some of our worst sailing has been the last 2 weeks before moving. It seems that everything that could go wrong surely did. Several attempts were made on our lives, but God has brought us through and we thank Him for His protection.

We get letters continually asking for us to defend ourselves against the many rumors going around. Brothers and Sisters, we just cannot constantly defend ourselves. All we can say in defense is that if you will wait and watch things will come to pass as John has said they will. A vicious rumor claims that John was saved before he said he was. The only thing John has to say about that is he wishes he had been. That would have given him more years to serve Christ. He might have accomplished more for the Lord Jesus Christ.

The rumors are only one more scheme to try to undermine and discredit what John has said. There will be some who will believe them. But then Jesus only had a chosen few who stood by Him. Even Peter denied Christ. We are determined to stay with Christ whatever the price may be. We know that because we are so close to the end, Satan seeks to destroy all those whom God has chosen.

If any of you don't have confidence in this ministry, please ask us to remove your name from our mailing list. It costs just too much to place our newsletter into ungrateful hands. And contrary to what some people may think, we only want to use Christ's money in a constructive way.

We would like to warn you to look out for this Jim Jones issue to play a part in what they'll start doing to the churches. First, they will try to get all churches to join a union so they will have a clear picture of those which will not join. In this way, the churches that are not a part of the World Council of Churches will be listed as cults. We are in the days in which everything that happens is shaping our future and this is not always good. We just ask you to pray that Jesus Christ comes quickly.

May God bless and keep you and yours,

Sister Sheila Todd
(signed)

The deadline came and went, and the Illuminati didn't attack. Ronald Reagan became President and things turned around. The hostages were freed, crime receded, the economy began its longest peace time expansion in the history of the United States. Americans became optimistic again. National paranoia seemed to evaporate, along with John Todd and his controversial claims. No one seemed to know where he went. Even Chick lost track of him.

All sorts of rumors surfaced: He was assassinated by the Illuminati this way or that. However, the truth is even more shocking. John Todd went to prison, but unlike some other famous fundamentalists, it was not for financial mismanagement — it was for sex crimes.

His attorney, Jim Corley, told a South Carolina paper, The State (June 10, 1987), "Todd had given up even Christian-survivalism by the mid-1980s when he plead guilty to incest with a niece in Louisville.

"Todd moved to Columbia in 1985 to live with his third wife, who was from St. Matthews. They have since divorced.

"He got a job as a carpenter on the Whaley's Mill apartment complex near USC. He was working there in the summer of 1985 when he stepped off a loft he was constructing and hit his head. The injury aggravated Todd's epilepsy, a condition he told very few about.

"Since his injury, Todd has supported himself with worker's compensation and conducted karate classes."

He also went under a new name, Jason Collins. He advertised he was looking for an editor for his new publishing company, 5 Winds Corporation. He offered $50K, plus other perks like a $5,000 wardrobe and a company car. One perk he didn't mention was mandatory sex. Danny Meyers, and Investigator for the South Carolina Law Enforcement Division (SLED), told the same paper that a female graduate student answered Todd's ad and went to his apartment on May 8, 1987, to discuss the upcoming publication.

Instead, Meyers said, Todd asked her, "What do you think the $50,000 is for?" and ordered her into the bedroom.

When she refused, Meyers said, Todd pulled a knife on her, forced her to swallow three white pills and threatened to kill her. He then made her undress, perform oral sex and had intercourse with her. Todd released her the next morning, Meyers testified.

After reports of Todd's arrest appeared on the local news, about 70 other incidents possibly linked to him were reported to authorities.

Saturday, January 23, 1988

Man gets 30 years for rape

'Survivalist' protests verdict

By DEBRA-LYNN B. HOOK
State Staff Writer

"Survivalist" John Wayne Todd was sentenced Friday to 30 years in prison for raping a graduate student after he promised to hire her as an illustrator for his publishing company.

A seven-woman, five-man Richland County jury deliberated one hour and 40 minutes before delivering a guilty verdict against Todd, who witnesses said had been seeking female "employees" through the University of South Carolina Career Center when he was arrested in May.

Todd, already serving a five-year probationary sentence on 1984 incest charges in Kentucky, was given the maximum sentence possible for a charge of first-degree criminal sexual conduct in South Carolina.

Todd

"Under the law of the state, this is probably one of the most serious crimes in the state of South Carolina," Circuit Judge Ralph King Anderson said before delivering the sentence. "The facts of this case, as outlined, reveal grievous conduct by the convicted. I must respond."

Anderson asked Todd if he had anything to say before the sentencing. Todd first shook his head no, but as Anderson proceeded with sentencing, Todd said he decided he did want to say something.

"The plea I originally entered — that is, not guilty — is the plea I stand by." Todd, 38, said. "This was not a rape that took place."

Defense attorney James Corley, who put no witnesses on the stand during the 1½-day trial, attempted to prove through cross-examination that the victim willingly had sexual intercourse with Todd.

The victim, a University of South Carolina student, testified during the trial that she met Todd through a colleague, who testified that Todd had molested her but she was too frightened of him to warn the victim. The victim said Todd called her after finding her resume in a file at USC's Career Center. He told her that he wanted a publicist for a publishing company he was starting in Columbia.

The third time she met with him, at his Percival Road apartment May 8, he demanded that she spend the night with him, she testified.

"He said, 'If you try to hurt me, I could have you killed,'" she testified.

→ See Jail. 6-D

6-D• The State/Columbia,

Jail

→ From 1-D

Todd gave the victim three white pills and raped her while holding a large knife used in jungle warfare she testified. He also stifled her with a pillow and she was groggy from the pills and didn't get up until the next morning

Corley pointed out that the victim willingly met with Todd the night of the incident. She met him at his apartment, had two drinks, then agreed to ride with him to pick up a ticket at the Greyhound bus station in downtown Columbia, Corley said in closing arguments. It was after midnight when they got back to Todd's apartment, and the victim willingly went in with Todd, Corley said.

"Does what (the victim) say happened actually happen the way she says it did?" Corley asked the jury in closing arguments. "Or did it become rape during a conversation between (the victim and two other women who knew Todd)? Is that when they cooked up the story? Is that when something that was fun became something else?"

Before the jury deliberated, Judge Anderson told jurors they shouldn't find Todd guilty if they believe there was any hint of consent in the victim's actions. Anderson also cautioned that the jury shouldn't confuse submission with consent.

"Yielding to overpowering force or yielding as a result of being put in fear is not the same as consent," Anderson said.

Todd has not been charged in the case of the victim's colleague, although that case is being reviewed along with several other incidents that were reported to police after Todd's arrest was made public, Fifth Circuit Solicitor Jay Ervin said.

Todd, however, does have two outstanding warrants against him that may come to trial in February, Ervin said. Those warrants charge him with two counts of lewd acts against a minor. In that case he is charged with having sexually molested two children at the karate school where he taught.

Todd disappeared from the public in the 1980s. He is now under the watchful eye of the state. The State/Columbia News ©1988, Jan 23.

Todd received the maximum sentence. According to the January 23rd, 1988 issue of The State, he told the Judge, "The plea I originally entered — that is, not guilty — is the plea I stand by. This was not a rape that took place." The 38 year old Todd received 30 years.

But the story doesn't end there. Todd has returned to making tapes, is still maintaining his innocence, and blames being framed by — you guessed it — the Illuminati.

To be fair, it should be remembered that the strongest evidence against Todd was testimony from the alleged victim. So it was his word against hers. Unfortunately for Todd, she wasn't on probation for a sex offense and he was.

Here's the highlights from a transcription provided by *The Netizen* website (2002, June) of Todd's latest — and perhaps greatest — tape to date:

"I am John Todd, and this tape is being made in a prison cell in South Carolina. It is very late at night. All the inmates are locked down in their cells, but you will still hear noise off and on. And if the guard comes by, I have to stop and be very quiet. The reason for this tape is that I have been framed and put in prison by order of US Senator from South Carolina Strom Thurmond. I'll go into all the reasons for that, and what happened to me. And only recently, in fact just about a week and a half ago did I find out how it was really accomplished.

"As I started to say, the reason for this tape is to get the word out about where I'm at. I've been in custody almost four years now. I've been in a prison cell for three years, and that time is a very closely guarded secret by the government, by the Illuminati, and definitely by the conspirators. The word of what has happened to me has not gotten out of the state of South Carolina."

What atmosphere! Hostile guards pace outside the cell while Todd attempts to whisper his news on tape. Audiences haven't experienced such dramatic on-the-spot reporting since Bernard Shaw dodged missiles in Baghdad live on CNN. How could any of Todd's previous lecture tapes compete with a scene like this?

Todd maintains that the media is owned and controlled by the Illuminati. *Spellbound?* ©1978 Jack T. Chick.

Todd is definitely correct about the under-reporting of his fate. The media usually makes a big deal whenever a famous Fundamentalist is sent to prison. How this trial and conviction remained relatively unknown is astounding. It had all the ingredients for national coverage: A controversial right wing religious survivalist accused of a violent sex crime. How did this remain a local secret for so long?

Todd talks about how the police stole his address book to cut him off from allies, then says:

"One of the things that seems to be very frightening to Christians is that such a thing could actually take place. Many who knew I was innocent could not believe that I had been found guilty. Not so much that - because-, it just wasn't there, it didn't take place, so therefore even the manufactured evidence wasn't even there. They just couldn't believe that a child of God in this country could go to prison. (I had stopped and came to the door. I can't let this tape be known that it is being made or it would never get out of here.) I want to say this now before I go on, whoever receives a copy of this tape I'm asking you to make a copy or copies and get the word out. Make phone calls. Let people know what has happened to me. Let them know that they can be of service to get me out of here. This is what is most feared about putting me in here, that the word will get out."

Todd rails against the injustice of his trial, then explains it was South Carolina senator Strom Thurmond who stacked the deck against him. He explains why:

"Now the reason that Strom Thurmond hated me, in case you're familiar or not familiar with this, is that when I was living in California working with Chick publications and preaching very heavily in '87 ['77] and doing mostly exposes on everybody, it had come out about Strom Thurmond being the highest ranking Mason in the world, and that he was also a member of the voting Board of Regents for the Bob Jones University. Now the first thing that Bob Jones University did was to deny that Thurmond was a Mason. But Thurmond wouldn't go along with it. He knew he was too well known as being a Mason. So he came out and tried to defend Masonic beliefs that Christians can be that. It blew up on him. And he became so outraged that ... they had to ask him to step down. "

Todd did in fact force the Senator off the University board by attacking his Masonry membership (Plowman 1979). How Thurmond chose to respond to the embarrassment isn't really known. Todd claims the Senator worked behind the scenes to settle the score and make sure he went to prison. He gives a long soliloquy itemizing the plots and cover-ups. Then he warns the listener about how the Illuminati are out to get Christians. He says they offered to let him go if he would tell them who is in the Christian Underground, but he refused.

"I expect for them to show up again trying to know if I will make a deal; the answer is 'no.' Isn't it amazing that I'm supposed to be this terrible rapist on a state charge that the Feds somehow have authority over ... and they are willing to let me just go, wipe it off the books for turning [over] Christians who are wanted for nothing, a lot of times nothing but misdemeanor warrants, or child custody warrants where the state wants to take the kids, or for violations of court orders. A lot of these people are on the run, from Christian schools where the state has sworn out warrants for these Christians because [of what] they were teaching the children, and the state decided that this was not right and so on. Little stuff, and yet they are willing to let me go for all these people plus the Christians who are hiding them out."

"I think you'd better wake up brothers and sisters, because I was sent to prison without the right to a fair trial and I want to tell you what. It could be done real easy. They control the media. They could say anything about you they want to say. They control the governments. They control the police forces. Wake up!"

Eventually, Todd makes a plea for contributions.

"I am asking you to help. I am asking you whether it is five dollars or a hundred dollars, or a thousand dollars. Please, we need desperately, we need to raise the finances. We need to get me free."

Todd compares himself to the Apostle Paul in prison. Let's hope he doesn't get the same treatment. *Why No Revival?* ©1986 Jack T. Chick.

He talks about the apostle Paul being in prison, and what it's like. Then he emphasizes how important it is to get him out.

"If the Illuminati, Strom Thurmond and them, put so much effort to do this to me, there is a reason. And I'm asking for your help. I'm asking ministers who hear this who have newsletters to just simply send out what is going on here, to make copies of this tape and to make it available."

Todd estimates the earliest he can get out without appeals is 2005. Either way, it looks like Todd's infamous tapes are back in circulation, even if he is not.

estant movement during most of its history. All this made Rivera's conspiracy theory seem very believable to Chick. It even had a scriptural basis as provided in the book of Revelation (according to traditional Protestant interpretations).

Chick met up with Rivera around 1978 during the height of John Todd's career. Todd owed part of his success on the lecture circuit to massive sales of *The Crusaders* comics that detailed his story. Rivera would face this same destiny. Rivera actually met Todd on at least one occasion in Chick's presence. The two argued over who was really behind the conspiracy to take over the world for Satan. Todd insisted it was the Illuminati; Rivera said it was the Vatican. In the end, Chick was convinced that the Vatican was manipulating the Illuminati and other organizations that frequently surface in conspiracy theories (Chick 1978, 29). The Club of Rome, the Council on Foreign Relations, and even the Ku Klux Klan are tied together at the top by the Vatican, according to Rivera. Chick was quick to trust Rivera because (unlike Todd) Rivera had several official looking documents showing he was indeed an ex-priest. The *Alberto* comics reprinted these documents as proof to doubters. Rivera claimed to have had many more documents, but most of them were left behind when he fled Spain and escaped to the West. Rivera said the Vatican then had all his prior records destroyed so that Rome could deny he was ever a priest. Any exposés by Rivera's critics were a waste of time, as far as Chick was concerned. They were only revealing what the Vatican wanted the public to know. Such attacks always seemed to originate from groups that were already playing "footsie" with the Vatican, and published in Protestant venues that openly urged reconciliation with the Catholics, including Billy Graham's *Christianity Today* and Walter Martin's *Christian Research Institute*.

©1980 Jack T. Chick.

Alberto, a.k.a. Alberto Romero Rivera

After publishing three *Crusaders* comics based on information from John Todd's Illuminati schemes, Chick met another person who said he had an even more explosive conspiracy to reveal. His name was Alberto Rivera, and he claimed to be an ex-Jesuit priest who left the Roman Catholic Church after realizing it was demonic. Rivera's conspiracy was far more controversial than anything else Chick had published, because it alleged that no less than 1/6th of the world's population was part of the Satanic plot (though most were unwitting dupes). Moreover, the "institution" he implicated was another denomination that officially recognized Jesus as the son of God.

Unlike the Illuminati—which was a secret society formed in 1776 and officially suppressed by the Bavarian government in 1785—the Roman Catholic Church is a high profile organization that has existed for nearly two thousand years and continues to grow in membership and financial strength. Its global ambitions have a factual historic basis, as demonstrated via worldwide missionary efforts and, on occasion, armed crusades into foreign lands. The Vatican has been openly hostile to the Prot-

Organized boycotts almost ran Chick out of business, but Chick publications bounced back stronger than ever. *My Name? In the Vatican?* ©1980 Jack T. Chick.

Based on stories supplied by Rivera, *The Crusaders* characters Jim Carter and Tim Clark would sit in a living room for six issues and listen to Rivera lay out Vatican plots to conquer the world for the Pope and reinstall the dreaded Inquisition. The resulting firestorm of Catholic protests would threaten the continued existence of Chick Publications, but when the dust settled, the company would emerge stronger than ever.

When Chick published volume 12 of *The Crusaders* series in 1979, he simply entitled it *Alberto*. The remainder of *The Crusaders* series were devoted entirely to Rivera's story on Vatican intrigue. The sequel, *Double Cross* (1981), evoked as much controversy as did its predecessor with new allegations that prominent Christians in the public eye were secret agents of the Vatican. Rivera continued his story in *The Godfathers* (1982), *The Force* (1983), *The Four Horseman* (1985), and *The Prophet* (1988). No further *Crusaders* series have been published since 1988, but rumor has it that another is planned after Carter completes his painting of images for Chick's movie.

At the center of the controversy is Alberto Rivera himself. Some say he was indeed an ex-Roman Catholic priest. Many others (especially Catholics) say he was a fraud. Some think Rivera was self delusional. If so, he certainly had a vivid and precise memory of his delusions. All the biographical details he provides about his life are much more concise than what most people could provide about their past. Any minor difference given in dates from the comic book and his public lectures can easily be written off as common memory lapse, especially in light of his claims to have undergone electric shock treatments at the Catholic sanitarium. (You can bet the doctor who discharged him had a lot of explaining to do!) And far from dodging critics, Rivera always seemed to seek them out and confront them. He would call up radio shows and debate with them (uninvited), or meet with them privately like he did with Dr. Walter Martin. However, these discussions and debates never seemed to improve Rivera's public credibility. He would give specific answers, but that's a far cry from hard proof. And whatever documents he did provide were always downplayed by critics (although never proved to be forgeries). Ultimately, the constant attacks on his claims and personal background made most of the mainstream public write him off as a fraud. Still, Rivera seemed completely oblivious to this and continued to engage doubters whenever the opportunity arose. He often offered tapes of such debates along with his religious materials.

Rivera said he intended on publishing four 500 page books giving additional details and documents to dispel critics, but he never got around to it. Was it because he couldn't provide those documents? Or was it because, like many of us, he got distracted with other priorities and procrastinated until it was too late? There is no way to know for sure.

On page 27 of the first *Alberto* comic, Rivera's national ID paper is reprinted in full color. The photograph on it shows Rivera wearing his priest collar. Chick correctly points out that fascist Spain was a police state at the time. Making a false ID to defraud the authorities would not be easy. If caught, the penalties would be severe. Chick states, "To obtain this document, Alberto had to supply his birth certificate, identifications papers, and positive proof from his Archdiocese of being a priest." Rivera also includes an official transfer document that he claims was issued by the Archbishop to authorize his travel. Both documents are dated 1967.

Rivera says on the same page that "I was made a Bishop in the Old Roman Catholic Church, receiving my Bull of Consecration under the Apostolic succession of Roman Popes." Rivera claims he was made a Jesuit agent and placed under Extreme Oath and Induction because of his espionage work.

Not listed in the comic books is corroborating testimony provided by Dr. Gerard Bouffard. He was a high ranking bishop born in Quebec, Canada. He rose from lower levels of his orders to become an assistant for many years to Popes such as Paul VI and John Paul II. He converted to Protestantism and claims he was the man who received the order to eliminate Rivera (AIC 1998, 9). In a documentary called *Unveiling the Mystery Behind Catholic Symbols,* Bouffard shows a fancy 18-carat gold plated pen containing a special disappearing ink with which the Holy Office authorities sign top secret documents. He claims, "With this pen that I am holding, I signed the order to kill Dr. Rivera." Pretty dramatic cloak and dagger stuff! His previous high profile position would make him an easy target for discrediting. Surprisingly, no such effort has been made. Is it a Vatican oversight? Or was he really a high ranking Catholic official that changed sides and the Vatican doesn't wish to call attention to him?

Another piece of evidence provided by Bouffard is a March 10, 1965 document which he claims is the official Vatican order telling him to organize Rivera's murder. It states:

"ALBERTO RIVERA, of Barcelona, Spain, having left the Holy Catholic Institution of Rome and not obeying the papal orders any more, is to be executed physically, eliminated, or placed so that he can not damage the Church any more."

The signature is supposedly that of the General Manager of the Holy Office. Oddly enough, the document is written in Quebecois, instead of Latin, the official language used in Vatican documents. That any official would actually put into writing such a potentially damaging memo is also suspicious. Then again, if Presidents made self incriminating tapes of phone conversations for their records, who's to say the Vatican might not do something equally stupid?

Chick reproduced Alberto's identification papers in many of his publications. *Alberto* ©1979 Jack T. Chick.

Manhattan personally vouched for part of Alberto's story.

Another piece of corroborating testimony comes from Avro Manhattan. He personally told Chick that he was in London driving the getaway car when Rivera ran in to rescue his sister from the Catholic convent (Lee 2002). Manhattan was a prolific writer and critic of Catholic issues, and often wrote articles in early issues of *Battle Cry*. He had substantial credibility in Chick's eyes.

Many fundamentalists think the Vatican has its own credibility problems to contend with. They feel that from a historical context, Rivera's claims to be a Jesuit working undercover to destroy Protestant churches is not far flung. The Jesuits were created in 1541 by Ignatius De Loyola for the purpose of fighting Protestantism (although some Jesuits claim their creation during the reformation was only a coincidence). Jesuits have been accused of involvement in many dirty tricks, including assassination plots. One example is the notorious gunpowder plot of 1605. Father Garnet, the highest ranking Jesuit in England at the time, was convicted of conspiring with fellow Catholics to blow up Parliament and their Protestant king. The execution of the Catholic traitors is still celebrated in England every November 5th during Guy Fawlkes day.

Although exact numbers are still debated, large scale atrocities during the Inquisitions are well documented. Chick's later comics often show these tortures in painstaking detail. *Alberto* ©1979 Jack T. Chick.

Jesuits were also involved in the infamous Inquisitions, which resulted in the torture and/or murder of countless innocents for the alleged crime of heresy. *The Office of the Inquisition* has been replaced with *The Holy Office*, but the Jesuits have never bothered with a name change. How much their goals have changed with time is also uncertain. Neither organization is very transparent and both serve the interests of the Pope. Bad reputations are not easily forgotten.

If Rivera's story is all fabrication, it's a brilliant piece of fiction with impressive consistency. There are certainly other conspiracies that have been dreamed up which are equally vivid and intricate. The JFK assassination conspiracy and the *Majestic 12* UFO conspiracy are similar examples. However, those conspiracies were created and improved by hundreds of people over a long period of time, then pieced together and rearranged until they formed a quality narrative. After years of public input and revisions, a semiofficial version is adopted. If any particular part of it is proven to be false, it morphs into a slightly different version without out the disproved parts.

Rivera may have drawn on a few other anti-Vatican conspiracy theories (like those told by Charles Chiniquy) but for the most part, his elaborate Jesuit conspiracy came from him alone. It wasn't revised and honed for decades by committee before Chick published it. On the contrary, it was published in its entirety and then sublimated with additional volumes (five more comics) giving more names and dates but no retractions. If nothing else, he deserves a prize for literary genius. Especially as far as his own biographical exploits are concerned (move over, Baron von Munchausen?).

After twenty years of investigations and criticism, all the Vatican's resources have failed to convince many of Chick's readers that Rivera was a fake. Critics like Gary Metz have amassed plenty of witnesses who will say bad things about Rivera, but witnesses can lie—especially if, as Rivera claims, they are really agents of the Vatican. One would think there should be *something* stronger than "he said/she said" testimony to make their case. (Rivera has his list of witnesses who make equally disparaging remarks against the Vatican, and that doesn't prove much either.) The most damning *hard* evidence that Metz presented has mysteriously vanished (assuming it ever existed). He said in a 1984 KBRT radio interview that he had a death certificate for Juan Rivera. Metz claimed Juan was Rivera's son, a child born when Rivera was supposedly a celibate priest in 1964. He said the son died in July of 1965 in El Paso. Rivera vigorously denied the allegation and that any such document existed. Metz brushed off the denial, saying anyone could get the death certificate from the Bureau of Vital Statistics.

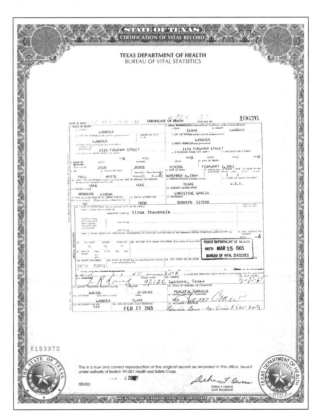

The questionable death certificate. The father's name is listed as Rudolfo, not Alberto.

Reverend Rich Lee attempted to do just that. At long last, both sides were on record agreeing that a certain piece of *documented* evidence from an official government agency proved which side was lying. Lee contacted the Bureau of Vital Statistics in Austin in 1985 and ordered the document. According the Metz, the mother was Carmen Lydia Torres (Metz 1981). The Bureau wrote back to say no such document existed. Refusing to give up on the "smoking gun" so easily, I ordered certified copies of the document myself...*twice*. The closest match they could find was Juan Jesus Rivera with a mother named Christine Garcia and a father named Rudolfo Rivera. I've also seen a non-certified copy of another close match, but that one has the father's name inverted and no mother listed at all. This episode gives the reader a taste of how frustrating this controversy can be. Just when you think one side has nailed the other, it turns out the accuser has credibility problems of his own. Another thing Metz never mentions is that he tried to get a job at Chick Publications, but was rejected (Chick 1981). Chick believes he was attempting to infiltrate Chick Publications and was always out "to get" his organization from the start. Not surprisingly, Metz denies these counter claims (Metz 2003).

Of course, Rivera failed to prove his allegations against the Vatican as well. So, in a way, the contest is still a draw. Maybe future developments will yield something dramatic. Don't hold your breath, though. Now that he's dead, Rivera can't confess anything, and it's not likely that the Pope will step forward and claim to be the Antichrist.

Rivera died in June of 1997 in Broken Arrow, Oklahoma. He was 61 and the cause of death was listed on the death certificate as an eighteen month battle with colon cancer (Cicchese 1997). He called Jack Chick before his death and told him that "the Jesuits finally got me." According to the *Double Cross* comic book, there were all sorts of failed assassination attempts carried out against Rivera throughout the years. His room was blown up in Ireland, ground glass was stuck in his food at a prayer meeting, and he became ill after eating poisoned food, etc. He was even shot at in Chick's presence, in a drive-by situation not far from Chick Publications (*Let's Make A Stand* 1981).

Rivera also claimed the Jesuits had a special poison that gave their victims a terminal cancer but left no traces of foul play. Years later, he succumbed to colon cancer. His wife, Nury Rivera, believes she knew when the poison was delivered (four years earlier). She claims it was supposed to kill him right away, and that it was a miracle that he survived another four years (Cicchese 1997). However, minor differences in her opinion and her husbands as to the timing of the poisoning do not seem to matter much. What is more interesting is her claim about a series of phone calls she received after his death. She told Chick that Catholic priests called her after her husband died and acted very sympathetic. They said they wanted to know where he was buried so they could conduct "a special service given to priests." She became angry and said they had denied he was a priest during his lifetime, and now that he was dead, they wanted to give him a priest's funeral. She said that she slammed the phone down in disgust. She figured what they really wanted to do was desecrate the grave.

Chick believes what they wanted to do was far more sinister. He told friends that he thought the Catholic priests wanted to exhume Rivera's body and "put it on trial." It was a medieval practice they used to perform on heretics that eluded their capture while alive. Jesuits would find the body, dig it up, prop it up, and hold a mock trial, excommunicating the corpse and condemning it to Hell. Torture and mutilation of the body is also rumored to have occurred (as if it could feel it!). But such practices were probably more effective as a deterrent. The living would hear about these after-death humiliations and become less likely to contradict the Church leadership.

We'll never know what the motive for the phone call to Nury really was, but it brings up an interesting possibility: She is either lying or the priests were admitting Rivera was once a Catholic priest (regardless of whether or not he told the truth about everything else). It also raises some other interesting considerations: Mental illness is not considered

Was Alberto crazy? He admits he was briefly treated, but says he had an epiphany while in the hospital. *Alberto* ©1979 Jack T. Chick.

contagious, and the chances that a husband and wife both suffered from the same exact illness and imagined similar delusions would seem unlikely. Of course, someone could have been playing a prank on her, but that seems a rather strange prank. Although she could be lying, she only made these claims in a private discussion with Chick. If the purpose was to provide greater credibility to her husband, why wouldn't she disseminate the tale in a newsletter or some sort of public outlet? It doesn't quite add up.

If Alberto Rivera consciously fabricated tales of Catholic conspiracy, he certainly worked hard to maintain the hoax all the way to his death. Unlike Todd, he never fell from grace or went to prison. Likewise, he never avoided critics as Todd often did, but instead, went out of his way to engage them. He continued to preach and try to convert Catholics months before his death, with little financial reward for doing so. Rivera refused royalties from *The Crusader* comics series and related tracts. If he was such a slick con man, one would think that he could have found a more lucrative line of work. His religious tape and video sales didn't appear significantly profitable. (Although he did charge a dime more for his tracts compared to Chick!)

Like many popular conspiracies, the *Alberto* conspiracy will probably never die. Despite all the common sense evidence to the contrary, there are always *just enough* unanswered questions and contradictory evidence to keep the suspicions alive. Many fans consider it one of Chick's most entertaining, if not frightening, conspiracy theories to date.

Rebecca Brown, a.k.a. Ruth Irene Bailey

A lot of Chick readers wondered where Chick would go after covering the John Todd and Alberto Rivera stories. Would he perform some sort of *mea culpa* and try to return to publishing less controversial mainstream Christian materials? If not, how could he ever top such incredible conspiracies as plots to take over the world by the Illuminati and the Vatican? The answer came flying in on a broomstick in the mid-1980s when Chick fell under the spell of Rebecca Brown.

Brown was a former physician who had left the medical profession to pursue a deliverance ministry. She claimed she was engaged in a spiritual battle with Satan and his various witches' covens. Brown believed they were angry at her successful efforts to drive out demons from patients and former witches. One person who had a foot in both categories was Brown's sidekick, a woman named "Elaine." Her last name was withheld, presumably for personal safety reasons.

Chick published Brown's amazing claims in the 1986 opus, *He Came To Set The Captives Free*. The book detailed how Elaine originally set out to kill Brown under direct orders from Satan. However, Brown converted Elaine to Christianity. Elaine then revealed sensational personal accounts of occult activities to her new found friend. These stories made exciting reading and garish headlines. In 1987, the two demon busters appeared on the syndicated talk show with Geraldo Rivera (no relation to Alberto) and repeated their amazing story.

Many of Brown's and Elaine's fantastic claims are chronicled in the *Closet Witches* tapes. Their testimony corroborates many of Todd's and Rivera's stories by confirming Chick's worst fears of witches, Catholics, and Masons working together for the common evil. Consider the following example provided by Elaine in the book:

"The Pope knew very well who I was. We worked closely both with Catholics — especially the Jesuits — and the high ranking Masons." (Brown 1986, 63)

Like Todd, Elaine claimed to be an ex-witch, only in her case, she said she had literally married Satan. In fact, he wore a white tuxedo for the ceremony (Brown 1986, 61). This provided Chick eyewitness testimony about the otherwise invisible mastermind behind *all* the conspiracies Chick was trying to expose. Like Alberto Rivera, Rebecca Brown claimed to be a doctor, but unlike Rivera, she was a *medical* doctor who could easily prove it. Physicians carry considerable credibility in our culture, perhaps more than any other profession. We often trust them with our lives. It is difficult to imagine a doctor trading a respectable and lucrative practice to pursue a career of demon exorcisms and ridicule...unless of course, that person is on a direct mission from God.

Brown claimed to be on such a mission, and more. God not only commissioned her ministry, he had personal conversations with her, sometimes via angels (Brown 1987, 17) and other times as Jesus Himself (Brown 1987, 226).

Both women sound completely sincere in their interview with Chick in the *Closet Witches* tapes. In the second tape, Chick makes an eerie prediction:

"I think the listeners should watch carefully who in the Christian circles will attack Rebecca and Elaine to destroy their credibility and the message on this tape... It is going to be very, very interesting to watch."

It was interesting indeed, because one of the Christians to spearhead the attack was none other than Paul Blizard, an ex-Jehovah's witness who worked with Chick to write the anti-Watchtower Society tract, *The Crisis* (©1985). Blizard teamed up with Richard Fisher and Kurt Goedelman to write a blistering critique of Brown and Elaine in the October/December 1989 issue of *The Personal Freedom Outreach Journal*. The report attempts to discredit both women with embarrassing revelations about their past.

For starters, it disclosed Brown's real name as Ruth Irene Bailey. It then printed excerpts from the September 1984 Indiana Medical Licensing Board's decision to revoke Bailey's medical license. It was a hearing that Bailey failed to attend and lost by default. They heard from 19 witnesses and decided that Bailey had intentionally misdiagnosed numerous ailments, blaming the cause of the sicknesses on demons and other evil spirits. She was also charged with writing inappropriate drug prescriptions (including narcotics) for herself, Elaine, and Elaine's 15 year old mentally impaired daughter (Fisher 1989, 14). The board appointed psychiatrist determined Bailey was suffering from acute personality disorders including demonic delusions and/or paranoid schizophrenia. The September 21st, 1984 *Indianapolis News* described Bailey after the board took her license as, "a woman plagued by drug addiction, religious extremism, and a belief that patients and colleagues were possessed by devils."

When Elaine witnessed demon violence in Satanism, she turned to Brown for help in escaping The Craft. A similar storyline occurs in *Satan's Master* ©1986 Jack T. Chick.

Brown says she was safe from spells because God protected her, but that didn't stop the witches from trying to hurt her. *Satan's Master* ©1986 Jack T. Chick.

Brown never denied that she lost her license, but she definitely disputed the cause. Her version of events is that the hospital where she worked was taken over by witches. When Brown started interfering in their efforts to help patients die, she says the witches set out to ruin her. Revoking her license was only one part of a wider campaign to harass and intimidate her. However, because of her covenant with God, the devil could not destroy her as long as she was faithful.

The published attacks on Brown failed to disrupt her popularity. Her first book was followed by another (*Prepare for War*, ©1987), and both continued to sell well for Chick Publications. So well, in fact, that she was wooed away by a competing publisher. Chick facilitated the separation by his refusal to print her third book, *Unbroken Curses*. He gives his reasons for his reluctance to do so in a letter written to Stan Madrak on August 25, 2000:

Yoder's first wife was supposedly abducted and murdered by the occult. A similar plot occurs in *The Poor Little Witch* ©1987 Jack T. Chick.

"I felt the Lord wanted me to print her first two books. I did that and her books became some of our best sellers. At a later date, she asked me to print her third book (I don't even remember the name of it now) but I did not feel led to do so. About that same time, she married (her last name is Yoder now), moved away and found another publisher for her new book. She then decided to place all of her books with the same publisher (Whitaker House in PA) and we simply gave her all of the negatives to the books we published and let her do what she wanted with them. We parted friends and I have spoken with her maybe two or three times since then. She says she is attending conferences, doing speaking engagements and selling her books. That is all I know."

One reason Chick does not mention for avoiding the third book is its content. Much of it was co-written by Daniel Michael Yoder, Brown's new husband. The two married in December of 1989 after only one month of acquaintance (Fisher 1996, 2). Yoder came across to some people as the consummate con artist. One such skeptic was Greg Baloun. Baloun was Chief of Police for Lake Park, Iowa, when the newlyweds moved there in 1990.

"From the very start, I knew something wasn't quite right ..." Baloun recounts, "He passed himself off, the first time I met him, as a neurosurgeon." Yoder also bragged that he sped across state lines to perform operations. "He told me how he had this Chrysler Cordova that would do 200 miles an hour and that he ran from California into Nevada to do a special surgery in a mere amount of time." Baloun asked Yoder how he managed the trip without losing time for pit stops. Yoder replied that he had a customized 40-gallon gas tank.

Baloun concluded, "He had an answer for everything. He was a big talker, but you could catch him in lies all the time." (Fisher 1992, 3)

The lies eventually reached critical mass in 1991, when Yoder was arrested and charged with perjury and fraudulent practice in the third degree.

Once again, *Personal Freedom Outreach* documented the embarrassing details for its readers. The 1996 article, *The Return of Rebecca Brown, M.D.*, was written by the same Richard Fisher and Kurt Goedelman as before, but without the help of Paul Blizard. Among the more tantalizing details was the fact that Yoder plead guilty and paid a $2,000 fine for one count of Fraudulent Practice in the third degree. He also admitted his real name was William Joseph Stewart, and that he had only completed seven years of grade school. The article also reports that authorities learned Yoder (Stewart) had a criminal record and had served time in Minnesota and Missouri and had admitted to receiving "Psychological evaluations, counseling, or hospitalizations."

These revelations were all in stark contrast to the impressive biography Yoder provided in Brown's third book, *Unbroken Curses*. There, he claimed he was born into a rich Jewish family of international bankers (the Rothschilds, naturally) and had completed graduate studies in Switzerland. He said he had become a powerful businessman and formed multiple corporations. Like Elaine, he said he was also the victim of occult abuse. He claimed he was sent to study under Rabbinical and Cabalistic teachers since the age of six. After trying to escape such a school, he was locked in a tiny pit and tortured with live spiders that were poured down on him (Fisher 1996, 2).

Yoder said his first wife was also abused because she was raised in Cabalism. She converted to Christianity and was therefore abducted. The bio states the kidnapped couple were "flown to Israel where Daniel was chained to the wall and forced to watch as Kai, his first and only love, was tortured to death!" Yoder escaped and supposedly fled to the United States and converted to Christianity himself before meeting and marrying Brown. (Fisher 1996, 2)

There's no way of knowing for sure what portions (if any) of Yoder's story are true, but it's easy to see why Brown was attracted to him. It's not every day that an unattached deliverance minister meets a well-to-do bachelor who's wife was murdered by cultists. Yoder must have seemed like a perfect match—until the court started punching holes in his resume.

In fairness to Brown, however, it should be noted that these revelations only prove that her husband was guilty of fraud, not her. Perhaps he was part of Satan's plot to make her look guilty by association? Whatever the case, at last check the two are still together and living off of Brown's successful book royalties. All three titles are still found in most Christian book stores, including the big chains. It is ironic that Chick's efforts to expose Satanic plots resulted in his materials being banned in many of the same stores that carry the conspiracy authors that he made famous.

It is impossible to determine what motivated those authors to make the claims that they did. However, Chick's own motivation clearly wasn't money. He not only risked losing his business by printing *Alberto*, but he knowingly forfeited millions by passing on Brown's third book. Her first two were very successful and there was every reason to assume her third would continue to generate big profits. She is supposedly earning more now than she would have if she remained a physician. Meanwhile, Chick continues to live in his modest 40-year-old home fighting off the termites (Chick 2001). But he is rich in one respect: The excitement he generates with his ongoing conspiracies is priceless!

"Marsha, there was a time in history when God cut off all communications with His chosen people, the Jews! They were rebellious; they ignored His laws, so He allowed them to suffer under the heavy hand of the Roman Empire."
Out of our way... you Jewish scum!
Roman pigs!
Clear the streets!
Run!... run!
Mama... mama, help!
"400 years had passed by since God had spoken to the children of Israel... (the Jews)... those who loved the Lord were heartbroken."

Why Collect Chicks?

Because they're a blast! Especially when compared to other collectibles.

Take for example, *Beanie Babies*™. Collectors pay a significant premium for recently manufactured items that were intentionally limited to create an artificial scarcity. Influenced by company hype and clever marketing techniques, eager customers scurry about hoarding small toy animals that will sit on shelves and gather dust. Heaven forbid they play with them: The ear tag might fall off and ruin the resale value! Yet *Beanie Babies* are tremendously popular years after the "fad" has died down. The varieties seem endless. Many a piggy bank went belly up trying to finance the stuffed animal farm. Newcomers can kiss their assets good-bye. Getting started is easy enough but finishing the collection is cost prohibitive for most people—especially kids. The space these critters take up is immense as well.

Chick tract collecting is the opposite in almost every way. Chicks are small and easy to store. They can be traded anywhere in the world by tossing them in a regular envelope and slapping a couple of stamps on it. Most of the tracts cost practically nothing. A mere 14 cents is the standard retail. A handful of the older, super-rare variations are expensive, but the vast majority of out-of-print titles are still below $25! (Most are only $2 to $5 each.) Lucky collectors have found rare tracts for free in public places.

With Chick tracts, there is no anguishing over whether to handle the item. Even the rarest tract can be read and enjoyed without depreciating the value. There are over 170 titles and hundreds more variations, yet finishing a collection of standard titles is still possible at a reasonable cost. Those who can't wait to "fill in the holes" can often find a collector willing to photocopy the tract for them, or download it from Chick's official website. (As long as it's not sold for profit.) Since only the covers of the tracts have color, this provides a cheap but faithful reproduction until the original turns up.

Chick tracts are the cheapest comics around, even when it comes to the vintage titles. They go all the way back to the early 1960s. They are excellent examples of American pop art. Their religious content discourages some from reading them because they think they are "for squares." But many of the hip crowd love Chick tracts for that exact reason. The tracts are so straightlaced and proper, they provide unintentional camp humor for much of their audience. Others avoid Chick tracts because they fear they may be converted by them. Such experiences have occurred with various collectors, but they claim to be grateful for it. If nothing else, it's a testament to the strong message Chick tracts can deliver. (But there are plenty of atheists who remain hostile to Chick's views in spite of collecting his work.)

Chick tracts have an added advantage in that they are educational. Many of them tell famous stories from the Bible, which is the most widely read book in existence. Like it or not, the Bible has influenced countless other works from popular novels to classic Shakespearean plays, and even the music of psychedelic rock bands like the *Grateful Dead*. Familiarity with "the good book" is essential for any educated person, regardless of whether or not he is religious.

The quality of the art in Chick tracts appeals to both the collector of primitive cartoons and the connoisseur of fine comic art. Chick's drawings are very stylized and cartoonish. His other artist (Fred Carter) draws and paints some of the best rendered comics ever made.

The Chick collecting base is still in its infancy, which is great for collectors who like getting in on the ground floor of a trend. As of this printing, Chick is over 80 years old. One can imagine what will happen to the values of his comics the moment he joins the "big guy" upstairs. (So don't procrastinate!)

The best part about Chick tract collecting is the pleasure in reading the tracts themselves. They are serious for those who believe them, hilarious for those who don't, and entertaining for everyone. The "Chick Universe" is a place where God and Satan are at a continual state of war. Chick reveals an invisible world of angels and demons as they fight it out around us, as well as many conspiracies we would otherwise never imagine. The Masons, the Vatican, the witches—it's us against them. With Chick tracts, everyday is Halloween and Christmas combined. Who doesn't enjoy at least one of those two holidays?

In short, Chick tracts are cheap, fun, and highly collectable pieces of Americana. Whether you swear by them or *at* them, Chick's tracts are wonderful conversation pieces sure to liven any discussion. (Asking people where they first encountered them and what they thought when they did is a source of many amusing stories.) Amass a small collection and you'll see how addictive they can be. And if you collect too many, you can always give them away. That is, after all, what they were made for.

The beautiful artwork is just one of the benefits of collecting Chick's comics and tracts. *The Gift* © 1977 Jack T. Chick.

Special tracts for special needs.

Many people, because of their religious or social backgrounds, need the Gospel ex lained in a special way for them to understand. Here are Chi k tracts that w ll ouch their hearts.

Roman Catholics

Have you ever been lied to? Millions have, trusting in "another Christ" to save them. Here is the gospel for Roman Catholics, proving that we have no other mediator but Jesus.

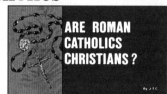

Roman Catholics trust in "another gospel," a gospel of works with no assurance of salvation. This tract shows that Catholicism cannot save ...only *Jesus* can!

Mormons

Two Mormon missionaries discover that the Mormon church is *not* what it claims to be. Only Jesus can save. To learn how to witness to Mormons, see books on page 14 of this catalog.

Jehovah's Witnesses

This Gospel tract for Jehovah's Witnesses will: shake their confidence that the Watchtower Society is "God's Organization," show that Jesus *is* Jehovah and tell them how to get saved (through Jesus, of course).

Muslims

A Gospel tract with a two-fold purpose: to stop Islam from gaining U.S. converts, and to reach nominal Moslems for Jesus.

Homosexuals

Homosexual life is not gay ... but a tragic life of insecurity and hopelessness. David discovers that Jesus can save him, but he must be willing to give up being gay.

For Christians

Satan has messed with your Bible. Find out how!

The exciting story behind the King James Bible, and how Satan tried to destroy it.

Rock Music Fans

They started as a "Christian" rock group, but soon the Green Angels found their lives shattered . . . they were slaves to rock. But Tom found that Jesus could change all that . . . and set him free!

Halloween

Halloween is not just a time of fun and candy. Worldwide, it is the high holy day of satanists. Here is the true story of Halloween, leading up to a great salvation message.

7

Tract Reviews &Values Guide

Welcome to Reviews & Values Guide section. This is where Chick's tracts are critiqued and appraised. These reviews may seem flippant to some, but remember, comics are supposed to be humorous. Chick demonstrates his talent in this regard when he includes sarcasm, social commentary, and visual gags throughout his stories.

These reviews are subjective since there is no scientific way to separate the best from the bad. Several reviews are written by guest reviewers, providing a completely different perspective. Some think Chick is great, others think he's nuts. A few believe both! Some reviewers are Christian (one is a minister), while others are not (one is a witch). You can judge them as they judge Chick accordingly.

Some reviews are a lot longer than others. Why? Certain tracts are more interesting to write about than others. Some are more controversial and generate more comment. Others are hard to find, so providing detailed descriptions may be the only way many fans get to know what they are missing. Also subjective are the Values Guide prices. They are determined by averaging prices of tracts sold in auctions as well as ones I've bought and sold privately. (Most of the recorded auctions occurred on eBay between 1999 and 2002.)

These prices are subject to change because many of the scarce titles are still available for reprinting. If a rare $30 tract is reprinted, 10,000 more can suddenly flood the market and prices can drop as the supply outpaces demand.

That is also one of the neat things about Chick tract collecting. If you wait long enough, even expensive tracts may come along at little or no cost. But just because a rare title is reprinted doesn't mean it will become readily available. A custom order is only offered in quantity to the public if it features a blank back cover. Most reprint orders are made with *custom designed* backs, and all of those are shipped to the organization that ordered it. That means all 10,000 can be passed out somewhere in the USA or overseas. It could be months or years before any of those make their way back into collector's hands. You just never know what to expect!

Another consideration is variations. A rare title may be reprinted, but changed from the original in slight or dramatic ways. So while the recently discontinued green cover version of *The Last Generation* is common and inexpensive, the blue cover version is still rare and commands a higher price. (It is especially popular because it features an image that was removed because it was apparently considered too risqué.)

In general, titles that have been permanently retired and are no longer offered for reprinting command the highest prices since their supply is finite. These titles tend to be popular anyway, since they were usually discontinued for being too dated or controversial. *Wounded Children, Kings of the East,* and *Kiss the Protestants Good-bye* are examples that come to mind.

And then there's the *Uncertainty Principle*. That's a concept used in physics to describe how the mere act of observing a phenomenon can change it. There has never been a price guide for Chick tracts before, and by publishing one, it can affect the prices it seeks to report. Interest may grow as more collectors read the book and enter the market, driving prices up. Or the supply may increase as "pack rats" see what tracts they've been hoarding are worth and suddenly offer them for sale, thereby lowering the price. It's difficult to predict.

Play it safe and don't bank on any of these tracts as valuable commodities or investments. They were originally obtained free of cost by those who passed them out. Ironically, that is also why many of them are rare. Since they were given away for nothing, many people who received them thought they had no resale value. Most of the public considered these tracts as worthless as the advertising supplement to last week's newspaper and tossed them away by the millions.

Nevertheless, these prices are included to give the collector some idea what they might expect to pay for various titles. They are based on public auctions and private sales made between 1999 and 2003. These prices are for excellent to near mint condition tracts. In other words, no holes, stains, rips, tears, writing, or other problems. If some prices seem too high, don't be dismayed. Remember the majority of Chick tracts are still available for next to nothing: 14 cents! Beginners can read the rare titles via photocopies or downloads until the real tract comes along. There are also cheaper reprints of *Kiss the Protestants Goodbye, My Name in the Vatican,* and *The Poor Pope* available from A.I.C. They're not priced here, however, nor is the cheaper version of *The Secret Weapon* (retitled *Missionaries Are Fools*) by the Bible & Literature Missionary Foundation. Only authentic Chick tracts are listed and valued.

Remember also that new tracts are being added every two months (sometimes more and sometimes less) so any list of titles on the printed page cannot remain current for long. (This list was updated through June of 2003.) All tracts that are **still in print** are valued at 14 cents. Super rare tracts that have not been publicly sold or auctioned have no price to reference and are therefore listed as **speculative**. All *major* cover variations are displayed, including oversized covers, but only if the differences in the design are significant.

Facing page: Spring/Summer 1993 Chick publications catalog.

©1994 Jack T. Chick.

©1999 Jack T. Chick.

THE ACCIDENT Review: (Art by Chick ©1999.) A tract drawn in a cartoonish style that tells the tale of a rich aristocrat who owns a castle full of treasures. His greatest item is a "carpet of snow" made from the hides of the (virtually extinct) white tiger. But in his zeal to show off the rug to a visitor, he opens the door and knocks over a bottle of ink on his priceless treasure. Now it is stained! The poor little rich man is so sickened by this disaster that he winds up ill in bed. He can't stand the thought of the stain, so he orders the rug burnt. (This must have been before the days of Goodwill Industries.) Lucky for his Lordship (get it? He's a British "Lord" just like God) he has a physician who is also an ardent fundamentalist. With a bedside manner learned at the "how-to-win-souls-but-offend-patients" School of Medicine, this doctor casually informs Lord Winthorp that he is scheduled to burn in Hell. An intense close-up shows Winthorp's face as his mouth drops, his hair stands on end, his eyes go cross-eyed, and his monocle pops out (page 11). We can either assume the physician has just stuck the thermometer where the sun don't shine or doc's threat of damnation has made an impression. Sure enough, it's the latter case. Winthorp wants to become a Christian and avoid the lake of fire. Five minutes later, he feels clean and declares "the stain is GONE!" And they all live happily ever after. Grade **A-** for Aristocracy. **Still in print.**

ALLAH HAD NO SON Review: (Art by Carter ©1994.) Not only does Chick step on Muslim toes here, he STOMPS on them! But what do you expect? They worship "the Moon God" and are destined for hell. So you could say Chick is just reaching out to a different kind of Moonie. The tract starts out with a Christian tourist explaining to his son how the Muslims are blasphemous to God. He just happens to do this right in front of a crowd of praying Muslims. (Typical Ugly American etiquette.) Not surprisingly, one of the Arabs understands English and *LEAPS* to the bait! The kindly Christian manages to avoid having his throat slit and winds up inviting the Muslim for tea. (Isn't that civilized? This must take place in one of the former British colonies.) By the time the Christian finishes explaining how Muhammad picked Allah out of 360 other pagan idols to manipulate followers and declare himself a prophet, the Muslim wants to convert. (Boy, that was easy!) The last panel shows a weeping Arab eager to witness to all his people about the "Moon God." The Christian warns him that it could cost him his life. The Muslim quickly responds, "It will be worth it, because I'll be with my loving Father in heaven for all eternity." Earlier versions include even more hostile criticisms of Islam on pages 10 and 11. They accuse Muhammad of statutory rape and blasphemy. (More on the Vatican/Islam conspiracy is covered in Chick's color comic *The Prophet*.) **A+** for Angry Arabs. Retired "child abuse" version (page 10) **$15.50.** Regular version **still in print.**

©1986 Jack T. Chick.

ANGELS? **Review:** This is a personal favorite. (Art by Chick ©1986.) Chick does a wonderful job showing the brainlessness of Rock 'N Roll and also lampooning all the hype and selling out that goes on behind the scenes. The story follows the exploits of "The Green Angels," a so-called Christian Rock band that teams up with manager Lew Siffer to hit it big. Lew brags to the band how he controls billions of souls with his music. He shows them a flow chart outlining how he started in the 1950s with Soft Rock, then Hard Rock from 1961 until his crowning achievement was unveiled in 1972 ... Heavy Metal Music! "My music pushes murder, drugs, free sex, suicide," he gloats, "to destroy country, home, and education... And man, ... is it doing it!" You would think he's revealing a little too much to a Christian band during his first meeting with them, but then again, they admit they're not really *rock solid* in their faith. In fact, they're so relaxed about it all that they sign Lew Siffer's contract in blood. (Although one member hesitates because it's "really gross.")

Thanks to Lew's Satanic blessings, they become a big SINsation. So much so, that Bobby gets a bit too big for his britches. He announces he plans to get married ... to another man! Lew balks at the idea because a queer wedding would ruin the band's image. Bobby smirks and tells Lew to shut up since he's more famous than his nobody manager. So Lew decides to give Bobby a nice wedding present: AIDS! Three months later, Bobby is skin and bones. The other musicians start dropping like flies — heart attack, drug overdose, Vampirism — hey, that's show biz! Only one escapes Lew's clutches (thanks to a fan slipping a copy of *The Contract* tract in his pocket). He rebukes Satan and saves the day. The splash of red Chick adds at the end as Lew turns into a demon is pretty neat-o! (A scarce version lacks the red.) Favorite Panel Award goes to page 17 where the band is playing and demons literally fly out of the speakers to seduce the crowd. The lyrics are priceless, "We're gonna Rock, Rock, Rock, Rock with the Rock!" (Oh no! I can't get that tune out of my head!) Another fun refrain is "Embrace Me, Love of Death." Don't be surprised if either of these lines winds up becoming hits. Grade **A+** for Atlantic records. **Value: $4.50**

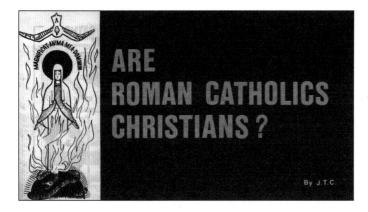

Helen is now a citizen of two countries. Helen has two flags, two presidents, two constitutions and two loyalties.

The Vatican is a government with its own money, secretary of state and ambassadors, and is a recognized nation, just like Germany, France, etc. If Helen is a *good* Catholic, her first loyalty will be to the Vatican.
Note: The pope has two powers – he's the chief of a political state and a religious leader.

©1981 Jack T. Chick.

ARE ROMAN CATHOLICS CHRISTIANS? **Guest review by Rev. Richard Lee:** (Art by Chick ©1981, 1985.) This is an inflammatory tract on Roman Catholicism that focuses only upon the doctrinal differences between fundamentalist Protestant Christianity and Catholicism. Interestingly, there are no wild-eyed conspiracy theories with cigar-smoking priests in this tract. Initially this tract was a promotional booklet for Chick Publications customers, and not intended to be a general release tract to be distributed to Catholics. The first promo version was printed in 1981. It has a black and white illustration of the Virgin Mary on the cover. The 1985 general release version has a red cover with rosary on it.

The tract begins with the question "Is there a slight chance that the Roman Catholic 'Church' is really not Christian? Think of the horrifying consequences! If it is not...then today, almost a billion people have been deceived. If it is not...then the ecumenical movement is not of God. If it is not...then the Roman Catholic charismatic movement is not of God. If it is not...then Roman Catholics are heading for a spiritual disaster."

One striking thing here is that Chick is careful to point out that only the Roman Catholic charismatic movement would not be from God, rather than condemn the entire charismatic movement (including Pentecostalism and its practices). Many charismatics (those who believe in speaking in tongues, miracles, and physical healings) are ardent Chick supporters.

The tract traces the life of Helen, a devout Roman Catholic from her infant baptism to her death. Due to the wordy nature of this tract, there are few drawings and more explanations of Roman Catholic doctrine. Each page gives some explanation of the Roman Catholic views of each of the Seven Sacraments. After Helen is baptized, we are told that she is a citizen of two countries: Her country of birth and the Vatican. Of course, the same criticism could be applied to American Jews (who become automatic citizens of Israel) but that's noticeably absent in *Love the Jewish People*.

One of the more interesting variations between both versions of this tract is over the origin of priests, nuns, monks, and popes. The earlier promotional tract is less tactful and very sarcastic in the use of words: "Did you ever wonder about the priests who look so holy? Where did they come from? The term 'priest' was stolen from the Jewish religion..." The later version intended for Catholic viewing reads: ""Did you ever wonder where the priests come from? The term, 'priest,' was taken from the Jewish religion..." "Stolen" vs. "taken" —is Jack going soft?

The earlier promo version continues with a scathing critique of the origin of nuns, monks, and popes: "The Bible NEVER mentions nuns, monks, or popes...it was all cooked up by the Roman Catholic Institution to razzle-dazzle their followers...only their leaders really understand the religious double talk and psychology used to control their 700,000,000 members." Compare the later version, wherein "cooked up," "razzle-dazzle," and "double talk" have been removed.

On the origin of the Roman Catholic version of the Eucharist, Chick doesn't get any better than this tract. Even *The Death Cookie* doesn't come close. Case in point is when Helen is about to take communion (the Lord's Supper or Eucharist). Earlier version says, "Helen is about to take Holy Communion. Now doesn't **THAT** sound Christian? But first, let's rip away Rome's false mask and show what's really behind **THEIR** communion." This distancing between Catholics and Protestants with the use of "THEIR" is anti-ecumenism at its best. It continues, "Let's watch Helen take her first Holy Communion. See if it's **TRULY** Christian, **ACCORDING TO THE BIBLE.**" (All capital letters and bold print are in the promo version). The wide distribution version omits the bold and capitalized lettering, to lessen the appearance of shouting. The "rip away Rome's false mask" remark is missing as well. As the tract continues, it concludes "IS THIS SYSTEM CHRISTIAN? **NO WAY!**" (Promo version). The later version's kinder, gentler approach renders the blurb "Doesn't this information upset you? **It should, beloved!**" The illustration depicts Helen as a child taking her first communion with the communion paten (a plate to insure the consecrated wafer doesn't drop on the floor) under her chin. The blurb in both versions reads "Note: If God should drop by accident, the communion paten will catch Him." The promo version has a variant here that is greater in its sarcasm. The earlier promo variant reads, "If God should drop by accident, the paddle will catch Him." Interestingly enough, many a theological problem was raised in the Middle Ages when rats would snatch consecrated wafers that fell to the floor and devour them!

As for poor Helen, she is "completely brainwashed." The promo version states "**THERE IS NO WAY HELEN COULD BE CALLED A CHRISTIAN—NOT ACCORDING TO THE BIBLE.**" This tract even has a variant in the wide release version meant for Catholic reading. This variant states, "Is Helen a Christian? She certainly thinks so!" The later version removes this statement.

Chick further drives home the point that he doesn't consider Catholicism to be a Biblical system in both versions. In the promo version he boldly states, "According to the Bible, there is **NO WAY** the Roman Catholic Institution was ever a Christian Church. **THEY JUST BRAINWASHED US INTO BELIEVING IT WAS.**"

Although this tract has very questionable historical data from controversial sources (like Hislop's *The Two Babylons),* this tract is pretty reliable on basic Roman Catholic practices on the Seven Sacraments. It is very accurate, although most Catholics would dispute the tracts more sarcastic remarks and the Chick charge that the doctrine of Transubstantiation is "magical" and originates with Satan. "Ahh, but Satan had other plans...Satan wants to show Jesus as a continuously "dying" Savior, or a dead Christ," we are told. This conclusion would certainly be denied by Catholics, but really, the conclusion logically follows from the premises that Chick establishes. Whether or not it is true is another issue.

When quoting the Council of Trent's anathema for Protestants, this should still shock modern Protestants because the Vatican hasn't renounced the famous Council of Trent's condemnatory pronouncements. Indeed, Chick is technically correct in saying that an inquisition could happen again because the Vatican hasn't changed its dogma and history has a tendency to repeat itself. Furthermore, Chick is accurate again in citing the Catholic position that if one has assurance of eternal salvation, they are "anathema," or cursed for committing the sin of presumption. No matter if one dismisses Chick's sensational conspiracy theories surrounding the Vatican, this isn't a misstatement of Catholic theology at all. The later version leaves out all of the hard-hitting comments on various popes' claims to being in the place of God. The promo version drives the point that many today think of the Pope as God. In rebuttal to this, the original promo stated, "Helen doesn't realize that the Pope is only a man dressed up in a religious costume." This remark isn't sarcastic; it's true to an unbiased observer and the force of Chick's point is totally lost in the later version.

This tract doesn't contain an entertaining story, and it's short on illustrations. However, it is a summary of basic Roman Catholic theology filtered through a fundamentalist Protestant perspective, albeit insensitive. If one wanted a pop level study of Catholic theology from a fundamentalist vantage point, this would be the tract to read. Favorite Panel Award goes to the page 19, a portrait of Purgatory with the caption "Based on II Maccabees 12:43-46 (found in Catholic and other perverted Bible translations)." Heck, even the parentheses are inflammatory! Grade "**A**" for Absolution. Retired Mary on snake cover version: **$4.** Regular red rosary cover version **still in print.**

THE
ASSIGNMENT

J.T.C.

©1972 Jack T. Chick.

THE ASSIGNMENT Review: (Art by Chick ©1972.) This tract raises more questions than answers about soul-winning. Charles Bishop is destined to die on November 22nd at 3:11 AM of a coronary. God's angels and Satan's demons both know this and fight over if he gets "saved" before his death. But if God knows when the old man will kick the bucket, wouldn't he also know if Bishop is going to save himself in time? If he's doomed, why bother sending angels to intercede? Predestination and Free Will don't seem to mix very well. But they make for great drama, as Chick demonstrates in this tract. The angels send Cathy to win Charlie's soul; the demons send an insurance agent to make sure he goes to hell. (So Satan's the reason those guys are so annoying. Figures.) The angels and demons try to sabotage each other's efforts. Demons send cute boys to distract Cathy, Angels cause flat tires to thwart the insurance agent. Cathy arrives and—as the angels say—"makes a penetration." (Alas, that suggestive language is omitted in more recent versions.) Charlie listens to her read from the Bible while an angel stands guard outside his home keeping the demons at bay. That night, Charlie considers becoming a Christian, but chickens out because he doesn't want to lose his friends. 3:11 AM arrives. As Charlie gasps for air, the demons breathe a big sigh of relief. "That was a close call—" they grimly observe, "but we got him." Ironic, isn't it? Charlie came *so close* to getting saved, but got cold feet. Now the rest of him is cold as well...except of course, his soul.

Weird Dialog Award: Little Cathy is reading to Bishop from the Bible, and he tells her, "Go on Cathy, you're getting through!" (Sounds natural enough...) Favorite Panel Award goes to page 20b. The sweating insurance agent is jogging down the highway after his tire went flat. A demon whispers to him, "Irving baby, look—There's a phone!" He runs to it but finds an old lady on the line relating her life's story to her friend. She's only at year 1932. Irving baby gestures to blow his brains out. The demon curses the smirking angel who arranged it all. *Haw-haw-haw!* Grade: **B+** for Bishop. **Still in print.**

THE ATTACK

J.T.C.

He's drinking it now.

Well done! His stomach cramps will begin in about three hours.

He should be dead by morning.

Bring me my medical bag.

Do you think you can help him, Doctor?

Oh, my stomach . . . I feel like I've been poisoned . . . Oh, Lord!

©1985 Jack T. Chick.

THE ATTACK Review: (Art by Chick ©1985.) This tract features an inflammatory cover of a Bible being set on fire! It outlines one of Chick's favorite themes: How the Satanic Catholic church has tried to pervert the word of God by destroying the King James Bible. Interestingly enough, much of Jack's historical information is correct (but cast in the worst possible light). For most of its history, the Vatican tried to discourage any translation of the Bible from Latin. Vatican II was the first time the Catholic mass was instructed to be given in English (or whatever the local tongue). That was relatively recently, in the 1960s! Before then, Catholics had to listen to a mass in Latin, a language that most of them couldn't understand. The King James Bible, on the other hand, was written in Shakespearean English. Many readers find it more poetic than any other version. The *Thees* and *Thous* make it sound romantic, like something from the days of King Arthur. And there's no denying the Vatican wanted to suppress it. But how many of the Catholic conspiracies outlined in this tract are accurate? Did Jesuits really attempt to secretly swap the "authentic word of God" with the "Satanic" Alexandrian version? Were Vatican agents responsible for slipping the "blasphemous" Apocrypha in the original King James translation until two Jesuits converted and confessed to the plot? True or not, these dramatic cloak and dagger tales are certainly fascinating. Queen Mary's efforts to execute Protestant leaders in 1553 and the Jesuit plot to blow up English Parliament in 1605 are true enough. On the other hand, Chick's claim that 68 million were tortured or killed during the Inquisition from 1200 to 1800 is probably inflated. But why quibble over numbers when the basic premise is correct? Countless innocents were ruthlessly tormented on behalf of the Pope for religious reasons. The last thing Chick wants is for Protestants to forgive and forget about it.

This tract does all it can to turn back the tide on the Ecumenical movement. It shows Catholics grinning from the sidelines as their victims drink poisons or burn at the stake. A dark room filled with scheming priests listen intently as their leader declares, "Now we must destroy the credibility of the King James Bible." The footnote asserts, "Jesuits were sent to infiltrate all Protestant theological seminaries and Bible societies." No wonder the Catholic Church has such a shortage of Priests. They're all working undercover! This tract is heavy on the text, but the generous helpings of conspiracy theory more than make up for it. Grade: **A-** for Attack! **Value: $1.50**

BABY TALK

J.T.C.

Eric's a bum!!

Bye!

Just *don't* get pregnant!

Did your teachers give you more free condoms?

Of course!

©1995 Jack T. Chick.

BABY TALK Review: (Art by Chick ©1995.) In terms of political incorrectness, you've GOT to love this one. Feminists will have spontaneous abortions reading it. The "Me" generation never looked as pathetic as it does here. Condoms are passed out at school, abortions are encouraged, and the main character—a boy named Eric—ditches his girlfriend the moment she tells him she has one in the oven. For a cartoon, it sure seems true to life! But when Uncle Mike hears about the stork, he decides it's time to put the fear of God into Eric. He pulls out all the stops. He takes his nephew to a doctor who informs Eric that abortion is murder, and that God will hold the father as responsible as he does the mother. (The doctor doesn't mention whether he performs abortions, but let's give him the benefit of the doubt and assume he does not.) Uncle Mike takes Eric home and starts preaching about the lake of fire (Rev. 21.8, King James version, natch). The next page shows Eric (with sweat pouring down his face) whining, "Hey, you're SCARING me, Uncle Mike!" (That's right Eric. Welcome to the World of Chick!) Of course, Eric is converted by the end of the story and saves the day. He marries Ashley and they live happily every after with child. Favorite Panel Award goes to page 20b: Trailer trash Thelma tries to haul her pregnant roommate to the clinic, but gets a flat tire. "@!!!**!" she swears, "No flat tire is gonna stop us from getting that abortion today." She's pretty peeved when Eric blocks the door to the clinic and calls off the procedure. But look at the bright side, Thelma. It should increase your monthly check amount for Aid to Parents with Dependent Children. Abortion protesters must LOVE passing these little darlings out. Grade: **A** for Abortions-R-Us. Recently retired: **$3**.

J.T.C.

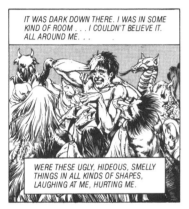

> IT WAS DARK DOWN THERE. I WAS IN SOME KIND OF ROOM . . . I COULDN'T BELIEVE IT. ALL AROUND ME. . .

> WERE THESE UGLY, HIDEOUS, SMELLY THINGS IN ALL KINDS OF SHAPES, LAUGHING AT ME, HURTING ME.

> THEY WERE LIKE SOME KIND OF DEMONS. MY GOD, IT WAS AWFUL!

> THEN ALL AT ONCE, THEY OPENED A BIG DOOR . . . (GASP)

> AND WHAT I SAW REALLY SCARED ME. PREACHER, IT WAS **TERRIBLE!**

©1982 Jack T. Chick.

BACK FROM THE DEAD Review: (Art by Carter ©1982.) This is the story of a man who is hauled into a hospital and pronounced dead, but who awakens in the morgue soon thereafter. He screams that he's seen hell and demands to speak to a preacher. At first, the preacher is incredulous that someone actually WANTS to get saved. But it doesn't take the preacher long before he starts— what else? Preaching: "When you're really dead, it's for keeps. There's no second chance! Want to talk about it?" The hysterical living corpse is only too glad to expound on his near-lake-of-fire experience. "It was dark down there. I was in some kind of room ... All around me were these ugly, hideous, smelly things in all kinds of shapes, laughing at me, hurting me." It wasn't the National Convention of Trial Lawyers, but you're getting warm ... It was HELL! His narrative includes flashbacks from down below. "All at once they opened a big door ... Beyond that door was an ocean, an ocean of fire! Flames everywhere and I heard screams." The preacher explains it is a Lake of Fire burning with Brimstone (Rev. 19:20). The patient wants to know why churches aren't warning more people about it. "Most preachers don't believe in hell. Of those who do, many sidestep it so they won't offend their congregations." The patient becomes outraged. The preacher explains that Satan wants to take as many as he can to hell. "He's got kids into punk rock believing that hell will be party time ... Some are so anxious to get there that they are committing suicide." (Now if only the Rap and Country music crowd would join suit, we could clean up the radio dial. But I digress...) The preacher lists various sins that will earn you space in hell. The list is too long to recite here, but it has most recreational activities in it, including drugs, drinking, fornication, and lying. (Is it getting kind of hot in here?) He also gives the standard Chick tract attack against the competition: "No church, saints, Buddha, Mary, Confucius, Allah — No religion can save you from going to the Lake of Fire. Only Jesus can!" Then we're told how the blood of Jesus washes our sin away. The patient prays, then turns to us to give the final pitch, stepping out of character like some cheesy actor in a 1950s TV commercial: "Now I'm

saved. My name is in the book of life. And by God's grace, I'm going to heaven." Corny? Absolutely, but effective! And during this entire tale, THE FOOTNOTE is working its subliminal magic. What's that you say? You missed the footnote? Go back to page 11 and read the fine print: "This story is partially based on a true story, *Three Men Who Went to Hell,* shown on *PM Magazine,* Channel 11, Los Angeles, Feb 24, 1982." (This is where the trumpets from *Dragnet* blast their dramatic flourish.) Grade: **A** for ALMOST dead. **Still in print.**

J.T.C.

> Did you hear about Bad Bob?

> Yeah, it's weird. Ever since the fire, he hasn't been the same dude.

> I hear he even prays now.

> Oh, well… we'll just hafta go find a new dealer.

"But it is an abomination to fools to depart from evil." (Proverbs 13:19)

©1983 Jack T. Chick.

BAD BOB Review: (Art by Carter ©1983, 1999.) Gather 'round children to hear of a slob who many Chick readers know as "Bad Bob." And yes, he is VERY bad. Why? Because his parents spoiled him. Or "parent" rather, since there is no sign of a father anywhere in this tract. Mommy gives little Brat Bob everything he wants and never spanks him. Fast forward and Bob has a beard, long hair and dark glasses. He pours drinks on the waitress if she doesn't give him what he ordered. The weenie bartender in the background yelps, "Call the cops, Bob's gonna tear this place apart again." His friends claim, "Bad Bob is crude, rude, and socially unacceptable, but we just love him ... Bob's the best connection we've ever had. He can get us acid, smack, dust, coke, speed, and black beauties." (You can bet they're not talking about African Americans either, because Bob's portrait on the cover features a prominent Confederate flag.) Fortunately, our boys in blue are ever vigilant in their efforts to remove society's trash from the streets. The cops nail Bad Bob and his cousin in an undercover drug operation. Once in jail, the two get a visitor. It's a pretty young boy who tries to witness to them. They cut lose with a string of @!!!**! and the jailer rescues the would-be punk just as the inmates nearly grab him. The jailer then lectures his captive audience that everyone deserves to "burn in hell ... You two have spit in God's face and rejected His gift of eternal life, so both of you are on your way to the lake of fire." (You get the strong impression that this is one guard who doesn't provide the inmates with free condoms.)

Later that night, the jail catches fire and the guard saves Bad Bob, but the cousin becomes toast. The kindly jailer offers his condolences to Almost Baked Bob by telling him "your cousin will be in flames like that forever and ever!" Bob declares he wants to repent right away. The guard says "I'm going to leave you alone so you can settle things with God." When he leaves the uncuffed criminal alone in the emergency waiting room, Bob escapes by breaking a window and jumping from the second story to freedom. (No wait, that was Bad *Bundy.*) Actually, the former Bad Bob begs for forgiveness in classic King James English, going so far as spelling "Oh Lord" as "**O** Lord" and "Savior" as "Saviour." Chick informs us that, "At this point, Bob becomes a child of God. He is born again and made spiritually alive. He will not go into the lake of fire, but will go to heaven." Happy ending, right? Not quite. The last panel shows Bob's former drug clients depressed because they now have to find a new dealer. (One of them is a dead ringer for Captain Kangaroo!) Oh well, God's gain is Lucifer's loss. Favorite Panel Award goes to page 3 where the fruity Child Guidance Counselor is waving his hands in disbelief that a mother could even THINK of spanking her child: "Good heavens, *NO!* Do you want to destroy his creativity? It could ruin his personality." Another must for your collection. Grade **B++** for Big Bad Bob. **Still in print.**

J.T.C.

The world becomes one gigantic witches' coven. Satanism is already saturating the world.

The bottomless pit is opened and demonic forces cover the earth. (Rev. 9:2,3) The unspeakable appears and mankind goes mad.

Occult murders, drugs, raping, sodomizing and looting is everywhere, yet these people will not repent. (Revelation 9:21; Luke 17:28)

The world is in Satan's grip! (Rev. 13:3,4)

For factual information on Satanism, read *LUCIFER DETHRONED*, the true story of ex-vampire William Schnoebelen. By Chick Publications.

©1988 Jack T. Chick.

THE BEAST Review: (Art by Chick.) This tract tends to be on many fan's list of favorites. It has everything: Conspiracies, controversy, violence, elaborate detail, and rare variations. It has remained in print since 1966 and there are four major variations. (We'll address the modern 24 page version here and the others afterward.)

The regular sized (©1988) tract's cover has a robed arm reaching out to bless a child's head. The child and his parents have 666 tattooed on their foreheads. (The sign of The Beast.) The inside cover opens to a scene of sinners drowning outside Noah's ark. Then we fast forward to a panorama of modern day depravity. Topless waitresses serve booze to drunkards who fight, curse, praise Satan, and try to seduce men and women alike. Chick warns, "Today's conditions are the same as it was in the days of Noah." Then it shows different religious leaders united to "serve the coming world ruler who is called 'The Beast.'" Chick warns

that Jesus foresaw the great tribulation. A graveyard scene shows saved souls rising from their graves and floating up to heaven. Long before *Left Behind* became a popular series of novels, Chick illustrated the rapture in tracts like these. The "four horsemen" (of the Apocalypse) are shown. The Destroyer of Peace is none other than the Pope (The Beast/ Anti-Christ). Although Chick never comes straight out and says it in a manner that can be quoted, he makes it very obvious with statements like "He is Satan's masterpiece and he rules from the Vatican." Another scene shows a man wearing the pope's white robe broadcasting on worldwide TV announcing everyone must wear his mark to buy or sell. One scene shows the Vatican on fire. "God moves ten leaders to rebel against the Beast. In their hatred of the great whore of Revelation, they destroy the Vatican by fire. There is great rejoicing in heaven." (Pretty *inflammatory.*)

In one of the more unusual statements, Chick states, "God allows the Beast to escape to Jerusalem because the Lord Jesus wants to take him alive and cast him into the Lake of Fire." Now what does this mean? Do you suffer *more* if you're tossed into the lake of fire alive instead of dead? It would seem if you're dead, you suffer the pain of dying PLUS the additional agony of having your soul tossed in the everlasting fire. Or if you're alive, do you get tossed in a *second time* after your soul is judged? Certainly Chick wouldn't want to suggest dead people feel hell less than live people. That would undermine the suffering in all those other lake diving scenes from his other tracts. We may never discover the answer (unless we take the plunge, that is).

A four-panel page shows various plagues yet to befall man. The fresh water supply becomes poison. The seas turn to blood. The land becomes desert. Are we leaving anything out? Oh yeah, the air becomes infested with a weird locust/ scorpion insect that attacks humans. It ain't pretty. Meanwhile, the Beast orders Israel destroyed. Orthodox Jews hiding in a cave weep as two-thirds of their neighbors are slain outside by soldiers loyal to The Beast. Jesus *gets even* and destroys The Beast's army during the Battle of Armageddon. Looking over the tiny detail in large epic scenes like the gruesome battle panorama, it's easy to see why Chick felt this tract hurt his vision. The detail is amazing and not found in later, more basic tracts.

The story ends on a hopeful note (if you're saved). "Jesus Christ, 'the prince of peace,' now rules over Earth. Swords are beaten into plowshares and there shall be war no more. The great millennium has come." Lest the sinners get too comfy, however, another couple of panels show the unsaved being herded up for the Lake of Fire. The closing shot promises eternal bliss to those who accept Jesus. This is what you might call the carrot and red-hot poker approach.

This tract is so chock-full of great images, it's tough to decide which wins the Favorite Panel Award. The three semifinalists are as follows. Page 12: Some poor Christian tries to buy food at the checkout counter without the sign of the Beast on his forehead. (He actually thought they wouldn't look under his hat. He was wrong.) The guards nab him and drag him to the dreaded mobile motorcycle-guillotine. Chick's ground level perspective shows a couple of jack boots standing over the last victim in the very close foreground, while the next execution takes place in the background. A true classic!

Page 13: A wonderful Halloween panorama showing Satan worshipers around a goat-headed priest removing a human heart. Also present in the full moon setting are bat-winged demons, a werewolf, and a vampire/ ghoul. "The world becomes one gigantic witches' coven. Satanism is already saturating the world ... Occult murders, drugs, raping, sodomizing and looting is everywhere, yet these people will not repent. The world is in Satan's grip!"

Page 18: The Battle of Armageddon. All the fighting and sword slashing carnage is painful to examine, even if you know the victims are the "bad guys."

Grade: **A+** for Animal Analogies. Regular-sized (24 page) version **still in print.**

THE TEMPLE OF SOLOMON IS FINISHED, SACRIFICES ARE AGAIN IN PRACTICE. - THE BEAST ARRIVES IN JERUSALEM.

HE'S OUR ONLY FRIEND!

UNSUSPECTING ISRAEL STILL DOES NOT REALIZE THE PLAN.

27

THE BEAST Early variations review: There are four major variations of *The Beast*. An original 52 page version, a 48 page version (both ©1966), a 40 page variation (©1966 or ©1981), and the modern 24 page version (reviewed above). This review focuses on versions with 40 or more pages. They all have an oversized cover with a big crowd cheering on a man in a dark suit. We cannot see the man's face, but everyone in the crowd has 666 printed on their foreheads. The 52 page version measures 5 1/4" x 3 1/2", whereas the other large format versions only measure 4 7/8" x 3 3/8". The 52 page version is extremely rare. Content wise, it only contains three different drawings from the 48 page version. Two are them are redrawn images of the first couple of plagues, and the differences are very minor. The big change is the scene of the rapture. The shorter versions have the souls ascending through clouds, but the original 52 page version shows them leaving their automobiles during rush hour on the freeway (page 17). This scene was changed to clouds because, according to Chick, the first version was too dark. The implications of the original version are much more frightening. As if driving on the freeway were not scary enough, now we have to deal with the prospect that the cars surrounding us could lose their drivers at any time. (Unless you're saved and abandon YOUR car instead.)

The 52 & 48 page versions are very popular. After all, they have twice the images and action of the modern 24 page version. But the 40 page version eventually went through a dramatic transformation that makes it just as interesting: The Beast is taken out of his dark suit and placed in the white vestments of the Pope. Remember, Alberto's comic book was printed in 1979. Chick apparently went back and revamped *The Beast* so it would dovetail with Alberto's claims of Vatican conspiracy. Oddly enough, the cover did not change; The Beast remains a civilian in a

dark suit on the outside of all large format versions, regardless of if he's the Pope inside or not. This added level of anti-Catholic fervor makes that particular variation of the tract desirable in its own right. (But remember, not all 40 page tracts have the change.)

Most of the missing pages in the 40 page version are reduced and crammed into multiple panels rather than being omitted altogether. Some noticeable exceptions are page 11, which shows members leaving church disappointed that their preacher has departed from the faith and instead gives "heed to seducing spirits and doctrines of the devil." In the background, we notice a new $39,000.00 wing being built. The inference is that mainstream churches compromise their message to expand their membership. Also page 27, "The temple of Solomon is finished, sacrifices are again in practice—the Beast arrives in Israel." The shorter versions ditch the image of a futuristic limo with UN flags pulling up to the temple as the crowd goes wild. Also page 33, where angels sound the trumpets to announce the upcoming plagues. Nowadays, they just don't give plagues the fanfare they deserve..

Nothing really valuable was lost in the 40 page version, but the reduction to 24 pages is another matter entirely. A wholesale slaughter of classic images ensues. Lost are such gems as page 2 & 3: The two page spread of bar room depravity from Biblical times. (Only the modern day bar scene survives in the 24 page version.) Also pages 4 & 5, images of Noah building his ark while others mock him, and the chaos of Judgment day erupting on the masses. Missing also are the next 5 pages, including a panel showing slimy communists planning to infiltrate the churches to destroy them, and a back-room image of the council of churches scheming to remove all gospel programs from the airways. (A Catholic board member raises his wine glass in celebration.) Also lost is the incredible image of an Israeli battlefield where dead Arab and Russian corpses feed hungry buzzards. Just as remarkable are missing pictures of (a) the Beast commanding fire to fall from the heavens, (b) his troops taking over the temple of Solomon and beating up the Jews who resist, and (c) the Beast commanding a statue of himself to come alive and speak blasphemies on international TV. The 24 page version makes a feeble attempt to recreate this last image in a fraction of the space, but without much success. Other images are edited out as well, but removing the five pages in a row is a tremendous loss. Indeed, this is one tract that should not have been reduced any further than 40 pages.

Yet those who only read the 24 page version are probably none the wiser. The modern abbreviated version is such a good tract, it's hard to imagine *any* version being better. (Even though they are!) Only collectors lucky enough to own the extended early versions can enjoy *The Beast* to its fullest extent. This is truly one of Chick's great masterpieces. Medium oversized version (5 1/4 x 3 1/2") with 52 pages: **speculative**. Medium oversized version with 48 pages: **$93**. Medium oversized version with 40 pages, **$31**.

BEST FRIEND

J.T.C.

They had **LOTS** of kids… and they were *naughty too!*

God called the naughty things they did… **"sin."**

God said that sin would bring death* and since Adam and Eve sinned, they **HAD TO DIE.**

Their sin was passed on to their kids, and on to us. Now *everyone* dies because of it.

*"For the wages of sin is death;" Rom. 6:23(a)

©1996 Jack T. Chick.

BEST FRIEND Review: (Art by Chick ©1996.) Another one of the "kiddy" tracts, designed to teach little ones about the love of Jesus. Two youngsters take a walk and one reveals to the other about her new "best friend." The other girl thought she was the best friend, but her hurt is quickly forgotten when she discovers the new best friend is Jesus. The first girl tells the second a brief overview about the history of Eden, the wages of sin, and Jesus coming to erase that burden. Of course, the second girl wants to be saved by the end of the tract. They both pray to Jesus for salvation and get it. Another happy ending.

This is not one of the better tracts, because it's so "dumbed down" for kids. Yet unlike other kiddy tracts, this one has generous details in the background, including lots of cameos by Fang, the recurring dog character. Grade **C+** for Cheesy. **Still in print.**

BEWITCHED ?

J.T.C.

Haw haw. Delightful! So disarming… so innocent… yet *so* effective!

Why are those old re-runs so important, Master?

Because, stupid, *that* show paved the way for all our occult and vampire programing viewed by **MILLIONS** today!

THE END

©1972 Jack T. Chick.

BEWITCHED? Guest review by Jayelle: (Art by Chick ©1972, 2000.) Well, it's obvious that Jack Chick believes in recycling, for one of his earliest tracts has been resurrected. *Bewitched?* is back and (barely) updated for the new millennium! In the 1960s version, Debbie is lost to drugs and occultism, all because she watched *Bewitched,* the devil's fa-

vorite TV show. Since there aren't so many teenage Debbies running around these days, the troubled soul's name has been changed to Ashley. *Bewitched* is credited for paving the way for all the devil's "occult and vampire programming viewed by MILLIONS today!" Chick proves for a fact that meetings are hell with a demonic conference. Ashley, whose drug habits, friends, and pad are charmingly '60s-retro (or just not re-drawn), gets involved in spiritism by contacting her dead mother. She seems to be well within hell's grasp—except that she has a "praying grand-mother." Will the forces of evil claim her with one last acid flashback—or will her grandmother be able to save her first? The suspense will kill you! This tract doesn't have the best art, but it's nostalgia-inducing and defi-nitely up to Chick's paranoid standards. Grade **A** for Acid flashbacks! Original "Debbie" version: **$15.50.** Recent "Ashley" reprint **still in print.**

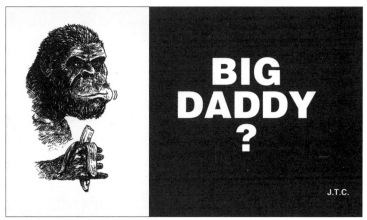

BIG DADDY ?

J.T.C.

How many of you believe in evolution?

OUR FATHER

©1992 Jack T. Chick.

BIG DADDY? Review: (Art by Chick ©1970, 1972, 1992, and 2000.) This is one of those tracts that fans love for a variety of reasons: First, it purports to refute evolution scientifically. Second, there are many differ-ent varieties of this tract as it evolves over time (creating an interesting paradox: If Evolution is false, why does it exist within the very tract that denies its existence?) Third, it features the way-out tale of how a student humiliates his teacher in class by proving evolution is bunk, making the teacher literally resign his post at the university in disgrace! What's more, all the other students convert to the creationists point of view. Is that a Fundy's fantasy or what?! (It's perhaps Chick's biggest believability gap ever!) But who doesn't secretly wish THEY had been able to turn the tables on the teacher who bullied them in class, making *the teacher* feel ashamed for being so stupid? It's the David vs. Goliath story within the story that makes this tale so much fun. At one point, the student asks the teacher what holds protons together when like charges normally repel one another. The teacher (sweating bullets) answers in tiny print, "I don't know". The Christian does what every teacher does at that point: He goes in FOR THE KILL! "I'm sorry sir, but I can't hear you" (making the teacher restate his defeat in bigger print). The balding bureaucrat meekly admits, "I said, I don't know. You tell me!" Then the authoritative Bible thumping begins. Teacher resigns, student becomes the BMOC, and the class is saved from Brainwashing and eternal damnation, all in one fell swoop. Not bad for an otherwise boring Biology class. The latest incarnation of *Big Daddy* was written in conjunction with Kent Hovind, a full-time Creationist spokesman and former Science teacher. Chick Publications sells a lot of his videos as well, which are heavily plugged throughout the tract. Grade: **A** for Anecdotal evidence. Original (©1970) version **$15.50.** ©1972 version **$5.** ©1992 version **$1.** ©2000 **still in print.**

©2001 Jack T. Chick.

THE BIG DEAL **Review:** (Art by Chick ©2001.) This is tract #5 in the new Bible series of 25, featuring the recurring character of "Bob". In fact, we also get to see Janet again. You remember Janet?—The shrill wife who was converted in the *It's Coming!* tract. (She's been a quiet and polite Christian woman ever since.) It turns out that she has a brother named Ronnie who is a dead ringer for Jack Nicholson. The story begins with her bailing him out of jail. (Notice the wanted posters in the background of page 2 featuring Frankenstein and Dracula.) Besides looking like Nicholson, Ronnie also *acts* like Nicholson. As Janet introduces him to Bob at a restaurant, she says, "I told him all about your sleazy deals, lies, and all the people you cheated." (Sounds more like an introduction given by an ex-wife, not a sister.) Bob uses the opportunity to segue into a sermon about another slime-ball, an ancient Jew named Jacob (son of Isaac). It's the same tale told in *The Scoundrel* tract by Chick in 1991. How Jacob screwed his brother out of his birthright and also deceived his father into giving him the blessing. Bob appeals to Ronnie's greed (and, presumably, the reader's) to tempt us into making a "big deal" with God. Bob says, "How would you like riches unspeakable ... Own a mansion and become a ruler of nations?" I'm not sure if souls in heaven actually get to *own* the mansion they reside in. I always thought it was God's mansion and supporters only get to stay there. And why rule a nation if you're dead? Of course, these finer points are lost on Ronnie. He quickly converts. He falls on all fours next to the dinner table and repents (page 22). Bob remains seated but places his hand on Ron's back. It must look pretty suggestive to other patrons in the restaurant who can't see under the

table! Ron emerges a changed man. His eyes are suddenly wide (instead of shifty), his shave is closer, and his wise-ass smirk is replaced with a gentle Sunday school smile.

Some especially interesting panels include an image of two men fighting. The caption reads, "That night God appeared as a man and Jacob knew who he was. They wrestled all night. [One says 'Let me go!' The other says, 'Not until you bless me!'] He then blessed him, changing his name to Israel (prince with God). Jacob never forgot it." This is one of the more perplexing scenes in the Bible. How is it that God can beat Satan but can't win a wrestling match against Jacob? (Heaven forbid he got tossed in the ring with Jesse "The Body" or Sting.) Favorite Panel Award goes to page 14, where Jacob wakes up shocked to discover he's sleeping with the sister of his fiancée. (Don't you hate when that happens?) The expression on Jacob's face is priceless. A reader could have a lot of fun replacing the dialog in that panel with humorous captions... Grade **B+** for Bad Brother. **Still in print.**

©1982 Jack T. Chick.

THE BIG SPENDER **Review:** (Art by Carter ©1982.) This is a modern retelling of the prodigal son. It's another "story within a story" tract and the Bible version of the prodigal son runs parallel to a similar story that occurs to the main character. Howard is a gambler who wins $250,000 at the casino. Like a brash young fool, he refuses a check. "Lay it on me in cold CASH, baby!" (Austin Powers would be proud! Yeah!) The teller warns him it could be dangerous, but Howard responds, "I'm a big boy. I can take care of myself." Unwiser words were never spoken. The very next panel he gets run off the road and two thugs beat the $%* out of him and steal the dough. Howie winds up on a respirator but eventually recovers ... at least physically. Once healed, he's broke and homeless. His "friends" want nothing to do with him. Page 6 is especially brutal. Howard goes to someone that he lent money to and gets turned away big time. "Try skid row, mission, you bum. And don't come back here any more. You're a loser." He limps to the mission and hears a preacher tell the prodigal son story. He gets saved. A tearjerker phone conversation soon follows with his father back home. The very last panel is full of unintended humor. When the son asks why the father forgave him, the dad doesn't say it's because he loves him. Instead, he makes it sound like it was an obligation. "I HAD TO SON, JESUS SAID, 'For if ye forgive men their trespasses (SINS), your heavenly Father will also forgive you.' SNIF" (Sniff misspelled, but he is under a lot of strain.) One can only imagine what the home life is like with a dad who provides translations within parentheses even during his most heartfelt conversations. You get the distinct impression he's quite the lecturer. As if that's not enough, he also provides footnotes in his heart-to-hearts. What a guy. There are plenty of interesting pictures in this one, a solid story line, and oceans of emotions. Grade **A** for Allowance. **Value: $35.**

©1991 Jack T. Chick.

***BOO!* Review:** (Art by Chick ©1991.) This tract is fun. It's one of several "Halloween is Satanic" tracts Chick produces for fans to pass out instead of candy. (Imagine the trauma they can cause kids who return home and read them. Some parents might miss the "good old days" when all they had to fear was pins, needles, and razor blades.) A group of guys rents an old camp ground for a Halloween party. As they plot to kill a cat as entertainment, Satan watches from afar. He's wearing a pumpkin head and has a rattlesnake on a leash. He curses to himself, "@!!** ... I forgot my chain saw!" But not for long ... He finds his rusty, trusty murder weapon in time for the climax. As the group prepares to kill kitty and mince him at midnight, in bashes Satan with his chainsaw blaring full blast! Forty minutes and nineteen corpses later, the police show up and Satan removes his pumpkin head, causing the cops to run like hell. Satan wanders around the valley looking for more victims. He finds a Christian to sneak up on for fun. The Christian gets the better of the demon by pointing his finger at him and yelling, "The Lord **rebuke** you, Satan!" The devil runs away screaming (@!!*#) as the Christian taunts, "I hate you! And I hate your lousy birthday!" (That's telling 'em!) Favorite Panel Award goes to page 18, which explains how the druids left Jack-O-lanterns at the homes where they drag off screaming victims for human sacrifice. (This was before homeowners started bribing them with treats.) There's also a "how to pray" section at the end, as well as an image of the devil wearing

his pumpkin head in hell saying, "Hi, Guys ... Welcome to the laughing place! heh-heh-heh!" A burning victim in the background clinches his fist and screams, "You rat!" (Careful pal, that rat controls the thermostat.) This is a fun tract with a good old-fashioned GHOST STORY going for it. **A-** for Apparition. **Still in print.**

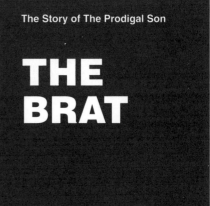

©1992 Jack T. Chick.

***THE BRAT* Review:** (Art by Carter ©1992.) This is the New Testament tale of the Prodigal Son. It's a pretty decent tearjerker. Even though most of us know the story already, it's hard not to get choked up when the arrogant little brat goes crawling back to daddy to ask for a servant's job, and instead gets the red carpet treatment. Hey, who wouldn't want parents like that? Chick's point is that God is a parent like that. This tract has plenty of great art, but Favorite Panel Award goes to page 14a, where slobbering hogs and hungry flies swarm around Joseph to get some of the delicious pig slop he's eating. Great dialog includes lines like, "The leeches move in for the kill, asking Joseph for expensive gifts and making him pay for all the good times." Another states, "Jesus died to save you from ... **the lake of fire!**" The ellipsis "..." pause is especially cute, no doubt included for dramatic effect. And putting the "**lake of fire!**" part in bold is also classic Chick. (Too bad he couldn't add sound. An organ flourish would really round out the effect.)

Chick is certainly obsessed with the burning lake concept. He references it constantly and draws it often in many of his tracts. It usually includes some poor soul being tossed into molten lava head first by an angel. (Sorry to cremate you buddy, but I'm just following orders.) Chick promotes the hell fire epilogue with such zeal, it undercuts his claim that "Sad to say, that's where *everyone* goes if they die without Christ." (Is it really that sad? One detects a little "holier than thou" smugness.) The cover is also one of Chick's funniest. It has a baby pushing his plate back and spitting out his corn. It would make a good promotional poster for birth control. Haw-haw-haw! Grade: **B+** for Bad Behavior. **Value: $3.50.**

© Jack T. Chick.

BREAKTHROUGH Review: (Art by Chick, circa 1971.) This is not a regular Chick tract. In fact, the back lists the company as "International Gospel Literature." (See *Kiss India Goodbye* for Chick's explanation about why he created this new Foundation.) This tract is exceedingly rare and announces the creation of *The Wordless Gospel.* This promo was an unknown title until a copy surfaced from inside Chick's archive vault in 2001. Nine of the pages are completely devoid of graphics and offer only sparse text. The inside front cover is a good example. It says, "There is an area which has been a heartache to missionary-minded Christians for centuries." It goes on to discuss the tribes in Africa that have never heard of Jesus. Since the chances of encountering this tract are next to nil, here's a reprint of much of the text from several pages:

"As the decades roll by, these tribes slip into Christless graves. The Wycliffe Bible translators are working diligently to crack the tribal languages. Their goal is every tribe by 1985 and they are doing a fantastic job. Could there possibly be a faster way to reach them? We tried. For more than ten years with countless sketches, struggling to work out a simple illustrated gospel message with a minimum of text. But, if they can't read—it would be useless.

"One night I watched a special TV program. It was on New Guinea. It drove me to my knees. In some areas these precious souls have no written word, greatly limiting their chances of hearing about Christ. I believe we got an answer to prayer. A new idea came to us. We started drawing a wordless gospel story. We made some very rough sketches and put them into a little booklet. We sent if off to New Guinea, to a missionary in a rather remote area. This was our big test. Could it really work??

"Months went by. We thought it was a failure. At long last we received word. The missionary told how he tried it out on his local natives. He showed them the sketches. The natives had never seen a picture before. The missionary explained it to him. Then the native took it and explained it to another native. What was the verdict? Could the missionary use these books for the uneducated natives?"

Chick then reprints a letter from the missionary saying he appreciates *The Wordless Gospel* and that the tracts help him reach natives who can't read. Chick continues with his thoughts about the importance of this new wordless concept: "I've shown the sketches to some missionary friends who work in Mexico. They feel it would be perfect for some of the Indian tribes there. We are praying that some day soon we will have versions of *The Wordless Gospel* for the Indians of Mexico and South America: Natives in Africa and those in New Guinea. Beloved, this is a brand new frontier and will not be an easy undertaking. This will require much prayer from you. We need all the wisdom we can get."

Then Chick describes a brutal tradition of certain natives to underline the importance of his mission. "In some tribes it is the custom at funerals to chop one or two fingers off the hand of little girls and present them as gifts to placate the ghosts. Lord willing, we will reach them with this Wordless Gospel, and stop some of these devilish practices!" He also includes a drawing of a crying little girl with her hand wrapped up in a makeshift cast. Her middle fingers have been chopped off.

Does Chick ask his readers to send money? No, that would be too much like the TV preachers. Instead, Chick asks his readers to ask the Lord if *He* wants them to send Chick money. "Please pray earnestly and see if the Lord would have you help us send out these *Wordless Gospels* to those who have no written word."

Chick also reminds his readers that the clock is ticking. His last pages states, "We believe we are now entering into the last great evangelistic thrust before the Lord returns."

This is a fascinating tract that reveals the story behind the making of another tract. How it remained undiscovered for so long is uncertain. It never showed up in any catalogs and was given away as a promo. It probably had a very short shelf life because it was tied so closely to the release of *The Wordless Gospel* (which first came out in 1971.) It includes some great renderings of various primitive natives. Favorite Panel Award goes to page 4, which features a full-page panel of a native praying before a wooden idol. Grade **B** for Breakthrough! **Value: Speculative.**

©1986 Jack T. Chick.

THE BULL Review: (Art by Chick ©1986.) This is one of those conversion stories that is so outlandish, it's especially entertaining. The story is about a bad-ass prisoner named "The Bull," and how he turns a hellish prison into a heavenly one after finding Christ. Sure, anything is possible, but there comes a point when credibility and probability split company. In this story, they run opposite directions screaming! That division occurs soon after The Bull finds a copy of *Somebody Loves Me* while rotting in solitary confinement. He instantly converts and demands a Chaplain with a Bible. Did I say instantly? According to the narration, it took 2 hours of reading the tract to finish it, even though he started crying the moment he saw it. (See top of page 11.) Granted, public schools are not known for the speed in which their graduates read, but 21 two-panel pages of cartoons shouldn't take more than 5 minutes max. Especially *Somebody Loves Me*, which contains a total of EIGHT different words of dialog (excluding the title and obligatory hic-up balloons of the drunkard father). So lets see, 2 hours divided by 8 words... that's 15 minutes per word. The teacher's unions should be proud. Anyway, The Bull calls a meeting of the prisoners once he's out of solitary. He delivers quite a speech. "I'm madder than I've ever been in my life! I hate sin and I won't put up with it any more! As of right now, all the killing stops! There will be no more raping, because I just found out that God hates sodomy!" A black guy in the audience looks especially shocked and exclaims, "What?" while a Mexican prisoner thinks, "Gasp!" The two probably had a date and some really big plans (although the Bull didn't really forbid sodomizing, he just said no more *raping*. But enough of the Jail House Lawyer.) The next panel says "Six Months Later", and The Bull still has the prisoners gathered in the meeting hall, only now he's reading them scripture. We can only hope he let them leave the room sometime in the last half year, at least for bathroom breaks. Then again, he does sound a lot like an Amway representative determined to make the sell. Check out his smooth closing technique on page 18: "Now, shut up or I'll break your legs. Listen good..." (He then reads from the Bible.) It must have worked wonders because the warden soon wins the coveted "Warden of the Year" award. (Oooh! Ahhhh!)

There are several interesting details in this tract. First, it clearly features Robert Redford as the warden, fresh from his 1980s role as *Brubaker*. (Except here, they call him *Blue Baker*. Subtle, huh?) The other unusual thing is that Chick seems to know how ridiculous this plot is, and actually calls attention to the fact with his closing line: "If you find yourself laughing at this story, think about this: Where will **you** spend eternity? In **heaven? Or in the lake of fire?**" (Sometimes you get the feeling Chick doesn't want anyone enjoying his cartoons for more than a few seconds without dreading the Lake of Fire.) Although this story won't win any points for realism, it is a fun tract never the less. Give it a Grade: **B** for *Brubaker*. Recently retired: **$2.**

©1991 Jack T. Chick.

BURN BABY BURN! Review: (Art by the third artist ©1991.) As the subtitle on the cover discloses, this is the story of Shadrach, Meshach, and Abednego. Who are they? They were three Old Testament Jews who were cast in the fiery furnace by King Nebuchadnezzar for refusing to bow down to his 90-foot high idol of Gold. The king orders the furnace be heated 7 times its regular temperature, but the Jews survive thanks to a fourth person who appears in the flames. The king gasps in disbelief, "His form is like ... the Son of God." How does an idol worshipper know what the Son of God looks like 600 years before Jesus is born? No details are provided regarding that mystery, but Chick does find room enough to include a footnote defining what a dunghill is for readers curious about its meaning. (He tells them to look it up in a dictionary. Haw-haw-haw!)

The king declares the Jews to be heroes and orders anyone who speaks ill of their God be cut into pieces. Chick warns that, "History will soon be repeated. Another world leader (the Antichrist) will set up his image. All who refuse to worship it will be put to death ... but God will take them to heaven." A group of people with the 666 tattooed on their heads face the reader. Chick continues his warning: "Terrible events are just ahead. Satan is setting up a one-world religion. Compromise is everywhere. Shadrach, Meshach, and Abednego were ready. **Are you?**" Readers are supposed to quake in their boots pondering the question, but chances are that most are more curious about what happened to the 90-foot image of pure gold. Perhaps they'll read the Bible in search of clues.

Favorite Panel Award goes to page 14. It features a beautiful panorama of the execution scaffolds leading up to the fiery furnace. Dozens of soldiers and spectators are drawn in the foreground and background with painstaking detail. If you're going to be executed, you couldn't ask for a more grandiose way to go. Grade **B+** for Burn Baby Burn! **Value: $3.50.**

The Story of Shadrach, Meschach, and Abednego

BURN BABY BURN

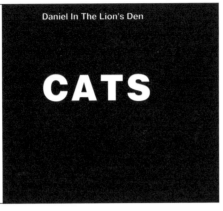

Daniel In The Lion's Den

CATS

CAUGHT!

⑬

Daniel's accusers were torn apart before they hit the bottom.

Daddy, why did you **do** this to us?

Mama, I don't want to die!

NO!

ROARRRR...

I'm **scared**, Mama!

There is also a pit waiting for those who reject Jesus Christ.
See Rev. 20:11-15.

©1999 Jack T. Chick.

Terrible!

Do you still love me?

As God is my witness!

You **betcha**, baby!

3 hours later

GASP!

What a surprise! Hi, Roger, where's Linda?

Who's Linda?

I just **love** this!

"...be sure your sin will find you out." Nu. 32:23

©2002 Jack T. Chick.

CATS Review: (Art by Carter ©1990.) Old Testament/Jewish tale of "I told you so" proportions. Chick's message here is one of his favorites: "Never mess with the Chosen Race." It's a message that continues to undermine Jews who claim Chick and other fundamentalists are anti-Semitic. If they hate Jews, then why do they promote them so much by repeating the Old Testament tales of vengeance against those who persecute the Jews? This is obviously pro-Jewish propaganda that Jack really believes, indicating his only problem with the Jews is that he thinks they're all gonna BURN unless they repent to Jesus—the Jewish Messiah. If Chick were really anti-Semitic, he would stop converting so many Jews to Jesus, because they're going to take over his heavenly neighborhood! (The same argument applies to Catholics, Muslims, Masons, and all of Chick's targets.)

Back to the tract: This story tells the tale of Daniel and the Lion's Den. Pious Daniel is promoted to high advisor status because he alone was able to read God's handwriting on the wall. His anti-Semitic enemies become jealous and conspire to get him tossed into the lion pit. Daniel survives (thanks be to God) and revenge is sweet: his enemies, along with their wives and innocent children, are tossed into the pit and ripped to pieces. (Daniel makes no effort to spare them—natch. And why should he? If there's one thing the Middle East doesn't need, it's more Gentiles.) Favorite Panel Award goes to page 20, which depicts the execution of Daniel's enemies and their families. The line of men, women, and children are being forced into the pit of starving lions at spear point. They scream and wail, begging for their lives as the giant cats consume the front of the line. (Hey! No push!) You'll never look at your kitty the same way again. Chick inserts a stern warning beneath the panel that reads, "There is also a pit waiting for those who reject Jesus Christ." Remember that the next time you hear a can opener. Grade: **B+** for Bottomless Pit! **Value: $7.50.**

CAUGHT! Review: (Art by Chick ©2002) This tract is number 13 in the series of 25 tracts that illustrate Bible stories with Bob. If you've gotten just a little sick of seeing Bob convert everyone by the last panel, this is the tract for you. The sinner not only refuses to see the light, he tells Bob to go to hell! Of course, we can guess who *really* winds up in hell, but that comes later...

The story opens as Roger is sneaking off to the *Motel Delight* to shag his latest girlfriend. Jessica is a little nervous, because, as she puts it, "I've never done this before." (Yeah, that's what they *ALL* claim.) But Roger assures her that no one will find out since they're alone. As they enter the room, they're followed by four demons, one angel, and a dog. (Bestiality anyone?) As if that's not kinky enough, the angel has a video camera and is taping the affair! Three hours later, the two are basking in afterglow at the restaurant and holding hands. A friend yells out, "Hey Roger, where's Linda?" Jessica wonders aloud who the heck Linda is. The ex-friend replies, "Linda is Roger's beautiful wife, and he's got three great kids!" The gig is up! Roger's been busted!

Jessica calls Linda and tattles about her one-night stand with Linda's husband. Linda leaves a note calling Roger a snake, steals their kids, accuses hubby of AIDS, and files for divorce. So Snake (I mean, Roger) gets angry at Linda, Jessica, God, and just about everyone else but himself.

Bob gets invited into the drama by Roger's cousin, who has to leave on a plane but wants someone to help Roger with his problem. Roger arrives and claims that he was only trying to minister to a younger lady. No wait, that was Clinton's claim. Roger claims he was "trying to comfort a lady in our church." Hmmm. They met at church and she never noticed he was married with kids? This must be one of those *swinging* churches!

Bob is unimpressed. Within three panels, he's telling Roger he's heading for the Lake of Fire. Roger gets defensive and tries the old, "Everybody's doing it. I came here for Christian love and comfort, not to be preached at!" cliché. Bob ignores the plea and launches into a long sermon about David, who killed Goliath, became a good King of Israel, but then committed adultery with Bathsheba and suffered the consequences. Well, sorta suffered ... He remained a rich King and had family problems, but he didn't suffer as much as the husband he had murdered so he could steal his wife. Chick's image of dying Uriah (who did nothing to David except serve him as a loyal soldier while the King banged his wife) is really gory. He has three arrows in his chest, a thick spear protruding from his stomach, and blood dripping out of his eyes, ears, nose, and mouth. It must really hurt when he laughs.

Roger stands up and puts his hands on his hips to tell Bob off: "I've had enough of this guilt trip! *I'm okay,* and I'm sick of people condemning me. You Bible thumpers can go to hell!" Bob tosses more scripture at him, but Roger stomps out the door yelling, "Drop dead, Bob!"

Eight weeks later, Roger is the one who drops dead from a heart attack. Roger is hauled before the Great White Throne of Judgment for some shouting (Matthew 25:41, of course). Then it's off to the Lake of Fire, just as Bob predicted. Smug Bob returns in the last panel to warn us that only the blood of Jesus can wash away our sins. Linda wins a moral victory but loses the alimony. The end.

Favorite Panel Award goes to page 13B. Six demons and an angel watch David and Bathsheba having sex. One demon in the background has to climb a bedpost to get a good view. (The angel's wings are in his way, darn it!) Grade: **B+** for Babes in Bed. **Still in print.**

©1997 Jack T. Chick.

CHARLIE'S ANTS Review: (Art by Chick ©1996.) This is probably the best of the handful of tracts directed specifically at children. What makes it better than most is a powerful analogy. Charlie is a kid who loves to watch his ants. A young girl and her kid-brother inform Charlie that the valley where the ants live will soon be turned into a lake. Charlie tries to warn his ants to move to high ground, but they don't listen or understand. (Probably both, since ants lack ears and brains.) The girl compares Charlie's frustration to how Jesus feels trying to save the sinners on Earth. While her kid brother tortures a kitty cat in the background, she delivers the gospel to Charlie, without the usual buckets of blood Chick tosses in to shock audiences. (We only get a silhouette of Christ on the cross this time.) She does mention that crucifixion was no picnic, however, when she states, "They arrested Him and hurt Him *REAL BAD!*"

This is one of the few tracts that uses the carrot of Heaven instead of the fiery whip of Hell. We don't see any panels showing or describing the Lake of Fire. The closest we get to anything like that is the sentence, "God cannot allow sin into heaven, so we *ALL* deserve to go to hell." (Though no explanation of Hell is given.) Plus, we get an image of a slobbering Satan carting Charlie off somewhere warm to consume his soul (page 12b). The classic expressions on both characters easily win the Favorite Panel Award.

It should be no surprise to learn that Charlie gets saved in the end, along with the "me too" kid-brother. The lovable ants, however, are doomed to wind up in The Lake (both in this life and the next.) Grade: **B+** for bunches of bugs. **Still in print.**

©1999 Jack T. Chick.

THE CHOICE Review: (Art by Chick ©1999.) This is clearly one of Jack's lesser efforts. The artwork is some of Jack's most plain, the plot is uninspired, several panels are recycled from other tracts. In fact, if you had to choose between this tract and another, the choice would be easy. (Pick the *other!*) It's another "sit down at lunch and witness to your neighbor" tract, with predictable (albeit unrealistic) consequences. The Christian corners his friend during the meal, sits down and tells him he's going to hell unless he accepts Jesus, and the heathen becomes instantly saved. (If it was this easy, Chick wouldn't have much of a demand for his recruitment literature—everyone would already be Christian.) Favorite Panel Award would be when the Christian picks up the tab! (It's the least he can do for letting the meatloaf get cold while talking about eternal damnation.) Sadly, this is pretty boring by Chick standards. It even misses an obvious opportunity to plug Chick tracts (something Chick usually slips into his stories whenever he gets the chance). At least that's one unique aspect to an otherwise formulaic tract. Grade: **C+** for Casual Cartooning. **Still in print.**

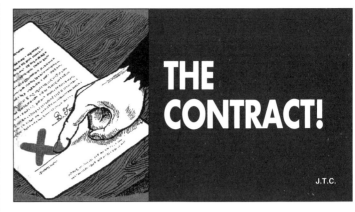

©1995 Jack T. Chick.

©1976 Jack T. Chick.

CLEO Review: (Art by Chick ©1995.) Remember those velvet paintings from the 1970s of dogs and cats with really big eyes and tears coming out the corners? You'll be reminded of those a lot while reading this tract. In fact, the cover has a similar dog with big eyes, giant eyelashes, and a bow in her hair. She has everything but the trademark tear. But don't worry; in the remaining 22 pages, 11 panels feature dog's tears, sweat, or droplets of drool. So if it's dog fluids you're after, this bud's for you.

The plot is pretty basic. Timmy's family goes on a 3-day trip to visit Grandma in the hospital, but their dog (Cleo) leaves the car to chase a butterfly and gets left behind. The dogcatcher snags her and she's slated for death in 4 days. The family returns and rescues her in the nick of time, just before she's put to death. Daddy uses the story to demonstrate to Timmy how Jesus came to Earth in order to reverse our death sentence. Timmy takes the bait and asks to be saved. Why daddy waited so long to redeem his son is hard to fathom, especially since they spend so much time on the highway and could have been killed (and tossed in the Lake) at any time. The last panel has Timmy hug Cleo and proclaim, "Hey Cleo. We both got redeemed on the *same day!*" (To preserve the happy ending, we'll avoid discussing where Cleo goes after she dies.)

There are plenty of images of quivering dogs throughout the story. These otherwise stupid creatures seem to know what's in store for them at the pound. In fact, Favorite Panel Award goes to page 13b, where some poor mutt is about to get his. The doctor prepares the poison syringe as the dog quakes in dire anticipation, while the assistant talks about needing to kill four more animals. Hey, it's just another *day o' death* at the pound, get in line and stop whimpering.

For those who own microscopes, check out page 7b and see if you can locate the rabbit. The bird's nest is easy to spot in comparison, but some of Chick's details are so small that they must be missed by 99% of his audience. Grade: **B-** for Back to the cage! **Still in print.**

THE CONTRACT Review: (Art by Carter ©1976.) Interesting plot insofar as you actually LIKE the main character, even though he sells out to Satan. He's a farmer who loses his crop in a hailstorm and sells his soul in order to keep his farm and feed his crippled kid. "B. Fox" gets him to sign a contract (for his soul) and makes him rich. A phony Christian cousin warns him that he's toast because he signed in blood. But a doctor who visits him on his deathbed informs Farmer John that getting "saved" in the last seconds of his life sends his soul straight to heaven. Boy, is the cousin pissed when he dies and winds up in hell without his kinfolk present. And to think the cousin spent all that time in church and doing good deeds. What a waste. One can't help but admire the farmer for cutting such a sweet deal. He had it all. Riches, a mansion, a deal with the devil, and in the end, heaven tossed in at no additional charge. Some folks have all the luck.

Favorite Panel Award goes to page 13b where John gets even with the banker who called in his loan. He goes to deposit his treasure but tells the owner his loan officer ordered him never to return to the bank. The owner fires the underling and shoves him out the door. The unemployed wretch complains he's too old to find another job. Too bad! Beelzebub snickers, "There's *nothing* like revenge!" He's right. Who can resist feeling good at seeing a ruthless banker tossed out on the street? Grade: **B** for Bargain. **Still in print.**

Then man multiplied and covered the earth...

but violence was everywhere.
Genesis 6:5-7

Because of man's wickedness, God destroyed the earth's inhabitants with water.
Genesis 6:13

Only one man believed and served God. He and his family were spared.

"Noah only remained alive, and they that were with him in the ark." Genesis 7:23

©1976 Jack T. Chick.

THE CRISIS

J.T.C.

Dr. Nelson... go with the transfusion! *Please!*

Let's do it!

She'll make it now, thank God.

Doug, are you out of your mind?

Not any more... I found out that **JESUS IS JEHOVAH!**

I've accepted Him as my Saviour and I've been set free.

For further information on Jehovah's Witnesses, see *"Answers to My Jehovah's Witness Friends"* by Thomas Heinze, published by Chick Publications.

©1985 Jack T. Chick.

CREATOR OR LIAR? Review: (Art by Chick ©1969, 1971, 1972, 1976.) This is one of Chick's earliest tracts (dating back to 1969) but it's still in print. The reason for its continued popularity is probably the simplicity of its message. It provides a very straight forward and easy to understand overview of the history of Christianity, going all the way back to its Jewish roots and Genesis. One of the highlights on page 16 states, "But Satan was defeated because three days later, Jesus rose from the dead. If the powers of darkness had known this would happen, they never would have crucified the Lord." The next panel states, "Having told His followers that He would return again, Jesus was taken back to heaven." Both statements are from the Bible, but when placed right next to each other, they raise the obvious question: If Jesus told his followers he would return, why didn't the devil also hear about it and know as well? Was he not listening? Or did he hear it but not believe Jesus would make good on his promise?

Whatever the case, the Negro version of this tract is equally amusing. It replaces most the characters with Africans. The first hand of God (the one playing marbles with the planets) is white. Then God's hand is black as it points down at Adam (who is also black). The angels are black, the dirty lepers are black, and all the Israelites listening to Jesus are black. You never see Jesus' face so you can't be too sure about Him. However, if you look really close at the hand of Jesus on page 13, you'll notice it's also black. Turn the page and the hand being crucified is white again. God's a chameleon! (Won't the *World Church of the Creator* be thrilled?) However, the virgin Mary is still white, from start to finish. (You can bet Joseph was surprised at delivery.)

Both versions are equally sparse on illustrations. Many of the panels have an overabundance of white space. It does include an early image of a sinner being cast into the Lake of Fire. Unlike the similar panel in *This Was Your Life*, this one looks less cartoonish and much more realistic. The sinner is covering his head with his hand (as if that will help reduce the pain when he hits the molten lava.) Another fun image is the protester panel on page 18. Chick loves to draw bitter-faced protesters carrying signs with ridiculous slogans. He usually reserves the most blasphemous signs for the Catholics. This one has a frowning priest carrying a sign stating, "God is Dead!" Meanwhile, the text challenges the reader to decide if Jesus was a fraud or not. It says, "If (Jesus) was a liar ... then forget it! But if Jesus IS who He claims to be ... your decision will determine where YOU will spend eternity." The last line of the tract is the most foreboding. "When you meet Him face to face, will He be your Saviour? — or your Judge?" (Chick's stacking the deck a bit by stating you WILL meet Him, so if you're not a believer, you better take plenty of tanning lotion.) Grade: **B** for Back to Bible Basics. Original medium oversized version (5 x 3 1/2") **speculative.** Regular size (5 x 2 3/4") **still in print.**

THE CRISIS Guest review by Rev. Rich Lee: (Art by Chick ©1985.) This is the only tract for Jehovah's Witnesses that Chick Publications has published to date. It was based on information provided by Paul Blizard, an ex-Jehovah's Witness who also gave an interview to *Battle Cry* in conjunction with the release of this tract. Blizard, now an ordained Southern Baptist minister, has assisted with an anti-Jehovah's Witness video from Jeremiah Films. He later did an independent article that claimed to discredit Dr. Rebecca Brown and Elaine. Ironically, Blizard assisted Chick Publications in the writing of this tract long before attacking Chick's biggest contributor since Alberto.

The tract, ostensibly based upon Blizard's own story, features a little girl on a gurney who needs a blood transfusion. Naturally, her parents Doug and Donna are both Jehovah's Witnesses (a.k.a. the *Watchtower Bible and Tract Society* in Brooklyn, New York) and do not believe in blood transfusions. The chaplain at the hospital, Chaplain Barnes, initiates a conversation with the parents. The doctor, faced with the little girl's life threatening prospects, remarks that if Chaplain Barnes "can't convince them in the next 30 minutes, we're going to have a little corpse on our hands." Of course, in 24 page tract fashion, it won't take this long.

Chaplain Barnes explains to the parents that he's studied the Watchtower Society and has several disagreements with their beliefs. He says, "I believe there are verses in the Bible to show Jesus is God Almighty. Can we look at them?" The girl's father Doug says nonchalantly, "Sure." (Why not? Beats fretting over his dying daughter.)

The tract overlooks the ethical dilemma real hospital chaplains face. Hospital chaplains are FORBIDDEN to debate the merits of a patient's or patient's family's religious beliefs. In fact, if the patient is a Jehovah's Witness and carries a card indicating that they are not to have a blood transfusion, then the patient's wishes are to be honored. Hospitals can obtain court orders overriding a JW's parents' wishes for their children, since the children don't have to be bound by religious practices not in the best interests of the child. But that's boring. This is a comic tract with a story that has to move forward.

Chaplain Barnes, our protagonist, is in a race against the clock. Not only is the child's blood pressure dropping, but the Elders from the local Kingdom Hall are on the way! In true conspiracy fashion, the JW Elders are tracking down Doug and Donna at the hospital. She's the weaker of the two because she read anti-Witness material. *The horror!*

Chaplain Barnes lays on the Bible quotations from the JWs own "New World Translation of the Christian Greek Scriptures" to prove that Jesus is Jehovah. The doctor orders a guard posted at the door to keep out interlopers from interrupting Barnes's witnessing to the Witnesses! He must know from prior experience that the Kingdom Hall thugs will bust in at any moment.

A classic moment arises in the conversation. Chaplain Barnes demonstrates that JESUITS were behind the translation of the New World Translation of Jehovah's Witnesses! "Doug," Chaplain Barnes intones, "maybe the Watchtower is tied closer to the Vatican than you've been led to believe." Chaplain Barnes does a knock down, drag out job of showing how the Watchtower falsely prophesied the end of the world and the return of Abraham, Isaac, and Jacob back in 1925. Space doesn't permit in the tract to show that the JWs were also wrong seven other times about the end of the world, the latest being 1975 in great detail, but at least the dates are mentioned. Chaplain Barnes' point is simple, yet very logical. "If they're wrong here, Doug, let's see if they're right on blood transfusions." He summarily shows Doug and Donna that the Bible verses that forbid the eating of blood have to do with consuming animal blood, not modern day transfusions. How is Chaplain Barnes so knowledgeable on this? We learn that he was a former Jehovah's Witness! Small world!

Meanwhile, the burly guard keeps out the Men In Black, a.k.a. the Kingdom Hall goons. Chaplain Barnes explains that he worked undercover to follow members who were suspected of not being good JWs, and the reports were sent to Headquarters in Brooklyn. No doubt traitors would end up at the bottom of New York harbor with bundles of "Watchtower" and "Awake!" tied to their ankles.

Chaplain Barnes goes for the *Coup de Grace:* "You can't earn your salvation by works like selling Watchtower materials." The sermon works. Doug and Donna defy their evil Elders and allow the transfusion. Let's hope that the blood she gets was free of contagions. Grade **B** for Blood transfusion. **Still in print.**

©1991 Jack T. Chick.

THE CURSE OF BAPHOMET Review: (Art by Chick ©1991.) This is a perennial favorite among Chick collectors because the basic message is that Shriners are demonic. Anyone who has attended one of those dull afternoon parades and witnessed aging men in red fez hats and vests weaving through the procession in miniature go-carts can certainly sympathize with that view. This tract begins with a knock on the door during a dark storm. Alex and Sally open up to find a rain-soaked cop. He explains that their son is in the hospital after shooting himself. They race to the I.C.U. but the doctor tells them that their son "has no will to live." They wait outside the ward racked with guilt, asking each other what they did wrong and why their boy would do such a thing. Three days later, Ed pops in, claiming he "just heard." The couple seems glad to see him ... at first. But then Alex makes the mistake of mentioning that he's a Shriner, Ed exclaims, "A lodge member? Alex, are **YOU** a Mason?" Alex proudly says yes. Ed drops his bombshell, "I had *no idea* you were into witchcraft." [Insert explosion here.] Alex and Sally almost go into cardiac arrest (good thing they're in a hospital). "WITCHCRAFT? *Are you crazy?* Masonry makes us *better* Christians!" they shout. They read Ed the riot act, explaining how they always sing Christian hymns and keep a Bible open at the lodge. Alex yells, "Ed ... you don't know what you're talking about!" But Ed has a snappy comeback. "Oh yes I do! I was a Mason until I found out about BAPHOMET!"

What's that, dear reader? *You* don't know who Baphomet is? Don't be embarrassed — neither do Alex or Sally, and they worship the S.O.B. Fortunately Ed has all the answers. He explains, "this 'Great Architect of the Universe' you pray to is NOT the God of the Bible. It's really Baphomet! And he's ugly, frightening, and completely satanic!" The parents deny any knowledge of Baphomet, but Ed is not surprised. Only the highest level Masons are let in on the dirty little secret. He just happens to carry a picture of Baphomet in his car for such occasions as these. Ed runs to retrieve it. Sally puts her hand on her husband's shoulder and opines, "This is scarey! [sic] What did you get us into, Alex?" (It's always nice to have a wife who blames you for everything.)

When Ed returns, he shows a drawing of a goat-headed demon with wings and women's breasts. They look like 36Ds. (Not bad for a goat.) "Here he is ... Baphomet. The old god of Baal worship AND Masonry." The couple are unconvinced. Ed reveals how the Eastern Star symbol of the lodge is really an upside down pentagram, which represents the satanic goat's head a.k.a., Mendez the "God of Lust." Alex disputes Ed's conclusions, but then Ed brings up Albert Pike. You know— *the* Albert Pike: Grand Commander Sovereign Pontiff of Universal Freemasonry! Listen to what he said!

"The MASONIC RELIGION should be, by all of us initiates of the high degrees, maintained in the purity of LUCIFERIAN doctrine. If Lucifer were not god, would Adonay (Jesus) calumniate (spread lies about) him? YES, LUCIFER **IS** GOD." Baphomet gets busted big time! Ed starts explaining various occult symbols, including how the all-seeing-eye on the back of $1 bills is from the Egyptian god, Osiris (so you may want to play it safe and burn your money). Moreover, the obelisk is a Masonic symbol of a male sex organ right out of Baal worship (so destroying the Washington monument might be smart as well). But wait, there's more! The fez comes from the 8th century when Muslims invaded the Moroccan city of Fez and butchered 50,000 Christians and dipped their caps in their blood to honor Allah. When Shriners are initiated, they swear a Moslem oath with their hand on the Koran, praying to Allah and calling that demon "the god of our fathers." What dupes!

Perhaps the greatest crime of Masons is their performance of so-called "good works." You know, helping crippled kids walk and that kind of thing. As Ed puts it, "The Word of God teaches that salvation comes by faith in Christ. But Masonry says good works will get you to that 'big lodge' in the sky. Unfortunately, that lodge is controlled by Satan! ... God will never bless a church led by Masons, whether they be pastors or deacons." Then Ed puts the finishing touches on his presentation. "Another witchcraft item is your cursed Masonic apron. Aprons worn by the high level Masons are packed with occult symbols ... Renounce Masonry, burn these objects and repent before God. So He can remove this curse you have brought on your family."

The couple runs home and burns all their Lodge paraphernalia in an open barrel, begging God to forgive them since they had no idea Masonry was witchcraft. The results are instantaneous. Alex feels suddenly different, and Sally remarks, "even the house feels clean and light." (So Chick tracts can also help clean your house.) The phone rings and Sally answers. She exclaims (with the obligatory tear drop), "It's the hospital. Tommy's awake and wants to see us. His depression is gone and he's hungry as a bear!" Another happy ending. "PRAISE GOD!" shouts Alex.

Praise God indeed, for this is a wonderful tract. Favorite Panel Award goes to page 18b. It's a drawing of a Shriner fez under a clear cake cover. Chick successfully transforms an otherwise dorky looking icon of geekdom into a sinister idol to Satan. As Ed puts it, "Your red fez under that glass dome is one example. It is actually a shrine to Allah." Scary! (Or should I say, "scarey"?) Grade: **A+** for Allah's Altar. **Still in print.**

master is a lady called Ms. Frost, but don't let the name fool you. Ms. Frost is hot, Hot, HOT! She's like the Penthouse version of Veronica from *Archie* comics. A snazzy dresser too.

Favorite Panel Award goes to page 11, where Debbie finds her ex-friend swinging from the rafters, leaving a ridiculous suicide note and impressive D&D collection. We can only see the bottom half of Marcie's dead body as it gently sways above the knocked over chair. (Nice legs! Shame about the neck.) Interesting note: later versions omit a footnote from page 19 which lumps C.S. Lewis and Tolkien books in with occult materials. Grade: **A+** for Anachronism Addict. Original "C.S. Lewis & Tolkien occult author" (page 19) version: **$8.00.** Version without reference on page 19 recently retired: **$1.00.**

©1984 Jack T. Chick.

©1988 Jack T. Chick.

DARK DUNGEONS Review: (Art by Carter ©1984.) A favorite souvenir among D & D players, this tract includes the worst demonic stereotypes about the famous 1980s role-playing game. Debbie loves playing D&D, but when Marcie commits suicide (in response to losing the game) Debbie has second thoughts. The Dungeon Master invites Debbie to join her witch's cult, and Debbie experiences power after casting spells on her father (to buy her more D&D stuff, of course!) but this doesn't quite fill the void. It takes a seminar where the speaker urges everyone to burn all their D&D material (plus charms, occult books, and Rock music) before Debbie repents and is set free. Ghost images of the demons can be seen leaving her body as she is saved. Soon, Debbie can be seen admiring the bonfire of satanic paraphernalia and praying aloud, "Thank you Lord for setting me free!" Another great scene is an earlier one where Debbie is introduced to The Craft. She enters a room with people in dark robes circling a giant pentagram on the floor. The unseen narrator states, "The intense occult training through D&D prepared Debbie to accept the invitation to enter a witches' coven." Does that mean the game really is educational? (Just curious.) Debbie's dungeon

THE DEATH COOKIE Review: (Art by Chick ©1988.) Apparently Chick wasn't very happy with the Catholic Church when this tract was written. Probably because they had been busy lobbying Christian Book Stores to remove his tracts. But why get mad when you can *EXPOSE THEM ALL AS SATANISTS!?!* (Or at least, Satan worshipers.) Chick goes way back in history to show where all the Vatican's bodies are buried in this tale. It has one of the best Chick covers of all time: a cookie with a skull and cross bones. (Try requesting **that** variety the next time the Girl Scouts come 'round.) What exactly is the "death cookie?" Why, the Holy Eucharist, of course. Talk about an inflammatory title, this one must really T-off the masses. (Get it? Masses? As in—never mind.) Chick's anti-Vatican zeal gets the better of him this time, making the premise of this tract ultimately self-defeating. This tract doesn't merely suggest the Catholic Church became corrupt over time, but that the earliest Pope created the church under the direction of Satan. The problem with this premise is that the very first Pope was (supposedly) Apostle Peter. And since the Catholic Church is the original church from which all Protestant churches are derived, it would mean that every modern Christian church is a spin off of a Satanic mother church. That's probably not the message Chick set out to deliver. (Then again, who knows? It wouldn't be the first time he was a rebel.)

Favorite Panel Award goes to page 9b, where a dark silhouette of Satan with glowing eyes offers the cookie with lightning striking in the background. (Talk about sinister atmosphere!) He states, "My friend, if we pull this off, our cookie will become a death cookie for anyone who opposes our Holy Work." The panels before allege the Vatican stole the idea of transubstantiation from Egyptian priests who said they could turn wafers into the flesh of the sun god Osiris. (He should at least give the Vatican credit for adding some wine to the ceremony to wash it all down.) I know a Catholic priest who says he finds these tracts left in the pews all the time. (Haw-haw-haw!) But don't look at me ... I treasure them too much to waste them on an audience who won't appreciate them. Grade: **A** for Anathema!

THE DEATH COOKIE Response by Rev. Richard Lee! Yeah, Jack goes to extremes here. However, I take issue with the popular claim that the Roman Catholic Church was the first church with Peter as the first pope, from which all Protestant churches came. Even Roman Catholic theologian Hans Kung admits this popular Roman Catholic claim is more mythical than true. Let us not forget the Eastern Orthodox Church on the other side of the world also claims Apostolic Succession going back to the Apostles. Each bishop was in communion with each other, and claimed succession back to ALL of the Apostles, not just Peter. Peter may have been bishop of Rome (although it's still disputed if he was the first). Regardless, he was not supreme over the whole church at the time. (Interesting Pope Trivia: Another challenge to the claim of unbroken Apostolic Succession is the fact that the Eastern Orthodox Patriarch excommunicated the Roman Catholic Pope in 1054 AD. The Pope quickly returned the favor and excommunicated the Patriarch. Succession of both sides was "broken" by each other.) **Still in print.**

Khadijah, a beautiful Roman Catholic, lived in a convent.*

* See **The Prophet** and **Islamic Invasion**, both available from Chick Publications.

Under orders, she married Muhammad, and the trap was set.

If the demonic conspiracy worked, the Arab world would soon be serving the pope.

©1990 Jack T. Chick.

THE DECEIVED **Review:** (Art by Carter ©1990.) A double slap at both Islam and Catholicism in one tract! (Like page 21 says, "No wonder the Vatican and Mecca blocked this good news. They used two dark religious forces, 'Allah' and the 'Queen of Heaven' to make us slaves.") Of course, you don't *have* to be a slave; you can get saved and be set free. But you'll have to ditch the idol worship of Mary & Allah (that's Semiramis and the Moon God to those of you not deceived by Satan). This tract follows two Arabs as they discover how the Pope created Islam in order to seize control of Jerusalem from the Jews. And hey, whadayahknow! It looks like the book they are reading it all from is exactly the size of a Chick tract! (Small world, huh?) Unfortunately, we can't make out the title of the tract. If we could, odds are it would read, *The Deceived.* Haw-haw-haw!

A sample of the narration states, "To destroy true Christianity, Satan moved his murderous religion from Babylon to Rome ... Roman idols were given Christian titles. Venus was called Mary ... who became the 'Queen of Heaven.' Roman Catholicism was born and Satan ruled from the Vatican." The Arabs angrily discover how Satan then expanded his kingdom by finding and financing Muhammad. One reads to the other, "Vatican spies were on the lookout for a potential leader for this new religion." The other shouts, "Those devils!" (He must know where this story is heading.) The Catholics discover Muhammad and hook him up with Khadijah, a beautiful Roman Catholic Arab who lived in a convent. "Under orders, she married Muhammad, and the trap was set. If the demonic conspiracy worked, the Arab world would soon be serving the Pope." Sure enough, it works. When Muhammad has visions, it's Khadijah's Catholic cousin who interpreted and influences them. (One hoof dirties the other.) Like Rosemary's baby, *Islam was born!*

Favorite Panel Award is a tie between the next to last panel and the one before it. The Arabs are beside themselves with joy after being saved. Now they finally feel "clean". Then they dedicate themselves to Kamikaze conversion careers — telling other Arabs about the Satanic conspiracy of Islam. No doubt, their fellow countrymen will love discussing it in a civilized and scholarly manner. (Yeah, right. By the way—how's that life insurance policy holding up? ... Just wondering.) Be sure to keep your eyes peeled for the "fisting" cover variation. Grade: **B** for Beguiled. **Value: $14.**

©1972 Jack T. Chick.

A DEMON'S NIGHTMARE Guest review by Dave: (Art by Chick ©1962, 1972.) This is one of my favorite Chick tracts. It's lighthearted, funny, and for a change the demons get punished in hell rather than the hapless sinner. It also has a rather cool subtext on spiritual warfare (for more on that topic check out Bill Schnoebelen's "blood on the doorposts" from the Chick site). I love the idea of demons fighting for man's soul. It's a classic theme that goes back to C.S. Lewis's *The Screwtape Letters* among many others. It also kind of reminds me of some of Frank Peretti's novels.

The tract is just great. It starts out with two demons perched on a building doing guard duty (note the headset one wears). They spot a Christian coming and immediately swing into action. The Christian finds one of Chick's "cool kids" in the park and breaks the ice with "say, did you ever hear of the time God was murdered by man?" (That would kind of make me a bit nervous but that's just me.) The story moves along nicely as the Christian guy fills the kid in with the gospel while the demons fume. Favorite Panel is where demon **A** regrets inciting the mob to crucify Jesus and demon **B** tells him to "SHUT UP ... Can't you ever drop that subject?" The kid goes home and his parents are of course *horrified* that their son is a "Christian". (Odd, my folks were actually pretty happy when I became a Christian.) Anyway, he goes out with a couple of friends (check out the striped jacket). They drink hooch and meet up with a couple of nice looking babes. He gets laughed at when he tells them he's saved. (Kinda sad.)

The next morning he gets up to go to church and the demons are there, trying to change his mind. They tag along to church where they make cutting remarks. They make a mistake when they decide to skip the Wednesday Bible Study though (they hang out at the kid's house to watch TV). The kid meets up with the guy in the park while their boss catches the poor devils. *They're in deep doo-doo!* Turns out the kid will become a missionary and lead many souls to Christ! I almost felt a little sorry for the two little demons as they ride the elevator down to deeper levels of hell. The last page is great as the demons ask us to burn this tract so the next person to find it won't turn to Christ since they "would miss having their company" (in hell). All in all a great story, classic Chick art, and a solid message. Grade **A** for Affirmation. Super oversized (8 x 5 3/8") with same story but different art, **speculative.** Regular size (5 x 2 3/4") **still in print.**

DON'T READ THAT BOOK Review: (Art by Chick ©1972.) This is one of the toughest Chick tracts to find, but fortunately, a copy of it can be easily obtained by the purchase of Chicks' paperback book "The Next Step." (It's reprinted in chapter Two.) There are not very many cartoons or images in it. Most of the panels are full of dry text explaining a strict routine you should follow to read the Bible. In fact, four pages are filled with nothing but lists of chapters along with what day you should read them. The basic premise is that you should read ten chapters per day. Easy you say? Just grab a Bible and a book mark, and stash it near the toilet or bed stand for convenient reading? Nah, that would be **too** easy. Chick has to make it **difficult.** First, you have to have your "tools," colored pencils, a notebook, and your personal Bible (King James version, natch). Then you have to pray each day *before* you read, asking for guidance and placing yourself in the proper frame of mind. No speed-reading folks; that would be cheating! You have to underline relevant passages and take notes as you go along. You have to keep this tract nearby also, because instead of reading from cover to cover, you're suppose to jump all around following a complicated formula of one chapter from ten different places scattered throughout the Bible. Why? I dunno. The Lord works in mysterious ways (or at least, Chick Publications does). The good news is that you'll be finished reading the Bible in just four months, at which time you're supposed to start all over again and again until you drop dead (and get eternal life, whereupon you will presumably continue the ritual indefinitely). Why is it so important to memorize the Bible from cover to cover? Well, page 5 gives one clue: Like Christians elsewhere in the world, you may soon be tossed into a dungeon and the only Bible verses you'll be able to enjoy are the ones you've memorized. Another reason is provided on page 12. "Won't you feel silly when you talk with Habakkuk in the next life and you have to say to him, 'Uh, no, I didn't read your book! I didn't even know it was in the Bible!'" (Talk about eternal embarrassment!) Let's face it, this is one of the most boring Chick tracts ever made. Chick's enthusiasm for the Bible and his determination to get everyone to read it becomes painfully obvious. However, even though the tract itself is not very exciting, the message within is what Chick tracts are really all about. Grade: **C+** for Christian reading. **$64**

©1972 Jack T. Chick.

"But the men of Sodom were wicked and sinners before the Lord exceedingly." Gen. 13:13

©1991 Jack T. Chick.

©1991 Jack T. Chick.

DOOM TOWN Review: Two different versions exist, both with different variations. The original one (©1989) was drawn by the third artist, while the more recent versions (©1991 & 1999) were redrawn by Fred Carter. Both rip into the homosexuals and warn of God's favorite gay bath (the Lake 'O Fire!). The first version is devoted primarily to the story of Sodom. The redrawn version sandwiches the Sodom story within a modern context of a cameraman trying to convert a homosexual at a gay rally. (He must be tired of working for the liberal media and *wants* to get fired.) Chick reveals his opinion of the media by only showing the last two of the network's call letters ... "B.S." (See page 5.) Both versions show plenty of sweating homosexuals looking and acting like complete perverts. The first version shows a crying kid and says, "the children (of Sodom) were all molested at a very young age" (page 10). When the same version gets revamped with a different cover, it tones down the molestation claim by leaving it more to the imagination. It says, "Even the children were not safe from their perversions." Carter's redrawn version ups the ante by showing a more graphic image. He draws a fat hairy brute in the foreground saying, "It's that time again," as a cowering kid trembles in the background!

Both versions are good, but Carter's version is more provocative in that it shows men kissing men, a priest chasing a child, and outlandish gay get-ups. It's also amusing to note that the idol in the first version is a fat fairy with horns (a horny fairy?) while the idol in the later version looks just like the demon statue in *The Exorcist*. (They're on page 9 in both versions.) Much of the same Sodom story was recounted in Chick's first controversial tract, *The Gay Blade* (©1972). That's when the death threats started. Perhaps Chick was feeling a little nostalgic and figured he'd kick the hornet's nest again to see if anyone was still home.

The original *Doom Town* cover was a graphic of Sodom burning, but it was later replaced with a skull & crossbones image floating above a modern city skyline. See Variations section for details. Many of the protest signs also change within different variations. Gay activists will have a hissy fit reading any version or variation of this tract! Grade **A** for Abhorrent. Original version with destruction of Sodom cover, **$20.** Skull and crossbones cover version without gay rally, **$15.** Gay rally with "Kill the Bigots" sign (page 2) **$5.** Gay rally with "Hate is not a family value" sign (page 2) **still in print.**

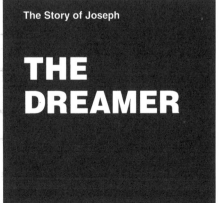

The Story of Joseph

THE DREAMER

THE DREAMER Review: (Art by the third artist and later modified by Carter. ©1991) This tract tells the story of Joseph, the favorite Jewish son that was stripped of his multicolored jacket and sold into slavery by his brothers. It gets a little risqué about half way through, once Joseph is bought by Potiphar and his wife tries to sleep with Joseph whenever her husband is away. Page 9 offers a sexy close-up of the Egyptian seductress looking out at the reader with bedroom eyes, saying, "Come to bed with me." *Ew-lah-lah!* Either Joseph is one straight arrow to resist her advances — or else he's not straight at all! Whatever his motive, she gets angry at being spurned so she concocts a plot to frame him for rape. Her husband believes her and throws Joseph into prison. But Joseph is blessed and his dream interpreting powers soon bring him to the attention of Pharaoh. He's freed and put in charge of storing and rationing food for the upcoming famine (as foretold in Pharaoh's dream.) Guess who comes begging for food when the famine hits? His sinister siblings, the ones who sold him into slavery. They don't recognize Joseph but he certainly recognizes them. He has them tossed into prison as spies but forgives them when they repent. Page 20 summarizes the happy ending thus: "Joseph sent them to bring their families to Egypt so he could protect them. So all the children of Israel dwelt safely in Egypt as long as Joseph lived." But there is no such thing as a free lunch! What the tract fails to mention is that the descendants stick around after the famine and multiply so much, that the alarmed Egyptians eventually enslave them all. (But why dwell on depressing details?) A quick salvation message is tacked on to the last couple pages.

This tract reveals a lot about the third artist and why he was let go. The very first version of this tract (Code A) shows more of the original art than the modified versions that follow. Chick was disappointed with this original artwork of the character's faces and had Fred Carter go in and redo the faces of Joseph and a couple other characters. The new Joseph is more handsome, and looks a lot like Michael Landon of *Bonanza*, *Little House on the Prairie*, and *Highway To Heaven* fame. Some of the original faces remain unchanged, including an impressive close-up of Joseph's crying father on page 7, and the beautiful unfaithful wife discussed earlier. The original artist could certainly do impressive faces at times, but at other times, fell short, like the Pharaoh's face on page 16 (which remains unchanged in both versions.) You can tell which faces are altered in later versions because Carter's faces are smooth and well defined, whereas the originals are more grainy and dark, and better match the surrounding images. Sometimes the difference is so obvious, it's almost amusing, making the new face appear like the character is wearing a mask. Page 20 is such an example. The new "modified" face is cut and pasted over the old grainy face, but the dark grainy neck remains unaltered. The skin tones don't match and it's really kinda creepy! (Fortunately, it's not that obvious to the casual reader.)

This also shows what a perfectionist Chick is. He'd rather go back and improve things than keep reprinting something he knows could be better. By letting the third artist go, he was slowing down the progress of the movie and putting *The Crusaders* on a hiatus that would last over ten years. The old adage, "Anything worth doing is worth doing right" comes to mind. Although the third artist was very talented and drew more realistic artwork than Chick's own cartoons, Chick still let him go. Fred

Carter's quality had spoiled Chick to the point where there was no going back. Carter and Chick would continue doing all the art themselves from this point on. Grade: **B+** for Bossy Brother. Original "A" code version **$25.** Redrawn version (Michael Landon as Joseph) **$4**

 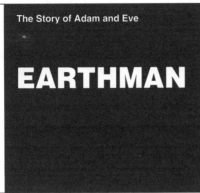

The Story of Adam and Eve

EARTHMAN

As a result of Adam's sin, the earth was cursed with thorns, poisonous snakes, insects, wild animals, wars, earthquakes, killer diseases, etc.

Satan uses **ALL** these miseries to ruin mankind.

©1990 Jack T. Chick.

THE EARTHMAN Review: (Art by the third artist and later modified by Carter ©1990.) This is the story of Adam and Eve. It's also one of the most redrawn of Chick tracts. The earlier versions (Codes A to E) were drawn entirely by the third artist, while later versions replaced over 25 panels with new artwork by Fred Carter. The opening narration is rather reactionary. "The world teaches that man is just a highly developed primate. We are told this took millions of years through the process of evolution. *Most people believe it!* But now, top scientists denounce evolution as a bad joke.* Yet godless media and public school leaders keep pushing it." The footnote sites a creationist book by Scott M. Huse entitled *The Collapse of Evolution.* The accompanying images show a panoramic shot of cavemen clubbing each other to death as volcanoes explode in the background. (The original version featured a similar image with apes using bones as weapons.) Chick takes a moment to bask in his own notoriety among public school educators. An angry teacher holds up a copy of *The Earthman* tract and screams, "Who brought this lie to school?" The narration surrounding the panel takes it further. "But there's one man they DON'T want you to know about! This book could soon be banned in public schools ... so read it now!" Pretty self-congratulatory ... The original version turns the hype a notch higher with a bold banner declaring, "It could change your life." The story then tells about Lucifer being kicked out of heaven with all his angels and exiled to Earth. Of all the planets in the Universe that God could have put humans on, he picks Satan's prison planet as the location of Eden. It doesn't take long for the trouble to start. Satan looks on in disgust as God creates Adam and chums it up with him, taking walks with the human through paradise. Once Eve is created, Satan makes his move. "Satan approached Eve as a beautiful serpent." To his credit, the snake has arms and legs, a Biblical detail Chick forgot in later Genesis tracts like *In The Beginning.* On the flip side, Chick misses an opportunity to place dinosaurs in Eden like he does in later tracts.

Eve follows the snake's advice and eats the fruit, convincing Adam to do the same. All hell breaks loose. The strategically placed butterflies and fig leafs get replaced with animal skins as the two feel shame for their nakedness. (Though they obviously get over their shyness in time to create Cain and Abel.) Chick doesn't blame Eve for causing sin, but instead, appears to place the responsibility on Adam. "Adam's sin started a horrible chain reaction. Now every man must die." As if that weren't enough, "The earth was cursed with thorns, diseases, insects, poisonous snakes, wild animals, wars, cancer, AIDS., earthquakes, etc." He later says, "Thanks Adam!" Cain and Abel's rivalry is outlined, along with Cain's murder of Abel. The last 4 pages introduce Jesus as the solution to our eternal damnation problem.

Carter's redrawn images are superior, but the original version is not bad either. Favorite Panel Award goes to page 15, which is one of the few *original* drawings that remains unchanged in the later version. An entire page is devoted to showing a modern day war scene from the perspective of a fallen soldier as tanks roll forward. Grade **A-** as in Able-less. Original Apes fighting (page 2) **version $25.** Cavemen fighting version (page 2) **$12.**

THE EMPTY TOMB

J.T.C.

What shall I do then with Jesus which is called Christ?

CRUCIFY HIM! CRUCIFY HIM!

See Matt. 27

Why, what evil hath he done?

Israel rejected their Messiah, and Pilate ordered his death.

I am innocent of the blood of this just person.

His blood be on us, and on our children!

See Mark 15

©1990 Jack T. Chick.

THE EMPTY TOMB Review: (Art by third artist, modified later by Carter ©1990.) This is the story of the rise and fall of Jesus—and rise again! It begins with the child Jesus confounding rabbis in the temple. When Mary finds the boy, she has a flashback of Gabriel proclaiming him as the Son of God. Scenes of Moses, Genesis, John the Baptist, and Lazarus are recreated. A sinister scene of Judas Iscariot is provided for readers to hiss at. (The original version calls him, "the world's greatest traitor!") The last supper and betrayal kiss are provided. But the showstoppers are definitely the images of Jesus being mocked, abused, tortured, and crucified. "When sentenced to death, they began to spit on and hit the Savior." (Chick removed any references to spitting or hitting in the later version.) Pontius Pilate's offering to free Jesus is also included, along with the crowd's demand that a murderer be freed instead. Close-ups of the barbed whip are offered for additional effect. "The whip tore away the flesh. Muscles were sliced wide open, and vessels spurted blood. Most victims died from the beating." Chick doesn't mince words, nor does he sugar coat the pictures. Jesus is ripped to shreds with blood dripping and spurting everywhere. The most painful image to view is the infamous nail-pounding scene. Chick provides an intense close-up and forces us to watch as the nail goes in and the blood shoots out. "They drove rusty spikes into His wrists instead of His palms because His weight would have ripped away the flesh of His hands."

To make absolutely certain no one escapes this tract without feeling significant loss of appetite, Chick devotes an entire panel to a *Medical view of His suffering by G. Bradley, M.D.* "This was the most agonizing death man could face... He had to support Himself in order to breathe... The flaming pain of the spikes hitting the median nerve in the wrists explodes up His arms, into His brain and down His spine. The spike burning through the nerves of the feet jerks His body erect, then the leg muscles convulse and drive His body downward... beating Him against the cross. Exhaustion, shock, dehydration, and paralysis destroy the victim." Just how Bradley observed and recorded all this graphic detail is somewhat of a mystery, as crucifixions are a long lost art.

Chick goes on to explain why a human sacrifice was needed and quotes scripture denouncing those who forego Jesus as hell bound (originally Matt. 10:28, revised with Rev. 20:15). The original version also contains a stronger attack on other religions that is noticeably absent in the revised version. "Beware! All religious systems can only give you false hope because they are satanically controlled. Remember: neither Mary, Buddha, Muhammad, Lenin, Confucious [sic] nor Ghandi died for your sins... and *all* of them are *still* dead." (Chick can't resist placing Catholics at the front of the pagan list.)

The differences between the original version drawn by the anonymous artist and the revised version modified by Carter are interesting. Most close-ups of faces have been redrawn by Carter (except for Judas and Pilate). Jesus is made much more handsome (except for the bloody crucifixion scenes). The baptism panel with John is completely redrawn. Several panels at the end are also replaced. But there isn't the wholesale replacement of art seen in other tracts like *Earthman* or the *Doom Town*. When it came to gore, the third artist's efforts made the cut! Favorite Panel Award goes to the nail through the hand scene. Not since the golden age of pre-code horror and crime comics have such gruesome images been available to kids. Grade **A-** for Awfully good. Original *"Whom* will you serve" version (page 22) **$25.** Redrawn "Who will you serve" (page 22) version **still in print.**

© 1972 Jack T. Chick.

ESCAPE (Art by Chick © 1972. See *The Great Escape.)* **Value: $20.**

©1998 Jack T. Chick.

THE EXECUTION **Review:** (Art by Chick © 1992.) This tract sports one of Chick's more provocative covers: A dangling noose! The contents, however, are far less serious. It's a rather cartoony tale about a bully who grows up to be a thug. The criminal kills a man in a robbery and is sentenced to death row. His mother visits him and brings cookies, which he feeds to his pet rat. He tells his mother he hates her but she keeps delivering the cookies despite his hostility. (He's probably going through a phase...) The execution date arrives, but he's lead to the front door and set free. He argues with the jailer that he's supposed to die for his crime. The jailer realizes the mix-up and hauls the criminal back into prison where he's properly executed. No, wait, that's *Life of Brian.* Yet this story is almost as surreal: What criminal would argue with the jailer not to be let free? The jailer explains that someone else was already executed in the thug's place—his mother! *Gasp!* But don't worry, she volunteered, so no one can be sued. (This must have occurred in one of those tough states where parents are legally responsible for the crimes of their children.) The tract then explains that this story is really about what Jesus did for his children. The last panel is the classic image of the Faceless God shouting Matthew 25:41 at a sinner to go jump in the lake (of fire). The very last sentence looks as ominous as it sounds. A black bar across the bottom declares in bold white type, "Receive Jesus while you still can."

Favorite Panel Award goes to page 6B. The judge is sentencing the killer to hang by the neck until dead. To lighten the otherwise downbeat mood (receiving a death sentence is usually a downer for most folks), Chick adds several upbeat details to cheer up the audience. The judge slams his gavel on a wayward ant, whose small corpse becomes stuck to the wood. If that's not funny enough, the judge's drinking water contains a fish in it. If all that fails to crack a smile, the smirking bailiff should do the trick. (He obviously loves it when people get sentenced to death.) Grade **B** for Bail...*Not!* **Still in print.**

©2002 Jack T. Chick.

son. He informs Bruce that he's heading to hell. "You're going down, Bruce!" Bruce squirms but there is no place for him to run. (Remember, he's a quadriplegic, and that means he's paralyzed from the neck down.) Bob pressures him for a decision to get saved, but Bruce tells him to come back in the morning. "Tomorrow may be too late, Bruce!" Bob whines, "But I'll come back in the morning."

The next panel explains, "Bruce Burke died in his sins at 3:10 a.m. His soul was taken to a screaming hell...lost for all eternity." So much for upbeat endings. Then again, Bruce was such a jerk, most readers are probably relieved he won't be taking up space in heaven.

It's a surprise ending alright. I expected Bob to show up at 12:01 a.m. and say, "Okay Bruce, it's morning. I'm back to close the deal." But, no dice. Bob wasn't pushy enough this time so Satan scores another soul for *The Lakers* (as in Lava). Let that be a lesson to all you polite Christians out there: people on life support *need* to be badgered to death to receive eternal life.

Favorite Panel Award goes to page 10b. Check out the shocked expression on Bruce's face when he realizes Bruno and his gang are behind him. *Haw-haw!* Grade **B+** for Bravo Bruno! **Still in print.**

The predictions of Juan's father-in-law proved to be true. Juan will now taste communist justice.

Carlos' most faithful follower is destroyed by those he trusted (Gal. 6:7).

FALLEN Review: (Art by Chick ©2002.) This is tract #19 of 25 featuring Bob Williams. It's another retelling of the classic Prodigal Son story, but in a modern context. It begins with an informal soccer match where the ball is a teenager named Bruce. The other guys are kicking the &*#@ out of him. His assailants indicate they don't need Bruce anymore because his money ran out. Bruce is left on the ground along with his mother's empty purse. The cops spot Bruce in an alley with a purse and stop him for questioning. They find an address in the purse and call it to see if the purse was stolen. The mother answers and is delighted to hear the police found her son. He took the purse and $26,000 when he ran away six months earlier.

Bruce is flown home but could care less for his parents. His father calls Bob Williams and asks for help. He explains that his son is "totally evil and laughs at God. He's into drugs, crime, and violence. He hates **everything** about us but our **money.**" Bob agrees to talk to the problem child and urges the father to pray for his son.

Either someone didn't pray hard enough or God wasn't listening, because Bruce gets into big trouble at a bar. The Bartender calls the mob and tells Bruno that Bruce is at his bar. Bruno arrives with the criminal equivalent of the Welcome Wagon. One of his thugs grabs Bruce and breaks his neck. They leave him for dead outside his parent's home.

Bruce is taken to the hospital and stuck in room 310. Chick regulars probably remember the last character who was in *Room 310* was a fellow named Danny O'Hara, and he didn't make it out alive. The prognosis for Bruce doesn't sound any better. He's a quadriplegic, and according to the footnote, that means he is paralyzed from the neck down. He also has pneumonia, but since there's no footnote, it must not mean anything important...

Bob finally shows up and visits. Bruce doesn't recognize him. Bob explains, "You were in my Sunday school class, years ago. Back in those days, you were such a tender boy before the Lord." (Good thing Bob isn't a Priest. The lawyers would be busting down the doors by now.)

Bob continues, "But you **never** got saved. Then you let Satan get his hooks into you. I'm gonna tell you something that will save your neck." (Sorry Bob, his neck's already broken.) Bob tells the story of the prodigal

FAT CATS Review: (Art by Chick ©1989.) This tract has a similar theme to *The Poor Revolutionist.* It follows the exploits of a loser who joins the communist revolution to improve society and is ultimately betrayed. But this time, the location is in South America, and the Catholics' involvement is front and center. The story begins in the dining room of a rich and powerful General. He and his cronies are feasting when news of unrest is reported. Rather than address the problems of starvation and unemployment that created the unrest, the General orders his soldiers to crush any resistance. A Catholic priest pats the General on the shoulder and blesses his wise decision (then burps). The village of San Marcos is attacked. One of the few survivors is Carlos. He decides, "the people must rise up and throw those criminals out of the palace." Juan is the balding El Stupido who actually believes Carlos and his commie chums will improve things if he joins their revolution and wins. Despite dire warnings from his wife and a six-page mini-sermon from her father (a Fundamentalist preacher), Juan goes to join the rebel forces. Carlos is delighted to have him. "When we win, you will *always* be at my side." Carlos introduces Juan to Father Dominic, "a good communist." Juan is taken back. He asks, "Excuse me, Father, but I thought the Catholic Church hated the communists." Dominic replies, "Not any more. Many of them have changed! ... Didn't you know that Jesus was a revolutionary **just like Carlos?**" Dominic shows Juan an 8 x 10 inch drawing of Jesus with an AK-47 which he just happens to have ready and says, "He said take from the rich and give to the poor. Jesus was a communist, you know." Juan disagrees and mentions his father-in-law. The priest becomes very interested. "Juan, your father-in-law is a dangerous man. His name is Perez and he lives in Santa Rosa? I think I will pay him a visit."

The revolutionary movement grows, due in a large part to the efforts of Father Dominic and his "connections worldwide." Carlos admits to Juan that Dominic was one of several children taken to Russia and turned into nuns and priests, then "trained how to implement Liberation Theology and socialism." The revolution reaches full force and the palace falls. Two days later, Juan learns that his wife and family were executed for being "enemies of the people and heretics." And, to make matters even more dramatic, it turns out his father-in-law was necklaced under orders of Father Dominic. (Chick provides a footnote to make sure everyone knows that necklacing means placing a gasoline filled tire around a person's neck and setting it on fire.) Juan gets predictably upset and swears revenge.

Dominic hears about the threat and convinces Carlos to "make an example out of him." The next panel shows a soldier blowing Juan's brains out with a pistol as Dominic looks on smirking. Chick's dry commentary is rather sardonic. "The predictions of Juan's father-in-law proved to be true. Juan will now taste communist justice." The execution is pretty graphic, too. Juan is knelling with his hands tied behind his back while the bullet goes through his head and knocks his glasses off. (Bastard commies! Don't they know you're supposed to let folks remove their glasses before you blast their brains out?) Juan then gets a double whammy as he's condemned to the Lake of Fire by the Faceless God for not accepting Christ as his Lord and Savior. The last panel is virtually a duplicate of the first, only now Carlos is the feasting General ordering his men to put down unrest while Dominic blesses his wise decision (and burps). This tract probably didn't get much distribution in Nicaragua or South Africa. Some of the comparisons are way too close for comfort. But it's classic Chick through and through, attacking both Communism and Catholicism at the same time. Grade: **A-** for Ammunition. **Value: $3.**

FIRE STARTER **Review:** (Art by Carter ©1986.) What a stunning and dramatic tract! It opens with a scene of a father surrendering his child to a high priest of Baal, who turns around and tosses the infant into a fire for sacrifice. Wide panel shots on pages 4 & 5 show various executions in all their gory glory. Then the story focuses on the prophet Elijah and his struggle to convince the evil King Ahab to abandon the Baal worship in favor of Judaism. Elijah promises a drought until Israel worships the one true God. He hides for a few years while the drought causes famine and public outrage. Elijah returns to order Ahab to gather all Israel and 850 prophets of Baal on Mount Carmel for a demonstration. Once there, Elijah challenges the Baal representatives to a showdown: Whichever religion succeeds in burning their sacrifice with fire from heaven is the *true* religion. (Why hasn't anyone thought of settling modern theological debates in this manner?) "The 850 prophets of Baal cried out from early morning until noon. But Baal didn't answer. They looked like fools! They slashed themselves, but Baal never answered. Satan ALWAYS double-crosses his followers."

Meanwhile, Elijah taunts the bleeding priests with snide remarks like "Cry louder. Maybe Baal's asleep!" When his turn arrives, the Baal priests are more courteous. (Perhaps they are too faint to taunt because of all their blood loss.) Elijah has his alter soaked with water, then prays. Fire shoots down from heaven and burns it. The crowd goes wild. Fat Baal priests are held as soldiers skewer them with spears. For his encore, Elijah prays again and the Lord sends rain. (Talk about a crowd pleaser, they end a reign of terror and start a real rain at the same time!) The last three pages explain, "Another showdown between God and Satan is taking place. The prize is YOUR SOUL!" The last image shows a wonderfully sinister image of Satan looking over his shoulder at the audience from beneath his Klansman-like robes with a rhetorical question posed, "Just like those in Elijah's time, we must choose between God and Satan. Eternal life in heaven with Jesus—Eternal pain in hell with Satan." (Gee, when you put it that way, curtain number one seems too obvious.)

Favorite Panel Award is a bit tougher to decide. There are so many great images in this tract: Baal priests feeding babies to the fire, or slashing themselves with knives, or getting impaled with spears. Page 5 wins the prize though, with a wide shot of a mass beheading in progress. Fat Baal priests triumphantly lift the bleeding heads of Jewish prophets in the background as future victims line up for their turn at the blood soaked chopping block. (Next! No pushing please!) Carter must have relished drawing the action images for this tract. It's another masterpiece of fine pencil images. The close-up of Elijah on page 6 is so detailed, you can practically count the whiskers in his beard! Grade: **A+** for Amazing Art. **Value: $3.75**

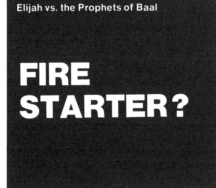

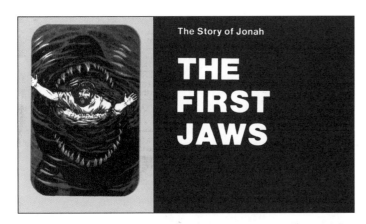

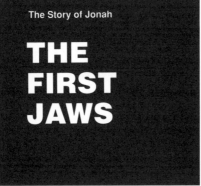

The Story of Jonah

THE FIRST JAWS

Look at the size of that fish!

GASP!

"The Lord spake unto the fish..."

Yuuuck!

and it vomited out Jonah upon the dry land."

©1985 Jack T. Chick.

FIRST JAWS Review: (Art by Carter ©1985.) This tract tells the Old Testament tale of Jonah and the Whale. It begins with a supposedly true story of a British sailor who was swallowed whole by a shark in the early 1900s, then rescued 48 hours later when the shark was caught and cut open. The narrative jumps back to Biblical times to relate the similar story of Jonah being swallowed and coughed up alive. Unlike sanitized versions of the story, this one has Jonah looking horrible after the ordeal. His hair is eaten away by stomach acid, his clothes ripped to shreds and seaweed wrapped around him. One image shows him crammed in the shark's stomach and he looks pretty miserable. The narration states, "He was in a type of hell." The confined space makes one wonder where the three days worth of air came from. Jonah is delivered to the Ninevites and reluctantly preaches for them to repent. Since he's a Jew and hates the Ninevites, the narration observes, "Jonah was the only evangelist who prayed that he'd get no converts." When the city repents, cows, kids, and cute puppies are draped in scratchy blankets. It states, "Man and beast were covered in sackcloth before God in true repentance. The ENTIRE CITY turned from their wicked ways!"

You can imagine how Chick would love for his tracts to succeed in converting an entire city, even if it was just a small rural bus stop. But Jonah is angered by his own success: "Jonah was furious! He wanted the

Ninevites DEAD!" Then it tells how God punished Jonah in the desert to teach him how saving everyone is important to God. It fast forwards to Jesus preaching to the masses. "When the Lord Jesus Christ began his ministry, his first word was REPENT! Jesus spoke more about hell than anyone else in the Bible. Out of love, He warned us that hell is real and gave us a way to escape." One gets the feeling that Chick is trying to justify his own heavy emphasis on hell and his constant call for readers to repent and be saved, *or else!*

Chick liked this story so much, he planned on making a full length animated cartoon out of it. (That project eventually snowballed into *The Light Of The World* movie.) The pictures in the tract are beautiful pencil rendering with incredible detail that few besides Fred Carter could provide. A close-up of the pierced hand of Jesus on page 21, for example, looks more like a detailed sketch from Leonardo De Vinci than something in a comic book. Each vein, every tiny bone and sinew is carefully included. Many of these same panels reappear painted over in beautiful color in the *Jonah* comic book, printed in 1991. That was the only Chick comic that was painted, instead of being inked and colored. It was then put on expensive slick paper and became the most costly comic book Chick ever produced. (The comic was discontinued for that reason in 2000.)

In short, this is a beautiful tract that jumps around between story lines but still delivers the goods. There are two different cover variations: One with an overhead shot looking down on Jonah in the water as the shark approaches from underneath, the other version shows a side shot of Jonah being devoured. The only thing better than the art in this tract is the painted art in the comic! Grade: **A** for Appetite! Bird's-eye view of Jonah being swallowed cover, **$8.** Side view of Jonah being swallowed cover, **$4.50.**

FLIGHT 144

J.T.C.

The Davidsons stand before God

I never knew you: depart from me...*

*Mt. 7:23

Hold on a minute!

You've made a HORRIBLE mistake, Lord.

Don't you KNOW who we are?

©1998 Jack T. Chick.

FLIGHT 144 Review: (Art by Chick ©1998.) Another grim reminder that those who believe in "good works" are damned to hell, while those who believe in Christ will go to heaven despite a life of crime. A "famous" older missionary couple are on a plane to the US and sit next to a recently saved but former felon. They brag about all their great accomplishments in Africa (5 schools and 4 hospitals), and the jailbird compliments them on how many souls they must have saved. Then the missionary makes a stunning confession: "No Ed, you don't understand. God called us to help these dear people to lead better lives." (In other words, social work is more important than converting people to Christ.) Ex-felon Ed starts to question if they're really ready to meet their maker, and the schmoozing quickly stops. But not because the jet engine is burning up outside and the plane is losing altitude. Everyone is far more concerned about the theological disagreement! (There's no screaming on board during any of this either, so apparently everyone else is enthralled with the debate as well.)

Finally, the missionary loses his patience and yells, "Just shut up! Can't you see we're going to CRASH!" (Remember this line if you need to change the subject from religion, because it seems to work in this tract.) The plane plunges into the ocean and no one survives. Guess who gets sent to the Lake O' Fire? Yes, our kindly little old man and his wife. (The jailbird goes straight to heaven without passing go.) The missionary starts to argue with God (kids, don't try this at home) and is tossed into the flames along with his main squeeze. At least they get the last word though. It's "YAAAAH!"

Favorite panel award is the final shoveling of bodies into the pit scene. That's always a good image, but seeing angels feed the flames with an elderly couple graphically demonstrates how totally unconcerned Chick is with appearances. Like the scripture he quotes says, "There is a way which seemeth right unto a man, but the end thereof are the ways of death." Eat your heart out AARP. Grade **A-** for Airlines. **Still in print.**

At last the jester had found a *greater fool* than himself!

©1992 Jack T. Chick.

THE FOOL Review: (Art by Chick ©1972, 1992.) This is not one of Chick's best tracts. It's drawn in a sparse style with simple backgrounds and few details. It looks like a kiddy tract, but it can also be directed toward an adult audience. The plot is also basic. In fact, the entire tract can be read in one minute. (Most of the pictures only have one or two lines of text with them.) A court jester is sent on a mission by the king to give a golden wand to someone in the kingdom who is a bigger fool than

the jester. The king becomes sick and calls the jester back to let him know he's preparing for a long journey (death). The jester asks if he's prepared for that journey and the king admits that he isn't. The jester gives the king the wand. (Get it? *Haw-haw-haw!* I bet the jester laughed all the way to the dungeon for that one.) So it's a one-joke tract, but a sobering one.

The style of the art is different from most of Chick's tracts. It's a fairy tale caricature style that makes many observers suspect someone else drew it (but folks at the factory say it was Chick). Whenever a full page is wasted on a hand pointing to the next page (like it does on page 19) and saying nothing more than, "Please read the following... **very closely!**" you can assume the story is being padded. Perhaps this is one of those times when the deadline came up too quick. However, the punch line dovetails nicely into Chick's salvation message: "What about you? Have you prepared for *YOUR* coming journey? If not, then you're in big trouble...just like the king!" The last panel sounds a little too smooth: "Would the little court jester give **you** that golden wand? Don't be a fool! Accept Christ and be saved...TODAY!" One gets the feeling that this tract could have been fewer than 24 pages, but that would derail the entire Chick formula. As Chick has indicated in his open letters before, sometimes the simplest message gets the best results. (This tract has remained in print for over three decades.) Grade: **C+** for Court jester. **Still in print.**

©1987 Jack T. Chick.

THE FOUR BROTHERS Review: (Art by Chick ©1987.) Four depression era kids are dragged to a Christian revival by their mom. They all become saved and get their very own guardian angel to watch over each. But one by one, three of the four brothers lose their faith and their angel. Frank loses his salvation the very next day. The devil convinces his subconscious mind that his girlfriend would flip if she learned he was a Christian. Chick observes, "In the years that followed, Frank attended church...to give the impression that he was religious. Notice the angel is gone." (Also notice that Frank's two kids have five freckles on their right cheek in the same exact place that Frank does. Apparently, it's a family trademark.)

Bobby loses his faith and his angel years later in business. His employer tells him that he'll have to choose between his religion and job advancement. He chooses his job and his angel splits. Chick remarks, "Bob continues to attend church to impress his old friends...a typical hypocrite."

Then there's Charlie. He becomes a successful preacher. Chick has some choice words for Charlie. "He's loved by millions, respected, charming, and has his own television program. Charlie is into the big time...but where's *his* angel? It was in his second year at the theological seminary that Charlie's angel left. Nobody suspected Charlie was into pornography and fornication. But the Lord knew." Sure enough, while Charlie checks out the centerfold, his angel zooms away.

Chick continues to show what a slick character Bobby is, brown-nosing his way to the top. Chick points out, "Charlie is introduced to those of the 'in' crowd. He never made enemies, and won them with a flattering tongue." In comparison, Chick makes enemies all the time by pointing out their hypocrisy and sin. This tract is a good example. Bashing religious phonies is only going to alienate them from buying his tracts, but Chick does it anyway because that's what the Bible preaches. Rocking the boat may be bad for business and personal success, but it's the duty of true Christians. The next brother in the story represents such a Christian.

Page 16: "Henry Sawyer is also a preacher, but he doesn't have a big church like Charlie does. Henry has a run down mission on the wrong side of the tracks.and works the streets. Henry is for real. His conversion was for real. He loves the Lord and honors the Word of God. Henry prays and weeps for the lost, and loves the unlovely." Chick Publications is literally across the railroad tracks in a less than ritzy location. Chick's conversion was for real and he's dedicated his life to promoting what he believes is God's true Word. He sincerely fears for The Lost because he believes they will burn forever in hell. Henry and Chick have a lot in common. As a black thug sneaks up behind Henry to stab him, Henry's guardian angel holds back the knife. In the *Closet Witches* tape, Chick is told how assassins were sent to murder him and his family, but a wall of angels held them back.

Henry visits his other brothers at their last family reunion. Henry's fanaticism causes problems with his siblings. He misses the meal for starters. Brother Charlie (the TV preacher) makes some snide remarks asking if Henry thinks he's too good to dine with his brothers. Henry replies, "I'm not allowed to eat with you. The Word of God says, 'If any man that is called a brother be a fornicator...with such an one no [sic] not to eat'." That goes over like a lead balloon with brother Charlie. He retorts that he's a man of God! But Henry doesn't agree. "No you're not, Charlie. God says, 'Woe be unto the pastors that destroy the sheep of my pasture ... Even so ye also outwardly appear righteous unto men, but within ye are full of hypocrisy and iniquity ... Cursed be he that doeth the work of the Lord deceitfully'." Ouch, that won't help the TV ministry ratings! Has there ever been a TV preacher who comes off looking good in Chick tracts? Not likely.

Brother Frank leaps to the defense of his slippery brother. "Shut up Henry. Both Bobby and I really respect Charles. Everyone says he's wonderful." Henry's response is typical Chick: "But if ye have respect to persons, ye commit sin." Once again, Chick is reminding his readers that being despised by the mainstream is actually a sign that you're on the right track (or tract, as the case may be). Is it any wonder the four brothers never have another reunion?

Charlie is too self-assured to listen to Henry's warnings. "God is love!" Charlie responds, then adds, "Henry belongs to the 'lunatic fringe.' Trust me. I have a Doctorate of Divinity. Henry is a nothing." These are classic criticisms of Chick, made by mainstream preachers with impressive degrees who don't want to offend wealthy patrons or influential friends of other faiths. When asked what they thought abut Chick's controversial tracts, they often make patronizing remarks about him, claiming he means no harm, but doesn't understand the complexities of the Bible because he lacks formal training. This tract can be seen as a scathing rebuttal to such snobbish dismissals of his work. Chick gets the last laugh with the

last two panels. The popular brotners are all sent to hell by the Faceless God while Henry is commended for his fine efforts and welcomed into the kingdom of heaven.

This title is discontinued and no longer offered for reprinting. One of the customer service ladies said it was because Chick received too many complaint letters from Calvinists after they read the tract. She says they didn't like the fact that three of the "saved" characters lost their salvation. Whatever the reason, it makes this relatively recent tract from the 1980s difficult to find for collectors. Grade: **A** for Adultery! Permanently retired: **$81.**

©2001 Jack T. Chick.

FRAMED Review: (Art by Chick ©2001.) This is tract #6 in the series of 25 Bible tracts. It chronicles the exploits of Joey Harris, a "law and order" man who gets framed by gang members for turning them in to the police. (They plant a gun in his pocket as he enters a metal detector on his way to jury duty.) Joey is thrown in the pokey and his mom goes running to Bob for help. Bob bails him out. Because of this big favor, Joey has to listen to Bob witness to him. He tells the Biblical yarn about Joseph being sold into slavery and being framed by his slave master's wife. Then Bob makes comparisons to how Jesus was also framed. As usual, the story goes on and on and on...by page 10b, Joey looks pretty tired of it. He gets home and Bob is still narrating. Joey politely insists that he's still listening. (Married Couple rule #456: Whenever your partner says, "I'm listening", they're not.) Ten pages later and Bob's still preaching. (Give him a break, Bob! Joey still needs to take a shower to wash off the jail stench!) Joey either honestly converts or pretends to in order to get rid of Bob. He falls to the floor and prays, "Oh, Lord Jesus, forgive me! And banish blabber-mouth Bob from my home for all eternity!" (Okay, so he didn't say the last part, but he probably *thought* it.) Thirty minutes later, the cops call to inform Joey that they've dropped the charges. Joey pumps his arm in the *Home Alone* movie gesture of "YES!" and all is right with the world. (Assuming of course, that Bob has finally left him home alone.)

Favorite Panel Award goes to the front cover. Joey is pinned against the jail bars as a big butch convict stands behind him with his arm around Joey's chest. Joey's cross-eyed expression looks like he just got goosed. (Do you think...? *Nah!*) Grade: **B** for Busted. **Still in print.**

©1972 Jack T. Chick.

FRAME-UP Review: (Art by Carter ©1972.) This is one of Carter's early tracts, drawn in the same basic style as *The Gay Blade*. Although the art is good, it is not as impressive or highly detailed as the fine line work from tracts and comics of later years. The story is pretty basic too. A prison chaplain visits a condemned man with 15 days to live. The prisoner wants nothing to do with religion, but the chaplain is able to pique his interest by talking about how Jesus was framed. The chaplain explains how Jesus was railroaded by Annas, a Sadducee and former Jewish high priest. (Annas was angry that Jesus had thrown his moneychangers from the temple.) Chick documents some of the eighteen laws violated against Jesus in order to sentence him to death. By page 21, the convict suddenly changes his disposition and decides, "If anybody loved me that much, to lay down his life for me...I'd be nuts to die in my sins...I want Jesus as my Lord and savior." He falls on his knees and recites the Sinner's prayer. The chaplain declares that his name is now in The Book of Life. (Even though he never bothered to ask what the prisoner's name is.) All prior sins are forgiven.

But things are not so rosy for those who framed Jesus. According to Chick, their future fate is ominous indeed. The narrator muses aloud, "I wonder what Judas, Caiaphas, Annas, Pilate, and the 23 Sanhedrin members will say when they face the Lord Jesus Christ as their judge?" What they say to the Faceless God may be a mystery, but what he shouts back at them is pretty certain: "Depart from me, ye cursed, into everlasting fire, prepared for the devil and his angels!"

Unless, of course, someone repented and accepted Christ before his death. Then Jesus would be obligated to forgive everything. Imagine the awkwardness of having someone like Pontius Pilate in Heaven. It would make for some unusual introductions. "Mary, this is Pontius, the gentleman who sentenced me to death. He tried to acquit me four times, but Annas was too clever for him. Now if you'll excuse me, I have some sentencing of my own to attend to. I'm sure you two have plenty to talk about..."

This is a surprisingly rare tract. Many collectors still need it on account of its age and because it is rarely if ever reprinted. (It was due for a revised copyright notice in 1999, but newer copyright dates have not been reported.) That could always change in the future. Until then, collectors should expect to pay a premium. Grade: **B** for the Big House. **Value $71**.

©1972 Jack T. Chick.

THE GAY BLADE Review: (Art by Carter ©1972, 2000.) With a name like this, it's gotta be good! Here Jack uses his most reliable weapon to bust some "homo-heads:" You guessed it, more tales of vengeance from the good Ol' Testament. Obviously, the outcome isn't very Politically Correct. (Can you say "death and damnation"? Sure you can.) After several opening panels featuring "in-your-face-fags" screaming at the reader, Jack turns back the clock to recount his favorite supernatural disaster (the destruction of Sodom). God sends two male angels to save Lot. Lot spots them on the streets of Sodom and realizes how handsome men fare in Sodom after sundown, so he implores them to spend the night in his house. The homosexual rape gangs gather around his home that night and demand some heavenly hiney. Lot offers the mob his two young virgin daughters instead (thanks dad) butt no! They want the angels. The crowd gets ugly and the angels blind them. Like some perverse parody of "Dawn of the Dead", blind homosexuals spend all night outside groping around for the back door. (Why not settle for each other? It's not like they could see anything.) The firestorm of Sodom soon follows, with only Lot's family escaping alive—all except his wife, who turns into salt for looking back. This tract fails to mention how later, Lot has incest with both his daughters and makes them pregnant. The Old Testament blames the girls for the rape. It says they wanted it, making Lot too drunk to know what he was doing. How times change! (Even Clinton would have a tough time spinning **that** defense.)

This tract offers plenty of interesting material. The 1972 version has a longhaired homo grabbing a reluctant straight man by the arm and saying, "You must understand that I'm sick—And *you* should have *compassion* on me!" The revised 2000 version is virtually identical, except the same panel now has a militant homosexual yelling at the straight guy, "You're offended by gays? Are you some kind of bigot?" Chick has basically documented a fundamental shift in social norms in a single panel. He shows how thirty years of activism moved the public condemnation of homosexuality from the perpetrator to those who reject it.

It was this tract that started getting Chick labeled a publisher of "hate speech" by gay activists. Militants would phone Chick Publications and threaten to bomb it, burn it down, kill the receptionist, etc. So much for taking the moral high ground. Instead of silencing Chick, the threats only seem to have hardened his resolve. He published two other anti-gay tracts (*Doom Town* and *Sin City*) as well as reprinted *The Gay Blade*. Homosexuality may be more mainstream, but Chick's not giving up without a fight. Just imagine what tracts we'll get if they legalize gay marriage?! Grade: **A** for Abomination. Original pink cover version **$11.50**. Lavender reprint cover **$2**

munes with spirits, especially a guide named "George." The invisible demon tries to shut her up, but Gladys is too much of a blabbermouth to heed George's advice. Bob mentions that the ancient prophet Isaiah was 100% accurate. Gladys thinks to herself that she is only 20% accurate. Then Bob explains how Moses said any prophet who is ever wrong is a *false* prophet, "and that prophet shall die." Gladys becomes offended and wants to call a ride. Holly Parker (from tract #12, *The Nervous Witch*) comes to her rescue. While driving off with Gladys, Holly admits she hates Bob and placed a death curse on him. Bob must not have prayed hard enough for his enemies, because Holly then drives her car straight into a fuel truck. Only the demon spirit guide survives the explosion. Holly's soul demands to speak with Lucifer. The angel on duty says she'll have plenty of time to visit with her master in the Lake of Fire. *(Ew, burn!)* The two women wind up shivering before the Great White Throne of Judgment. The Faceless God shouts Matthew 25:41 at them and they are plopped into Lava Lake. (You can bet that wasn't one of Gladys's predictions!)

Favorite Panel Award goes to page 9B, where demon George tries to plug Gladys's ears, but only succeeds in tickling her. She chuckles, "Oh, stop it, George ... You're such a silly boy!" George is probably tickling her now...with his pitchfork. Don't be surprised if her laughter has taken on a decidedly higher volume and tenor. Grade: **B** for Burning Astrologers. **Still in print.**

©2002 Jack T. Chick.

"God is angry with the wicked every day." Psalm 7:11b

See Bible tract #2, **"It's Coming"**.

©2002 Jack T. Chick.

GLADYS Review: (Art by Chick ©2002.) This is tract #17 of 25 featuring Bob Williams. Getting your name placed on the cover of a Chick tract is like being featured on "60 Minutes;" you can assume you are not going to look so great by the time the show is over. Such is the case with poor Gladys. She visits her niece, Sandy, (from tract #7, *It's the Law*) in order to avoid the expense of staying at a hotel during her Astrology convention. Sandy's Bible study group shows up. Bob Williams is the leader of the pack. He starts to talk to Gladys about her powers of prophecy, and (as always) stirs the conversation around to the Bible. He asks Gladys if she is a psychic. She proudly claims that she is. She says that she com-

GOD WITH US Guest review by Andie Kittab: (Art by Chick ©2002) This is tract #18 of 25 featuring Bob Williams. It begins with a couple of punks in a skating park swearing at each other. "Where the *?!@ have you been?" asks one. The other snorts, "#!&?! Get off my case!" But look, coming around the corner; it's a bird, it's a plane, it's BOB WILLIAMS! He scolds the kids for taking the Lord's name in vain. For the first time since *Murphy*, Chick translates one of the swearing blurbs for readers. It turns out that one of the punks said "Jesus Christ," only he wasn't praying or evangelizing.

Bob asks the kids if they even know who Jesus Christ is. The kid with the nose ring says that Jesus is "The Christmas kid in the manger," while the longhaired punk protests "I don't know **nuthin'** about **that** little dude." (Really Jack, your use of slang to connect with the kids has been rather smothering lately. Moderation, that's all I'm saying.) Anyway, the skaters "got nuthin' to do" so they're more than happy to let Bob give a sermon about who Jesus is and why they shouldn't say naughty words. "What I am about to tell you will **blow** you away," he warns. In real life, most kids would respond to that warning with a wisecrack that incorporates the word "blow" in a somewhat less scriptural context, but hey, we're in *Chickland*.

Bob starts the skaters out with Intro to God 101: God is real. He created the universe in 6 days. ("Wow, he's something else!" says Long Hair.) He made heaven and hell, and He's going to decide where you're going to go when you die. ("Hey, that's scary stuff!" whimpers Nose Ring. "Who is he?") Bob brings it home: ***"His name is the Lord Jesus Christ!"*** Now the skaters are sufficiently frightened.

Bob tells the skaters about the Great Flood and how God drowned everyone except Noah because they were wicked. Then Bob explains how people were just as rotten even after the Flood. "He (God) saw many of them turning into perverts. Jesus made Adam and Eve—not Adam and Steve." Bob adds, "There were some cities where these sickos were doing every evil thing they could think of." Long Hair asks, "Then being gay is a no-no?" (No-no? What grade are these skaters in, anyway?) Bob replies, "Absolutely, stay away from it. It smells of devils and death—and **God hates it!**"

Whoa. "Sickos?" "Adam and Steve?" "Smells of devils and death?" Nobody could ever accuse Jack Chick of hiding his true feelings. When it comes to the gay issue, it appears that Chick is getting crankier in his old age. Either that or he's started jogging with Fred Phelps in the morning.

So now that Bob's helped the skaters take their first steps toward faith-sanctioned homophobia, he takes the skaters through each of the Ten Commandments. Then he moves into the story of Jesus, pausing to explain some things about Mary. It turns out that Long Hair doesn't know what a virgin is. Now when I was a kid, my mom taught me that if a strange man with a mustache walks up to you in the park and asks if "you know what a virgin is?" your wisest course of action is to scream and run like hell. Then again, this is the world of Chick. Bob defines a virgin as "a young lady who has never made love to **anyone,**" which makes me wonder what the biblically accepted term is for a young **man** who's never made love to anyone.

Anyway, we all know the rest of the story: Jesus was born, grew up and got crucified, then rose from the dead so that people like Long Hair and Nose Ring could weasel their way into heaven. We don't actually get to see the kids say the Sinner's prayer, but the last panel shows the two skaters basking in Just-Been-Saved afterglow. Nose Ring says he feels clean and he **never** wants to cuss or tell lies again. Long Hair has loftier goals; he says he wants to be like Jesus (minus the crucifixion, presumably). Bob should be proud. I wouldn't be surprised if these kids show up in a future tract, minus the piercing, long hair, and evil t-shirts.

Favorite Panel Award goes to page 10A. It's a picture of costumed wicked people who "swore at God and **hated** Him. Apparently, pre-Flood earth looked a lot like the back stage of the World Wide Wrestling Federation. This tract lacks classic elements like invisible demons and someone laughing "Haw-haw-haw!" However, it sports increased vitriol with the "Gayness is Bad" segment, and that's always worth the price of admission. Grade: **B** for Bad Boys. **Still in print.**

©1991 Jack T. Chick.

***GOING HOME* Review:** (Art by Carter ©1991.) Talk about a downer, this one has it all: a dying patient, a dying doctor, a dying nation! It takes Chick just three panels to set the depressing tone. An African man limps to hospital to beg admittance, but there is no room. He starts to walk away. Then another patient croaks, and the nurse calls out, "Hey, come back! We found a bed for you!" (And it's still warm, too!) So here's the scoop: Most of the Africans are dying from AIDS (1 in 3). According to the doctor, "The US could be like this in just a few years." The big wigs at Atlanta disease control secretly admit to one another, "It's a death zone! No hope left!" One of them suggests telling the media. "No you idiot! That could trigger a world wide panic!" (So why is Chick spilling the beans? He must want to start a *world wide panic!*) While everyone loses his cool in Atlanta, back in Africa, the good Christian doctor happens to mention to his patient that he also has AIDS—because of a lab accident (yeah, sure bud, whatever you say). The doctor tells the dying VD victim—whose name happens to be "Peter" (seriously!) that Doc plans to go home and live with his loving father the moment he dies. Before Peter can ask what in the world he's talking about, Doc has to run and perform surgery. Maybe when he gets back if Peter is still alive he can hear the rest of the story. The entire tract reads like this. It's surreal! There's some wonderful dialog too. When Doc answers the phone, his boss asks how he's doing. Doc responds, "I'm rich in Christ." His boss snaps back, "Stop preaching! @!!**" At least his patients like him. Peter tells the nurse that his doctor is "almost nice enough to be an African." What's that supposed to mean? That he'll take foreign aid instead of giving it? (Sorry, I forgot. We're supposed to feel guilty for being white.) Speaking of guilt, the nurse dispenses it almost as much as she does medicine. After Doc pressures Peter to get saved, Peter politely postpones the decision, saying, "Let me think about it, doctor. It sounds too good to be true." The nurse swoops down and lays into him, "Peter, what's wrong with your head? You could die tonight! Haven't you suffered enough? Why choose to die in your sins...and suffer forever in the lake of fire?" Now that's what I call a real assistant. Not only does she take the temperatures and bedpans, she clinches the deal for Doc's evangelizing efforts. Will our patient make the right decision in time? Or will the lava lake level rise another few gallons? Get this tract and find out for yourself! Grade: **A-** for AIDS Awareness. **Recently retired: $2.**

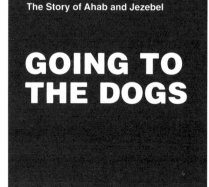

The Story of Ahab and Jezebel

GOING TO THE DOGS

©1992 Jack T. Chick.

GOING TO THE DOGS Review: (Art by Carter & third artist. ©1992.) God comes across as pretty brutal here, full of anger and wrath. The opening narration sets the stage nicely. "There was a rotten king, who married a rotten queen. They had a rotten little brat named Ahab, who became king of Israel. Ahab married a foreign princess named Jezebel, who had a little problem...*she was into devil worship!*" A dramatic beheading is rendered for our viewing pleasure. Then a smirking priest with a demonic statue behind him leers at us on the next page. "Being a witch, Jezebel had the prophets of God destroyed. She imported 450 prophets of Satan to set up Baal worship...God hates idols (graven images) because demons operate behind them, deceiving the worshipper. So God declared war on Baal." The story of *Fire Starter* is quickly recapped, telling how Elijah challenged the prophets of Baal and won, having them summarily executed. Then Jezebel finds out about it and demands revenge. Elijah conveniently disappears for a while.

Years pass and Ahab lusts after his neighbor's vineyard. He asks Naboth to give it to him, but the old man gently refuses. Ahab cries about it to Jezebel, who promised to take care of the problem. She writes letters to Israel's leaders to knock off Naboth. They arrange for a surprise party. Instead of a naked woman popping out of a cake, two men stand up and declare, "Naboth cursed God and the king! He is worthy of death!" The onlookers are in a party mood and ready to rock, so they stone Naboth to death as a blasphemer. The dogs lick up his innocent blood. (Yummy.) God sees this and decides a little payback is in order. He sends Elijah to deliver a curse. Elijah finds the king in his newly acquired vineyard and says, "Thus saith the Lord, In the place where dogs licked the blood of Naboth, shall dogs lick *thy* blood. And the dogs shall eat Jezebel by the wall of Jezreel." Ahab gulps in fear...but then seems to forget about it as time passes. He decides he wants to take land belonging to Syria (some things in Israel never change). He asks his prophets if the invasion will succeed. The yes men say "yes," but Micaiah says, "If you come back alive, I'm no prophet!" Ahab turns to the reader to give a hilarious deadpan expression and says, "I just *knew* he'd say that." Ahab throws Micaiah in prison and goes to battle anyway, "*which was dumb, dumb, dumb!*"

Sure enough, Ahab catches an arrow in his back and croaks. They just happen to unload the blood soaked corpse where Naboth was murdered. The dogs return for a second course. Jezebel gets twenty more years of royal splendor before she has to face the music. Her servants tolerate her that long before throwing her out of a palace window to her death. Chick warns, "Then the dogs ate her body. **GOD DOESN'T PLAY GAMES.** Ahab and Jezebel both went to hell. As God watched Ahab and Jezebel...*God's watching us too!*"

If that's not scary enough, consider this: They look like the **same three dogs** licking up leftovers as the earlier canine clean-up crew from twenty years before. Could they be vampire dogs that stay young from all the blood? (Sorry, no Fang sightings.)

Readers are warned that, "Every person's entire life is recorded for the Day of Judgment." On page 20, we spy on angels as they spy on us from the clouds. One asks, "Did you get that?" The other replies, "Of course!"

So in essence, Big Father Is Watching! A random sinner is shown standing before God and weeping, "Why didn't someone warn me?!" Chick's cold footnote states, "ATTENTION READER: You've just been warned!"

Fortunately, the last panel offers hope. Recite the Sinner's prayer and you'll be saved. (You might also play it safe and replace Fido with a feline.) Plenty of "I told you so" moments and "he who laughs last, laughs best" endings.

Favorite Panel Award: There's lot to choose from, but it's hard to top page 12. We get to see Naboth getting stoned in one image, and the snarling dogs chowing down on the crime scene in the next shot. (And you thought the Bible was boring?) Grade: **A+** for Aggressive Animals! **Value: $3.50.**

©1996 Jack T. Chick.

GOMEZ IS COMING Review: (Art by Chick ©1996.) This is sort of a Hispanic version of *The Bull.* Only this time, the saved con gets *out* of prison and converts fellow gang membèrs. It contains all types of Hispanic stereotypes, creating a future demand for this tract similar to the Negro postcards of the Jim Crow area. The offensive stereotypes are not intentional. Most are *unintentionally* funny. Like when a victim is told by his Hispanic tormentor, "Tonight, we'll serve you a taco supreme ... Because tomorrow, you'll *never* have to worry about eating again!" Talk about a silly sounding threat ... It would be like a Mafia guy telling his victim, "Tonight, we're a-gonna serva you-ah BIG plate of Spaghetti. With a LOTS-sah red tomato sauce, to hide all the-ah BLOOD-dah stains!"

Check out this plot and decide yourself if the Anti-Taco Supreme League has a case: A predominately Hispanic gang sets out to execute a drive-by shooting. The kid says, "Which one (do I shoot)?" The driver says, "It doesn't matter!" The gun says, "Pop! Pop! Pop! Pop!" The crowd scatters and someone screams they are hit. The proud shooter brags that he shot three innocents, only to discover one of the dead is Luis Gomez! You know, Luis—the BROTHER of Carlos "THE BUTCHER" Gomez!?! And he gets out THURSDAY! (Sorry, no T.G.I.F. this week.)

The shooter's name is Valdez, a smart-ass kid with a backward baseball cap and a perpetual smirk on his face. That is, until Butcher's gang kidnaps him and places duct tape over his mouth. They can't wait to see what their boss will do to Valdez. They tease him, "Guess how Gomez got his named 'The Butcher.' Because he LOVES to slowly torture his victims until they die!" Sure enough, Gomez orders his gang-bangers to leave him alone with little Valdez. Gomez warns the hog-tied Valdez, "You can't DREAM what I'm about to do!" Does he prison rape the boy? (Naw, that's the *Trust Me* tract!) But we're all left wondering during the unbearable pause it takes to flip the page. His partners get impatient also and throw open the door to find the boy on all fours with Gomez's hand on his waist. The boy prays, "Thank you, Lord Jesus, for coming into my heart." Hey, you'd be thankful too, if a gang member who's brother you murdered just happens to get saved before kidnapping you. Talk about luck! The part that really gets surreal is the rest of the gang's reaction: When Gomez tells about Jesus and asks who else wants to be saved, they all raise their tattooed hands. (What's the underworld coming too?) This is one scene where a loud "Haw-haw-haw!" would seem like more realistic dialog.

Speaking of tattoos, check out some of the stereotypical Mexican styles: Gomez has tear drops etched next to his eye and a spider on his neck. One of his henchmen has a web tattooed next to his eye. My favorite is the guy with number "13" next to his eye. What's with all the eyes? *Eye-eye-eye!* (Maybe Chick's a fan of the *Frito Bandito.*) Number 13 goon also has perforation marks tattooed along his neck. It looks like the words "cut here" are tattooed beneath it in Spanish. (Haw-haw!) Another funny detail is the placement of Catholic "idols" in the Valdez home (page 8). It's like Chick is suggesting that unleashing such demons in your home is bound to turn your kids into criminals as well. Expect the new and improved fundamentalist Valdez to evict Mary the moment he gets home!

Check out how Gomez looks related to recurring character Bob Williams from the 25 tract Bible series. He's got the same albino eyes and straight black hair. The way he's able to convert groups of people at a moment's notice could also be a family trait. Perhaps they were separated at birth? Grade: **B** for "Badges? We don't need no stinking badges!" Recently retired: **$1.**

GOOD OL' BOYS Guest review by "WiseAss!": (Art by Chick ©2003.) Tract #22 in the series of 25 featuring Bob Williams. The story starts with a "Shining Path" terrorist story, presented as an actual occurrence, but open to question as far as I'm concerned. After all, *The First Jaws* tract repeats what is universally considered an URBAN LEGEND, the survival of a sailor from inside a giant shark! Frankly, I doubt very much that Chick concerns himself with accuracy in the newspaper sense. It's whatever will save souls! I'm actually surprised that he never referred to the "Missing Days" nonsense, wherein a NASA computer "goes crazy" while "going back in time" because of Joshua stopping the sun and another Old Testament miracle (II Kings verse 20).

We see the ultimate *O'Henry* finish in this segment when revolutionaries not only decide to spare the intrepid pastoral couple (surprise!) but then gun down those who agreed with the terrorists and renounced Jesus. (Bet you didn't see that one coming.) "Disgusting cowards," indeed! And if you are wondering how they'll fare with "Ol' Light-bulb-head," just read on!

Bob Williams suddenly appears. It seems the whole first segment was just a narrative flashback, told to get some friends' attention. Young Robbie can't believe the courage of the Christian couple. (It turns out he was among the unsaved, although that was unclear early on.) But the big fish is actually John, who said he was already saved. (Emphasis on "WAS"!)

Astute Chicklets will spot in panel 8B that John scowls too much to be a faithful Christian. His Masonic ring gives away that he has already DENIED CHRIST, as much as he, in contrast to Robbie, can't imagine ever personally caving in under *any* circumstances.

I must say, I can't fault the JTC logic in this instance: if it is indeed true that all Mason members ceremonially agree (if only by silence) to living in darkness before initiation, then it certainly seems fatal to the witness and credibility of Born Agains (and also their salvation). Bob claims that praying in Jesus' name is forbidden in lodges. I'm too old to take such statements without proof, but again, the logical consequences based on the premises seem to hold up.

The conclusions of this tract are far from predictable. I expected Mason Man to remain in his sins, though I suspected Robbie would receive The Word. After all, there have been only four cases of obstinacy in the series so far. But, Lo and Behold, we have not one but *two* repenters.

Which brings me to another general observation: Ever since *The Four Brothers,* Chick has displayed a stance against *Once Saved, Always Saved* (OSAS). Now it's Once Saved, KEEP IN LINE, LOSER! Trust me, this was not his original conviction. Even in *Sabotage?* the backsliding hippie (fooled by the non-KJV Bible) was not warned about re-damnation, and only seemed to fear embarrassment if JC should return that very moment — and neither Tim nor Jim objected.

I'm not that impressed with this particular entry in the series. It has a dramatic Urban Legend-like intro, but it's too unbelievable. It doesn't even attempt to support it with the otherwise plentiful footnotes. Favorite Panel Award goes to page 7, where the entire congregation bites bullets blasted from communist machine guns. For that reason alone, I'll give it a C+ for Christian Carnage. **Still in print.**

©2003 Jack T. Chick.

Then we go to **A.I.D.S.** – wiping out entire regions in Africa. There is no cure in sight. It could be the last great plague, wiping out civilization. Nations are going bankrupt… and race riots are ending in global wars…

and you still think there is an escape?

Absolutely! I know it!

Watch me block *every* exit, mister!

©1991 Jack T. Chick.

THE GREAT ESCAPE (a.k.a. *Escape*) Review: (Art by Chick ©1991.) The original version is easy to spot with the large ecology symbol floating above the graphic, but both versions scream 1970s. Remember those "hip" years when saving the planet was all the rage? This story recreates the fashions and ideals of the wild and crazy time! A teenager with long sideburns jumps in front of a Christian's car and tries to kill himself. Unfortunately, the driver is too quick with the brakes. The disappointed dude yells, "@!!!***! He missed me!" The good Christian invites the wanna-be road kill for coffee. It turns out that Sideburns-boy is suicidal because the environment is going to the dogs. "It's too late, mister! It's all over—there's no way out! No escape!" Sideburns proceeds to recite a litany of end-of-the-world predictions. Too many people, not enough land, 40,000 babies starving to death daily, the sea is dying, the fish and phytoplankton are dying, air pollution is causing cancer and killing plants…even global warming is mentioned (though not by that name). Christian-man agrees, sorta: "Without the Lord, it looks impossible." Sideburns barks back, "C'mon, ***don't*** give me any of that religious stuff!" But Christian points his finger back at Sideburns and orders, "I heard YOU out—now you hear ***me*** out! (Or what? You're gonna run him over?) Christian explains that all this was predicted in Revelation and starts to preach about the Great Tribulation, the Beast, WWIII, attacks on Israel, and the overall end of the world. Sideburns is excited to finally find a kindred gloom-or-doomer. "OK, OK…I'm convinced!" he exclaims, "Now, you mentioned an escape. If there is a way out, I want to be in on it!" The Christian smiles and says, "Easy kid! Next time jump in front of a semi. They can't stop as fast!" No wait, that's the lawyer's answer. What the Christian does is explain about the rapture. "Jesus Christ is about to remove his true followers from off the earth. That's our only escape!" Sideburns looks kinda stupid and says, "How? Some kind of spaceship?" (Not too bright… But what do you expect from someone who can't even calculate when to jump in front of a car?) Christian recites scripture and tells how all the dead shall rise and float up to meet Jesus in the sky. Sideburns suddenly believes it all—not just the prophecy, but in God and heaven and all the rest. He wants a piece of the action and quickly agrees to recite the Sinner's prayer. **"Man! I feel clean!** Even with everything caving in, I have ***peace!"*** That's right, **peace.** And that's what the '70s was all about, man! It's one groovy tract!

The original *Escape* featured more dire predictions than *The Great Escape* version, including page 9 which states, "At the present rate of pollution, by 1999 all twenty-two of our water systems will be gone." Plus, page 11b has Sideburns look the reader straight in the eye and declares, "So there's your big black picture. It's all over, man! There's **no exit!** Those who can really see what's coming are blowing their minds with drugs or booze, the rest are turning to the occult or sex!" So ***that's why*** the '70s were so experimental! But you gotta admit, it makes more sense than jumping in front of cars. Grade **B+** for Baby Boomer Bumper Bender. **Still in print.**

Daddy, I'm begging you to trust Jesus.

Never!...

Religion is only for the weak.

…the heart of fools proclaimeth foolishness. Proverbs 12:23

©1999 Jack T. Chick.

THE GREAT ONE Review: (Art by Chick ©1999.) At last! A tract with artwork worse than *A Love Story.* This is probably the worst art of any Chick tract ever. So bad, it deserves a Worst Panel Award for the very first panel! It features a bird's-eye view of a city that looks like my 5 year old nephew drew it. (No offense to my nephew.) Even the clouds are bad. We're talking simple lines with lots of blank white backgrounds. If I were cynical, I would theorize that this tract was drawn during Chick's recovery from a stroke. But the copyright date doesn't support that theory. When Chick dies and is recognized centuries later as a genius, scholars will probably speculate that the super basic style of this tract is actually a brilliant artistic statement. The masterpiece visually depicts the *simplicity of grace* in an abstract manner. While the subject matter deals with a great intellectual who thinks he is too smart to believe in God, his simple-minded daughter is smarter than he because she has faith in Jesus. All the Great One's advanced learning and sophistication distract him from the simple truth that Jesus died for his sins. Maybe the artsy fartsy experts would be correct. But to paraphrase a famous judge's view on pornography, "I can't define what **bad art** is, but I know it when I see it." And this is bad art.

The story, however, is compelling—probably more for adults than kids. Especially pages 11-16. The daughter asks her father if he knows where he will go when he dies. He puffs up and declares he's too educated to believe in God. She gets on her knees and begs him to trust in Jesus. He says that religion is only for the weak. She pleads, "I love you, Daddy. Please don't think you're smarter than God." Chick tracts often have aggressive witnesses pressuring the unsaved to convert out of fear of the lake of fire. Mocking such fanatics is great sport for many. But who could laugh off their own daughter's pleas when her only motive is wanting to be with her parent for all eternity? (The phase soon passes once they reach their teens and can't wait to leave both parents.) Just when you think Chick has changed his trademark *fear formula* into a more politically correct "save yourself for the children" angle, you flip the page and he's back to tossing sinners into the lake of fire. Oddly enough, this is one of the few times the sinner is still wearing his clothes! Imagine a fate worse than suffering hell in long black pants and a thick tweed jacket. That's gotta be *extra* uncomfortable. So despite the bottom of the barrel artwork, this tract earns some redemption. (Which is more than the main character gets.) Grade: **C** for Cooked to the Core. **Still in print.**

THE GREATEST STORY EVER TOLD Review: (Art by Carter ©1987.) This is the abbreviated story of Jesus. It begins with the three wise men observing the star of Bethlehem. They set out to find and worship the newly born King of the Jews. A couple of pages attempt to explain the holy trinity concept, but it's tough going: 3 = 1 logic is confusing enough for most readers to comprehend, and to make it even *more* complicated, Chick uses the old King James medieval English to explain it all. Try this on for size: "In the beginning was the Word, and the Word was with God, and the Word was God. All things were made by him; and with him was not any thing made that was made." Okay, now repeat it five times *real fast* without getting dizzy!

The prophecy of Jesus is recounted, along with Mary's visit by an angel telling her she will give virgin birth. A special panel explains how Joseph had a dream assuring him Mary wasn't fooling around on the side. The birth in Bethlehem is shown, along with Herod's slaughter of the innocents. Several scenes of Jesus publicly preaching are presented. He's shown as a youth and also as a young adult. The bloody crucifixion and Sinner's prayer round it out. The story isn't that original, but much of the artwork is top notch. Grade: **B** for Bethlehem. **Still in print.**

THE GUNSLINGER Review: (Art by Chick ©1997.) The adventures of Terrible Tom, a gunslinger sent to murder The Preacher, but who instead becomes born again. Meanwhile, The Marshall [sic] comes to town and gets the drop on Tom. (Not that Tom would ever hurt anyone again, seeing how he's "seen the light", but The Marshal doesn't take any chances. Into the pokey goes (now Terrific) Tom, and the following morning they hang him high. The Marshall looks on grinning while The Preacher covers his eyes. The audience appreciates the loud CRACKing noise as Tom's neck snaps. The Marshal gloats "At last! Terrible Tom got EXACTLY what he deserved!" But what's this? In heaven, Faceless God welcomes Tom home! Oh yeah, God forgives everyone, even the mass murderers... (How could I forget, it's one of Chick's favorite themes.) The Marshal doesn't get the message though. The Preacher offers to save him, but the lawman says nothing doing. He's too honest and law-abiding to need Jesus. "If I'm not good enough for heaven, then NO ONE is." Poor fellow. He lived before Chick tracts and didn't know how the system works (until it's too late, that is). Three hours later, a rattlesnake strikes The Marshal square in the face! (Now that's GOTTA hurt!) Evil spirits in black Ku Klux Klan outfits pull his ghost down a desert pothole to hell. Within minutes, The Marshal is covered in flames, screaming at the top of his lungs. "I was a GOOD man! I UPHELD the law!" Of course, we all know Chick's response to such claims: "But you NEVER received Christ as your savior." He's totally toast.

Favorite Panel Award goes to the last shot as The Marshal is CONSUMED in flames, yet you can still see his face and recognize him. (How come the burn victim's skin never peels in Hell?) Some folks will probably think sending the killers to heaven and the lawmen to hell is like something out of Catch-22. But John 3:16 (Whosoever believeth in him should not perish but have everlasting life) gives Chick plenty of ammo for this interpretation. The bottom line is this: If you sin all your life and convert the very last minute, you're much better off than those who waste their lives living like angels but don't accept Jesus. A thought-provoking and controversial comic. Grade **A-** for Amnesty. **Still in print.**

©1996 Jack T. Chick.

HAPPY HALLOWEEN Review: (Art by Chick ©1996.) It's tracts like these that make me wonder if fundamentalists really hate Halloween, or if they really love it but condemn it anyway out of a sense of duty. Chick clearly relishes the monster scenes and they're a lot of fun to behold. Like the "Boo!" tract, the first two-thirds of this tale recount a great horror story. This time we follow the haunted house experiences of Timmy and his friends. They get so scared by the carnival type spook house, that they dash out and ... "Timmy! Look out for that car!" (Screech! *Thud!*) Timmy meets Jealous Jesus, and Jesus DOESN'T like sharing the stage with satanic exhibits. Naked Timmy is fed to the fiery flames, while his buddies are saved by a Sunday school teacher back on the Earth's surface. By the end of the tract, the Joy of Jesus so overwhelmed his buddies that they've completely forgotten about Timmy! (Hey, he was yesterday's news.)

There are some wonderful panels of witches, demons, and various spooks in this tract, but I have to give the Favorite Panel Award to page 14. It shows Timmy standing there with his arms crossed and a shit-eating grin while Mrs. Baxter tries one last time to explain why Jesus is the only way to heaven. Of course, Timmy's arrogance is rewarded one day later with fire and brimstone. Mrs. Baxter wins the debate by default and the reader is reminded once again that God always gets the last laugh. A good read. Grade: **B+** for Blistering Boy in hell. **Still in print.**

©1976 Jack T. Chick.

HAPPY HOUR Review: (Art by Chick 1976.) A pretty depressing tale of a father that drinks like a fish and leaves the kids at home to starve. Did I mention that he beat his wife to death while trying to rob the cookie jar for drinking money? Yeah, a real nice guy. The perfect target for converting to Jesus and making a born again Christian. All it takes is for him to go to ONE church service and suddenly it happens. He gives up drinking, (presumably) gets a job, and the family becomes happy again. Such is the power of God. And to think he did it all without the help of a Chick tract. Amazing! Grade: **B+** for Brutal wife Beater. **Still in print.**

©1993 Jack T. Chick.

HE NEVER TOLD US Review: (Art by Chick ©1993.) Only the first seven pages of this tract look like a typical tract. The art isn't quite up to typical standards, either. There's little detail and an over abundance of white backgrounds. It begins with a funeral where the friends of the deceased are shocked to discover the victim was a Christian. "He never said a word to me!" At judgment day, his pals are all missing him while waiting in a place that looks and feels like hell, but isn't *technically* purgatory or hell. (It's Hades, the warm-up act.) They complain to the angel about his absence and are told Charlie is in heaven because he was saved at age 9. They're escorted to the Great White Throne of Judgment and grumble along the way how he never witnessed to them. God tells them all to go jump in the Lake (of Fire). Charlie watches in horror from a balcony above. He wrings his hands about how he never had the guts to warn them. A nearby angel folds his arms and states the obvious: "You could have given them the gospel, Charlie." Another passing spirit chimes in, "Why didn't you give them tracts?...*That's how I got saved!*" (Heaven may be paradise, free from hunger and want—but don't expect to escape guilt trips provided by those more perfect than you.) Just in case you're confused which brand to buy, the heavenly helper spells it out for us. "The most effective tracts I used were the illustrated ones. They're called Chick tracts."

The story cuts to various testimonies of people saved by Chick tracts. Most of the art is robbed from other Chick materials. We see Jerry, Janet, and a traffic cop from *Going Bananas.* We see the kid with the striped shirt from *Somebody Goofed.* We also see the blond chick from the cover of *Who Me?* There's other recycled art as well.

The inspiration for this tract may be quite old. In an open letter issued with *The Trap* (1988), Chick mentions how he and a friend named Clair Powell used to discuss hell during their lunch hour at the aerospace company. (And to think some guys blab about sports. Boring!) Clair made a big impression on Chick by saying how determined Christians would witness if they got so much as a glimpse of how horrible hell really was. Chick stated, "I dread thinking of standing before the Lord and seeing a parade of people pass before me, pointing their finger [sic] at me and saying to the Lord, 'He never told me.' There will be a great number of us feeling very upset because we didn't love our neighbors enough, or our friends or relatives or anyone who crossed our lives, to have the courage to witness as we should." (Thanks to Chick, we don't have to wait until heaven to feel guilty about it!)

Despite these pure motives, this is not one of Chick's better tracts. It's brilliant salesmanship, but the quality isn't up to usual Chick standards: The rough Chick sketches, the recycled Fred Carter art ... Then again, what do you expect from a free promotional tract? Grade: **C** for Creative Marketing. **Still in print.**

©1999 Jack T. Chick.

HERE HE COMES! Review: (Art by Chick ©2003.) This is the last of the 25 tract series featuring Bob Williams, and also the last tract published in time to be included in this book. In an incredible "last act" for Bob Williams, Chick pulled out all the stops for this tale of the Rapture. It begins with Bob, Helen, and Damien driving down the road. Helen leans forward to say, "Damien, there's something *really* important you should know!" Ex-Catholic priest Damien responds, "OK, Helen... what is... *whoa!* (gasp!)" What stuns Damien is the sudden vanishing act of the other passengers as they are raptured up to heaven. The car skids out of control and smashes head-on into a telephone pole (which displays a "lost dog" poster for Fang).

Cut to an interior shot of Helen and Bob sneaking into Damien's bedroom wearing their bathrobes. They claim they heard him cry for help. (Yeah, right, I'll have to remember that line to use on the Nanny.) Damien tells them about his terrible nightmare of the Rapture. Bob assures Damien he won't be left behind, because he accepted Jesus. "Jesus will rapture His church **before** the 7-year Tribulation, but **after** the Rapture, the tribulation saints will be beheaded." In other words, the present day Christians get a free pass on all the unpleasantness, but ones who become Christian *after* the Rapture have to pay for it with their lives. (So by the time you see proof that the Rapture is real, it's too late to convert and avoid the suffering.)

As Damien nurses a cup of coffee, Bob goes over the Rapture highlights. Russia, Germany, and the Arabs attack Israel. (What about France? They seemed pretty chummy with Saddam before the war.) The Muslim's Dome of the Rock is destroyed, the Jews rebuild their temple in Jerusalem, and "The pope and his Jesuit general watch from Rome—drooling, waiting to grab it for themselves."

Pope John Paul II and his Jesuit general, Peter Kolvenbach, are seen signing documents. "A deceitful 7-year peace treaty with Israel is signed. Israel is thrilled. At long last they feel secure." It's only a feeling though, because "The Great Whore of Rev. 17-18 by this time controls every nation on earth. The Jesuit general and the pope (the Beast and the False Prophet) now openly rule the world." So Chick is stating the Pope is only a False Prophet. The real "Beast" is his Jesuit general, a.k.a. "The Black Pope." (He's been promoted!) But the pope appears to be the top dog in public because "the world faiths pull together, as one massive world religion is created during the Tribulation." And guess who's given the position as the spiritual leader of the world? That's right, Pope John Paul II. (And you thought he wouldn't last much longer. According to this, he has at least another 7 years left in him.)

Satan's spirit is shown taking over Kolvenbach. "Then Satan enters the Beast giving him tremendous power." This means Kolvenbach isn't the Beast yet, but will one day become him. (Maybe his family and friends will take consolation in knowing he's still human for now.)

Naming the Jesuit general as the Beast is a significant change for Chick, who previously quoted Alberto as saying that it was the final **pope** who becomes possessed by Satan in the end times (*The Four Horsemen,* page 22). In that comic book, Chick also quoted famous Protestant patriarchs as stating the pope was the Antichrist (page 17), who is also the Beast (page 32). Ironically, he even refers readers to *The Four Horsemen* comic for more information on the Beast, even though it contradicts the identity of the Beast in the tract.

Bob continues his narration of the end times... The Beast defiles the Jewish Temple, has the ark destroyed, and a statue made of himself. He proclaims himself as God. His statue comes alive and speaks, so that "many as would not worship the image... should be killed." The giant image of Kolvenbach is rather amusing. He has one hand on his hip and the other making the goat-head symbol that heavy metal fans flash at concerts, when they extend their pinky and index fingers. (See the cover of *Angels?*)

The pope orders everyone to receive the mark of the Beast. Those that do not have their heads lopped off by guillotines and stuck on spikes for easy display. The executioner wears a priest collar and says, "C'mon! Lets get this over with. I don't want to miss my lunch!"

Angels are shown in heaven lining up to literally dump God's wrath on earth below. The wrath is stored in seven heavenly test tubes.

Meanwhile, it's hell on Earth. "One-third of the earth goes by fire. The sun scorches the multitudes. Water becomes undrinkable. Famine, death, and wild beasts are everywhere." A panel shows lions, rats, and flying scorpions attacking the hopeless sinners. Ten leaders rebel against the Beast and destroy the Vatican by fire. ("There is great rejoicing in heaven.") The Beast escapes to Jerusalem and commands his armies to destroy Israel. The Chinese march down the dried up river Euphrates. Jesus leads his army from heaven and defeats the bad guys at Armageddon. Pope John Paul II and Kolvenbach are shown being tossed into the lake of fire. The devil is judged along with the rest of the sinners.

Bob turns and warns readers that if they reject Jesus, they will probably take the mark of the Beast and wind up in the lake of fire. **"THIS IS NO JOKE!"** Bob admonishes. "This may be your last chance."

There are so many incredible images in this tract, selecting the best one is tough. There are cameos by the pope and his Jesuit general, plus wonderful battlefield images, and so many others to chose from. But my choice for the Favorite Panel Award goes to the guillotine scene with all the severed heads neatly lined up in rows. The priest moonlighting as the executioner is icing on the cake. Grade: A for Antichrist. **Still in print.**

Granted, his clothes are all rags, but they're the same rags he wore 1,000 years in Hades. (They must be fire retardant... and pretty darn stinky.) Lest anyone accuse Chick of not trying to scare the audience, his next to last panel features death waving to us from a dark graveyard and saying, "I'll be seeing YOU!" (Subtle, huh?) Other Trivia: There is also a Chinese version of this tract with everyone's eyes (except the angel) being given Asian slants. Grade **B+** for "Back to work, Boys!" **Still in print.**

©1975 Jack T. Chick.

©1979 Jack T. Chick.

HI THERE **Review:** (Art by Carter ©1975.) An unflattering rendition of redneck construction workers, one of which meets his maker after making many anti-Christian remarks. The poor soul's name is Charlie Conners. We see him cook his goose during a lunch break, when he explains to all the other rednecks that, "We came from Monkeys. In fact, we started out in the ocean as a blob of goo! So actually the ocean is our mother. And when you're dead, you're DEAD, and that's it, baby!" The other losers sit around and pick their teeth as Charlie pontificates, nodding in agreement. When lunch is over they return to work. Charlie is walking down a catwalk when death appears and announces "Hi there!" Charlie responds by cussing "@!!**!" and falling backward. He drops several stories and lands on a spike. His final words are a fitting "gurgle...ugh... help me...I ...uh... I'm starting to bur... ugghhh!" Kinda sums it up nicely, doesn't it? One of his comrades waxes eloquent with, "All his troubles are over, now." Chick responds with "Oooh? Are they really? Lets see..." And sure enough, Charlie is down in burning hot Hades. Interestingly enough, he's not guarded by a demon, but an angel. One wonders what this angel did to get assigned to this kind of duty. He appears stuck with Charlie for over a thousand years, until after Jesus returns to Earth and reigns for ten centuries. (I think I'd rather have toilet detail.) Finally Charlie makes it before Jesus to face judgment. Surprise, surprise, it's Lake of Fire time! (I'm guessing that's a few degrees hotter than the caverns of fire where he spent the first 1,000 years, but I'm not sure.) Unlike other Faceless God judgment scenes, the accused remains dressed in this story.

HIT PARADE **Review:** (Art by Carter ©1979.) The theme of this tract is "Anger God and you'll get what's coming to yah." It chronicles how Jehovah always smites the enemies of Israel, but sold the Jews into slavery the moment they misbehaved. The gays get special attention in this tract also. Sodom is compared to modern day America. One panel ends with the ominous line "This time the US will feel the sting of God's Awful Judgment." The reader turns the page and WHAMO! It's the mushroom-shaped cloud of Thermonuclear Attack! (Scare tactics, anyone?) This tract is depressing but an accurate reminder of how bad things seemed during Jimmy Carter's presidency. (It was printed in 1979.) As page 15 puts it, "Patriotism is a joke—the dollar is dying—Russia has overtaken us militarily—our population is defenseless and the smell of war is in the air." It's hard to imagine now, but like many "boomers", I remember having nightmares of nuclear war during those very years. Nothing seemed secure. Inflation was amok, unemployment was high, gas prices soared, and Iran had us by the short and curlies. This tract was probably VERY SCARY during its day. Plenty of its gripes are still current, but enough are outdated that it will (probably) never be reprinted. The fine line art is superb, but the graphics are somewhat crowded out by text. Grade **B+** for Big Boom Boom. Permanently retired**: $40.**

©1984 Jack T. Chick.

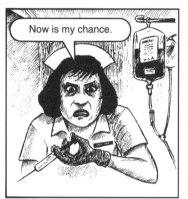

©1993 Jack T. Chick.

THE HIT Review: (Art by Chick ©1993.) Chick often takes popular movie titles and names tracts after them (see *Terminator* and *Superman*). This tract may not be named "The Godfather," but it is certainly a take off on it. It starts out with a mobster named Tony bombing a home and killing the husband and two kids of Rose. Fast-forward 15 years and Tony is in the hospital for gunshot wounds. Guess who his nurse is? Rose tells Tony she's waited 15 years to kill him and hovers over him with a menacing syringe. Unfortunately, she can't because Jesus told her she should forgive him. A sermon ensues, reducing Tony to tears. His wounds recover miraculously. The Catholic priest comes to visit but is turned away. Tony is saved and returns to his old gang. He meets all the other mob dons and proclaims (page 19) "I know you godfathers are reasonable men...so I'm going to make you an offer you can't refuse. Either accept Jesus Christ and go to heaven or die in your sins and burn in hell." Tony looks just like Brando at this point, complete with the godfather hand gestures. Your Godfather collection is not complete without this tract. You better collect it or someone might stick a horse head in your bed. Grade **B** for Brando. Retired: **$6.**

HOLOCAUST Review: (Art by Carter ©1984.) This tract probably upsets the Vatican more than *Why Is Mary Crying?* and *The Death Cookie* combined! It implicates the Vatican with the Nazis, claiming the Holocaust was just another Catholic Inquisition—a Papal public relations nightmare! Of course, Chick knew *exactly* what he was doing. He was providing payback for the Alberto comics ban the Catholics had engineered in Canada in 1983. (This tract is released in 1984.) If they were going around labeling Chick a bigot and hate-lit publisher, why not open the Vatican's closet and reveal a few of *their* skeletons? Say, *six million* of them!?!

The tract starts out with an elderly Holocaust survivor yelling at the American Nazi Party as they march in a parade behind the Daughters of the American Revolution float. The crowd also yells at the Nazis, but their attention shifts to the Jew when he starts screaming, "You filthy Christian swine!" Fortunately, a helpful Christian named Bob escorts the Jewish gentleman away before a pogrom erupts.

Back home, Grandpa complains over a cup of coffee while his daughter and Bob listen to the gripes. "Those !@#%** Nazis brought it all back. Somebody has to speak up."

Rather than let the old man vent, Bob seizes the opportunity to lay out his Catholic conspiracy theories. "You're right, Mr. Weiss. There ARE things that must be told...the truth about World War II has been covered up long enough. YOU were in an inquisition." Grandpa nearly regurgitates his Java after that, but Bob piles on more: "And in all probability, you will experience another inquisition being set up right here in the U.S." (Someone call 9-1-1! Grandpa's going to need resuscitation!)

Bob explains that the Jesuits masterminded the Holocaust, but instead of the Dominican monks wearing robes, the Vatican used Nazis to carry it out. Bob asserts, "It's a documented fact that the Gestapo was run by the Jesuits, and that Hitler was a faithful Roman Catholic simply following the laws set forth in the Council of Trent." (A footnote discloses that Alberto's *The Godfathers* comic is the source of the documentation.) Page 9 gives five statements from the Council of Trent defining heretics. These definitions are still in effect and apply to almost every Protestant. Perhaps the most embarrassing image in the tract is actually a photograph on page 12, which shows future Pope Pius XII signing a concordat with the Nazis in 1933. Bob says, "Germany signed a concordat in 1933 and according to Catholic law, the Council of Trent gave Hitler the authority to put the inquisition into effect and slaughter Jews and non-Catholics alike to purge the land of heretics."

Now done with the coffee, the three retire to the living room. Heaven forbid they change the subject! Who needs television when they have Bob on a roll? He continues, "Today the Vatican is a tremendous political and religious power. It has one billion citizens, and it controls the wealth of the world. It's goals are to make America Catholic, to set up diplomatic relations, destroy our Constitution, negotiate a concordat and work through our legal system which would make it possible to carry out their plans to 'purge' the U.S. of all Protestant and non-Catholic opposition."

The footnotes are as conspiratorial as the regular text. Bob says, "The Department of Immigration* has been bringing Catholics into the United States by the millions." The footnote adds, "*Assisted by Notre

Dame University." Another good example is page 17. Bob states, "Catholic controlled media deliberately downplayed the appointment of an American ambassador to the Vatican, to prevent strong Protestant opposition. The last wall of defense to keep the U.S. from signing a concordat was removed." The footnote says, "Interesting note: Billy Graham aided Reagan on Vatican recognition. Chicago AP 1/22/84." Turn up the ominous music!

Imagine the fireworks that exploded at the Holy See when *this* little dandy started making the rounds. Talk about irreconcilable differences! The Vatican was already fighting pressure from Jewish activists alleging collaboration with the Nazis during WWII. This tract undoubtedly turned up the heat. It's still an issue and won't be going away anytime soon (especially with hungry lawyers eager to tap the Vatican's deep pockets.) This tract is no longer in print, but if you want to make sure Chick and the Vatican never sign a concordat, custom ordering and distributing this title in Yiddish should certainly do the trick.

Favorite Panel Award goes to page 11. A gaunt Hitler stands before a skull & crossbones and is quoted as saying, "As for the Jews, I am just carrying on with the same policy which the Catholic Church has adopted for 1500 years when it regarded the Jews as dangerous and pushed them into ghettos, etc., because it knew what the Jews were like." It then points out that as early as 1212, Papal edict required Jews to wear a distinctive badge and not hold public office. (When it comes to antagonizing the opposition, this is bringing out the heavy artillery!) Grade: **A** for Anti-Semitism. **Value: $35.**

©1972 Jack T. Chick.

HOLY JOE Guest review by Terrible Tommy Murray: (Art by Chick ©1964, 1972, and 2002.) This tract is a true classic in the Jack T. Chick universe of Fear and Fantasy. It is filled to the brim with historical inaccuracies and fantasies that have absolutely NO basis in reality. Classic Example: Even though this tract came out during the Vietnam War, it is screamingly obvious that the "enemy" soldiers are actually Korean. (I'm a Veteran and I checked with experts on this very thing.) Wrong war, Jack! Once again, JTC is WAY off track, both in a historical context and in mere reality.

The Christian in the story is a buck private who is consistently persecuted for his beliefs. Just like the Prophet Daniel, he gets picked on by his sergeant and the company for praying openly and is saddled with the nickname "Holy Joe," hence the title. The sergeant, while laughingly lighting up a cigar (all sinners in JTC's comics smoke) throws muddy boots at Holy Joe while he prays with the requisite chorus of "HAW HAW" from the other soldiers in the background. The next day, the sergeant wakes to find that Holy Joe has shined the boots for him. What a humble little angel Holy Joe is!

When the sergeant maliciously sticks Holy Joe with K.P. in a futile attempt to break his "holy" spirit (as opposed to S.O.P. like the other poor slobs), Holy Joe performs the degrading task of washing out trash cans while singing (with a big smile on his face) "There's Room at the Cross for You" with sweat pouring down his face. The sergeant asks the cook, "How is Holy Joe taking it?" The cook replies with a cuss word and says that the more work he piles on Holy Joe, the harder he works. Later, Holy Joe is witnessing to a fellow soldier, who expresses his doubts of the Scriptures with the prerequisite "@!!**!" cuss words. Holy Joe, naturally, quotes the verse, "The preaching of the Cross is, to them that perish, foolishness." What a brave little soldier of Christ Holy Joe is!

Finally, poor Holy Joe gets sent out, like Uriah with King David, to almost certain death on a one-man patrol (something that is absolutely against every procedure in the Army Ops manual). The company corporal begs the sergeant not to send Holy Joe out to die, but to no avail. Holy Joe waves goodbye and calls back: "I'm still praying for you, Sarge."

Later, the sergeant and the corporal find Holy Joe's body which has a very graphic hole in his little Christian head. The look of beatific peace on Holy Joe's face so impresses the sergeant that he falls to his knees and prays the JTC Prayer of Repentance right then and there. The unsaved corporal, however, gruffly responds, "I could care less!" Like most soldiers, he's a little more concerned about the enemy he sees sneaking through the trees than he is with religious or philosophical questions. The Yellow Menace mows down the Americans and the blonde white guy angel arrives to retrieve the two souls. Once before the Big White Dude with No Face, the corporal gets his comeuppance (even though he stuck up for Holy Joe). Pointing away to the Damned Left, God thunders "Depart from Me, ye worker of iniquity, I never knew you!" (Remember, Jesus fried a number of towns for failing to be sufficiently impressed with his powers and once zapped an innocent fig tree just because it had no figs, being out of season. Such childishly inappropriate fury is one of the recurring themes with the God of Jack T. Chick.) The corporal is dragged off to the fiery basement, while the sergeant, who was a lifer JERK and basically arranged Holy Joe's death, is welcomed to heaven with open arms! All because he said the magic words at the last minute. (What ever happened to the notion of judging someone by their actions instead of their words?)

As a non-Christian who served in the military with honor and medals, I can tell you that *Holy Joe* is pure unmitigated meadow muffins. I have NEVER seen any religious person persecuted or denied anything. I know many soldiers who got on their knees every night. The only ones punished for it were the ones who bent over for reasons OTHER than praying! (Now *that's* persecution.) My father, while serving in the Air Force during the Korean War, conducted his own Bible study after he was "born again." He had a few debates with people of other beliefs, but he never had muddy boots tossed at his head.

If you want an accurate portrayal of what the born again guy in the barracks was really like, check out the character of Frank Burns, from *M*A*S*H*. The "preacher" of the bunch was very frequently a snitty butthead who delighted in tattling on other people and was universally despised. Give it an "**A**" for "A-hole above and beyond the call of duty." **Still in print.**

There is also a super rare medium oversized version of this tract (5 5/8 x 4 1/4") which features the same story except the unit is sent to combat via a boat instead of plane. **Value $200.**

©1978 Jack T. Chick.

HOW TO GET RICH AND KEEP IT Review: (Art by Carter ©1978.) This title consists of several stories in one tract. The first tale is 8 pages long and funny but frustrating. It shows an ailing Uncle John on his deathbed, accusing his groveling nephew of wanting him dead in order to collect his fortune. Herbert insists, "Oh, nooo, Uncle John. I've *enjoyed* waiting on you 18 hours a day for 20 years—just to take care of you!" Uncle John misses the sarcasm and calls for his lawyer to write out his will. Herbert literally drools as his uncle tells the lawyer he wants to leave EVERYTHING to him. The old man is about to sign the will when...gasp!...Gurgle! He expires! Herbert is hysterical but the lawyer doesn't seem to mind much. (He collects a fee either way.) He reassures Herb, "Since there was no will, your uncle John's fortune will go to the state. Of course, there will be some *minor* court and attorney fees... I'm sure you'll get something." Sure enough, a year later, Herbert receives something: A bill for back taxes of $4,980.21. Bummer.

Story number two involves a rich fellow who builds a safe to hold his money since he doesn't trust banks. Late one night, he decides to go down to the vault and count his cash again (beats counting sheep). The money is gone! He's been robbed! The cop tells him the safe installer was, "Dirty Joe. He's wanted in ten states." Maybe he can stop payment on the installation bill.

A few other panels tell similar tales of woe. A lady's $9,000 mink coat is eaten by moths. Chick observes, "Great Civilizations have fallen to the simple little moth." (That was probably the nation of Minktania.) Another panel features a tombstone and the statement, "With all his billions—Howard Hughes lies in a grave without a single thin dime in his hand." (The silver dollars probably fell between his fingers as the bones decomposed.) Another panel with pyramids says, "Even the mighty Pharaohs buried with their treasures have been picked clean by grave robbers." (Unless they were protected by mummies.)

All kidding aside, the various vignettes get you thinking about the pointlessness of life. Chick then points out, "The Bible tells us we can put our treasures up in heaven, where thieves can't break in or moths or rust can't destroy it." A cartoon character complains he was tricked by the title of the tract. Chick responds, "Not really—but I hope you're greedy enough to go on with the message!"

That message is, of course, how belief in Christ will provide anyone eternal life and a mansion in heaven. "Starting now, all the good works you do for Christ, like helping others, will start putting riches in your new bank account in heaven." You don't want to go to heaven and not be able to keep up with the Joneses do you? Here's some other unusual statements from the last page. "Jesus, who, incidentally, created this planet..." Oh, *THAT* Jesus!

"In heaven, you'll have eternal life, you will reign with Christ, Judge angels," Stop the tape! *Judge angels?* Does that mean they will be committing crimes and have to be put on trial? Will Jesus need a jury? This is getting interesting. Roll tape again. "become a joint heir with Christ. Then when Jesus soon returns to this planet—" (The same Jesus, who, incidentally, created this planet? Just checking.) "—to take over the governments of this world, you'll come back and reign with him." Imagine the lawsuits the ACLU will file when Jesus runs the government. They can't even tolerate prayer in schools. *King* Jesus will drive them bonkers!

No tract is complete without a little fire and brimstone. Sure enough, the next to last line states: "And one of your **BIGGEST** benefits is: You'll miss out on hell!" (This threat helps motivate folks who otherwise lack the ambition to work for a heavenly mansion.)

Favorite Panel Award goes to page 18. A three star general pounds his desk and declares, "The world's financial picture is so bad, the only thing that can save us from total collapse...is an all-out, full scale, thermonuclear war!" Eat your heart out, Dr. Strangelove. This tract uses a shotgun approach to get its point across, but ultimately succeeds. There's also an Asian version with slanty eyes added to most of the characters. You probably won't get rich reading this tract, but at 14 cents a pop, you shouldn't go broke. Grade: **B** for Bankers. **Still in print.**

©1995 Jack T. Chick.

HUMBUG Review: (Art by Chick ©1975, 1995.) A surprisingly faithful adaptation of *A Christmas Carol.* There's only room for one ghost (Marley), but all the other major elements seem present. There's also more talk about Jesus than there is in the novel, but hey, it's a Chick tract, so whadaya expect? This story still packs a punch. When you stop and think about it, *A Christmas Carol* probably inspired one of Jack's other tracts: *This Was Your Life,* complete with an alternate happy ending. *Humbug* may not be very original plot wise, but it's well executed. Readers will learn that getting salvation not only removes the ugly scowl from your face, but also the dark razor stubble.

Favorite Panel Award goes to page 13: An older woman in the snowing street begs Scrooge, "I've been quite ill. Could you PLEASE extend my loan for ten more days?" Scrooge replies, "**NO!**... Not for *one extra minute!* You can expect **FORECLOSURE,** madam!" Merry Christmas to you, too. Grade: **B** for "Bah, humbug!" Original "?" cover version **$3.** "!" version **still in print.**

©1987 Jack T. Chick.

HUNTER Review: (Art by Chick ©1987.) This tract is to comics what "Reefer Madness" was to movies: Hard-core antidrug propaganda taken to the nth-degree! And it's full of the conspiracy paranoia that makes Chick tracts so much fun. The cover sets the tone: Young Bobby is pictured inside the center of a rifle scope's cross-hairs. Satan commands his slaves to bring him more souls on the next page. They race up to Earth and threaten their rich mortal collaborators, who quickly hold meetings to discuss how to increase their quotas. They decide to lean on Curt, a high school football captain and class vice president who's the Big Man on Campus. Curt has a constant smirk on his face and looks suspiciously like Bill Clinton (see page 8). Curt targets Bobby and Jimbo, two new youngsters at school. They are thrilled to get attention from "the Big Man." He invites them to a party that is filled with dolls, drugs, and the devil's rock & roll. Curt offers them something to smoke with "happy powder" in it. (He thinks to himself, "One drag on that primo and you're mine, stupid!") Some girls give Bobby a PCP cocktail, and he goes bananas! ("Poor baby. He can't handle it. He's freaked! Haw, haw.") They decide to dump Bobby on the side of the road somewhere. He winds up in the hospital screaming at the top of his lungs. A month later, his brother Doug meets with the doctor (a dead ringer for Billy Dee Williams) to hear the prognosis. "All his insurance is gone," the doc explains, "You'll have to admit him to a state mental institution for long term care. His mind is gone; he'll

never recover." Doug responds with classic understatement: "This is terrible." Yes Doug, it is. And so is the rest of the script. But fortunately, it is so campy, it is fun nevertheless.

Rather than dwell on medical options, the doctor then launches into a sermon about Jesus and the second coming. Within minutes, they are both on their knees in the doctor's office and praying—not to heal Bobby, but to save Doug. (I wonder if Medicare is paying for this?) Back at "high" school, Clinton—I mean Curt—is lining up Jimbo with a fix. Since Jimbo made a threat about turning Curt in, Curt decides to give him some "pure stuff to take him out." As he delivers his going away present to Jimbo, Curt smiles and says, "It's been real nice knowing you kid (may you rot in hell!)" Jimbo injects the drug and promptly o.d.'s. The last page shows Curt getting congratulated by his evil mentor. He wins a football scholarship (or was it a Rhodes scholarship?), a fancy new sports car, and a firm handshake. He'll make a great politician...

Meanwhile in Hell, Jimbo is shocked to discover he's standing naked in a pillar of flames. Satan rubs salt in the wound by taunting him. It's a downbeat ending, but that's why they call it "dope!" Favorite Panel Award goes to page 12. Bobby is FREAKING OUT and racing toward the viewer with THAT CRAZY LOOK in his eyes! *Kids! Don't try this at home!* Grade: **A** for Addiction. **Value: $10.**

"*But* of the tree of knowledge of good and evil **Thou shalt not eat of it.**

"For in the day thou *eatest* thereof **thou shalt surely die.**" Gen. 2:16-17

Adam got the message... He was busy naming all the animals and God saw that he was lonely.

So God created Eve to help him... **And now the drama begins.**

©2000 Jack T. Chick.

IN THE BEGINNING Review: (Art by Chick ©2000.) This story follows the intellectual awakening of Jason, as he's alerted to the sinister brainwashing that evil eggheads have perpetrated on him. His roommate "Bob" sets him straight: "There was *nothing* 'prehistoric.' That word was created to brainwash us." Bob informs Jason that the world is roughly 6,000 years old. Jason is shocked. "Then what I've been taught in school, films, and magazines **is all phony.**" Now you're catching on, Jason, but just in case you haven't, let's have Bob restate it one more time for any of the less bright comic book readers: "There were no prehistoric men, Jason. Before Day One, there was no world." The good news here is that Christians can flunk Paleontology and wear that failure as a badge of honor.

There is NO MIDDLE GROUND. It's all or nothing folks, the Bible said it and that settles it. At one point, Bob reminds the reader that according to Genesis, on Day 3, grass and fruit were created. Only on Day 4 was the Sun, moon, and stars made. So "they had to be real days or the plants and trees would have died." So much for non-literal Creationists. But if you're like me, this kind of hard line interpretation makes Chick tracts all the more enjoyable. One can't help but admire the ultra enthusiastic hard-line faith of defending every word, dash and period in the Bible as if it were Holy Writ. Which, I guess it is—so maybe that's the entire point.

Favorite Panel Award goes to page 5, where Bob declares "There was no big bang!" This news is so startling, that not only does Jason give a double take, but so does his model dinosaur! (Abiogenesis anyone?) Also note the "JTC" cover credit has been replaced with the number one. That's because this tract is only the first installment featuring Bob Williams, who will return in 24 more tracts to tell more stories of the Bible in the months that follow. Grade: **A-** for Anthropology. **Still in print.**

IS THERE ANOTHER CHRIST? **Guest review by Rev. Rich Lee:** (Art by Chick ©1983.) Two versions of this tract exist. The earliest version has a fat, unshaven monk hiding behind the Jesus mask on the cover while the latter version shows a priest.

Unlike *The Death Cookie,* this tract's treatment of the Roman Catholic version of the Eucharist is not inflammatory. In fact, most Protestant denominations hold the opinion against Catholicism's views of Communion found in this tract. It is wordy with few illustrations. Unlike Chick's other anti-Catholic treatises, this one confines itself to Roman Catholicism's sacred central doctrine, the "transubstantiation" of the Eucharist.

The opening frame shows a slick salesman trying to sell an elixir, and is obviously lying. Chick's point is that some people believe their newscaster, rabbi, priest, or pastor no matter what they say. Since they are only men, who is the public to turn to for absolute truth? The Bible, of course! The tract points out that His Word, the Bible, is put above even God's own name. The point is logical: "If you've been taught one thing, but the Bible says something else? WHO'S RIGHT? GOD in His Word, says: 'let God be true but every man a liar...' Romans 3:4 GOD'S WORD IS FINAL!"

After the tract quotes John 14:6, "I am the Way, the Truth, and the Life: No man cometh unto the Father, but by me," it makes the point that Jesus can't be separated from the written Word of God, because the Bible says that Jesus *is* THE WORD of God. Then, the reader is told that, "Jesus warns us about **another** type of Christ, a very **dangerous** type of Christ." In Matthew 24:4 Jesus said "Take heed that no man deceive you." This page also has the monk/priest cover variations. It's unclear why the cover and illustration were changed, but unlike the scruffy monk, the priest is clean cut and probably less offensive to most Catholics.

The tract continues Jesus' warnings against deceivers who claim that Christ would appear: "For there shall arise false Christs, and false prophets, and shall shew great signs and wonders; Insomuch that if it were possible, they shall deceive the very elect," Matthew 24:23-24. In a moment of self-appreciation, the tract states "When you see people who are deceived in this religious battlefield...WHAT DO YOU DO? If you love them enough, you stick your neck out to warn them, and tell them the truth." After Jesus left, it was the Holy Spirit's job to lead Christian believers into all truth. We are then given the tag line: "ARE YOU READY FOR THE BOMB?...CAN I SHOW YOU A VERY SCARY THING?" An incident from the life of Jesus recorded in John 17:11 says that he used a term so reverent that it appears only once in the Scriptures. That term is "HOLY FATHER," a sobering truth when we see how that reverent term is used when applied to the Pope! The Pope claims to come to us in the name of Jesus, and bears the title of Holy Father, sits as Christ in the Vatican (citation to Dogmatic Canons and Decrees, pg. 256), and can even speak for the Holy Spirit. Chick is very bold in pointing out this foible, but the Pope of Rome is just as bold in claiming these functions for himself. "NOW, ISN'T THAT JUST A LITTLE PRESUMPTUOUS?" Perhaps, but there are more quotes to bolster this claim.

The earlier version carries a lengthier quotation from Pope Boniface VIII, whereas the later version carries a truncated version so more presumptuous quotes from other popes can be cited. Pope Innocent III: "He [the Pope] judges all and is judged by no one." Pope Boniface VIII: "We declare, assert, define, and pronounce: To be **subject to the Roman pontiff** is to every human creature altogether **necessary for salvation.**" Pope Leo XIII: "We hold upon this earth the place of God Almighty." The Scripture warns about a man of perdition that will sit in the temple of God **shewing himself that he is God,** (II Thessalonians 2:3-4). The clinching quote in the tract comes from *Time* magazine when Pope John Paul II was shot in 1981, "It's like shooting God."

Chick believes that the dynasty of popes from history is a direct fulfillment of Bible prophecy in the words of Jesus himself. Many will come in his name, deceiving many. This looks pretty convincing, especially seeing the artistic portrayal of popes standing single file coming out of St. Peter's Square.

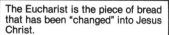

The Eucharist is the piece of bread that has been "changed" into Jesus Christ.

That wafer is adored as God, and is placed into the tabernacle sitting on the Roman Catholic altar.*

*MODERN CATHOLIC DICTIONARY, by John A. Hardon, S.J., pg. 530

When children are being questioned by the priest, he asks:

WHERE IS JESUS CHRIST?

THERE, FATHER.

THERE IS CHRIST.

Over 50,000 times a day, Jesus goes through the unbloody sacrifice of the mass.** According to Roman Catholic doctrine, Jesus Christ can be *physically* found in every Roman Catholic "Church," world-wide.

**DOGMATIC CANONS AND DECREES, pg. 135

©1983 Jack T. Chick.

The tract goes on to undermine other Catholic beliefs with more quotes from scripture. This tract is missing the fun and sometimes obnoxious **bold words that give the appearance of shouting** that can be found in other tracts like *Are Roman Catholics Christians?* Several pages have photos instead of drawings, but the information in its contents can be corroborated through official Catholic sources. This is not offensive fare, and certainly not as entertaining as the Alberto conspiracy theories. However, as a tract Fundamentalists can whip out to (literally) illustrate the differences between Catholic and Protestant theories of the Eucharist, it's very provocative. A surefire antidote to any dull dinner party. Grade: **A-** for Altruistic Arguments. Monk cover version: **$25**. Priest cover version: **$10**.

Janet is stunned by this presentation. "*GASP!* My professors **lied** to me!" (That's college, babe.) Jason warns her, "It's evolution or Jesus. What is your choice?" Can you guess her answer?

Favorite Panel Award goes to page 13 where some dude is riding a Triceratops and waving to the reader. It looks like more fun than a barrel full of ancestors. Grade **A** for Aquifer. **Still in print.**

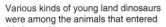

Various kinds of young land dinosaurs were among the animals that entered this huge ship.

It was big enough to haul 50,000 animals with room to spare.

God called Noah and his family into the Ark.

Once inside, God shut the door... and the world RUMBLED!

©2000 Jack T. Chick.

You **flunked!** I gave you an "F"! How **dare** you write about the 10 Commandments?!

But it's **true,** Miss Crawford. They even made a movie on it.

It's all a **lie,** Tim Johnson! This is the last straw!

I don't believe a **word** of it. Who do you think you are? I know how to deal with **your** kind...

I'm coming to talk to your parents tonight. I could **suspend** you for this.

©2001 Jack T. Chick.

IT'S COMING Review: (Art by Chick ©2000.) Here's proof that Chick doesn't make tracts like he did in the good old days. He makes them *better!* (Or at least more entertaining.) This is tract #2 of a series of 25 tracts, which converge history with the Bible. It even uses the same two characters from the last tract (Jason and Bob). This time, Jason drags his cousin Janet into the debate. They argue with Bob about the Noah's Ark story. Bob believes the world is 6,000 years old, and that all animals and humans alive today owe their survival to an ancestor who climbed aboard the Ark. Noah built the Ark despite taunts from his evil neighbors. They watch in disbelief as twosomes of animals and dinosaurs line up to enter the Ark. (There's a Woolly Mammoth, a couple of T-Rexes, and a Pteranodon—just to mention a few. What happened to their offspring is not mentioned.) God's giant arm is shown reaching out of heaven to shut the door of the Ark as the waters rise. Every living thing outside the ark drowns in a giant whirlpool. "Billions of dead creatures became trapped beneath millions of tons of rock and mud. Huge layers of sediment were formed. The skeletal remains of these creatures became the fossils we find today." (No explanation for why the human fossils are not buried in the same layers as the dinosaurs is offered.) The happy ending shows the Ark safely perched on a mountain top with a rainbow above it. "God promised never to destroy the Earth again by water..." (Hurrah!) "...the next time it will be by fire." (Oh joy. I think I preferred the water.)

IT'S THE LAW Guest review by UK Dave: This is tract #7 in the series of 25 Bible tracts. (Art by Chick ©2001.) It's an interesting tract for those of us readers on the other side of the pond where the issue of religion in state schools doesn't really occur. (I went to a *Church of England* state school after all.) Here we see young Tim Johnson flunking his examination for making mention of the 10 Commandments. Miss Crawford (note her unmarried status) in her dinosaur-decorated classroom is most upset about this and informs Tim that she will be calling on his parents that same evening. Suspension looks imminent.

Now Tim is a resourceful lad and the nephew of none other than our old friend Bob. Bachelor Bob's singleness so worries Tim that he sets up his lonesome uncle on a blind date of sorts with Miss Crawford. When she turns up, Tim's parents are nowhere to be seen (at the 'hospital' apparently). Only Tim is home (making himself scarce) with a tray of tea and cookies (that's biscuits, fellow Limeys), and of course Bob, in a rather fetching open shirt. Bob and Miss Crawford's eyes meet over the steaming cups and they fall into a passionate embrace. No, no, I'm losing the plot—what we actually learn here is possibly why Bob hasn't been such a great hit with the ladies. Instead of a few sweet nothings and perhaps an invitation to dinner, Bob produces a large leather bound Bible (KJV of course) and we're straight into the heavy theology neatly dovetailed with a whistle stop tour of Egyptian cultural history. At this stage Miss Crawford begins to wonder how she got herself into such a mess.

Meanwhile, we're treated to an explanation of how the plagues of Egypt demonstrated the powerlessness of the various Egyptian gods. My eyes usually begin to glaze over at this point in a Chick tract—I much prefer the end-of-the-world stuff, but this was actually quite interesting: Darkness discredited Horus the sun god, boils discredited Imhotep, and so on. Whether it's correct or not I don't know (this is always a slightly infuriating thing with Chick tracts because the references are either from his own books or nonexistent).

But I digress. This quick trip through the book of Exodus seems to be enough to convince Miss Crawford. (Where do the years of University education and logical debate go with these people?) Before you know it, we're into the, 'have you ever stolen a paper clip from the office?' debate. Why are vicars so obsessed with paper clips? I have heard so many sermons on this. (Chick uses the same example in *The Next Step*.) Is it projection? Is there a paper clip fetish among the clergy? It would appear that breaking the slightest law is enough to send our representative of the teaching profession to a much hotter classroom for all eternity. *Good works* will not be enough to spare anyone, because Martin Luther said so. (Although Jesus didn't address the issue, but why sweat the details?) So sheriff Bob fires the gospel message from the hip, Tim holds his head in his hands outside the door (presumably praying), and it's high noon for Miss Crawford's scientific logical positivism as she does the usual all fours position on the carpet (though this may be out of frustration with having had to listen to Bob). What we tantalizingly don't see in this tract is Miss Crawford going back to school and explaining to the governors why she is teaching fundamentalist Creationist theology in the classroom. She better do a lot of praying before that meeting...

All in all, this is an enjoyable tract. Favorite panel goes to (page 8) Moses' cool Ju-Jitsu stranglehold on the Egyptian slave master. (**Editor's note:** Bob turns out to be married in the tract, *The Outcasts*.) Grade **B** for Bold Beliefs. **Still in print.**

©1984 Jack T. Chick.

IVAN THE TERRIBLE **Review:** (Art by Chick ©1984.) Yet another Cold War relic, but this time, the emphasis is on how the commies were bamboozled by the Vatican. It begins with an American passing a Soviet diplomat a small piece of paper at the United Nations Building. In real life, the CIA would swarm in and tackle both men in an attempt to prevent the unauthorized transfer of military secrets. But this is *Chick's world*, and the small piece of paper is—you guessed it—a Chick tract. Normally, accepting this tract automatically does one of two things: (1.) It results in the imminent death of the recipient who then goes to hell for ripping up the tract and refusing to believe in Jesus, or (2.) It "saves" the recipient after they read it with an open mind and are immediately converted by its contents. These "born again" readers usually go on to live long and rewarding lives, though we do get previews of their eventual death so that we can witness their glorious entrance into heaven. But *Ivan The Terrible* is a rare exception. We never learn whether Ivan becomes saved or not! He doesn't tear up the tract though (a wise move, for a Russian). Instead, he gives the classic "Haw-haw-haw!" and decides to invite the Christian to lunch in order to humiliate him. The Russian girl friend says, "Oh Ivan, you're terrible!" Ivan grins and admits, "I know!" The two meet at dinner and the taunting begins. The Christian's vast knowledge of behind-the-scenes Russian history quickly turns the tables on the communist. It seems this diplomat wasn't very well briefed on how the Vatican really created communism to destroy the Eastern Orthodox Church. What an idiot! This Red didn't even know that Lenin and Stalin were closet Catholics, or that Marx and Engels were converted from Judaism to Catholicism and controlled by Jesuits (page 7). But the Christian knew all this and more from reading Chick tracts and Alberto comics, especially *The Godfathers* and *The Force*.

The theory gets a little complicated, but intriguing once you understand it. (It took me a couple of rereads to appreciate the convoluted GENIUS of it all.) It goes like this: The early bishops in Rome and Constantinople both claimed to be the true inheritors of apostolic succession. This split resulted in rival catholic churches (The Eastern Orthodox and the Roman Catholic Church). Both the Eastern Patriarch and the Roman Pope declared the other's church false. This started a long history of hatred between the two, resulting in a Roman Catholic attack on Constantinople in 1204. The Christian mentions (on page 11) that both Churches "are basically the same, but Rome wants to control the governments of the world, while the Orthodox are willing to coexist with the state. Eventually, the Orthodox church came under the protection of the Czar of Russia." So the Jesuits "worked with Engels and Marx to develop the Communist Manifesto (page 13) ... That way the world would see it as a political action instead of a religious war that it was." On page 15, we learn Rasputin was a "faithful Jesuit working undercover." (Surprised? Me neither.) But it turns out that the Eastern Patriarch is pretty sly too. He snatched the dead Czar's gold and used it to bribe the communists. (Page 18) "When the Red Army came to kill the old chief patriarch, he greeted them with open arms and cried, 'We've been holding the Czar's gold for you, my true comrades'." So now the communists decided to let the Orthodox live, since they would help legitimize communist control. They took their gold, as well as the Roman Catholic gold and double-crossed the pope by letting the Orthodox Church survive. "To get even, [the Vatican] built a new machine called the Nazi Party." (page 19)

And there you have it. The Jesuits not only created the communists to destroy their arch enemies (the Orthodox) but they also created the Nazis in order to destroy the communists, who befriended their earlier arch enemies (the Orthodox) and thereby became their NEW arch enemies! So let's see, the Vatican started the Civil War to get even with Lincoln (*The Big Betrayal*), and then WWI to get even with the Orthodox, and then WWII to get even with the communists... You can bet they'll be blamed for WWIII.

Favorite Panel Award goes to page 6, where Ivan bangs his plate with his fist. (There's something about Russians in the U.N. that makes them want to pound on things and shout.) Unfortunately, this tract is outdated and out of print, but it's well worth hunting down. Grade **A+** for Advancing Armies. **Value: $30.**

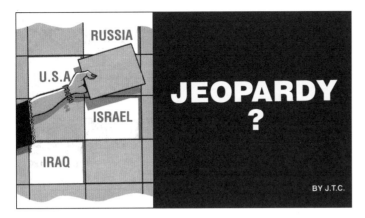

JEOPARDY (Art by Carter ©1992. **A.k.a. Support Your Local Jew,** see *Love The Jewish People.*) **Value: $4**

The animals were all brought aboard.

The people watched, completely unaware of what was ahead.

Then God ordered Noah and his family into the ark.

There they go! *Haw! haw!*

The fools!

In just seven days, it would start to rain… and only Noah knew it.

KILLER STORM Review: (Art by the third artist. ©1991.) This tract begins with a Russian WWI pilot spotting what he thinks is a submarine atop Mt. Ararat. His supervisor also flies over it and decides it's Noah's Ark! They alert Czar Nicholas, who in turn, orders a scientific expedition. One of the members of the team never heard of Noah, so the Old Testament tale of the Great Flood is related in flashback: God decides ancient humanity is wicked and tells Noah to build a giant 300 cubit Ark (the size of an aircraft carrier). The onlookers think he's crazy and say, "he should be put away." (But where? Mental institutions haven't been invented yet.) Noah continues to build and warn his neighbors of the upcoming flood. They laugh at him, because "it had never rained. God watered the earth with a mist." Then two of every kind of animal show up and climb aboard the ark, including dinosaurs. "The people watched, completely unaware of what was ahead." You would think someone might

suspect *something* was up to make all those animals climb inside the Ark. But no, they only get worried when they witness the first ever thunder mist —I mean, storm. They get quite a demonstration, too: Forty days and nights worth. Flash forward to the expedition. They climb the mountain and one of the two groups makes it to the top. They enter the Ark and find giant cages covered with pitch. They return and send the documents proving their discovery to the Czar via a soldier. (No mention of photographs is made.) Alas, the soldier happens to run into the communist revolution and gets himself executed. "Rumor has it he was shot, and the documents fell into the hands of Trotsky, the Communist leader. All the documents **disappeared!"** A three page summery of the upcoming judgment is provided to motivate readers to get right with Jesus. The basic theme is: If God saved Noah, he'll save you too—if you accept him before it's too late.

This is a pretty cool tale. It contains a mystery/conspiracy/Urban Legend, plus a Bible story, all in one tract. The flashbacks are neat as well. As readers, we know what's going to happen long before the victims do. The characters in the tract don't believe in God, so they'll perish. Likewise, modern society doesn't believe either, and will likely suffer the same ending. We *almost* get hard evidence to convince the disbelievers, but like the hero in *The Invaders* TV series trying to warn the world about aliens, the proof mysteriously disappears before anyone can see it. Frustrating...yet exciting!

Favorite Panel Award goes to page 12. The shocked expression of the future floater as the rain starts falling is pretty priceless. (Didn't *anyone* have a boat back then besides Noah?) Grade: **A** for Ark. **Value: $3.50.**

AFTER WORLD WAR II, CHINA GOES INTO A CIVIL WAR.

IN 1949 THE COMMUNISTS WIN! MAO BECOMES THE CHAIRMAN OF THE PEOPLE'S REPUBLIC OF CHINA.

IN THE PURGES THAT FOLLOWED, AN ESTIMATED 60 MILLION CHINESE WERE KILLED. HUMAN COST OF COMMUNISM U.S. SENATE 1971, 63-549-0.

THE GIANT OF ASIA, WHO MANY HOPED WOULD STAY SLEEPING, WAS NOW AWAKE.

KINGS OF THE EAST Review: (Art by Carter ©1975.) A fun romp through Jack's red-under-every-bed world-view. This is basically a rant on how the Chinese are out to take over the world. Released in 1975 and discontinued soon thereafter, it must have really seemed paranoid. Since that time, however, the Chinese have made major territorial and political gains through their use of spies, intimidation, and bribery. They've taken over Hong Kong, threatened to invade Taiwan, and received permanent World Trade Organization status. And don't forget the $6 million illegal campaign contribution to Clinton's re-election, or their successful snatching of nuclear secrets from our weapons labs, or their stealing of our rocket technology from joint venture satellite launches in Asia. Chick must have really flipped whenever he heard Clinton refer to China as our "Strategic Partner." (With allies like that, who needs adversaries?) If Chick wanted to update this tract, he'd probably need more than the standard 24 page format! But this tract is pretty juicy as is. Check out page 5, for example: "Tibet falls in 1959. No one cares, including the U.N. What kind of Masters are the Chinese Reds? In the village of Ba-Jeuba the inhabitants were forced to watch the crucifixion of 25 wealthy people. In the same village, men and women had to watch 24 parents being killed by having nails driven into their eyes—because they refused to send their children to Chinese schools." (*Hey!* That's our Strategic Partner you're talkin' 'bout!) Don't miss the Red-baiting scene directed down-under: "In the classrooms of China, the map has a new name for Australia." An instructor points to an Australia map with NEW CHINA printed over it. (But will the *Outback Steakhouses* go Chinese as well?)

The rest of the tract warns of the domino theory and commie plans to move on Israel. First, the Russians attack it. "World War III begins with the U.S. and Russia at war. It's a one day fire war. One quarter of the world's population dies as a result. Israel survives the Holocaust." Then the Red Chinese invade seven years later. (No one seems that interested in the Arab countries rich with oil.) Page 16 shows an endless formation of Chinese foot soldiers marching in unison on tiny Israel. Two-thirds of the Jews die. The attack on the Chosen triggers the rapture. Jesus jumps into the fray and all hell breaks loose.

Favorite Panel Award goes to page 18, a red color insert of the resulting river of blood. It states, "Jesus cuts them to shreds. The blood in this 130-mile valley is 4-feet deep up to the bridle of horses. The greatest slaughter in human history, 1/3 of the world's population is gone." (That's a lot of Red blood.) But not to fret, because the good guys win. "Jesus sets up his kingdom in Jerusalem as the ruler of the Earth... Peace comes at last." The only problem is that one-fourth of the world population was blown up in WWIII, another one-third cut to shreds by Jesus, two-thirds of the Jews destroyed by the Beast, plus "the ecology is ruined and the plagues are hitting everywhere." So the odds of enjoying that peace don't sound good. But it sure makes an exciting tract! Grade: **A+** for Asian Adversaries. Permanently retired: **$20.**

© 1970 Jack T. Chick.

***KISS INDIA GOODBYE* Review:** (Art by Chick © 1970.) Like *Breakthrough*, this is an exceptionally rare tract that lists its origin as "The Gospel Literature Foundation." It is also from the same time frame, and was an unknown title until a copy was unearthed from inside Chick's archive vault in 2001. This tract also has something in common with *Operation: Somebody Cares.* It's a Red-baiting tract that predicts a Russian invasion (of India, instead of the US) within a few years and it never occurred.

The cover is one of Chick's most bland. There is no color or graphic, just the title. The inside front page demonstrates a rare case of cynical candor. It says, "If you are a typical 20th century Christian, you will NOT be interested in missionary work. If this is true, then please close the cover and throw this book away. We are both wasting our time!" Wow! Chick is taking a bold gamble here. He's actually telling the reader to throw away his tract *before* reading it. He quickly follows up with some bait to keep the handful of guilt-ridden readers turning the pages: "But if you are a soldier for Christ and ARE concerned for the lost and for missionaries, you will find this to be of special interest." It shows a map of India and China. Then it warns, "China has built a super highway that starts at Peking and moves southwest. It goes through Tibet, Nepal, and connects with the Indian highway system. Its bed is made of thick concrete to support heavy military vehicles. A LAUNCHING POINT FOR THE INVASION OF INDIA!"

Why the communists would bother with a country that is even more crowded and poor than China is not addressed. Instead, a large bamboo wall with a steel door is drawn. It is labeled "Bamboo Curtain." The dire predictions continue. "People in the know say that India has less than 1 year before the door slams shut—Never to be opened again to the Gospel. Most people are unaware that Calcutta has already fallen into Communist hands. Over 100 political assassinations took place in West Bengal last year. This cancer is also spreading into the states of Bihar, Orissa, Assam, and Kerala. One-seventh of the human race is at stake."

Chick stirs the discussion to one of his favorite topics, that being how successful the communists were in using printed propaganda to brainwash everyone. "Did you know that the population in India increases by ONE MILLION every month? THE ONLY THING THAT CAN REACH THEM IS LITERATURE! The Chinese know this and they are doing a tremendous job. Did you ever see a copy of 'Evergreen?' It is published in China for India and it's on par with our leading magazines. Incidentally, it sells for a few pennies. At the cost of millions of dollars, Red China pumps in tons of literature to India, telling them of the utopia behind the Bamboo Curtain. Can **WE** counteract this?"

Chick repeats a claim also made in *Operation: Somebody Cares,* that a leading communist said in 1930, "The only force that can stop us is the Gospel of Jesus Christ."

The tract discloses an interesting bit of company trivia that is normally hidden behind the scenes. It says, "We now have available: A huge Cottrell web press, capable of printing 1,000,000 books a day." Have you ever wondered how Chick covers the globe with tracts? Now you know. Blame Cottrell.

Chick places a mirror before Christians and exposes an ugly image. He states, "Out of Fundamental Evangelical Christianity (whose testimony must be an utter disgrace to our Lord Jesus Christ) is a multitude of sleeping, prayerless, self-satisfied Christians playing Church. And yet within that body, which represents Christ on this Earth, are only a few sincere Christians of God, completely sold out for the cause of Christ. It is those few we are calling upon to help back up this work." This may be the only time when being labeled a "sell out" is meant as a compliment.

Chick says half of India has never heard of the name of Jesus. He also pleads, "One of their gods is a Cobra. We MUST tell them about Christ! Beloved—the heathen are going to hell! I just received a letter from one large Bible-believing church begging for $32,000 to pay for an organ. GOD HELP US! We play games while our missionaries sleep in mosquito infested trucks as they pass out Gospel literature." This may give some insight why Chick doesn't attend church. You can imagine how popular he is with the ministers whenever they ask the congregation for a raise.

Chick states 16 out of 20 houses that received his books in India decided for Christ. "Did that number really sink in? Read it again—it's unbelievable! WE KNOW IT WORKS!"

Page 21 shows a drawing of sinister Chinese military officers planning their invasion of India. "The Chinese Red Army and you both know what is ahead for India. We dare not be indifferent. When the door is shut, it will be forever!" This image is a serious contender for the Favorite Panel Award, but is edged out by page 17, which shows the trembling pagan offering a bowl of food to the hungry cobra.

Page 22 reveals the rationale behind the creation of the Gospel Literature Foundation. "The many requests for free literature from overseas and at home have caused a serious drain on Chick Publications. In order to offset this problem we have formed a tax free foundation called the 'International Gospel Literature Foundation.' Its purpose will be to supply free illustrated gospel booklets to missionaries and workers in India, Africa, New Guinea, and many other foreign fields." Grade **B+** for Blasted commie Bastards! **Value: Speculative.**

©1981 Jack T. Chick.

KISS THE PROTESTANTS GOODBYE Review: (Art by Chick ©1981.) Once The Whore of Rome (Chick's pet name for The Vatican) started fighting Chick Publications over the publishing of the *Alberto* series, Jack responded with several counterattack tracts. They included *The Poor Pope, My Name... in the Vatican?, Is There Another Christ?, The Death Cookie,* and *Kiss the Protestants Goodbye.* This particular tract sports a tombstone on the cover inscribed "Rest in Peace." Chick reminds readers that Rome executed millions of Protestants during the Inquisition for refusing to bow to the Pope, and that the origin of the word "Protestant" means to protest. Then he launches into Vatican conspiracies to infiltrate the Protestant seminaries, corrupt the King James Bible, and turn one Christian church against another. You can tell that Chick feels DEAD CERTAIN that he is right and is BURSTING AT THE SEAMS to tell the reader of ALL the various Catholic behind-the-scenes intrigues. Ninety-nine percent of the writing is in BIG CAPITAL LETTERS as if he's SHOUTING from the ROOF! As a result of all this information, very few illustra-

tions are included (a definite minus to an otherwise A-1 comic). But this obscure tract is still very desirable on account of all the inflammatory language and "Jesuit under every bed" conspiracy claims. There's no telling how much of it is accurate or not, but it certainly gives insight to Chick's biblical beliefs and how hot the feud between Chick Publications and the Catholic Church got during the early '80s. In Chick's words, after *Alberto* was published, "IT HIT THE FAN!" (page 18). Grade: **B+** for Blasphemer! Permanently retired**: $50.**

©1992 Jack Chick.

THE LAST GENERATION Review: (Art by Carter ©1972, 1992.) It's Carter's artwork, but drawn in a different style from his fine line illustrations. (This art looks painted.) The subject matter is the New World Order. A bleak and depressing future is depicted where pollution and crime are rampant. Smiling news anchors cheerfully report from One World Government headquarters that "All opposers of the Church of World Brotherhood are now officially **enemies** of the state!". Everyone lives in concrete block houses, and schools brainwash kids with New Age beliefs. Parents who try to discipline their children are arrested for Child Abuse. (This may sound like typical H.R.S. tactics by today's standards, but must have seemed like sensational science fiction when originally published in 1972.) Little Bobby wears a Nazi-esque brown shirt outfit and turns his grandfather in to the authorities for claiming that Jesus created the universe. The "New Age Healers" then toss Grandpa in an agony chamber and turn up the power. When he refuses to recant, they curse him and say, "Take this heretic away. Dispose of it, or use it for food." Black helicopters chase down the escaping parents (who get turned in by their brother-in-law for the reward money.) But just as the ATF (or whatever the agency) kicks down the door, the Christians are Raptured. Call it the ultimate *Deux Ex Machina* ending. All that is left is a pile of clothes! (It will probably get recycled along with the corpses.) You won't look forward to the wonders of the 21st century after reading this tract. There are blue cover (©1972) and green cover (©1992) versions. The original blue cover version seems more influenced by John Todd's *Illuminati* conspiracies, with Jews like "Supreme Chancellor A. Jablonsky" running the courts. The more recent green cover version supports Alberto's anti-catholic beliefs, with "Supreme Justice Mahoney S.J." calling the shots. (S.J. = "Society of Jesus," the Jesuit order.) The later version also censors the pile of clothes on the floor after the rapture. The empty bra must have been too suggestive, making readers think impure thoughts! This tract has recently been discontinued, so you better hide a copy before the One World Government orders them all destroyed or recycled.

Favorite Panel Award goes to page 8: Brat Bobby holds up pictures of a puppy and kitten and shouts, "My teacher said these are **great** for Halloween sacrifice!" (The blue cover version says, "The teacher gave us pictures of these two extinct species.") Grade: **A-** for Adorable Brat. Original blue cover version: **$26.50**. Green cover version recently retired: **$1**.

©2002 Jack T. Chick.

THE LAST JUDGE Guest review by Rich Lee: (Art by Chick ©2002) This tract is number 11 in the series of 25 tracts that illustrate Bible stories with Bob.

Bob is assisting Kelly with her laptop computer when an elderly man with a walker approaches. Uncle George is distinguished looking and wears a patch over his left eye. After Kelly introduces Uncle George, we learn that George was once a judge that criminals feared. This is just the segue into Bob's Bible Story (we saw that coming!).

The Bible story for this tract is from I Samuel in the Old Testament. Eli, an ancient judge and high priest, ruled in the days before Israel had a king. Everyone did what was right in his own eyes. Eli observed a woman praying to God, promising that if she had a son that he would be dedicated to the service of God. Indeed, he was born and named Samuel. As a child, Samuel had prophetic tendencies that Eli readily observed, and he was destined to become Israel's judge. Later, Israel lost the famous

Ark of the Covenant in battle against their enemies the Philistines. Israel assumed that God would be with them in battle just because they possessed the ark, carried by Eli's two wicked sons Hophni and Phinehas. The Philistines killed both sons and kept the ark. When Eli heard this, he fell backwards in his chair and died of a broken neck. Samuel became Israel's new judge, but in time the people demanded a king like other nations. Samuel warned the populace that a king would demand more of them than they were willing to give. Nevertheless, Israel wanted a king to rule over them. King Saul was appointed by Samuel, and in a short time, Saul committed sacrilege by offering a burnt sacrifice that was only lawful for a priest to give. The last straw for Saul was when he didn't obey a "word from the Lord" through Samuel. Under orders from God through the judge and prophet Samuel, King Saul was to kill Amalek and all of his people, including women, children, and cattle! Saul disobeyed, and kept the spoils of invasion including sparing Amalek's life. Samuel was upset, and proceeded to kill Amalek himself by hacking him to pieces with a sword. Because of Saul's disobedience, he forfeited his throne and Samuel proceeded to anoint the legendary David as the new king.

Despite his brutal tendencies, Samuel ruled as a judge for 40 years and died a peaceful death. All Israel mourned his passing. Bob tells the retired judge George that "Samuel was a godly and righteous judge. He never took a bribe and never let people influence his decisions...because he knew that one day he will face the **greatest** judge of all time." (Samuel only advocated the killing of women and children under orders from God, but at least he never took bribes!) Uncle George asks, "Who is that? Tell me!" Bob says that this ultimate judge will sit on His throne with all the world gathered before Him. All that we've ever done is going to be played back for all to see, including our secret thoughts. During Bob's presentation, Uncle George thinks back to a time when he took a bribe from an ostensibly seedy lawyer named Richard. "Gulp!" Uncle George begins to worry...

Bob tells George what's in store for all those who sin before God. George gets nervous. He admits that he wasn't perfect. Bob emphasizes that George is guilty before God and without hope. George asks what way is there to escape this sentence? Bob tells him to pray the Sinner's prayer. George gets saved. Now he can look forward to being in that Great Courtroom in the sky without facing an angry Judge. Let's hope that Samuel won't have that sword handy, either!

Favorite Panel Award goes to page 16, where the crooked lawyer bribes the judge. We even get to learn the lawyer's name. (It's Richard, the same as my name. He looks the same as me, too. Hey, that **IS** me!) Grade **B** for Bribe. **Still in print.**

Missionaries are locked into constant warfare with spiritual wickedness in high places. These dark powers are *always* working against the Gospel.

Oh, Prince of Darkness, weaken that missionary. Kill him and his family.

Hinder his work . . .

Evil forces cause many problems unheard of in nations where the Gospel has made an impact . . .

©1987 Jack T. Chick.

THE LAST MISSIONARY Review: (Art by Chick ©1987.) This is another of several self-promotional tracts showing the importance of buying tons of Chick tracts. You see, it basically boils down to this: Satan HATES Chick tracts because even after the devil drives out and/or kills all the missionaries, Chick tracts continue to stick around and win souls for Jesus. The cover shows a couple of soldiers marching a missionary away at gun point. Inside, the REAL fun begins. It's war between the Christians and the Godless commies from the very first line on the very first page! The commander starts out by saying "By the end of this month, I want every missionary in this country either dead or gone." These soldiers are obviously Red because they look like unshaven Cubans with thick black mustaches. But just in case that hint is too subtle, Chick slams the reader over the head with a communist manifesto by having the lieutenant respond, "Yes, comrade!" Keep in mind this tract was published in 1987, while Ronald Reagan was in the White House and Oliver North was secretly aiding the Contra "Freedom Fighters" in their war against Sandinista communists. This secret mission was later exposed by the media and labeled a scandal. We'll never know if a worldwide communist blood bath was barely avoided or never in the cards to begin with. But we do know this: many Americans were paranoid that the Reds were slowly working their way from Cuba to South America and up to our borders. One of those worried was clearly Jack Chick.

Chick figured Satan had a four-pronged approach to fighting Christianity by promoting Communism, Catholicism, Islam, and the New Age movement. He devotes a full page to each theory. Here are just a few of the juicy highlights: **Communism** (page 5) "When the communists show peaceful coexistence with 'Christian churches,' the pastors or priest are party sympathizers taking orders from the K.G.B....The communists want Bible-believing Christians and their missionaries six feet under." **Islam** (page 6) "Woe to anyone caught in a jihad (a holy war). Recently some 30 churches were burned in Africa by irate Moslems... Bible-believing missionaries are not tolerated in many Moslem countries. They are called infidels." **Catholicism** (page 7) "The Vatican wants a Roman Catholic world... The pope claims 'there is no salvation outside the Church of Rome.' The office of the Inquisition is alive and well. Many missionaries died in Latin America standing against Catholicism. And many will in the future." **New Age Movement** (page 8) "The new age movement is actually a westernized form of Hinduism which has invaded every aspect of life in Western cultures. It is directly hostile to Bible-believing Christianity through its deceptive teaching of supposed sciences such as yoga, Transcendental Meditation, and mind control techniques. It has opened up millions of people to direct contact with demons."

The very next page shows a blindfolded prisoner getting shot in the head by a Fidel Castro look-alike goon. It says, "These massive forces under Satan's command have set the stage for the Antichrist and there WILL be war against the saints of God. Time is short. We MUST go on the offensive and pluck the brands from the burning." Do you get the feeling we're at war yet? If not, check out page 11 where he compares sending missionaries to preach without tracts to sending solders to war without ammunition. Or page 12, with the heading "Read this carefully,

the enemy means business." It contains a small font full-page rant by some commie declaring how they intend to bury the Christians because Reds dedicate "all our free time and part of our holidays" to propaganda purposes.

Another sensational section is page 15. "Africa will soon be gone... AIDS and famine are stalking the land. Africa is ripe for a blood bath! Forces are massing to enslave every African nation, one at a time." Alas, this is one prophecy that probably seemed far-flung in 1987, but now appears plausible as the AIDS epidemic continues to spread like wide fire throughout Africa. But did you know the *real motive* behind AIDS is to "close Africa to the Gospel and throw out Bible-believing missionaries!"? (At least it makes more sense than Al Sharpton's theory that AIDS is a racist plot to make blacks wear condoms and reduce the birth rate.)

All in all, this a great tract. What it lacks in pictures, it more than makes up in elaborate conspiracies. Favorite Panel Award goes hands down to page 3, where a demonic witch doctor holds a snake staff in one hand and a skull in the other while chanting, "Oh, Prince of Darkness, weaken that missionary. Kill him and his family. Hinder his work..." (Interesting Factoid: killing someone and his family usually hinders their work, or at very least, weakens them.) And for the record, who exactly is "The Last Missionary"? Why, the Chick tracts themselves! Once the missionary is gone, the tracts carry on the missionary work via autopilot. So remember, you can send a cannibal a missionary and you've fed him for a day, but send him a Chick tract and you've fed him *FOREVER!* Grade: **A** for African Outreach. **Value: $25.**

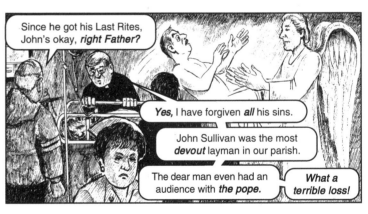

Since he got his Last Rites, John's okay, *right Father?*

Yes, I have forgiven *all* his sins.

John Sullivan was the most *devout* layman in our parish.

The dear man even had an audience with *the pope.*

What a terrible loss!

©1994 Jack T. Chick.

LAST RITES Review: (Art by Chick ©1994.) If you've ever wondered why the Catholics hate Chick so much, this tract is a good starting point. There's nothing sensational inside it, no scenes of the Pope conferring with the Devil or child molesting Jesuits helping the Nazis or anything like that. The story line is rather basic: A catholic named John dies and goes to face judgment.

One has to admire the simplicity and effectiveness of this tract. Even though the Catholic/ Protestant debate basically boils down to two different interpretations of the same book, the Protestants win the debate in this tract because God says so... Literally! When John pleads for his soul and starts listing good deeds, God quotes the Bible, "For by Grace are ye saved through faith; and that not of yourselves. It is the gift of God: Not of works, lest any man should boast." (Talk about a policy wonk.) John presents other arguments as well, but all of them seem to lower him further in hell. He mentions he prayed to the blessed virgin, just like the pope does. God responds, "That's idolatry, John, and no idolater shall enter Heaven. Thou shalt not make unto thee any graven image. Thou shalt not bow down thyself to them, nor serve them." Chick inserts a photo of Pope John Paul bowing before a Mary statue at this point, as if to say "the Fish Eaters rot from the head down." John really steps in it when he mentions he attended Mass twice a week, and Mass is the unbloody ongoing sacrifice at Calvary. God yells, "*THAT'S A LIE!* The sacrifice was completed on the cross when I cried 'It is finished'." Keep in mind that no one really knows how loud God shouts, but it's enough to knock John back a full body length and have him hide behind the angel for the next few panels. God certainly **sounds** pissed, but it's difficult judging his faceless face expressions to determine how mad he really is. On top of everything else, the queue behind John is probably backing up the longer he argues. Millions die every day, and one-sixth of the world is Catholic. No doubt a lot of them are surprised like John and want to debate theology with God (if Chick's version of the hereafter is correct).

Then John makes a major *faux paux:* He tries to blame God for his ignorance about everything wrong with the Catholic system. He whines, "Why didn't you warn me?" God (and Chick) pounce on the question: "*I DID!* My servant, who loved Roman Catholics, gave you a tract that warned you about your false religion." A panel shows John ripping up the tract and shouting at the good Christian, "This is **hate** literature! How dare you attack my church!" (You know Chick loved drawing that picture. It earns the Favorite Panel Award.) Ironically, if Chick's theories are correct, this would make yet **another** reason for Catholics to despise Chick tracts. By passing them out, Chick is virtually assuring all Catholics who read them that they are losing their only good argument to prevent going to hell. No one will be able to say they didn't know any better, thanks to Chick and his legions of dedicated human tract dispensers. It also provides a sinister motive for why Catholic apologist groups like *Catholic Answers* send Chick tracts to fellow Catholics: Perhaps the Vatican really **IS** demonic and wants to make sure all its members have no excuse to avoid damnation. (I never thought it was possible to come up with more elaborate and sinister conspiracies than Alberto, but this theory might qualify.)

Either the timer goes off indicating hell has reached the proper preheating temp, or Chick realizes he's running out of tract pages. Whatever the reason, God decides to conclude this episode of the Papal's Court and send John sliding down the fire pole to join the rest of the Catholic congregation. John asks one more question (not a very smart one either): "Don't you love the Roman Catholic Church?" God answers, "How could I, John? Her false teachings are why you are going into the *lake of fire.*" As if that weren't enough, Chick really gets the last dig in with the final page. It shows a priest giving John's funeral service back on Earth. The priest says, "John is now reaping the rewards of serving the one true church. And I'm sure he can't wait for all of us to join him." (Now *that's funny,* unless you happen to be the 1 in 6 readers that this tract is directed to.) Grade **A-** for Absolution. **Still in print.**

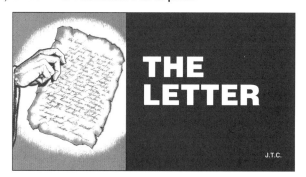

© 1982 Jack T. Chick.

THE LETTER Guest review by Richard Lee: (Art by Carter © 1982.) This tract is a very entertaining story, and is one of two tracts (*Reverend Wonderful* being the other) with the real-life personality of "Chaplain Dann" as a main character. He has been the subject of several Battle Cry articles. The first panel shows Chaplain Dann passing out (what else?) Chick tracts. As he attempts to hand a copy of *Somebody Loves Me* to a woman named Mildred, she chews him out for being a fanatic; "I'm a Christian and what YOU'RE doing cheapens the Gospel! I let people SEE how I live. I don't cram it down their throats like YOU do! You, sir are a fanatic and an embarrassment!" Mildred is dressed in fine clothes, wears a Martha Stewart hairstyle, and lives in a mansion. She must be a well-to-do Episcopalian or Presbyterian. She's not an undignified blue collar fundamentalist who would pass out tracts in a Chaplain Dann-like manner. It seems obvious that Jack Chick wrote *The Letter* with such mainline Protestants in mind, since they are not exactly known for their Evangelical fervor, but better known for their upper middle class socio-economic status and having more at stake in the wider culture. Her last caustic insult to Chaplain Dann is "How dare you place yourself with the Apostles! YOU'RE SICK! Get away from me or I'll call the police!" The Holy Apostles are in a class by themselves, and would not be a bottom-of-the-food-chain, blue collar Chaplain Dann type who hands out religious propaganda in an actual attempt to convert anybody!

As Mildred falls asleep mumbling about how she is so glad she is not like the protagonist Chaplain Dann, she starts to dream about the regions of the damned. Somehow, someone in hell manages to write a letter without the paper burning up. (One wonders how a tormented soul could have enough light to write a letter in the blackness of hell, but this is only a dream sequence.) Two demonic/angelic messengers (not the cute demons with horns that Jack usually draws) take the letter and pass through the nether regions as others writhe in hellish torment.

They reach Mildred's gated estate (she definitely ain't a Pentecostal or Baptist!) while she finishes a telephone call from her pastor thanking her for her "generous gift" to the church. Mildred says that it was "her Christian duty." (This is a not-too-subtle jab at mainline Protestants who relegate generous gifts to their churches while ignoring the larger Christian duty of evangelism.)

One of the demonic messengers enters her master bedroom to deliver the message while the other one waits outside the gate. Judging from the scream "EEEEEEK!" the waiting demon knows that contact has been made. The messenger tells Mildred "here is the letter I was to deliver. It's from a friend...IN HELL!" She reads it, and it's a poem from a friend: "Though we lived together here on Earth, you never told me of your second birth. And now I stand this day condemned...because you failed to mention Him." As she continues to read it, the demonic messengers are shown returning to their domain, again bypassing the souls in torment. She finishes the letter, "And yet in coming to this end, I see you really weren't my friend. Signed Frances." Mildred wakes up from her dream, horrified and shaking. She reflects how Christ died for the sins of the whole world, and how she'll share Christ with Frances on Monday night. When Monday night rolls around, she calls to find out that Frances died the previous Saturday when her car hit a tree. The final frame is classic: Mildred's eyes are open in horror, realizing that she was ashamed to tell her friend about Jesus Christ, and now it's too late!

This tract undoubtedly has frightened many Christians into being more zealous in sharing their faith and preventing others from taking deep dives into the lake of fire. The scenes of torment with a touch of sulfur smell added to the ink on the tract adds to the overall ambiance. A true tract classic! Grade **A** for Aggressive witnessing. **Still in print.**

ished except the victim. (I guess that's more realistic than most of us like to admit.) This tract is currently out of print, but it's a favorite. Grade: **A** for Adult Content. Permanently retired: **$100.**

©1984 Jack T. Chick.

©2001 Jack T. Chick.

LISA **Review:** (Art by Carter ©1984.) This has GOT to be the most uncomfortable Chick tract ever written. Not because it's insensitive, but because the topic is SUPER sensitive: Child Molestation—by the parent! The story follows a jobless, henpecked husband as he stays at home and watches pornography. His beer-bellied next door neighbor comes over to watch with him, then drops a bombshell: "I know what's going on with (you and your daughter) Lisa... That's pretty juicy gossip. I'll keep quiet, old buddy, if we can share and share alike!" WHOA! The story suddenly kicks into hyper-gear. The very next panel, henpecked Henry is catching another bombshell, this time from his doctor who just ran tests on Lisa. She has Herpes! And she told the doctor how her daddy and his neighbor are to blame! He screams that she is a liar, but the wise old doctor doesn't buy it. Just when you expect the police to arrive and cart Henry off, the doctor launches into a sermon about Jesus and forgiveness. Henry instantly converts (hey, it beats the big house!) and mums the word on daddy's dirty deeds. Henry races home and tells his wife he's saved. She admits she knew about the molestation all along, because her *!%* uncle did the same thing to her (so it's a family tradition). They pray together and tears flood from every eyeball. They call Lisa and we see how young she really is for the first time. It's shocking. She still carries a teddy bear and looks maybe five years old. We're talking MAJOR molestation and rape here, but all seems forgiven. Never mind the incurable child Herpes, or the unrepentant next door neighbor. The important thing is, another saved soul. I must be vindictive, because I wanted to see someone dive into the Lake, or at least get raped in prison. Giving the perp a good dose of AIDS would have been poetic justice. Instead, nobody is pun-

LITTLE GHOST **Review:** (Art by Chick ©2001.) I had high hopes for a tract with "Ghost" in the title. Unfortunately, it turns out this is one of the dreaded kiddy tracts, drawn in the same simplistic style as *Best Friend,* but with even less detail in the background. In fact, I can think of only one other tract that leaves as much blank space, and that would be *The Great One.* (Which was anything but!) This tract's plot involves a couple of boys who try to scare a girl by wearing a devil and ghost Halloween costume. She gives them an earful about how nothing scares her because Jesus loves her. At one point, she breaks out in spontaneous song, singing *Jesus Loves The Little Children.* It's painful enough to watch, I can only imagine what it must sound like. I don't think kids like primitive art and plots devoid of detail. (I know I didn't when I was that age.) But since most adults *think* kids are stupid, Chick is probably wise to make a few tracts like this, because let's face it: The adults are the ones buying the tracts for the kids. The other marketing motive behind this tract is that parents can pass it out during Halloween instead of candy—not a bad idea at all. (It's certainly cheaper than a *Snickers* chocolate bar.) And who knows? Maybe kids like the blank white areas to color with their crayons. All the characters have big wide eyes, which —big surprise— are crying tears of joy once they realize how much Jesus loves them. My eyes were crying too—but only when I considered all the talent and trees that were wasted creating this tract. Still, as Clinton would say with his trembling lower lip, this was "for the children." So let's be generous since Chick's motives were good. Grade: **C** for Cutesy. (Follow up trivia: This tract sold 300,000 copies in the first couple months of release. Once again Chick's shrewd market sense hits pay dirt!) **Still in print.**

THE LITTLE PRINCESS

J.T.C.

Just think, that's four Christians saved due in part to Halloween. Maybe it's not such a bad holiday after all? Especially if you use it to distribute *Death Cookies* (the tract version, not the food.) The German version of this tract is noteworthy because it has a different cover and title (*Sandras Grosster Wunsch*). She doesn't wear a costume and neither does her brother. Many panels are redrawn to reflect this change and the absence of a crown.

A rather depressing story, except for Josh, who inherited a bigger bedroom out of the deal. Grade: **B+** for Beaming Brother. **Still in print.**

©1998 Jack T. Chick.

THE LONG TRIP

J.T.C.

©1994 Jack T. Chick.

THE LITTLE PRINCESS Review: (Art by Chick ©1998.) If you like the sappy tracts best, then this is probably one of your favorites. It's also one of the few Halloween tracts that doesn't call the holiday Satanic. In fact, it owes the happy ending to the trick-or-treat tradition. Little Heidi is dying and her big wish is to celebrate Halloween before she dies. (She must be a Druid.) She goes as a princess and her brother goes as a cowboy. The last house she visits belongs to the Smiths. They spike their candy with Chick tracts! As she leaves the Smiths, the husband observes that Heidi is "in trouble." His wife decides, "Let's go pray for her **right now.**"

Later that evening, Heidi gets saved reading the tract. But what about mom, dad, and brother Josh? She screams for them and they come running. False alarm... She just wants them to ask the Smiths over so she can talk to them. Daddy delivers the summons and the Smiths race over. Heidi tells them, "I only have a few days left to live, so if you hadn't given me that little book, I might have ended up in hell." She continues, "Mom, dad and Josh don't know any of this. Would you *please* share it with them?" (This is the Christian equivalent to inviting a vampire into your home. Once someone *asks* for preaching, they can't take back the request!) The Smiths are more than happy to oblige. "Folks, it's no accident that Millie and I are here tonight. This is a *divine appointment.*"

You can guess the rest of the story. The family coverts and Heidi goes to heaven that very night. (She thought she had several more days left. Sorry kid, Josh gets to eat all your candy!) The next-to-last panel shows Heidi running to God in three forms: A Faceless God (regular human size, not the usual giant from Great White Throne of Judgment), Jesus with the pierced hands, and the dove hovering over them both. No telling which one she's going to embrace first. (If she's like most kids, it will be the pigeon. And she'll probably squeeze it too hard.) The last image shows Josh putting Heidi's crown on top of her tombstone. "My little sister is in heaven because she trusted Jesus." Chick's warning, "How about you?"

THE LONG TRIP Review: (Art by Chick ©1994.) Here's a tract with a pretty good twist ending. It has a rather depressing premise, epitomized briefly on page three: "Sometimes it's a long, long trip from the cradle to the grave." The tract follows the progress of the baby as he grows. "At one year, John has a mind of his own. Only 69 more years to go." John enters a big freeway of pedestrians marching toward their deaths. He's surrounded by Muslims, Jews, Chinese, Catholics, Hindus, etc. "By age 20, John has all the answers... just ask him. He has 50 years left." (A pretty sarcastic but accurate portrayal of youth.) John grows older and gets a wife and kids who join him on the highway of life. "By 50, John no longer has all the answers. He's only got 20 years left." (This is where the stress starts to build up.)

Then they pass a detour with a Christian holding a sign saying "Good News." He warns the other travelers that they are heading toward destruction. John's wife and kids leave him on the highway and take the path to heaven. They call after John to join them but he says the path is too narrow and he needs time to think about it. An older man with a goatee agrees with John that the rest of his family was too hasty. The white haired man looks like Col. Sanders of *Kentucky Fried Chicken* fame. He reminds John that he has eight more years to think about it, so why rush? Six months later, John reaches the end of the road and gets pushed off by the crowd of humanity behind him. As he falls into Hades, the mask of Col. Sanders flies off and reveals Satan. John complains that he was supposed to live until 70, and Satan laughs: "I lied! I tricked you! And now you're mine...FOREVER! Haw Haw Haw!" (So John gets fried until he's finger-licking good.)

This tract is brief but powerful. What makes it especially interesting is the way we are also tricked along with John. We also thought he would live until he was 70. And if we can be tricked like John was, that means we can also wind up in the same place. But wait a minute—the reason we believed he would live until 70 is because the narrator (writer) told us that from the very start. That means the liar was Chick! Haw-haw-haw! You can't trust *anyone* these days... Grade **B** for plan B (the other path). **Still in print.**

assumes the position and recites the sinner's prayer, adding an extra prayer request for strength to face the bullies. The two thugs approach Tommy and notice he looks different. When he says he now has a very powerful friend protecting him, the bullies suddenly want to become his buddy. (Kids, I urge you not to try this tactic at home. Not unless you have a good dental plan.) It's another *Leave It To Beaver* happy ending!

Favorite Panel Award goes to page 8. A pagan priest plops an infant into a pit of fire before a giant idol of a hooded cobra. Pretty spooky! Grade: **B+** for Busted Baal idols. **Still in print.**

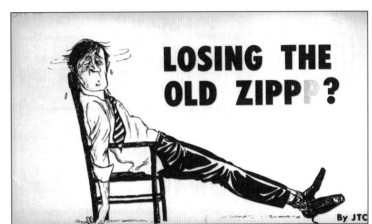

©2002 Jack T. Chick.

THE LOSER Review: (Art by Chick ©2002.) Tract #10 of 25 Bible tracts starring Bob. Two kids are terrorizing Tommy. (One of thugs looks like the bully from *Toy Story*, complete with the trademark skull & crossbones black t-shirt. Tommy resembles the lead in *Leave It To Beaver*.) Tommy runs away and bumps into Bob, who happens to be raking some leaves. Bob takes the kid inside and starts to evangelize. He tells how the Jews escaped Egyptian slavery but soon turned away from God. They backslide into Baal worship and become terrorized by the Midianites. One of those most afraid of the Midianites was a Jew named Gideon. God sends an angel to tell him to rebel against the Midianites. Gideon tears down a Baal statue. He kills the ox he used to destroy the idol and sacrifices it on the empty altar. (That's gratitude!) When the locals find the idol vandalized, they set out to punish the culprit. It's eerily reminiscent of the outrage felt by the international community after the Taliban destroyed a Buddhist statue—except God didn't help defend the Taliban like he did Gideon's warriors. In fact, God orders Gideon to *reduce* his army from 32,000 to only 300, to make the victory all the more impressive. Countless Midianites gather to attack. Gideon's 300 troops surround the pagan camp at night and light lanterns to scare them. The scheme works. The Midianites panic and kill each other in the chaos.

What does all this have to do with Tommy? Well, according to Bob, both Gideon and Tommy are LOSERS! (So much for self-esteem.) The good news is that God loves losers, providing they accept Christ. Tommy

©1972 Jack T. Chick.

LOSING THE OLD ZIPPP? Review: (Art by Carter ©1972.) This tract is one of the five super rare promo tracts produced around 1970. Unlike the others, however, this one was drawn by Fred Carter and is one of his earliest efforts. It opens with a two page story of a smug Christian explaining why he no longer uses tracts. They were ineffective, he says, and a waste of his time. The other fellow in the panel disagrees. He says he was saved by tracts. When the first Christian asks the second one who gave him the tract, the guy answers, "You did!"

Occasionally, Chick gets carried away with the military analogies and they cross the line beyond good taste. An example is a panel on page 6 showing a jet dropping bombs. It says, "In warfare, some bombs are used with a delayed action—the pilot never knows the results." Didn't Princess Diana campaign against tracts like these? It's hard to imagine a more politically incorrect comparison. The best I could make up was, "Leave these tracts lying around like land mines. Then when a sinner stumbles across one, it will BLOW HIM AWAY!" (Yeah, I know, Chick's version is better.)

The booklet gives several testimonials of people who were saved by tracts, pointing out how most readers take time before they convert.

One such story devotes six panels to showing what happened when a hitchhiker left a tract in a car. "He had sown the seed. Notice the driver was not impressed. He threw the copy of *This Was Your Life* in the glove compartment. It was soon forgotten. Weeks passed. Beset by problems, this man came to a state of despair. He connected a hose to the exhaust pipe of his car. He put the hose through the window, turned on the ignition, and at that point he remembered his family. He searched the glove compartment for paper to write a farewell note and found the copy of *This Was Your Life*. He read it and found Christ just in time!" It's quite a tale, all the more exciting because it's true. But then Chick includes an ending that is a bit of a downer. "A few months later, he died of cancer." So much for the happy ending!

Readers are told that three tracts a day equal over a thousand per year, at a cost of just five minutes a day. More testimonials are provided, including one with a hippie girl wearing a headband. "We know of one 20 year old girl who was a revolutionist. She was with a group that tried to blow up a police station. Somewhere she found a copy of *Bewitched*. It led her to Christ. Now she is a radiant soul-winner!"

Several more stories are crammed into a box without graphics. "A 15 year old girl came to my house for dinner. She was reading a horoscope book and was interested in witchcraft. I gave her *The Thing*. She read it. She threw away her book on astrology and said she wanted nothing more to do with it. And she gave her heart to Jesus. Thanks to your wonderful booklet this girl was changed."

"I gave a copy of *The Poor Revolutionist!* to a long-haired, rebellious fellow who was full of anti-American hatred. He was sharp, real sharp. A very hard case. He read the booklet and came to Christ that night."

"One year ago a boy was at my house and read one of your tracts and at the time he was on L.S.D. and that night God saved him and he is called to preach. Praise God." Imagine giving someone hallucinating a copy of *Demon's Nightmare* or *Somebody Goofed*. Talk about a bad trip!

Page 19 says, "Make sure you continue your outreach to gas station attendants, neighbors, even by mail if you're shy. But make sure NO one will point a finger at you at the Judgment and say..." Below, an angel drags a sinner away to hell while the victim screams, "Why didn't they warn me?" His friends turn away in shame and think, "We were too occupied with things."

The tract also includes a postage paid order form which readers can fill out and order tracts for just 5 cents each. Isn't preventing embarrassment in the afterlife worth a nickel? If that's not incentive enough, read on to the inside back cover. It's the only known tract to replace the Sinner's prayer with a four-panel cartoon explaining that the more people a Christian converts on Earth, the bigger the Christian's mansion is in heaven. It's quite amusing and wins our coveted Favorite Panel Award.

This is a fun and interesting tract, probably outdated by too many references to tracts that were soon retired (like *The Poor Revolutionist!*) It's also neat to see a sample of Carter's early work. Grade **B+** for Big potential! **Value: Speculative.**

© 1977 Jack T. Chick.

A LOVE STORY **Review:** (Art by Chick © 1977, 2002.) This is one of Chick's worst efforts. The artwork is generic and features long shots of planets, clouds (with souls rising), close-ups of eyelids, anything that's easy to dash off. Even the text is sparse. One page says nothing but: "Now... If you've done that..." Another page is blank except for the sentence "Only God Almighty". Talk about wasted space! Perhaps this one was done under a deadline or something. (The contractual obligation tract?) The only good panel is the one with a Christian walking down the street and an angel holding back a criminal. We know the crook is evil because he has a bad haircut, didn't shave, and smokes. It's not really a story, but a basic questionnaire asking the reader who loves them the most, who died for their sins, who wants them to go to heaven, etc. It answers each question with a big JESUS! If you want to see how bad other tracts on the market are, read this one because they rate about this (bad) quality. Then read any other Chick tract and see how much better they are in comparison. We expect much better work from Chick, and 99% of the time, we get it. Everyone deserves a little slack now and then, so this must be Jack's *slack tract*. Grade: **D-** for Disappointing. **Still in print.**

© 1998 Jack T. Chick.

LOVE THE JEWISH PEOPLE **Review: (A.k.a.** *Support Your Local Jew* **and** *Jeopardy.* Art by Carter ©1976, 1992, & 1998.) Here's a tract that Chick critics usually ignore, because it shows Chick is **not** anti-Semitic. In fact, his support for the "Chosen Race" is so fanatical, some consider it humorous. Did you know that God promised the Jews, "I will bless them that bless thee, and curse them that curseth thee"? (Page 8.) God was actually talking to Abraham, but Chick applies it to the entire race forever and ever. (A good Jewish lawyer could have broken that contract easily.) This tract is full of similar one-sided interpretations. "Egypt built her empire using Jewish slaves, and look what a backward country THAT is!" (Page 5.) They're so poor, they're the second largest recipient of US foreign aid, requiring nearly $3 billion a year. *What losers.* But guess who's the **largest** recipient getting $6 billion a year? That's right, Israel! Such obvious counter arguments get left out of this tract, but I'm sure it's only because of space limitations. (*Haw-haw-haw!*) Instead, we get other juicy nuggets of Jewish trivia (page 6): "When mighty Rome ruled the world the Jews were mistreated under its iron fist. Where is the Roman empire today?" True, the Roman Empire has broken up. But only after lasting longer and prospering more than any other nation in history. Undaunted by such facts, Chick plows ahead. Germany killed 6 million in the holocaust so— "Judgment fell on Germany! It is now a divided nation, never to rise again. 1/2 is now under communist slavery." This info gets removed in later tracts after Germany not only reunites, but becomes the richest nation in Europe. There's plenty more examples: Britain, Russia, Africa, and, of course, the Pope. (Page 7.) "Israel's deadliest enemy is the Vatican. To date, she has **never** recognized Israel as a nation." This statement is later altered after the Vatican **does** recognize Israel. It's converted into a terse statement that, "Israel will regret any agreements with Rome".

Basically, Chick picks and chooses the facts to support his premise and ignores everything else. It's a process he utilizes in *many* tracts, but normally, to **criticize** a group or religion rather than to support them. (I guess there's a first time for everything.) But the most glaring problem with this instance is what happens if you apply the same logic to Israel itself. Not many people have suffered more than the Jews. If the holocaust is God's idea of blessing his chosen race, gee, I dunno... I think I'd rather be cursed! And Israel certainly has its own sinister streak. Few modern nations mistreat their minorities worse than Israel. Palestinians are treated much the same way as blacks were under Apartheid. So presenting Israel as an innocent little nation that deserves our blind loyalty is a bit of a hard sell. However, Chick is not one to shy away from a challenge.

This tract offends about every foreign nation EXCEPT Israel, and even **they** probably despise it for its last page effort to convert Jews to Christianity. (Chick can't resist tossing in that final pitch.) In summary, you gotta love this tract, simply because everyone else **hates** it. It's even printed in Arabic! You know that one must go over really well! Grade: **A-** for Antagonism. **Still in print.**

©1982 Jack T. Chick.

MACHO! **Review:** (Art by Carter ©1982.) You might describe this tract as *Alberto* meets *Iran Contra!* A group of communist rebels take over the US embassy somewhere in South America. The US Secretary declares the hostages are basically dead meat because, "those who were captured knew in advance that we would not pay ransom nor negotiate with the rebel forces."

Meanwhile, back at the embassy, we get our first look at the rebels. It's the usual cast of misfits, except one happens to be wearing a priest collar under his combat fatigues. Sure enough, it's a Catholic priest who preaches and practices Liberation Theology. (You know—Jesus was a communist rebel. Rise up and revolt for Rome. That sort of thing.) The priest can't wait to kill the Protestant missionary found in the embassy. But the missionary is unafraid and explains, "You can't kill me unless your father gets permission from my Lord Jesus." The priest asks who his father is and the captive shouts, *"The devil!"*

One of the Catholic commies is unamused by the answer and yells, "Holy mother of God! *I'll kill him!* Tie him to the chair." He then does some heavy duty dentist work on the missionary's mouth using the butt of his machine gun. The missionary willingly accepts the beating rather than call the priest "Father," (which is a big fundamentalist no-no according to Matthew 23:9).

The rebel leader calls off the torture. "You're very macho," Carlos tells the battered evangelist. "Lots of guts. You would have made a good communist." The missionary says he **was** a communist, until he discovered that communism was created by the Jesuits for the Vatican. Carlos is outraged and doesn't believe it, but listens to the missionary for the next 16 pages anyway. Not much action occurs, but plenty of Alberto allegations and footnotes advertising anti-Vatican books cram the remaining pages. Carter's artwork is great, but how many different ways can one draw two guys talking Catholic conspiracies locked inside a room? We see close-ups of his bloody face, we see exterior shots of the embassy, we see rebels guarding the exits. It gets rather ridiculous after a while. We even get a bird's-eye view from above the compound on page 20! My favorite variation shows a long shot of the two men in dark silhouette with a large desk fan looming in the foreground. (This tract must have really hit the fan!)

Bet you'll never guess what happens in the end: Carlos converts to Christianity and commits his life to Christ. (Okay, so maybe you *did* guess.) The hostages are set free and it's another happy ending. (Except for Carlos, who will probably meet Jesus sooner than he expected when his commie commanders learn he surrendered the embassy.)

Interesting trivia: Page 19 seems to toss the leftists a bone when it states that the wealth will be distributed to the poor and hungry, but only after the thousand year rule of Jesus Christ. (Sorry Hanoi Jane, but not in **your** lifetime!)

Favorite Panel Award goes to page 3. It shows a bullet-ridden embassy with Carlos barking orders to captives strewn across the floor. Other panels have little to offer the eye but plenty to feed the imagination. Page 10 features a big swastika (which is always good for grabbing attention).

It states, "Communism was rebellious (against its Papal parent). So the Vatican created another strong daughter to bring communism to her knees. The Jesuits, with Vatican money, built Hitler's 3rd Reich to serve Pope Pius XII, not only to murder 6 million Jews but to whip the communists and convert them to Catholicism. Hitler lost the war. So the Vatican used another approach." That *other* approach was the wooing of Russia by picking a communist Pope from Poland. The missionary explains, "Vatican experts today have written off the United States saying it will lose the war against Russia. The Vatican will only back a winner!"

If that's true, the Vatican is sure on a losing streak when it comes to picking a winner. Not only did Hitler fail, but the Soviet Union went belly up as well. (Perhaps if we can get the Vatican to support Cuba, we might finally get rid of Castro!) Seriously though, times have changed a lot since this tract was written. More Americans are worried about heart attacks than they are Russian military attacks. Such claims made this title dated, so the company stopped offering it for custom printing in late 2002 due to lack of sales. However, it's still a treasured tract for collectors and is tough to come by. Grade: **B++** for Big Bad Bolsheviks. **Value: $35.**

cerned if patients have insurance rather than if the therapy is working. They apply so much electroshock treatment, that recipients literally jolt off the tables. Inmates are pumped high enough with drugs that they appear to fly around the rooms. When one patient asks the psychiatrist how she can alleviate the guilt she feels from sin, he answers, "Sin is outmoded. The solution is simple. Blame it on your mother."

The correct answer, according to Chick, it to turn your life over to the Lord. A reporter interviews such a Christian whose husband has died. She has no relatives, no money, and suffers from cancer. He listens in disbelief as the woman claims to have peace of mind and no stress. In a glowing testimonial reminiscent of late night infomercials selling miracle products, she turns to the audience and beams, "I have eternal life and will reign with Christ throughout eternity. Now I call *THAT* real good therapy!"

This tract was published in 1975 after Watergate. Inflation, unemployment, and low national self-esteem were rampant. That feeling of hopelessness was begging to be exploited by someone and Chick was obviously up to the task. Favorite Panel Award goes to page 11a where a reporter interviews a chemist. The caricature of the dorky scientist with thick glasses is even more hilarious than its geeky chemist counterpart in *The Simpsons.* Grade **B** for Bad Medicine. **Still in print.**

©1975 Jack T. Chick.

After Noah's flood,* Satan created the Whore in ancient Babylon** by Nimrod and his wife, Semiramis.

Their occultic religion had priests and confessionals to control the people.

*See "It's Coming" **See "The Two Babylons" by Hislop

After Nimrod died, Semiramis gave birth to a son who she *claimed* was Nimrod reincarnated. She was worshiped as the "Queen of Heaven"…

Pray for us now…

…and at the hour of our death.

SEMIRAMIS

…and a billion people still do today.

©2003 Jack T. Chick.

THE MAD MACHINE Review: (Art by Chick ©1975.) Here's an optimistic tract. The basic premise is that the world is going crazy and falling to pieces. Stress and despair are everywhere. The only way to find happiness and inner peace (especially when you're dying) is with Jesus. There are plenty of comic punch lines to keep the audience amused. Page 3: A frustrated man exclaims, "I've had it! Everything is caving in on me. I'm going to see my shrink!" His wife responds, "You can't! He's seeing *HIS* shrink today!" Page 6b: A lady complains, "My husband ran off with someone else." Her friend responds, "That's terrible! Who is she?" The first lady replies, "It wasn't a 'she'. It was a 'he'!" Page 16b: A nurse asks a co-worker, "Where's Dr. Hyde (the shrink)? He's late!" The other nurse answers, "Didn't you hear? He committed suicide!" These little vignettes serve as dark comic reminders that everyone has problems, including the mental health "experts." Many of the secular cures are presented as jokes as well. The staff at *Happy Halls Asylum* is more con-

MAN IN BLACK Review: (Art by Chick ©2003.) Tract #23 in the series of 25 featuring Bob Williams. Bob Williams is driving across a bridge when he notices a drunk Catholic priest about to jump to his death. He stops to intervene. He talks the priest out of suicide, but not without a price. In exchange, he gets to lecture the priest about how the Catholic Church is really The Great Whore of Babylon. At first, the priest thinks it's disrespectful, but he doesn't put up much of a fight. After all, Bob saved his life, gave him a ride in his car, and bought him a hot cup of Joe. (So I guess he owes him.) Bob recites a long list of Catholic conspiracies, including the one where Queen Semiramis evolves into the Queen of Heaven, A.K.A., the Virgin Mary. Scenes of religious persecution are illustrated, including an image where a grieving Christian forgives Roman Centurions as they finish killing the Christian's family…and their dog, too!

(Don't be deceitful—tell him where the cat is hiding.) Bob explains how Emperor Constantine pretended to be a Christian but also worshipped the sun. Satan's agents rewrote the Bible in Alexandria, so as to create a counterfeit church. "In just 25 years, the Whore was in control. The first pope died and shortly the world was plunged into the Dark Ages." It's been downhill ever since.

Bob skims over a few centuries. "Civilization collapsed. Life became a nightmare. Vandals plundered, raped, and destroyed Europe. Rome built monasteries and cathedrals. The ignorant masses looked to them for help but were taught only idolatry and superstition. The popes were the new Caesars, and each one claimed to be Christ on Earth. Even the kings served the popes, believing that they ruled as Christ. Satan had created his own **anti-christ**, who blasphemed the Word of God."

The backsliding priest finally pipes up, "Then Peter was **not** the first pope?" Bob fires back, **"No!** That was another lie. They uncovered his body in Jerusalem, ***not** Rome. (*See *The Crusaders: The Four Horsemen*, pg. 20.)"

Another panel shows a rogue's gallery of thugs glaring at the reader. The unusual thing about these cruel criminals is that most of them are Catholic priests, monks, and popes. Oh sure, there's a few Mafia Dons and Ku Klux Klanners thrown in the batch for good measure, but most of them are clearly Catholics. (Sorry, no Nazis. Chick must have run out of room.) "Because Vatican City controls the wealth of the world, she can create wars to enhance her power, making all the world leaders shake in their boots. She is the greatest enemy of Jesus on this planet."

And you thought Chick was getting mellow with age? *You don't know Jack!*

Two dynamite images juxtapose the horrors of the Inquisition with scenes of lecherous popes fondling whores and priests kissing one another. "The unbridled lust of the popes: intermarriage, pedophilia, incest and occult murders—all this filth has been swept under the rug." (These two scenes of perverse pleasure and pain deservedly win our treasured Favorite Panel Award.)

The priest confesses to Bob, "A priest I knew said he actually saw those files in the Vatican. **It's all true!**" (That unnamed priest must have been Alberto.)

With a little prompting from Bob, the priest soon falls to the floor to squeeze out a tear and recite The Sinner's Prayer. Of course, it could just be the booze talking. There's no telling what the priest will think after he sleeps it off. But Bob can proudly carve another notch in his Gun of Salvation. Lock the doors and hide! *The Gospel Gunslinger is a-coming to town!*

There's plenty of action, violence, conspiracies, and vivid images to keep this tract interesting from start to finish. (Check out the cool seven-headed dragon and sexy harlot on page 6.) It wins an **A** for Audacity, because not too many folks would have the *chutzpah* to try and convert a priest! **Still in print.**

***MISS UNIVERSE* Review:** (Art by Carter ©1987.) This is the Old Testament story of Esther, a Jew living in the Persian palace of King Ahasuerus. Uncle Mordecai tells Esther to keep her Jewish roots secret. The king divorces his queen and holds a beauty contest to select the next queen. He picks Esther, unaware that she is a Jewess. Mordecai protects his royal investment by snitching on an assassination plot against the king. The assassins are executed, but nobody rewards Mordecai for tattling. An official named Haman arrives on the scene. He's an Agagite who hates the Jews, and with reason: "Almost 500 years earlier, God commanded the first king of Israel, King Saul, to utterly destroy Amalek. But Saul didn't kill them all [the Agagites]. He disobeyed God... Because of this sin, the Agagites survived and multiplied, and eventually Haman was born, to serve Satan." (In other words, Saul's big crime was refusal to carry out genocide. Good thing no one mentioned this at Nuremberg.)

Haman decides its time for some payback. He convinces the king to have the Jews executed on a certain day. Mordecai urges his niece to intervene. She plots to have Haman invited to her banquet and embarrass him before the king. Haman unintentionally helps by sticking his foot in his mouth about Mordecai, forgetting it was he who blew the whistle on the king's assassination plot. At the party, Esther reveals she is a Jew and begs the king to spare her life from the enemy Haman. The king is furious at Haman. Haman begs Esther for his life, but she shows no mercy. He's hung on the same gallows he prepared for Mordecai. "A new law was sent out showing the king and his army were now on the side of the Jews, giving the Jews authority to kill anyone who threatened them... Many of the people became Jews for the fear of the Jews fell upon them." (Love us *or else!*)

The last few pages tell of Jesus and warn about other enemies of Israel. "Like Haman, another enemy of the Jews will come to power. The Bible calls him 'The Beast,' the most evil man to walk the Earth." The picture shows a man dressed in Catholic robes. Armageddon is outlined. A final challenge is issued to readers to join the winning side and accept Jesus. "Who will you serve? Jesus Christ? Satan? The Choice is Yours."

It's fun to watch the "evil Gentile" getting trapped by his own schemes, but there is also a disturbing subtext here. The Jews win the day by being sneaky and conniving... not to mention Esther was acting like a whore by offering herself to the King for reasons of power and wealth. It seems opposite of the "proclaim your faith no matter the consequences" message expressed in other tracts like *Burn Baby Burn*. Should Jews lie about being Jewish or not? And what does this mean for Christians? Should they do as Peter did and deny their faith when it benefits them? You won't find the answer in this tract. Favorite Panel Award goes to the banquet scene on page 2. It's a gorgeous panorama of royal splendor. Grade: **B+** for Beauty contest. Value: **$8**.

©2002 Jack T. Chick.

THE MONSTER Review: (Art by Chick ©2002.) This is tract #16 of 25 featuring Bob Williams. A.J. is a very nasty boss. He's arrogant and he throws coffee at his secretary—who happens to be Shirley Shepherd, the former prostitute who turned herself over to Jesus in tract #8. Now she's all prim and proper and wears her hair in a tight little bun. The new outfit looks good on her and she would probably earn top dollar if she went back to turning tricks. But let's not go there...

Shirley doesn't like being a hot coffee target and calls Bob to complain. "My boss is a **monster!** I can't stand him. He's **so** awful that I've stopped praying for him!" Bob reels. "You mustn't stop, Shirley," Bob implores, "This is a battle for his **soul.**" That night, Bob calls his Gang of Four together: *The Last Judge, the Outcast,* the *It's Coming* babe, and of course, his dutiful wife. It's a *Who's Who* of Chick tract celebs. They combine forces and pray as a power pack to conjure up some holy mo-jo and direct it toward A.J.

The next week, his life falls apart. He loses his big business deal, his son gets arrested for drugs, his daughter gets knocked up, and his wife demands a divorce. Shirley phones Bob to announce the good news. "Man, is God ever working on Mr. Jennings! He's a wreck. He's even asking me what he should do. I told him about you guys. Could you come over here?" Does the I.R.S. like taxes? OF COURSE! Bob races over to

console the weeping A.J. and slip in a sermon or two. He tells about how king Nebuchadnezzar was arrogant and God made him go insane for seven years, reducing the leader to a mental case who ate grass like an ox. Once Nebby-the-nut repents, he returns to being a great king. A.J. doesn't take the hint. Bob has to explain that A.J. is hated by everyone and is on his way to hell. A sweating A.J. retorts, "You're scaring me to death. What shall I do?" A few panels later, A.J. is reciting the Sinner's Prayer. All the employees rejoice and the world becomes a better place. Bob turns to us and announces, "A.J. got **saved!** Jesus **took over** his life and He can do the same for **you!**" With ringing endorsements like that, who can resist such a fabulous deal?

Favorite Panel Award goes to page 16B. Nebuchadnezzar grabs his head with his hands and goes cross-eyed as God drives him insane. It's the same expression many motorists give when trapped in gridlock. Grade: **B+** for Big Bad Boss. **Still in print.**

©1999 Jack T. Chick.

MURPH Review: (Art by Chick ©1999.) This anti-Vatican tract is about two policemen, a good cop and a bad cop. The bad cop isn't really *that* bad. He just happens to be a member of a Satanic cult, also pronounced *Catholic* (according to fundamentalists). Actually, this tract isn't anywhere near that inflammatory, but there's still plenty of little digs to work up the Irish in many Roman readers. It begins with a typical police stereotype: Two cops with Irish names are snacking at the donut bar when a bank robbery is reported. Murph (the Catholic) complains, "@!!!**! This happens **every time** I order a sprinkled donut." Donovan (his Christian partner) admonishes him, "How many times have I asked you not to take the Lord's name in vain?" (Relax Donovan, this will be the *last* time. Murph's about to bite the big one.) The litterbugs leave their unfinished coffee and donuts in the parking lot and take off in the patrol car.

At the bank, the two cops barge into the robbery in progress. Not surprisingly, the robbers shoot at them. Donovan jumps in front of his partner. Both are hit. The doctor at the hospital informs Donovan he was lucky because he only has flesh wounds. Murph, however, isn't going to make it. Doc doesn't say how long the partner will last, so Donovan takes his time before checking on him. Thirty minutes pass before he makes it up to see his dying buddy. (Maybe he had to stop off to finish that half-eaten donut.) Murph is plugged into I.V.s and receiving oxygen through a nose tube. He asks Donovan why he intercepted some of his bullets. Donovan says, "Because I'm ready to die, Murph... and *YOU'RE NOT!*" (So much for tact.)

The two debate the finer points of Christianity over Catholicism. Donovan informs Murph that purgatory was an invention of the Catholic Church. He says, "Think about it. Would a God who really loves you want you live not knowing if you were headed for an eternity in a lake of fire?" Murph admits that would be pretty cruel, but he wants to check with his priest before making any hasty conversions. When the priest gets around to visiting, he tells Murph that any Protestant guarantees of salvation are really wicked sins of presumption. Murph counters that he saw it in the Bible. "You need MORE than just the Bible," replies the priest, "You also need the magisterium and the traditions of the church. And church tradition says that NOBODY, not even popes, can know where they will go when they die." The priest admits that the Catholic Church invented purgatory, but insists that such traditions are infallible.

All this doesn't wash too well with Murph. The priest leaves Murph alone to die, which is a big mistake, because Donovan is waiting in the wings to intercept another soul from Satan. He pops in with a big surprise: He tells Murph he used to be a Catholic also! But one day... "a real friend loved me enough to open his Bible and show me that salvation was a Free Gift! When I received that gift, my spiritual eyes were opened... I also saw how deceptive Catholicism is. Rather than offering people freedom in Christ...it keeps them in bondage to the church." Murph starts breaking out in a hot sweat. (Maybe he feels the fires of hell closing in on him.) Donovan seizes the opportunity and applies the hard sell: "It's time to choose, Murph. It's Christ or dead religion. And your time is running out." Murph agrees. "I'd be a fool to trust in man," he gasps, "I gotta go with the word of God." Donovan helps him pray. The fever suddenly breaks and Murph is all smiles. "WOW! Now I know what you were talking about... I'm READY to die!" Good, because the very next page, *Murph* is not of this *Earth*.

Although Chick's disdain for the Catholic system is still quite noticeable in this 1999 tract, he makes a more subtle attempt to persuade potential converts by using the carrot as opposed to the whip. Heaven and the Free Gift of Salvation are repeatedly emphasized, whereas the Lake of Fire is only mentioned once. Strident terms like "The Great Whore" and "Death Cookie" are nowhere to be found in this tract. This is probably the closest Chick gets to *Détente*. He's still at war with Rome, but it's calmed down from *all out attack* mode to cold war status. That's good for getting along, but alas, it's just not as enjoyable as the hard-core in-your-face tracts. Interesting note: The German title for this tract is *Harry*, and the Spanish version is *Pancho*. Grade **B+** for Banks & Bandits. **Still in print.**

MY NAME?... IN THE VATICAN? Review: (Art by Chick ©1980.) Forgive me Father, for I have sinned...I read the forbidden text of *My Name in the Vatican* and loved it! But how could anyone resist this tract? It's so thrilling and conspiracy filled that even ardent Catholics can't avoid turning the pages. Oh sure, they condemn it, just like they condemn abortions. But that doesn't mean Catholics never **get** abortions. Likewise, I suspect millions of copies of this scarce tract are in the private collections of Catholics. They tend to either hate it or find it hysterically funny. Or both! Either way, it's a great conversation piece and fun to show the priest while the kids are outside running around during their confirmation party. Protestants get a kick out of this one too. To say it's dramatic doesn't begin to do it justice. Check out these opening lines: "Yes! The name of every Protestant church member in the world is being recorded in the Big Computer in the Vatican. This is being done by the dreaded Roman Catholic 'Holy Office' (Office of the General Inquisitor)." Sure enough, the next panel shows a group of hooded clergy in a dungeon area, pointing accusing fingers at an innocent Protestant as the torches burn ominously from the walls. "Big Brother wants to keep you in the dark about it, but you should know that the Holy Office is alive and well in the 20th century, and will soon be back in business as usual." What does that mean? Turn the page and see for yourself. Christians get *BURNED AT THE STAKE* as the Pope looks on and others hold a banner of Mary (who is probably enjoying the show as well). Chick warns, "Ever hear of the Inquisition? From 1200 A.D. to 1800 A.D.? It's never mentioned any longer. We hear a lot about the Jewish Holocaust when six million Jews were murdered under Hitler. But most people don't know that Adolph [sic] Hitler was a Roman Catholic and an instrument of the Holy Office. Nor did they know that Pope Pius XII called Hitler the 'Defender of the faith'... Why has the Inquisition been covered up? Because the total number of victims of this atrocity reached 68 million people." Now THIS is what you call an *IN YOUR FACE TRACT!*

The next panel shows a bound victim quivering as the priest points at him and declares, "Burn the heretic." Chick explains, "The victims were ALWAYS found guilty. They never knew who accused them. They never had lawyers, and no one would dare lift a finger to help." Then he rhetorically asks, "You mean this nightmare will be repeated?" Okay—lets pause for a moment and predict Chick's answer before turning the page. All the optimists can stay after school and clean the erasers. The answer is (naturally) *HELL, YEAH!* Chick states, "According to the Bible it will. We always figured in the far distant future, right? **WRONG!** The Holy Office is getting ready for action NOW. Big Brother never dreamed one of their top undercover agents who worked in their intelligence division would truly find Christ and blow their game plans wide open." Enter Alberto! His proud profile adorns the very next page. "The man who broke away is Dr. Alberto Rivera, an Ex-Jesuit priest whose job it was to infiltrate and destroy Protestant churches."

Believe it or not, it keeps getting better. How the Vatican tried to silence Alberto, Chick publications, and blackmail Christian bookstores from carrying the Alberto comic. "Satan is so upset about this book that he will stop at nothing to kill its message." Sure enough, high-ranking, cigar-chomping priests are pictured huddled around a conference table plotting ways to suppress Chick's comic books. "Rome moved like lightning as soon as the first copies of Alberto arrived in the Vatican. And so the machine went into action!" The very notion that the most powerful organized religion in the world was having back room emergency sessions in order to put Chick out of business is somewhat self-congratulatory to say the least. But what would **you** think if it happened to you? Chick lost two-thirds of his business virtually overnight. Otherwise democratic nations like Canada banned his comics from crossing their borders. The phone lines lit up with angry callers threatening to destroy Chick Publications. Chick probably figured that if it walks and talks like a well organized and heavily funded attack campaign, it is one.

How much of this tract is true and how much of it is Bull (that's Vatican humor) is something each reader will have to decide for himself. But even Francis E. Dec would have to admire the elaborate conspiracy theory that is meticulously cataloged in this hard-core rant (complete with footnotes, no less). For me, the tantalizing thing is imagining how much of it MIGHT be true—though I admit, I have a pretty vivid imagination. But even if he's exaggerating, and say only one-fifth the number of people he claims were murdered in the Inquisition actually were, that's over 12 million people—and that's back in days when a few **thousand** people comprised the largest of cities! Hitler was born a Catholic and continued to tithe to the Church until his death, that's a historical fact. But was he really considered a "defender of the faith" by the pope? And does the Holy Office (of the General Inquisitor) really still exist? (That would make me a little nervous, even if it is just for office parties.) To write it all off as complete nonsense would certainly make it easier to sleep at night, but equally close-minded as to accept it all as fact. I'm not saying I would base my history dissertation on its underlying premise, but without rendering a decision on the most controversial aspects of it, let's just say it's essential reading for any serious Chick fan. It gives Alberto a grand entrance on the scene and goes a long way in explaining what the feud between the Vatican and Chick is all about. What little art is provided is mostly Chick's. It's the alarmist text that makes this tract great reading. Grade: **A+** for Amazing! Permanently retired: **$25**

*1 Sam. 28:12,15

©2001 Jack T. Chick.

THE NERVOUS WITCH **Review:** (Art by Chick ©2002.) Tract #12 in the Bible series of 25 featuring "Bob". This tract does for *Harry Potter* what *Dark Dungeons* did for *D&D*. It identifies the Potter phenomenon as a tool of Satan and urges burning all the merchandise. This creates an interesting dilemma for *Harry Potter* fans: They need the tract to complete their collections, but by reading it, they might be convinced to torch their investments. It's a risk, but well worth it. Nobody—especially *Harry Potter* freaks—should be without this tract.

It begins in a car with Maggie blabbing on her cell phone when she should be concentrating on driving. She's alerting her teenage daughter that she's bringing Bible Bob Williams home. Samantha is bummed when she hears the news. She complains to Holly (a fellow witch), "He makes me nervous because he reminds me of Jesus." Holly smirks and exclaims, "He's an enemy! I'll take him down with a powerful love spell!" A ghost demon behind her smiles in approval, but Samantha rejects the idea. "Don't even try," she warns, "You have *no* idea what we're up against." The two retire to Holly's room to conjure some spirits to help them deal with Bob. Witch icons adorn the walls, including a poster of Harry Potter. Holly is confident and brags, **"Witches rule!** God is dead and the churches are powerless. Old 'Bible Boy' won't stand a chance against our black arts!" But an hour later, she's whistling a different tune: "Something really powerful is blocking my spell." The doorbell rings and they scurry to blow out candles and unroll the rug over the pentagram on the floor.

Mom introduces Bob to the witches and announces she's just become saved. Samantha freaks and Holly nearly vomits. Mom exits to make a phone call, leaving Bob alone with the girls. He dares them to listen to a Bible story, and since teenagers always accept a dare, they listen. He tells how Moses punished witchcraft with death. Then he tells how King Saul was made the first king of Israel. God would only speak with Saul's prophet, a man called Samuel. Saul panicked when Samuel died on the eve of a battle with the Philistines. He went to a witch to conjure up Samuel so he could find out who would win the battle. Some neat séance panels feature demons and the ghost of Samuel returning to confront Saul. The ghost tells Saul both the king and his sons will become dead meat during the battle. Brave King Saul faints. Bob attempts to bring the story home with a happy ending: "The next day, Saul died in combat. Later the witch died and went to hell."

The two girls are unimpressed. Holly hollers, "I **hate** your @!!!**! Gospel!" Bob responds, "That's your **spirit** guide talking. Let me cast him out!" Holly turns into an ugly, grotesque version of her former self. **"Never!"** She snarls, "I'd **die** without him! I **curse** you Bob Williams. May you suffer a **horrible** death!" Bob takes it all in stride. "Careful Holly. Take back your curse. It can't hurt me but it'll come back on you with a vengeance." Holly and her demon leave in a huff. Bob then turns around and orders the demons to leave Samantha. A goblin flies out and Samantha feels stunned. "What happened, Uncle Bob?" She wonders, "Everything has changed. I feel different." She falls to the floor and recites the Sinner's Prayer. She later reveals to Bob that Harry Potter books lead her to witchcraft. "We wanted his powers, so we called for spirit guides. They came **into** us." She admits, "They led us into stuff we found in the Harry Potter books—tarot cards, Ouija boards, crystal balls." Bob credits the Potter books with leading millions of kids to hell. Samantha asks if Bob thinks she should destroy all the occult junk in her room. Three guesses what he decides...

One bonfire later, the two watch demons flee in a dark plume of smoke. Samantha points at one and says, "The spirits are leaving. Do we really have power over them?" Bob reassures her, "As long as we walk with Jesus." Bob warns his niece that she needs to read her King James Bible every day, because all the other versions have been perverted by Satan. She agrees and they live happily ever after.

Rebecca Brown may have left Chick Publications, but her spiritual guidance lives on in this tract. There are more witches and spiritual warfare references than you can shake a wand at. Don't be surprised if fundamentalists start planting this title in Harry Potter video rentals. They make good book markers, too. They have better pictures than anything in the novels. There are so many cool images in this tract, it's hard to select a

Favorite Panel Award. But action, dialog, and imagery all reach a wonderful climax on page 18 when Bob rebukes Samantha's spirit guide and casts it out of her. The demon, by the way, looks just like the banker Goblin from the movie. Grade **A** for Alchemy. **Still in print.**

©1997 Jack T. Chick.

NO FEAR Review: (Art by Chick ©1997.) Teenagers sure come off looking stupid in this tract. But hey, sometimes art imitates life! The defiant teen on the cover has a semitransparent demon smirking behind him. Similar demons appear throughout the tract egging the teen on to kill himself through subliminal suggestion. They call him brave and say "Amen" when he contemplates suicide, then applaud him when he finally carries it out. Misery loves company, so Lance took the advance precaution of convincing his girlfriend to kill herself during his funeral. When he finally snaps his neck, one of the demons gleefully proclaims, "now for the BIG surprise!" It's BURNING HELL, Lancey-poo, and you're TOAST for *ALL ETERNITY!*

Meanwhile, back home, everyone pays their respects at Lance's funeral. Everyone except Dolly, who climbs her makeshift gallows and prepares to join her boyfriend in the great beyond. Her sister approaches the preacher after the service and tattles on Dolly's suicide plans. (Ratting on a sibling is a time-honored tradition in most families. Although this instance may look altruistic on the surface, the squealer not only waits for the funeral to end before informing on her sister, she *just so happens* to forget her keys! One has to wonder if she didn't secretly want to be the only child!) *Super-Preacher* quickly springs into action. He leaps into his salvation-mobile and races to the crime scene. He literally KICKS DOWN the front door and catches Dolly as she jumps to her (near) death. Angry demons flee the holy-roller's arrival, but Dolly stands her ground. She puts her hands on her hips and demands an explanation. Man-O'God vividly describes the **SHOCKING TRUTH** (Chick's italics, not mine) about Lake-o'-Fire Land. Demons shake their fists outside the window, but that doesn't stop Dolly or her sister from assuming the position for *Minister-man* and praying for their salvation.

Lance, however, continues to bake below. Out of sight, out of mind...

Favorite Panel Award goes to the three-panel sequence starting on page 8b. Lance is in hell asking questions when his leg catches on fire. The demons make insincere apologies about how they can't change his fate, and the flames completely CONSUME Lance. He looks like those Hollywood stunt men who douse themselves in gasoline and walk out of burning buildings. The third panel is completely black except for a scream and shout of "I'm burning!" (He must be burning on the INSIDE now, since there are no more flames to give off light.) Grade: **B+** for Burning Boyfriends! **Still in print.**

©1972 Jack T. Chick.

ONE WAY Review: (Same story as **The True Path.** Art by Chick ©1972 and 2002.) This tract is similar to *Somebody Loves Me,* in that it is practically all pictures and very few words. It takes less than a minute to read the entire tract. The story shows Adam and Eve in Eden walking with the Faceless God. God points to the Forbidden Fruit and says "No!" But they eat it anyway and dirt rains down on them from the tree. Now they're dirty and God avoids them. He builds a wall to keep them away. They bathe, but the stains of sin won't come off. They have kids who are also born dirty. A crowd of stinking humanity approaches a cliff overlooking flames. There's only one detour with a sign that says, "God's Love Gift Inside." A few kids enter the detour and see pictures of the Virgin birth, the wise men, the crucifixion, etc. They see the image of Christ on the cross. Those who pray to it get bathed in God's blood and become clean. Those who refuse return to the dirty crowd heading toward hell. The clean children run up a stairway to heaven and are welcomed by the Faceless God, Jesus, and a dove (the Holy Spirit). The end.

There are two other ethnic versions to this tract. A black cast in featured in the African version and a Native American cast is featured in an Indian version. The Indian version has a different cover entitled *The True Path.*

It's difficult to get excited over this tract since the art and plot are both very basic. At least *The True Path* has some interesting Indians tossed in, as well as a few non-Indians. One example is a white Cavalry officer on page 8 who was probably slain at Little Big Horn or some such massacre. Not to worry. A few hours in hell and he'll be as red as all the others. Grade: **C** for Cleaners. **Still in print.**

©1985 Jack T. Chick.

THE ONLY HOPE Guest review by Alan: (Art by Carter ©1985.) This is a primer in eschatology, promising that God destroyed the earth once with water, and next time it will be with fire! (Maybe God did such a great job creating the earth that He needs to destroy it twice.)

The tract opens with a group of men during the time of Noah engaged in horrific conversation: "I love drugs. Do you?" "No, incest and murder are my thing." "Let's kill someone just for fun..." "Can I torture them?" A guy yells at two men who are fondling each other, "Take your hands off him. @!!!**! He's my wife!" Another fellow leans back, drink in hand, and unleashes Chick's trademark "HAW HAW" at the proceedings. All this on just the FIRST panel!

The tract states, "It had never rained on earth, but in faith, Noah built the ark." Exactly one panel after the flood begins, somebody asks what's happening. He's told, "It's raining...lets go to the mountains for safety." Boy, people were sure smart in those days. That fellow knew exactly what rain was and advised people to head for high ground. (But then, these ancient people also used "drugs," so maybe their minds were expanded.)

Most of the tract is King James Bible verses that crowd out Carter's excellent line art to almost postage-stamp size. But as a bonus: the narrator reveals himself for the first time! He's a white man with thinning hair, high cheekbones, and a small mustache. He's describing the Rapture with a cold, detached expression common amongst cancer doctors. Two panels later, he's sitting in his leather swivel and looks straight at us, saying "The next question usually asked is: when is all this going to happen?"

Has Chick finally made his appearance??? I was told that this is not him, but it does resemble the portrait of a young Chick addressing a group of convicts included in an early issue of *Battle Cry!*

The unnamed narrator makes a third appearance, leading up to the accusation that the pope is the antichrist who will unite all denominations together. The wrath of God is fully illustrated over the next few pages, although some scenes look like they were lifted from other Chick works, including *The Killer Storm* tract and *The Ark* comic book. The Faceless God is shown three times on His throne. The last panel concludes stating, "Moral conditions today are the same as they were at the time of Noah." I love drugs, don't you?

Grade **B+** for Big Boat. **Still in print.**

©1970 Jack T. Chick.

OPERATION SOMEBODY CARES Review: (Art by Chick ©1970.) This is one of my personal favorites. What a shame it's so rare. Its existence was only a rumor until a copy was found in Chick's archive vault in 2001. It has everything a great tract should have. It has sensationalism, end-of-civilization predictions, and plenty of Red-baiting.

It all starts with the outrageous cover. A sign on the wall states, "Instant Anarchy Inc." It has a meeting between a militant black, a fat unshaven peace protester, and a hook-nosed communist complaining about Chick's tracts. "Let's pray that 'Operation 'Somebody Cares'' doesn't catch on!" Meanwhile, the shadow of Satan looks on in the background and chimes in, "Amen!"

The tract gets even better inside. The opening page states, "THE PLAY PERIOD IS OVER! Either the Christians go to work as soul-winners or expect to see the following. Communist timetables for the U.S. —1973. Spreading riots—too late to evangelize!" The drawing shows mobs pouring into a white, middle-class household to shoot the husband, strangle the kid, and scalp the screaming wife. Policemen burn in flames in the background. Page 4 continues, "A leading communist said in

1930—'The only force that can stop us is the Gospel of Jesus Christ.' Missionaries tell of the Red Chinese presenting their propaganda in cartoon booklets-WITH FANTASTIC SUCCESS!" What follows is a litany of war analogies, comparing the witnessing to an armed assault. (It's a fight to the death, but the other side started it!)

Chick suggests a program of visits and tracts that will convert the country back to Christianity before the Communists have a chance to take over and end civilization as we know it. The tract states, "the average citizen is frightened, lonely, [and] thoroughly brainwashed. He is steel against the Gospel, and is ready for an argument! Our attack begins with a smile, a free gift, [and] an invitation. The contact is caught off guard! After the 3rd visit the resistance breaks. At least one in the combination of six books will hit every member of the family." A survey conducted by Chick showed that out of 100 people who received the visits and six tracts, 23 accepted Jesus as their savior. In India, the results were even more dramatic. "16 decisions for Christ out of 20 homes."

Things get real inflammatory on page 19, when the stakes are raised to the limit. "Satan has launched his greatest offensive—the tribulation is on its way. As Christian soldiers, we must move now to counterattack by invading the neighborhoods with 'Operation: Somebody Cares' and offer them the light of the world as darkness engulfs our land."

A clean cut man in a funeral director's suit grimly states, "We felt it was our solemn duty to print a terrible quote on the next page—it was made by one of the nation's top communists." Across the bottom of the page is scrolled a dire warning: "PLAY TIME IS OVER—WE ARE NOW AT WAR!" Do we dare turn the page? Heck yeah!

The top of page 20 blares, "IF YOU DON'T BELIEVE IT-READ THIS!" What follows is some of the most violent language of any tract. "'I dream of the hour when the last Congressman is strangled to death on the guts of the last preacher—and since the Christians seem to love to sing about the blood, why not give them a little of it? Slit the throats of their children and drag them over the mourners' bench and pulpit and allow them to drown in their own blood, and then see whether they enjoy singing hymns.'—Gus Hall at the funeral of Eugene Dennis, February 1961. This statement was made by the top communist in the United States."

Readers are urged to fill out the attached mini-postcard and mail it in to Chick Publications and support *Operation: Somebody Cares*. How many people obeyed and vandalized this valuable tract is uncertain. What *is* certain is that this is one of Chick's rarest tracts. It predicted such an early onslaught for communist revolution, it was outdated within three years of printing. Chick apparently learned his lesson. Other tracts tend to avoid specific deadlines or push them back decades instead of years. Then again, Chick could always say the reason the 1973 deadline came and went was because his tracts were so effective, they prevented the revolution from occurring. Whatever the cause, we can all take comfort in the fact that our Congressmen have yet to be strangled to death with the intestines of preachers. Favorite Panel Award goes to the riot panorama on page 3. Grade: **A+** for Alarmist Alert! **Value: Speculative.**

| I finally stood up to Hank and exposed him. He beat me up and threw me out of the house. | I got into drugs, got hooked… |
| That's when I hit the streets and died inside. | did tricks to pay for my habit… and I gave up on God. |

©2001 Jack T. Chick.

***THE OUTCAST* Review:** (Art by Chick ©2001.) Tract #8 in the series of 25 Bible tracts. Jack sure loves to make the stuffed shirts squirm. This time, he does it by retelling the story of Rahab, the "good" prostitute. The tract begins with a badly beaten Shirley knocking on Janet's door for help. (You remember Janet, the blond that Bob converted in *It's Coming!*) As she opens the door, Janet's look of wide-eyed **SHOCK** is worthy of an EC horror comic cover. (Good Lord! (Choke!)) Shirley's really roughed up. She looks even worse when she takes off her shades. Who did this to her? Why, her pimp, 'coz Shirley's a whore!

Being a *real* Christian, Janet accepts Shirley anyway, despite her sordid past. Bob and Helen soon arrive with medicine, clothes, and the Word of the Lord. Is Helen Bob's main squeeze? Stay tuned for future tracts and clarification. Being Chick's main protagonist, it's a safe bet he ain't gay.

Shirley launches into the story of her life. It's rated PG13. We don't get to see her turning tricks or anything, but we do see her buying drugs from a black thug with shades and a nose ring. (Cartoon translation: He's one *bad dude*.) Shirley claims it all started with her stepfather "making bacon" with her while mommy was away earning it. When she finally tattles about this incestuous relationship, she gets tossed out on the street and turns to drugs and prostitution. Now she feels "absolutely filthy."

Tactful Helen asks innocently, "I know of a prostitute that God loved. Wanna hear about it?" Shirley takes the bait. Helen then relates "the beautiful story about a prostitute." (I've heard of beautiful prostitutes, but never beautiful stories *about* prostitutes.) Helen tells of Rahab, the prostitute who betrayed Jericho and helped the Jewish invaders kill all her neighbors. (They must not have tipped well.) But since the invaders are God's chosen race, we're supposed to jeer those defending the city and cheer for the ones destroying it. (I'm sure the Old Testament makes a better case for Rahab than that, but in the limited 24 page comic, it's hard to give the traitor much of a make-over.)

Back to the tract: The Jews conquer Jericho and kill all the families except Rahab's. They honor her for her treachery (I mean, *assistance*) and a Jewish man named Salmon falls in love with her. Page 12 says, "But God wasn't finished blessing her. She became the great, great grandmother of King David, and best of all... an ancestor to Jesus Christ Himself."

Bob, who had stepped out earlier so the girls could discuss the dirty details of Shirley's sex life without crossing gender lines, returns to bring it all back home to Jesus. Clueless Shirley asks, "Was Jesus Christ a man of God?" Surely, Shirley, you jest! He *was* God! Bob sets her straight and goes on to tell the tale of the cheating wife who was about to be stoned until Jesus said, "Let he who is without sin cast the first stone."

Bob delivers the main message of this tract on page 18: "Jesus came to this Earth to die for sinners... That includes prostitutes, pimps, Sodomites, religious phonies, liars, thieves, murders...everybody." This convinces Shirley that Jesus really loves her. She drops to the ground and prays. The results are immediate. "I can't believe it! ... I'm clean! Oh Jesus, thank you! Thank you!" They all embrace in a smarmy group hug and it's another happy ending.

Favorite Panel Award goes to page 6B with Shirley handing her hard-earned (whore) money to the drug dealer for a small packet of pleasure. Grade **B+** for Brothel. **Still in print.**

The Story of Ruth

THE OUTSIDER

Ruth said:

Whither thou goest, I will go…

thy people shall be my people, and thy God my God.

Where thou diest, will I die, and there will I be buried…

…the Lord do so to me, and more also, if ought but death part thee and me.

©1991 Jack T. Chick.

THE OUTSIDER Review: (Art by the third artist. ©1991.) This is the Old Testament story of Ruth, the gentile who gives up her homeland and people to live with her Jewish mother-in-law in Israel. Ruth is also the woman who is often quoted at weddings, when brides go beyond the usual script and say, "Whither thou goest, I will go. Thy people shall be my people, and thy God my God. Where thou diest, will I die, and there will I be buried. The Lord do so to me, and more also, if ought by death part thee and me." Of course, it takes a lot of the romance out of it when you realized this was originally spoken to a mother-in-law. But despite this minor detail, the story of Ruth is actually a compelling love story.

Ruth's husband dies, as does the husband of Naomi (her mother-in-law). The two widows return to Naomi's Jewish homeland. Ruth is rather unwelcome because she is a Moabite. However, an older landowner named Boaz admires her because she's been good to his relative (Naomi). Boaz also likes her because she's *hot!* Like most Jewish mothers, Naomi can't resist playing matchmaker. She tells Ruth to work only in Boaz' fields. When that doesn't solicit a proposal, she tells her to go lie at his feet while he sleeps. Boaz awakes to find this beautiful babe laying at his feet. He does the opposite of what most men would do given that situation: He respects her and agrees to marry her. It's a happy ending for husband and wife, as well as manipulative mother-in-law.

There are several interesting details about this tract. It states, "Naomi's two sons disobeyed God and married Moabite women." Marrying Moabites is bad for the sons, but when it comes to Boaz, no such condemnation is given.

Another interesting note is the evolution of Boaz. In the original version of the tract (Codes A and B) he looks remarkably similar to Sean Connery with a beard (like he looked in *The Hunt for Red October*). Just a

coincidence? Perhaps. But is it also a coincidence that the catalog number for this tract is 007? (Just kidding.) But seriously, the resemblance is really striking, especially on page 16b. And why else would they mysteriously change the face to make him look different in later versions of the same tract? (Codes C and beyond.) Did Connery complain? Did too many readers point it out and give Chick's lawyers the jitters? We may never know for sure. (Perhaps Mr. Bond thought it was time for a disguise?)

One of the funniest details is one that is missing from this tract. In the original story, Boaz must first ask another kinsman if he would rather buy Naomi's land and marry Ruth instead. This scene is included in the tract. What is *not* included is the Jewish custom of the day where one man pulls off his sandal and gives it to the other man as proof of the transaction. How does a stinky sandal prove anything? Are they designer sandals with names embroidered on them? Or if challenged, does the recipient say, "If you don't believe this belongs to Boaz, take a whiff! I dare yah!" It all sounds like something out of Monty Python's *Life of Brian*.

Favorite Panel Award goes to page 6. It's a close-up of Ruth in all her beauty, as she recites her promise to stick by Naomi during thick and thin. She's quite the looker! Grade **B+** for Beautiful Babe! **Still in print.**

PARTY GIRL

J.T.C.

Lord, **YOU** are going to have to get me to Jill in time.

I better report this.

I just **KNOW** that Satan wants her *dead!*

Back at Satan's Headquarters

Master, we a have a **BIG** problem. *Rita Jones* is on her way.

She's coming to *steal* her granddaughter away from you.

©1998 Jack T. Chick.

PARTY GIRL Review: (Art by Chick ©1998.) The story opens with Satan preparing for his festival. A demon reports, "We've *loaded* the city with drugs and alcohol. You're music is also ready. We've booked the *hottest* groups in the world. You're warehouses are *PACKED* with *low-grade* condoms. And *hundreds* of volunteers are ready to give them away." Satan is pleased. Three thousand miles away, Rita Jones is awakened by a dream. God has warned her that Satan is after her granddaughter. She calls but learns that Jill has already left for the festival. She leaves to save Jill in person. A demon reports back in hell what Grandma is doing. "*Grrrr.. I HATE that old* @!!!**! She's been a thorn in my side for *TWENTY YEARS*," Satan steams, "For sweet revenge, I'll kill her granddaughter *tonight!*" Meanwhile, Jill is having the time of her life at Mardi Gras. The bartender is replaced by Satan, who poisons her drink. Grandma arrives just in time to tear her daughter out of the arms of her date. The date decides not to waste the poison and downs it. He dies in his sins. Jill finds out about his death later when she calls her friend to apologize for her crazy grandmother. When she realizes Grams saved her life, she listens to her wise Christian advice. She recites the Sinner's Prayer and gets saved. The last page offers juxtaposing images of Satan and Grandma urging different behavior from readers. Ugly Satan says, *"Listen!* Don't believe **any** of this. *Keep on partying!* You'll **NEVER** regret it. *Trust ME!"* Kindly old Grandmother urges, "Stop believing Satan's lies. Trust Christ *today!"*

Favorite Panel Award goes to page 5b: A demon stands in a tight spotlight surrounded by darkness, telling Satan about events on Earth. The lighting is both creepy and surreal. Interesting trivia: If Rita is 3,000 miles away from Satan, and the planet is 4,000 miles to the center, that would suggest hell is about 1,000 miles from the middle. Grade: **B+** for Barf up that Beer! **Still in print.**

THE PASSOVER PLOT? Review: (Artwork by Chick © 1972.) This tract has several blood red inserts, which certainly add to its novelty factor. It tells one of Chick's favorite Old Testament Tales: God's vengeance against Egypt. The ten plagues are all outlined with typical Chick glee. Venom oozes from every panel as the Egyptian misfortunes are added up like trophies. Hey, they asked for it, so they got it! Then again, it also mentions that God hardened Pharaoh's heart, so in a way, he was just "following orders." (Details, details!) Then it compares the Passover blood smeared on the Jewish doorways to the blood Jesus gave on the cross for Christians. (Same God, but a different Chosen.) How the Jewish Pharisees tried to cover up the resurrection is also outlined.

The Favorite Panel Award goes to just such a scene: A sneaky Jewish leader is paying off a corrupt Roman soldier with a fist full of coins. He whispers, "Say his disciples stole his body! Matt. 28:12-13." Normally, biblical references are provided with * and a footnote, but by actually including it *within* the word balloon, it makes it look as if an ancient Jewish Rabbi is quoting the New Testament to the Roman—long before it was written! Grade **B+** for Bible Background. **Value: $20.**

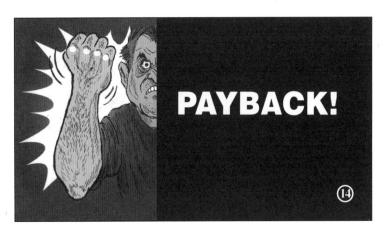

PAYBACK! **Guest review by Andie Kittabb:** (Art by Chick © 2002.) This is tract #14 of 25 featuring Bob. We begin in front of a luxurious mansion. Fang the dog makes an appearance in the front yard, barking ferociously at the copyright statement on the side of the panel. Meanwhile, a kind but sickly old man, Mr. Banks, waves goodbye to his favorite nurse, Kelli. Apparently, she's an exemplary nurse because she reminds him to take his medicine. A medical aide telling a patient to take his medicine? Talk about going above and beyond the call of duty!

But Kelli isn't the angelic caretaker that Mr. Banks thinks she is. Her grumpy husband Alan is whining because "We should have a house just like that (Banks'). We deserve it." Kelli, instead of telling her husband to get off his butt and get a job, decides that exploiting her client's trust "may be our doorway to riches." Oh *YEAH,* sinners; can I get a HAW-HAW?!

Our heroine spends the next 3 months, 2 weeks, and 4 days worming her way into Mr. Banks' life. She isolates him from his family, tricks him into signing some legal papers, and stops taking care of him. I especially like how Nurse Ratched, er, Kelli, tells Mr. Banks' family that he can't come to the phone because he's sleeping, then tells Banks that his family hasn't called. I think the message that we're supposed to get is that Kelli is evil for keeping his family away. Not to make excuses for Kelli, but what kind of family stops checking in on a sick relative just because his nurse says he's taking a nap? It's not exactly a heartwarming portrayal of family devotion. But I digress. When Banks dies and leaves all of his worldly goods to his "good friend and saintly nurse, Kelli James," his children (a ragtag bunch of brats all wearing unsaved sneers on their faces) are angry to discover that they didn't inherit anything and that the will is incontestable. Haven't these people ever heard of nuisance lawsuits?

Fast forward seven years: Kelli is living in Mr. Banks' old house and dying of cancer, and her husband Alan is nowhere to be found. (He probably dropped dead while reveling in his newfound riches and was whisked away by cranky angels for a terse meeting with the Faceless God.) Kelli receives a visit from Bonnie, a precocious young Christian who looks more like a Gelfling from *The Dark Crystal* than a girl. Bonnie, with wholesome childhood naiveté oozing from every pore, announces that, "My big sister had cancer, but God took it away!" Awww, isn't that sweet?

Bonnie asks Kelli to come to church with her that Sunday. Pastor Malcolm (played by Walter Cronkite's black twin) regales the congregation with the story of Ahab and Jezebel.

Okay, we've all read Chick's other tract, *Going to the Dogs*, that dealt with this story, so I'm not going to rehash it here, but I should mention a few highlights. First, when evil Ahab cries into his pillow because Naboth won't give him his vineyard, we find that Jack Chick has replaced his traditional "Sob sob!" with the newfangled "Snivel snivel." Is nothing sacred? Jackie boy, just promise not to mess with the "HAW-HAW-HAW!" That would be blasphemy!

There are some other great sound effects, like the arrow going "Thud!" into Ahab's chest, the "Grrrr" of dogs waiting for Jezebel to hit the pavement, and of course, the classic "Yaaaaaa!" as Jezebel approaches terminal velocity. The Favorite Panel Award goes to the scene where a group of people mull around the spot where Jezebel was eaten by dogs. One guy says, "Yuk!" Just in case the point isn't clear, the caption at the bottom reads "It was pretty gross." What really makes the panel though, is the picture of a bulldog in the foreground. The dog's belly is distended and his mouth is full, but not so full that the dog can't let out a healthy "Burp!" Not surprising, really, since one would expect Baal worshipers to cause gas in canines.

At the end of the sermon, Kelli has an epiphany: "I did the same thing to Mr. Banks that Jezebel did! I'm going to hell too!" Whoa! You mean it's *wrong* to kill an old man and steal the inheritance from his family? Get outta town! She kneels, prays, gets saved, then tells Malcolm what she's done and asks if she's really forgiven. This is also a break from tradition, because usually after saying the Sinner's Prayer, the newly saved person gets up and gives the Chick trademark "Oh my God, I feel different, I feel clean!" speech. I guess Kelli still feels a little soiled. Malcolm offers a bit more advice than most other Chick messengers. He doesn't just say, "Congrats, you're saved, hallelujah." He asks Kelli what she thinks God would have her do now. Normally, dying Chick characters only have a few hours or even minutes to say "Jesus save me" before they croak. Kelli's lucky though; she has a week to make arrangements with lawyers and call "a lot of people and ask them to forgive me for the terrible things I've done" before her friendly neighborhood angel comes to cart her off to heaven.

Overall, this is a neat tract written in the classic Chick vein. I was especially happy to see Fang; it seems like he's making more appearances now. Too bad he missed the free meal on the palace pavement. He must not have heard the Jeze-Bell. Grade: **B+** for Belching Bulldog! **Still in print.**

NETONI LELO TUNG'ANA NEINASAKI ALAIRRITANI ILOMON LE NGAI.

ORE APA TENGAITER NETII ENGAI, WENGERAI WENGIYANG' ET SINYATI.

© 1997 Jack T. Chick.

PICTURE GOSPEL, AFRICAN (Art by Chick © 1997. **See Wordless Gospel.**) **Value: $3**

20 minutes later

Attention, please…

We are about to make an emergency landing.

Oh, no!

Gasp!

Please brace yourselves and keep your heads down!

Dr. Ali… I'm *AFRAID* to die.

Be of courage, my brothers. If Allah wills it, we may be in paradise in just a few minutes.

© 1999 Jack T. Chick.

THE PILGRIMAGE Review: (Art by Chick © 1999.) The last tract of 1999 pulls no punches explaining how all Muslims will toast in hell for rejecting Jesus. It all starts when some Muslims fly on their pilgrimage to Mecca. They start talking religion and the aircraft develops equipment problems. They crash on the runway and all 246 perish. As the relatives at the airport witness the tragedy and burst out in tears, one says, "It was the will of Allah! Thankfully, their sins were forgiven because they performed the hajj." The head pilgrim discovers differently. Abdul gets the shock of his afterlife to hear Matthew 25:41 shouted at him by a Faceless God. When he objects, Faceless God delivers the double 1-2 punch. He reveals, "Allah is a Satanic counterfeit. He is one of many false gods that have deceived millions!" Naked Abdul complains that it's unfair since no one ever told him about Christ, but not so fast Abdul! J.C. counters that he sent one of his faithful servants to witness to Abdul in his earlier years. What a pity Abdul didn't convert, and all because his family would disown him. (Perhaps if his friend had presented Abdul with some Chick tracts, it might have turned out differently.) Interesting note: This tract quickly sold out after September 11th, and had to be reprinted.

The Favorite Panel Award clearly goes to the next to last panel when Abdul grovels before God and begs, "But I was a very sincere Muslim", to which God retorts, "I'm sorry Abdul, but you were sincerely WRONG!" Try to look at the bright side, Abdul: Surf's up in the Lake O' Fire! Grade: **A-** for Apology unacceptable. **Still in print.**

 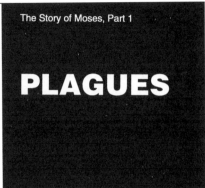

The Story of Moses, Part 1

PLAGUES

Every Hebrew boy born in Egypt will be cast into the river *to die!*

Pharaoh has spoken!

This is a true story. Read Exodus, chapters 1-14.

©1991 Jack T. Chick.

PLAGUES Review: (Art by third artist, revamped by Carter ©1991.) Like *The Passover Plot?*, this tract also tells the story about Egypt and the Plagues. The artwork includes fantastic detail that makes Fred Carter's work so wonderful. The subtitle is "The Story of Moses, Part 1", so it presumably goes with the *Sin Busters* tract subtitled "The Story of Moses, Part 2". Instead of focusing on Passover, it gives more attention to how Moses was discovered as a baby on the Nile, grew up to lead the Jewish revolt, and how Pharaoh's army was held back with a pillar of flame and eventually drowned in the Red Sea. It's basically an Old Testament tract, but a good one at that and well worth obtaining. Two versions exist. The first one was drawn by the third artist and can be distinguished by a servant with a covered head bowing before Pharaoh on page 3b. The other version has a bald servant bowing before Pharaoh on page 3b. It has several panels redrawn by Carter (mostly of Pharaoh). Carter probably had a hand in the first version as well, as beautiful panoramas like page 19 suggest. It's hard to be certain.

The cover features a great graphic of a vulture staring at two dead feet on a dried up mud flat. Ten toes to taste, but which will be first? Creepy! Grade **B+** for Boat Babies. Original servant with covered head bowing (page 3b) version: $25. Revamped version of bald servant bowing (page 3b), **$18.**

THE POOR LITTLE WITCH

By J.T.C.

Our most Holy Father . . . accept this sacrifice . . .

WAAAHH

Gasp . . . This can't be! **HAIL SATAN!**

Note: Police estimate between 40,000 to 60,000 ritual homicides per year occur in the U.S. (Dr. A. Carlisle — Homicide Investigation Seminar, Las Vegas, Nevada, 1986)

Here Mandy, you **MUST** drink of the child's blood and our Father will bless you and give you increased powers.

Drink Mandy! OR DIE!

No . . . No! I can't . . . I'm sick.

O.K., O.K . . . I'll do it.

©1987 Jack T. Chick.

THE POOR LITTLE WITCH Review: (Art by Chick ©1987.) A delightful tale of witchcraft, conspiracy, and teen angst. It begins with the trials and tribulations of Mandy, a teenager who would "give anything to be like the other girls." Unfortunately, she can't play volleyball worth a damn and her teammates despise her. Her tacky wardrobe doesn't help matters much either, especially her hideous hair bow, which resembles a dead fish (see page 4.) Mrs. White, her teacher, sees the vulnerable Mandy as easy-pickin's. She invites her for a "sleep over." Mandy's divorced mother doesn't seem to have a problem letting her daughter spend the night with strangers. As Mandy approaches the party pad, Mrs. White urges the other young vixens, "We have a new girl. Mandy. Go easy on her. She doesn't know!"

Mandy arrives and the older girls are already in bathrobes and nightgowns. One has her leg draped suggestively over a chair and her other leg spread open toward Mandy. She smirks and asks, "Hey Mandy, do you want to learn some really neat things?" Mandy foolishly agrees. Do they rape her? Naw, that's another tract (see *Lisa*). Instead, they use their broom handles for an equally evil purpose: Witchcraft! They show her a trick or two and she eagerly joins up. Now pause and ask yourself what you would do if you were magic? Whatever it is, it's too clever for Mandy. Obtaining money and power don't even occur to her. She uses her magic to make the other girls drop the Volleyball during practice. (Pretty ambitious, huh?) Unfortunately, even this mild request unleashes demons. Mandy soon discovers she got more than she bargained for. She attends a black mass where witches murder a baby and force everyone to drink the blood. A footnote warns us that police estimate between 40,000 and 60,000 ritual homicides per year occur in the U.S. (and the cops should know. According to *Broken Cross* and *Spellbound*, they're in on it!) Mandy resists at first, but then agrees to an itsy-bitsy taste. (Teenagers love to experiment.) During the drive home, Mrs. White warns Mandy not to even THINK about going to the police, because their high priest **IS** the Chief of Police! Mandy wants out, but where can she run? The witches have infiltrated the Church and bought off the minister with large cash "love offerings." Rev. Chuckwyn gives a special sermon attacking witchcraft as Mrs. White gloats from within the choir. Mandy takes the message personally and feels completely isolated.

In desperation, she visits Mrs. Grayson, a true Christian that Mrs. White warned her to avoid. Mrs. Grayson turns out to have all the answers and knows how to send the demons away screaming. Mandy becomes saved and "feels clean," but she's still clueless when it comes to common sense. Her new Christian friends warn her that the Satanists will try to kill her, but she insists she'll be all right. She walks home alone under the full moon and gets abducted and murdered by the Satanists. (Where's Romans 8:31 when you need it?) Not to worry though, she stands firm in Jesus and goes straight to heaven. (So does that make it a happy ending?) To make things even more exciting, Rev. Chuckwyn *just happens* to die the exact same night and gets tossed in the lake of fire. (So it's really a win-win situation, since Jesus and Satan both win a soul.)

Another footnote tells us to learn more about the occult by buying Dr. Rebecca Brown's books (published by Chick). Mrs. Grayson is probably modeled after Rebecca Brown, demon fighter extraordinaire. The role of Mandy reflects the personal experiences of Elaine Moses, Brown's ex-witch turned Christian colleague. Even though Elaine claims Satanists kill ex-witches all the time, this dramatic ending was apparently too much of a downer for most readers. The last version of this tract (the Code "G" variation) has the Christians assure Mandy she needn't worry about Satan any more, since God will protect her. Then it quotes scripture to prove it. ("No weapon that is formed against thee shall prosper.") It creates a rather uncomfortable paradox. Either the first tracts were wrong, and evil things can happen to good Christians, or the last version of the tract is whistling in the graveyard. Only the faceless one upstairs knows for sure, and he's certainly entitled to change the rules of the game whenever he sees fit. But my advice is to play it safe: If you happen to be a young woman who witnesses a child murder and then decides to leave The Craft, don't tempt fate by walking home alone under a full moon. (The next cup of blood your ex-friends drink could be yours!) Grade: **A-** as in Type: A *Negative*. Original "Mandy dies" version **$80.** "Mandy lives" version **$45.**

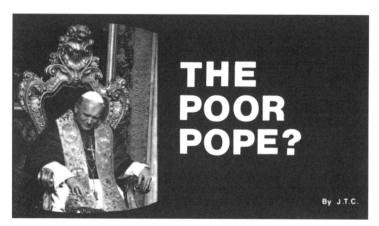

©1983 Jack T. Chick.

THE POOR POPE **Review:** (Art by Chick 1983.) It doesn't get more politically incorrect than this! Even the cover sports a picture of the media's favorite Pope John Paul in a gilded chair, adorned in gold. This is one of Chick's best anti-Catholic rants, pulling all the skeletons out of the closet for everyone to see. Included is the historically factual story of how Pope Stephen II forged a letter from Heaven to King Pepin of France to convince him to stop the Arabs from raiding Rome. This juicy bit of history is taught in most Western Civilization courses and proves that even an infallible Pope can be caught in a lie (unless of course, Saint Peter really did give Stephen II a letter from Heaven). Pope Hadrian 1st repeated the con with Pepin's son, King Charlemagne, claiming Constantine had made the Popes heir to the entire Roman Empire. Another piece of historical trivia is how the Spanish soldiers plundered South American kingdoms, demanding gold payments for the centuries the natives lived on the Pope's land without paying rent. Then things get somewhat personal as Chick reminds Protestants when *they* were the targets. "The most vicious, dirty technique used by the Roman Catholic System to raise money was **The Inquisition.** The victim could be a landowner falsely accused of some crime such as eating meat on Friday. His family was hauled away by the inquisitors, never to be seen again. The landowner was tortured until he confessed. Then he was tried for heresy and burned to death for his crime. His land and possessions became the property of 'mother church.' She did very well considering there were 68 million victims." (Note that he doesn't say 68 million were actually killed, but infers it by calling them "victims.")

Truth is often stranger than fiction, and even Chick's most ardent conspiracy theories can't upstage some of these incredible historical events. If nothing else, this tract proves the old adage, "Absolute power corrupts absolutely"—even when that power is religion. Of course, Chick goes well beyond fact and ventures into wild speculation. Prostitutes selling themselves to earn money for the Pope? The Vatican arranging the assassination of Lincoln and the starting World Wars I and II? (These allegations *might* be true, but the evidence requires more than a motive and the testimony of an ex-Jesuit priest to prove them.) They make great reading however, and heck, it's fun to be the victim for once instead of being blamed for everyone else's woes. (It seems every race and religion competes to see who suffered more throughout history. The Inquisition is the Protestants' only claim to victim fame.)

Favorite Panel Award: Jack's rendition of a monk selling bogus Holy Relics. He assures the crowd, "I personally know this thorn was stuck in Jesus' head. Would I lie?" Such shams were big business during the middle ages and provided extra income for many Catholic officials. (Check out Chaucer's *The Canterbury Tales* for more amusing examples.) It's short on 'toons, but long on good gossip! Grade: **B+** for Bitter & Bombastic. **Value: $30.**

©1972 Jack T. Chick.

THE POOR REVOLUTIONIST Guest review by Terrible Tommy Murray: (Art by Chick ©1971, 1972.) This is an early Chick tract that purports to show how the secret agents of Soviet Communism, a.k.a., Hippies, were on the verge of taking over the country for Stalin and Castro. This tract has been out of circulation for some time, mainly because, as with many another JTC tract, the words of the Prophet St. Chick turned out to be a total crock. When the Hippie Era faded and the Disco Era oozed onto the stage, Mr. Chick quietly phased *The Poor Revolutionist* out of existence and came up with *That Crazy Guy,* a condemnation of the Disco Era, promiscuous sex, and Steve Martin. I remember running across this particular tract back in the early '70s, when Chick was just seriously firing up. I can still remember very well the feelings I got from this tract.

I also remember a book being published around then, entitled *None Dare Call It Treason* that dwelt on this "Hippies are Commies" theme. The motifs are practically identical. If Jack doesn't have it somewhere on his shelves, I'd be very surprised.

Now, on to *The Poor Revolutionist:* As with Star Trek's famous split infinitive ("To boldly go..."), the grammar of the title is incorrect. It should be *The Poor Revolutionary.* But, hey, we're dealing with a guy who firmly believes that the public schools are ruled by secret Jesuit witches planning to take over your children's minds with D & D, rock music, and algebra. Maybe Jack be done think-um that thar grammar stuff is Say-TAN-ik.

At the time that *The Poor Revolutionist* came out, the Hippies were in full swing, Woodstock and the anti-war movement were current events and there were any number of Fundie preachers making their money by going around to Fundie churches and showing the undeniable links between the Hippies and the secret agenda of the Communists. (Nowadays, they preach Creationism, "reformation therapy" for homosexuals, and accuse Catholics, Wiccans, and everyone who likes Rock music — even Christian rock music— of being secret Satanists.)

As I recall, the art work was very good, which means it's probably a Carter effort. The story centers around a longhaired, grungy-looking hippie, complete with headband, mustache, and peace-symbol patches on his denims. (I think his name was Bobby. I'm not positive on that, but that's the name we'll use for the sake of convenience.) As the tract opens, we see an exterior view of a house where Bobby the Hippie and his Commie friends are holding a "cell meeting," while a Joan Baez look-alike strums a guitar outside and sings: "Will you take my hand a year from now, when the land is ours?"

Bobby has a brother who is a Christian. Like most Christians in Jack Chick's fantasy world, Bobby's brother is a Ken doll clone, complete with sweater and perfect blonde haircut that looks molded on. It seems that Bobby's born-again brother has interrupted the Communist insurgents' cell meeting, so Bobby decides to beat the crap out of him to ensure that he'll never do that again. As Bobby pounds the little Fundie, the other Commies go "HAW HAW!" and shout "Get 'im, Bobby!"

But does having the crap beat out of him stop this little Christian? Why, heck no. This is a JACK CHICK Christian! With blood pouring down his battered face, the poor little martyr continues to preach to his Commie-rat brother about how he's being fooled by the Reds and needs Jesus. Two of Bobby's cell-mates drag him away and kick him out with the prerequisite "HAW HAW" chorus so relished by Chick.

The Commie brother's controller, a secret Soviet agitator, is so stereotypically Jewish that it's a wonder they didn't meet in a synagogue. It's interesting that, while not overtly Anti-Semitic, most of Chick's Commie-traitor characters (like Gertrude in *Operation Bucharest*) are Jewish. He tells Bobby that he will have great status in "our brave, new Communistic world."

Then, next page, THE REVOLUTION HITS! Police and firemen are gunned down in the street. Commie "revolutionists" attack people in their homes. One particular panel is a real work of ultra-paranoid fantasy art: In a scene straight from White America's worst nightmare, the panel depicts a white family being murdered with guns and axes by mostly-black revolutionaries. In Chick's paranoid fantasies, America falls in practically no time, due to the masses of Communist sympathizers that have infested America.

Soon, America is under Soviet control. Bobby walks by a row of gallows where the Christians are being executed. One of these is Bobby's Fundamentalist brother. Looking remarkably fresh and unruffled, Bobby's brother tells him: "I'm going to be with the Lord, now..." and puts in one last plug for Jesus before the executioner kicks the box out from under him. Walking away, Bobby grumbles about what a pest his brother was and how he's glad the little creep is dead.

Then comes the shocker: Bobby's Jewish controller tells Bobby that he and his cohorts are going to be executed. The reason? "If you couldn't be trusted not to turn against a free democracy like America, how can we trust you not to turn against US?"

As they are led away, Bobby and his Commie buddies grumble that they were used. One of these revolutionaries is the spitting image of Angela Davis, bushy afro and all. Bobby is shot in the back of the head, with the peace symbol prominently displayed on his back. The inevitable flight with the white, blonde angel and condemnation by the faceless white man to His favorite fiery playground naturally follows. A spate of anti-Communist statements accompany the "Get Saved" blurbs on the back, which, although hilariously laughable now, probably seemed reasonable when this tract was published. Grade: **A+** for Anarchy in the U.S.A.

[**Editor's Note:** Tommy's recollection of this tract is amazingly accurate, despite the passing of decades. The main character's name was not Bobby, however, but Paul. Another correction worth noting is that the artist was Chick himself (not Carter). Despite Tommy's obvious disdain for Chick's views, it's clear this tract made quite an impression on him. Whether you agree with Chick or not, he does a remarkable job at grabbing your attention and making you remember his message. This is a tough tract to find.] **Value: $150.**

THE PRESENT

J.T.C.

©1993 Jack T. Chick.

THE PRESENT Review: (Art by Carter ©1993.) This tract features an unusual art style for Carter. The first seven pages have characters drawn as goofy cartoons from a fairy tale book. That's also the tone of the story. It tells how a good king sends his beloved son to the village to tell his people he has prepared some apartments for them in his Castle. But the villagers don't believe the son and kill him. The king is outraged and sends his army to destroy the village. Then Chick reveals that this story is really the true story of Jesus. He shows scenes of the same story taking place, only the characters are no longer cartoonish and goofy looking. Instead, they appear as skeptical Jews confronting a generous Jesus. An angry Pharisee yells out that they should "Crucify him!" And so they did. The sacrifice, judgment, and eternal torment are summarized using panels seen in previous tracts. Then the usual "how to pray and get saved" panel concludes the story. This is a decent enough tract, but probably not anyone's favorite. However, it is effective at communicating Chick's main message, and for that reason, it is probably pretty popular with missionaries and other witnesses. Grade: **B** for Bland but effective. **Still in print.**

THE PROMISE Review: (Art by Chick ©2001.) This is tract #4 in the new Bible series, featuring the recurring character of Bob. This time, he's visiting Israel and gets to watch a bus full of people explode. Let's cut straight to the chase and say up front that the Favorite Panel Award goes to the very first page. It features your stereotypical Arab villain with explosives strapped all over his body. As he squeezes the detonator, he proudly proclaims, "Death to all Jews! This is for Allah and his prophet Muhammad!" Someone screams "NO!" in the background, but to no avail. The bus explodes and everyone runs late. (Late, as in, the "late" such and such.) If you thought Bob looks creepy with his pale albino eyes, you'll love this Arab. How any bus driver would be stupid enough to let a maniac with wild crazy eyes climb aboard is beyond comprehension. Not much is left of the bus after the tragedy. As the crowd gathers around and looks for free tokens, you would expect some sort of "Oh, the HUMANITY!" speech. Not so. Bob uses the opportunity to preach his latest sermon on God's Chosen People. He tells two tourists that the entire Arab/ Jewish conflict was caused by Abraham fathering Ishmael and Isaac. Of course, he completely ignores the current conflict, which probably has something to do with the Arabs being pushed off the land they've lived on for thousands of years. But for some reason, Bob thinks Arabs are more angry about a 4,000-year-old Biblical injustice to Ishmael, rather than all of them losing their country 55 years ago. (Maybe in another 3,945 years, they'll get around to resenting what happened in 1948.)

The funniest part of this tract is how hard it tries to justify what Abraham did to his first born. The story (for those unenlightened heathens in the audience) goes like this: Abraham and Sarah were two elderly Jews wanting children. Ninety-year-old Sarah tells Abraham he should use their Egyptian servant as a sex slave and father a child through her. (Funny how the Jews can own Egyptian slaves, but when the Egyptians enslave Jews, it's suddenly the crime of the century!) The servant has a child but then the unexpected happens: ninety-year-old Sarah gives birth to Isaac! Sarah gets jealous when the Arab stepbrother teases her son, so she pressures Abraham to send the servant and his first born into the desert to die. The tract doesn't mention mother and child would have died had not an angel appeared to save them. Instead it states, "Ishmael and his mother were angry and humiliated. They were cut off from God's Chosen people." Okay, so let's pretend you've been sent off to die in the desert with your baby... Are you going to be more upset over losing your sex slave job and the company of God's Chosen people? Or would you be more disturbed about watching your child being eaten by vultures while they wait for you to die? (It's only a rhetorical question.)

After reciting Biblical history, Bob gets to the REAL message of the tract: God's promise that "If you refuse God's love gift and reject Jesus Christ as your personal Lord and Saviour, you *will* be cast into the lake of fire." The two tourists do the math and decide heaven is definitely better than hell. They fall to the pavement and accept Jesus. (Lucky for them, the Jews in Israel are more considerate drivers than the ones in New York. No one runs them over for blocking traffic.) Well worth the 14 cent price of admission. Grade: **B+** for Bomb Blast! **Still in print.**

©2001 Jack T. Chick.

©1970 Jack T. Chick.

©1995 Jack T. Chick.

PSSSSSSST! ISN'T IT TIME?? **Review:** (Art by Chick ©1970.) This is one of five super rare promo tracts released around 1970 that urges Christians to support tract ministries. Chick uses a series of biting social commentary cartoons to show readers how desperately we need a revival. Page 2 shows a schoolyard where the children are smoking pot, popping pills, and shooting up on drugs. A little girl flies through the air flapping her arms, while a boy on the swing hiccups in a drunken stupor. The next page shows a street lined with adult movie houses. A thug carries off a grandmother, a gay couple cuddle, and a dirty old man chases a kid. The next scene shows cops trying to arrest a mugger, but his lawyer is running interference. A couple in the background appear to be next on the victim list, even while the cops look on. The next page show racial riots in progress. The National Guard and police stand in front of the burning buildings, unable to stop the destruction. "Student unrest is spreading. Incidentally, have you read the black manifesto? If you did, you would be praying for revival! We received a phone call from a pastor in Hollywood telling of a rapid growth of black magic and witchcraft among teenagers-IN THE ATOMIC AGE?—YES! Have believers lost their influence? Antichrist movements are steadily gaining momentum! While all this is going on, let's look at the valiant defenders of the faith!" Chick shows a confused Christian watching *Bewitched* on TV and wondering aloud if Luke is in the Old or New Testament.

A group at church plan for their annual revival. They decide to get the same Evangelist that they had last year, a man who only succeeded in saving two people at a cost of $2,412.02. Chick suggests that tracts are a cheaper and much easier way to convert the lost. All the excitement over Vietnam must have really activated his military metaphors. Even though this is the same year as *Operation: Somebody Cares* was being launched, Chick also initiated a new campaign he calls *Operation: Wake Up!* It consists of three publications: *Why No Revival, This Was Your Life,* and the 64 page oversized booklet, *The Last Call.*

For the nay-sayers in the audience, Chick states, "Some Christians say there will be no revival. As a result of the spiritual awakening in Indonesia, more than 2,000,000 Moslems have been led to Christ in the last three years. It CAN happen here!" (If it does, let's hope the religious massacres that resulted there don't happen here as well.)

There are so many wonderfully sarcastic cartoons in this tract, it's tough to select a Favorite Panel Award. It could be any one of the first four cartoons described earlier. My vote is for the race-baiting cartoon on page 6, because it's so stridently politically incorrect. The angry expressions on the Negroes faces as they watch the town burn down make it obvious who lit the flames and why. The Rev. Jesse Jackson would label this tract racist faster than you could say "out-of-wedlock love child." But it's too rare to create any controversy. Once the civil unrest of the early 1970s died down, this tract no longer seemed relevant and was quietly retired. What a pity. Grade **A** for Agitate! **Value: Speculative.**

RANSOM Review: (Art by Chick ©1995.) There are some Chick tracts that are so unrealistic, they are hilarious. This is one of those. It's so exaggerated, so stereotypical, so unbelievable—you gotta love it. The plot is pretty basic: two thugs (one complete with a pirate eye-patch and gold ear-ring hoop) kidnap the poor sister of a rich couple. The rich folks are total snobs and could care less. When the kidnappers tell their victim that she hasn't been ransomed, she jumps on the opportunity to preach about Jesus. "Oh Yes I have!" She declares, "My ransom has been paid in full...and I've been set free!" (Children please note: Don't try this line on your kidnappers if you are ever abducted. They will probably kill you just to shut you up.) But in *Chickworld,* the criminals want to hear all about it as they untie her. Both crooks instantly convert to Christianity and not a moment too soon, as the cops have traced the ransom call and are surrounding the building. They bust in and arrest the thugs but the victim refuses to press charges. Instead, she screams "How DARE you invade our Prayer meeting! Have you no respect? These are my new brothers!"

Favorite panel award goes to page 19. As the Christian crooks devoutly pray, a teardrop falls from the Pirate's eye patch. Now *that's* gross! Grade: **B+** for Botched Badness. Recently retired: **$1.50.**

In prison

I *cannot* deny Christ and His Gospel. God will help me bear the pain.

If God gives you the strength to withstand the pain... give us a sign.

I will.

Hawke told his friends... if the pain was bearable, he would lift up his hands toward heaven as a signal before he died.

The crowd had *no idea* what they were about to witness.

©2002 Jack T. Chick.

REVEREND WONDERFUL

J.T.C.

Yes, God cares about souls, but He also cares about *SOCIAL JUSTICE*... the poor and needy!

He's right!

Amen!

We must *UNITE* to fight ignorance and bigotry.

Praise God!

He's wonderful!

Oh, how it must hurt God to see Protestants, Jews and Catholics bickering over incidentals...

We must *pull together* to usher in a great New Age, for the glory of God.

©1982 Jack T. Chick.

REAL HEAT Guest review by Rev. Rich Lee: (Art by Chick © 2002) This is tract #15 in the series of 25 Bible tracts featuring Bob. The melting man on the cover does not quite convey what JTC has in mind in this story about a man injured in an auto accident. A huge semi truck hits a car head-on, killing the driver. The passenger screams "AAAH! I'm burning!" while the paramedics put out the flames. Two months later, Bob Williams visits Rick (the recovering passenger). He is eager to speak to Bob since he knows Rick's mother. Rick can't get the fire of the accident out of his mind. Bob says that fire was an ancient method for execution. "Throughout history, thousands were put to death that way... The fear of fire is a terrible weapon to control people..." Hmm, some non-Christian critics would accuse the Christian faith of controlling people with the threat of burning eternally in Hell. However, this irony does not dawn on Bob as he proceeds to work toward that exact goal.

Bob relates the story from the Protestant classic *Foxe's Book of Martyrs* wherein Thomas Hawkes was burned at the stake. Hawkes refused to have his infant baptized as a Roman Catholic, and refused to convert to Catholicism. For this, Hawkes faced death by burning. In fact, Bob says that the Roman Catholic Church's most effective weapon during the Inquisition was the fear of being burned to death. Bob also relates the story of King Nebuchadnezzar in ancient Babylon from the Old Testament book of Daniel. He explains how the three Hebrew slaves Shadrach, Meshach, and Abednego refused to commit idolatry against God by bowing down to Nebuchadnezzar's golden statue. For punishment, they were cast into a fiery furnace while the king watched. However, he saw four men in the furnace, and the fourth one looked like "the Son of God!" (How a Pagan king would recognize Jesus centuries before his birth is not addressed.)

Bob segues into the message of the Gospel. Bob explains that Jesus was with the three Hebrews in the furnace and protected them from being burned up. Likewise, Jesus will protect anyone from eternal Hell fire if they accept him as their Lord and savior. If not, you can expect plenty of blisters. Rick takes the hint and repents on the spot. He even recites a "Sinner's prayer" without being told what to say. Rick ends his prayer with "I've had enough fire. Amen." (Then he better stay away from Chick tracts, because hell fire is in practically every tract!)

Favorite Panel Award goes to page 8 where Hawkes is burning at the stake. Although completely engulfed in flames, he claps for the audience to show that the pain is bearable with God's help. It's pretty dramatic stuff. Protesters should remember this stunt the next time they set themselves ablaze. It's a real crowd pleaser and sure to get them on CNN! Grade **A** for "AAAH! I'm afire!" **Still in print.**

REVEREND WONDERFUL Guest review by Rev. Richard Lee: (Art by Carter ©1982.) This tract appears to be a sister tract to *The Letter,* wherein the real-life Chaplain Dann guest stars in both tracts. The opening page displays politically correct religious diversity as one of the characters appears to be a Hindu. The people are fawning over a Rev. Dr. Westhall, a slick highly educated respectable clergyman who obviously is not a born again Fundamentalist. As often as Jack Chick is able to do so, he addresses Catholicism in his tracts. This one is no exception. Dr. Westhall has just had a private audience with the Pope, and is scheduled to give a dinner speech after speaking with reporters. Thirty miles away, Chaplain Dann is praying for boldness to share the Gospel with the one whom he hopes God will lead him to. Sensitive to the instruction of God, Dann is led to the location where he is destined to meet Dr. Westhall. Meanwhile, Westhall is at a prestigious dinner party where his accomplishments are announced. He is voted "the most loved man in America...He's so humble...one of today's GREAT men of God." Chick is implying in a not-so-subtle manner that TRUE men of God are never loved or accepted. In fact, although Westhall is fictional, Chick is implying that Westhall is based on "Pope-lover" and most loved preacher Billy Graham, who in fact WAS considered one of America's most loved men, and seldom slandered in the news media. (Chick indicates in *Smokescreens* that he believes Graham to be a pawn or knowing agent of the Vatican.)

As the story continues, Dr. Westhall gives his speech: "Yes, God cares about souls, but He also cares about SOCIAL JUSTICE...the poor and needy! We must UNITE to fight ignorance and bigotry. Oh, how it must hurt God to see Protestants, Jews, and Catholics bickering over incidentals...We must PULL TOGETHER to usher in a great New Age, for the glory of God." Like *The Letter,* this tract is a swipe at liberal mainline Protestants who tend to emphasize social justice over evangelism and the literal Second Coming of Christ. Furthermore, Chick considers the union of Protestants, Jews, and Catholics to be a compromise of Biblical doctrine, and such a unity will constitute a super church in the end times, which foreshadows the return of Christ. As Westhall leaves in a limo, he converses with a Catholic priest whom he calls "Father." Chick refers the reader to Matthew 23:9, which seems to forbid the use of such religious titles. Westhall's assistant forgot his notes, so they are forced to go back to the office to retrieve them. The slick limo is to be compared with Chaplain Dann's humble Ford truck, which drives up nearby with "I HOPE 4U" on the license plate. Again, as in *The Letter,* Chick highlights the subtle socio-economic angle that separates the likes of Chaplain Dann, a lowly Fundamentalist, with the high and mighty types of a Dr. Westhall, a prestigious mainline Protestant.

As Westhall descends from his office stairs, Dann confronts him: "The Lord sent me to talk to you about your soul...If you died tonight, are you sure you would go to heaven?" You can barely see the Chick tracts in his shirt pocket. As Westhall's assistant and priest-friend come to his rescue, they extol his pedigree: "THE Dr. Westhall...D.D., M.A., B.A., Th.D., D.R.E. Come on, Dr. Westhall, or you'll miss your plane." As he leaves, Chaplain Dann shouts, "But you never told me...are you SAVED?" To further add insult (with the added socio-economic elitist angle), Westhall exclaims "How HUMILIATING! People like that are SICK! ... We should talk to the Governor about passing a law to keep people like him off the streets."

Dr. Westhall boards his plane and dies in a midair collision. On the Day of Judgment, Jesus tells Dr. Westhall that his name is not in the Book of Life, because he never accepted Christ while he was alive. The weeping reverend is sent to hell.

I especially enjoy the earlier version of *Reverend Wonderful* because it contains a lengthier speech by Jesus of Westhall's faults. Westhall is condemned for preaching a gospel of love and unity rather than separation and holiness. People spent time in "YOUR books, tapes, etc." rather than in the Bible. Not only that, the earlier version is more vocally anti-Catholic than the updated version. Westhall is condemned for not calling Catholics out of the false religious system, and hating Dann in his heart for witnessing to him. That was his only chance before the plane crash, and he blew it. Therefore, it's luau time in the Lake of Fire forever! This tract features class envy at its best, with plenty here to offend everyone including Hindus, Jews, Catholics, non-Fundamentalist mainline Protestants, upper middle class people, and charitable workers who donate money, time, and effort to social causes, but neglect to preach salvation through Christ. **A** for Aloof. Original version with *The Contract* tract visible (page 13): **$6.** Recent reprint without *The Contract* (page 13): **$2.**

ROOM 310 Review: (Art by Carter ©1973 and 2002.) In many ways, this is one of Chick's most sobering tracts. Not because the protagonist dies via some dramatic car crash or airline accident, but rather, through a disease we all know and fear: The Big "C"... Cancer! Danny's friends go to visit him at the hospital. Like most folks, they don't like hospitals and can't wait to leave. They try to act cheerful around Danny but the reassurances and optimism ring hollow. "We're pulling for you!", "We'll keep our fingers crossed!", and the classic cliché, "Keep your chin up Danny. They could come up with a cure for cancer tomorrow!" (Yeah, right.) The moment Danny's three buddies get out of there, they agree Danny looks terrible and they don't want to go back because it's too depressing.

Meanwhile, Danny is passing the time by yelling at the hospital minister and throwing him out of his room. The Chaplain made the critical error of offering to leave a Bible. "@!!!***!! You get out of my room right now—or I'll call the nurse!" Danny shouts, "—and you know what you can do with that Bible!" (No Danny, we don't. Our minds are pure from reading Chick tracts.)

Danny calms down after the incident by thumbing though a porn magazine and smoking some of the cigars his buddies were considerate enough to drop off for him. (Maybe he'll kill the cancer with fumes.) His black roommate starts to witness to him. Danny tells the bro to go to hell.

A week later, Danny is a little more desperate for company. He asks his roommate why his friends never came back. The roomy tries to witness again, but Danny gives him the brush-off. "Shut up!" he yells, "Stop trying to convert me! My friends would *never* forgive me if I became a Christian!"

But time is on the roommate's side. As Danny's condition worsens, his resistance to witnessing weakens as well. The Christian senses his target is vulnerable and launches another advance. He tells a story of two Chinese brothers, one who sacrifices his life for the other. The ruse works. Danny is touched by the tale but not quite ready to commit to Christ because he fears his friends would laugh at him. Still, success is so close the roommate can taste it!

Finally, the agony of dying combined with constant preaching wears down Danny until he agrees to say the sinner's prayer. (He's got nothing to lose, his friends have already found a new bowling buddy.) Before croaking, Danny makes an unusual confession. He says he's glad he's dying slow from cancer instead of quickly with a heart attack. "This way I had a chance to find out how much God loves me," he confides, "and how I'll be in his love throughout eternity."

It's a bittersweet ending to an otherwise depressing scenario. You have to give the roommate credit though: If he recovers, he'll make one hell of a salesman.

Interesting note: Chick treasurer Ron Rockney appears in this tract as the Chaplain who gets thrown out for trying to dispense Bibles. He should have tried Chick tracts instead—they get read! Grade **A-** for Agonizing yet Amazing grace. **Still in print.**

©1973 Jack T. Chick.

The unseen hosts of heaven and hell were all in the viewing audience.

That night David broke 3 of God's 10 Commandments:

1. He coveted (lusted after) Bathsheba, Uriah's wife. 2. He stole her. 3. David committed adultery by having sex with her.

THE ROYAL AFFAIR Review: This tract relates the Bible story of King David's adulterous affair with Bathsheba. There are actually two versions of this tract. The first one is by the mysterious third artist and ©1990. It was later updated and completely redrawn by Fred Carter in 1993. The differences between the two are significant and interesting. The 1990 version has all the action occurring in Biblical times. But the Bible story tracts were not selling as well as the tracts set in modern themes, so Chick had Fred Carter redraw the story and encapsulate it within a modern context. Whereas the original begins with a Biblical battle scene, the newer version opens in a modern courtroom during a sexual harassment trial. The bulk of both tracts outline the basic tale of how King David had everything, but blew it by staying home from the war one night and playing hide the sausage with another man's wife. He first sees Bathsheba bathing in the moonlight. Then he sends for her, porks her (which isn't very kosher for a Jewish king), and completely ignores the fact she's married to one of his soldiers. *When the soldier's away, the generals play!* The plot thickens when she becomes pregnant. David realizes her husband will know she was cheating on him because he's been off fighting the war all the while. David orders the husband (Uriah) home in hopes he'll have sex with his wife and assume the baby is legitimate. No such luck. Uriah sleeps outside the king's door. David tries another scheme: get Uriah drunk and tell him to go home. (*Good old alcohol!* It's nature's answer to abstinence.) Unfortunately, Uriah becomes too drunk to cross the street and go home. David resorts to murder. He gives Uriah a sealed letter to deliver to his commander. It says to send Uriah into battle and abandon him to die. The commander obeys, Uriah becomes an arrow cushion, and David marries his widow. Everything looks *hunky-dory,* until the prophet Nathan shows up and blows the whistle on David's dirty deeds. Rather than punish the *actual sinners,* both David and Bathsheba continue to rule in royal splendor. Instead, their *first born* dies and their additional *children* engage in murder, rape, and incest. (And you thought soap operas were kinky.)

The 1990 version features juicer details than the '93 version. Most of the drawings are medium shots, providing much more background than the close-ups in the later tract. We get to see Bathsheba naked in the tub (if it weren't for a few strategically placed bath bubbles.) When Uriah bites the big one, we watch him getting skewered. (The later tract only shows his arrow-riddled corpse.) One gets the feeling the sex and violence was toned down in response to various complaints. However, the newer version wins the coveted Favorite Panel Award, since it alone features the hilarious image of a senator getting throttled by his wife as she screams for a divorce (page 3b).

On a more philosophical note, both tracts make a big deal out of the fact that David's baby goes to heaven, **as do *all* babies.** We'll skip over to question of why God killed an innocent baby for the sins of the parents, since only God knows and he's taken the fifth. But how does Chick reconcile babies going directly to heaven when other tracts clearly state NO ONE goes to heaven unless they accept Jesus? Maybe we'll get another tract addressing that paradox sometime.

Until then, this is a catchy tract with a timeless message. About the only thing that could be done to update it more is to make the Senator a President. Grade: **B+** for Bathing Beauty. Original version without courtroom intro, **$15.** Redrawn version with courtroom intro, **$4.**

The Story of Abraham and Isaac

THE SACRIFICE

I don't think we heard God correctly.

He must have meant someone else would give birth to Isaac.

Abraham, I have a wonderful idea.

My Egyptian servant could bear a child for us.

THE SACRIFICE Review: (Art by the third artist ©1991.) This is one of those Old Testament stories that make you wonder about the family values of Israel's founding fathers. (It's an unintended interpretation if you read between the lines. Weigh the evidence and decide for yourself.) God promised Abraham that his 76-year-old wife would bear a child named Isaac. Sarah doesn't believe it's possible, so she offers up her Egyptian slave Hagar to conceive the child. Hagar supposedly agrees, but she obviously had little choice, as Sarah's fierce temper soon demonstrates. Once Hagar becomes pregnant, Sarah doesn't like the way her slave looks at her and demands that Abraham throw her out. Abraham agrees and sends his yet-to-be-born baby and its mother to the desert to die. An angel visits Hagar and tells her that the child will become a great nation, but she must return and submit to Sarah. She returns to her owners and the son is born. They name it Ishmael, despite the original plan to name it Isaac.

Fourteen years later, 90-year-old Sarah gives birth to a boy and they name him Isaac. Like most older brothers, Ishmael makes fun of his sibling. Once again, angry Sarah demands her slave be abandoned to the desert, along with her stepson. (Where's the Slave's Union during all of this?) Wimpy Abe agrees and the two are exiled to the burning sands. They run out of water and wait to die beneath the brutal sun. An angel calls out to Hagar, and a well suddenly appears. The mother and child are spared certain death. Ishmael grows up and marries an Egyptian and becomes the father of Arab nations.

Meanwhile, God tells Abraham to sacrifice Isaac as a burnt offering. Always one to follow orders, Abe takes Isaac to a secluded mountain and prepares to murder his son. God stops him before the knife falls and lets him sacrifice a ram instead. It was all a test to see how obedient Abraham really was. But this creates an obvious paradox: If God knows in advance what everyone is going to do, why does he carry out such cruel tests?

Keep in mind that Chick raises none of these embarrassing questions. He puts the best possible face on slavery, sexual harassment, and Abe's failed attempts at infanticide. One thing's for certain: No one will ever accuse Chick or the Old Testament of being politically correct! Favorite Panel Award goes to page 11. It's a desert scene showing a crying Hagar in the background while a hungry vulture waits in the foreground perched atop a dry skull. Grade **B+** for Bloated Bird. **Value: $4**

©1986 Jack T. Chick.

SATAN'S MASTER Review: (Art by Carter ©1986.) This is one of the anti-witchcraft tracts inspired by Rebecca Brown. (See also, *The Poor Little Witch*.) It tells the story of four young girls who are initiated into a witches' coven by an evil high priestess. The group is systematically killed off except for one (who gets saved) following the same Chick formula used in other stories like *Angels?* The first victim is Ann. The high priestess sends a demon after her that tosses her face first from a third story window. (She had whispered something naughty behind the priestess' back.) The second victim is the high priestess herself. She made the mistake of summoning her demon "Ri-Chan" to go after Judy, a born-again ex-witch who exposed other witches who tried to infiltrate the local Bible study. The demon returns yelling, "You dirty @*#:! You dare send me against a true, born-again believer. Her angels almost killed me, and I'm going to beat you to death." The battered priestess begs help from Satan himself, who shows up only to mock her. "Me help you? You stupid @*#j! You got yourself in this mess. Now get yourself out. Haw! Haw! Haw!" Chick provides a footnote at this point that reads, "What a sweet daddy!" In what is perhaps the worse timing of all time, in walks Hannah, the so-called "white witch," right when Ri-Chan is still whipping the near dead priestess. Hannah is shocked. As Chick mentioned earlier, "the white witch believes her powers are only for good. She believes that she is pure." But as Ri-Chan strangles the life out of her, he lets her in on a secret: "You little fool. We demons supply the power behind **all** forms of witchcraft. This is for your failure to handle Judy."

These brutal events send Sarah running to born-again Judy for advice. Judy tells her, "Simply ask Jesus to forgive you for all you've done, and to cleanse you and take away all your powers of witchcraft. Then

your contract will be broken and your name will be in the Lamb's Book of Life." So there you have it. The Christians triumph and the sinners die an agonizing death. Everything is tied up in a neat little bundle.

Heyyyy, wait a sec! There was **another** girl in the group that mysteriously disappeared without explanation... But not to worry. She wore a hippie headband and no bra. So she's probably dead by now from a drug overdose or AIDS—or both! After all, we can't have any loose ends left over. (That would be so un-Chick.) And like the high priestess warned, "There is **no** escape. You leave the craft only one way, and that's feet first." (Except for Ann, who went head first.) Grade **A** for AAAAAIIIEEEE! (splat.) Permanently retired: **$56.**

©2002 Jack T. Chick.

THE SCAM Review: (Art by Chick ©2002.) Tract #9 in the Bible series of 25 starring Bob. The tale of Joshua getting tricked by the Gibeonites is told in this tract. It starts with a guy named Frank getting conned by an elderly couple. He gives them $500 cash for their car but then loans it to them and they drive off with it. After overhearing Frank whine to police that he's broke, Bob offers him a free meal. (You would think after being recently conned, Frank would have learned there is no such thing as a free lunch.) Sure enough, Bob starts preaching faster than you can say, "Check please." He tells the Old Testament story of how a Jewish soldier stole some precious metals and clothing from Jericho after the Israelite army invaded it and murdered everyone. God didn't appreciate the soldier's recycling efforts and made the Israelites lose the next attack until they found the thief and killed him. This story is actually Bob's warm up act. The real sermon is about how Joshua was tricked into a treaty with a future target of Israel. The Gibeonites dress poor and approach Joshua claiming to have come from far away. They flatter him and ask for a treaty. He grants it. Later, he realizes they were next on his conquest list but feels obligated to honor the treaty. (It's hard to believe he ruled over 3 million Jews at the time, and there wasn't a single good lawyer who could have wormed out of that treaty.) Bob says that Satan was behind the Gibeonites scheme to stay alive, just as he was behind the thieves who stole Frank's money. (He fails to mention that Frank's greedy desire to buy a car for pennies on the dollar was also a factor in the scam.)

For dessert, Bob offers the Satan sandwich. That's where Bob lifts the outer crust and reveals what the meat of the matter really is. As always, it's Satan. Those who fail to give their life to Jesus will suffer heartburn for all eternity...along with every other burn imaginable. The Satan sandwich is Bob's specialty, but he wraps it in different bread and passes it off as something new in each tract. The listener thinks they are hearing a tale about some ancient folks when it is actually a story about the listener and how they can avoid damnation. This ploy has worked nine times straight and will probably work another 16 times before Bob is through. Frank assumes the praying position and starts the Sinner's prayer. As if to show approval from above, the cops return in 15 minutes to announce that they've caught the crooks and retrieved the stolen money. Crime may not pay, but reciting that Sinner's prayer sure does!

Favorite Panel Award goes to page 10, where the thief is getting stoned to death. (If that's what he gets for confessing, one wonders what the punishment would have been for lying.) At least it doesn't appear too painful. It looks like he's the cook getting pelted with a barrage of burnt biscuits! Grade **B+** for Butter those Biscuits! **Still in print.**

his second born instead of his first. Esau is justifiably infuriated when he discovers the plot, but Jacob sneaks off to stay with his mother's brother until his angry brother cools off. While there, he falls in love with his cousin Rachel. His uncle Laban doesn't seem to mind the incestuous relationship, and says he can marry his cousin in exchange for seven years labor. The sleaze factor seems to run thick on Rebekah's side of the family. As Chick puts it, "Though Jacob was a scoundrel, he was **no** match for Laban." When the wedding night arrives, Laban slips the **other** sister under the sheets and Jacob discovers the following morning that he married the wrong wife. As Chick puts it, "Laban had outfoxed the fox." Laban claims it's their custom (What, to cheat?) and Jacob agrees to work another 7 years for Rachel. They finally marry and Jacob is exchanging body fluids with **both** his cousins. (Talk about all in the family!) Jacob returns home after 14 years as a rich man. Esau welcomes him and his in-laws/ cousins. Chick warns, "But their offspring became deadly enemies. Esau's line became the Arabs of today." Scoundrel Jacob is renamed Israel. Chick states that eleven of the twelve sons of Israel were all scoundrels, "But God loved and blessed them in spite of themselves." (Sounds like our support of Israel today.) The closing panels explain how *everyone* is a scoundrel, but God loves us, too. The last panel says, "Only **a scoundrel** would turn down God's love gift and spend eternity in the lake of fire." (Wait a sec. It told us earlier we *are* scoundrels, so is this some kind of *Catch 22?*) Grade: **B+** Back Biting Brothers. **Value $2.25.**

The Story of Jacob
THE SCOUNDREL

SCREAM!
㉑

Esau became a cunning hunter....
He was Isaac's favorite.

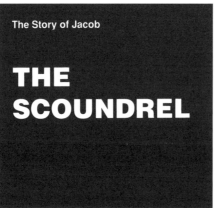
But Rebekah loved Jacob...
who had his own special skills. *He was sneaky... like his mama.*

©1991 Jack T. Chick.

"There was a certain rich man, which was clothed in purple and fine linen, and fared sumptuously every day:"
He had it made!

"And there was a certain beggar named Lazarus, which was laid at his gate, full of sores,
And desiring to be fed with the crumbs which fell from the rich man's table: moreover the dogs came and licked his sores." Luke 16:19-21

©2002 Jack T. Chick.

THE SCOUNDREL Review: (Art by Fred Carter © 1991.) This tract tells the Old Testament tale of Jacob. Rebekah gives birth to Esau and Jacob. Esau grows up to be a great hunter, and Jacob turns into a real snake in the grass. Together with his conniving mother, the two scheme a way to defraud the blind father into giving Jacob the birthright that really belongs to Esau. Step one is to get Esau to trade his birthright to Jacob for a bowl of stew. Step two is to wait until daddy is about to die and ready to give his blessing to his eldest son. Sneaky mom outfits slimy son with goat fur to cover his arms and neck in order to trick her handicapped husband into thinking it's Esau. Jacob enters the tent with dad's meal and asks for the birthright. Not realizing what a lying cheat he's created, Isaac blesses

SCREAM! Guest review by Emby Quinn: (Art by Chick ©2002.) Tract #21 of 25 featuring Bob Williams. The story begins with two would-be arsonists entering a warehouse to torch it. The owner is paying $2,000 (half in advance, the rest "when it's nothing but ashes," gloats Charlie, the man in charge). With a liberal amount of gasoline, Charlie starts the blaze and his partner, Sonny, hoofs it out of the building. Charlie trips on his way out, the flames engulf him, and we get a wonderful one panel shot of Charlie covered in flaming death. (This is similar to another firewalker scene in *Real Heat,* just six tracts earlier.) The Fire Department is called and arrives to put out the flames—of the warehouse, not Charlie. Sonny is in the crowd watching nervously. He's sure that Charlie is dead because *"**Nobody** could* live through **that!**" One of the firefighters, Fred, falls through the roof into the burning building. He is rescued, alive but badly burned.

Fast-forward a couple of weeks to the hospital, where Fred is told how lucky he is—the arsonist's remains were found on the floor below. Fred's devoted wife brings in Our Hero Bob Williams, presumably because Fred isn't suffering enough already. Fred complains about his flashbacks ("The flames, the smoke...it was **hell!**"). Now come on, how could we expect good old Bob to resist an opening like that? "You got a **taste** of hell...but it's a lot **worse** than that!" With little further preamble, Bob launches in on the by-now-familiar boilerplate about Jesus being God, how He created all things including Hell, yadda yadda yadda. Then the actual "Bible story" part of the tract begins, telling the story of the rich man and Lazarus. I'm sure that some people out there aren't entirely familiar with this story, even though it was rehashed in an earlier tract (see *The Trap*), so for the sake of those two people unfamiliar with it, I won't spoil the ending, except to say that the phrase "you can't take it with you" doesn't even begin to cover it for our poor little rich dude.

Anyway, after terrorizing the fire-traumatized burn victim about the eternal flames of hell for most of the rest of the tract, Bob dangles the "pray to Jesus and repent" panacea, which Fred eagerly gobbles down (at this point I'm wondering if he was really sincere or if he just wanted Bob to shut the $#%@! up about the "Lake of Fire" and its various torments). Bob then looks out at the reader with this really creepy negative-eyes effect and tells YOU that "To get **saved** is the **most important** thing in your life. You **are** going to die, and don't kid yourself...you **will** be judged!" Thanks for the heads-up, buddy. The concluding text backs Bob up on this, telling you that "You can't squirm out of this...you really got nailed when you read this story. You've got **no excuse** now!"

Other than the fact that I certainly wouldn't recommend giving this tract to a burn victim in the hospital no matter what concerns you may have about the state of their soul, I must admit there are some loose ends that rather annoyed me. What about Sonny, the doomed arsonist's sidekick? Are we going to see him either come to Jesus or get what he deserves in a future tract? And what about the genius who got himself flash-fried by his own accelerant? Shouldn't we have seen his just punishment for his misdeeds? Why no scene of Charlie-the-arsonist burning in Hell for eternity? Maybe Charlie accepted Jesus in the last moments of his fiery agony and his name is now in the Book of Life. Grade: C+ for Charbroiled Charlie. **Still in print.**

THE SECRET Guest review by Rev. Rich Lee: (Art by Chick ©1999.) The woman on the cover wearing a scarf and sunglasses says it all. She is harboring a secret, but what could it be? Two police officers find out when they respond to a domestic violence call. A drunk opens the door and denies that any violence occurred, but then his son attacks him with a knife and yells, "I HATE YOU!" (Move over Norman Bates!) The police demand to see the wife. She appears with a black eye and bloodied face. In typical codependent fashion, she says, "I fell down, officer. It was an accident." Sure thing, lady—and *The Jerry Springer Show* is for intellectuals!

The man is carted off in the squad car while the son growls, "When I grow up, I'll KILL YOU for hurting mom." Why should he wait until he grows up when he just tried to commit patricide two panels earlier? He should finish the job sooner and take his dad's place in the slammer.

In jail, the heavy-handed husband admits to God that he wants to change, but he can't. Interestingly enough, he makes this confession on his own without the prompting of any Chick tracts. (That's a first.) Across town, the mother prays that God will solve her dilemma. At least she doesn't bail his sorry butt out like most dysfunctional codependent wives do. *But I love him!*—Yeah, right. Tell that to Mr. Fist.

Two days later, Pastor Hunt is feeding the jailbirds free Bibles. The wife beater takes one and asks to talk with the pastor. He tells Hunt that his name is Roy Davis and "The secret is out! I'm a drunk and a wife-beater!...no matter how hard I try to change...I can't!" The pastor tells good ol' Roy that he can't change because he's "dead," meaning that he's dead in his sins due to Adam's transgression. Funny, Adam was punished for *obeying* his wife, while Roy is punished for making his wife obey him! Men can't win either way!

Fang (the dog) appears as a tattoo on a prisoner's arm as the pastor continues. "Because sin brings death, we are ALL dead spiritually." Roy responds, "Then it's hopeless, preacher...We're all **doomed!**" Hey, wait a minute, it's the pastor who should be doing the preaching. Hunt assures his captive audience that he isn't doomed after all, because of the sacrifice that Jesus gave frees everyone from sin, including wife-beaters. After praying the obligatory Sinner's prayer, Roy tells the pastor "Wow! I feel different!... I can't wait to get out so I can tell my wife and son what happened." (Translation: Hey Pastor, are you stupid enough to post my bail?)

©1999 Jack T. Chick.

Upon release, Roy goes home and says "Guess what I have behind my back" to which the son replies "A fist?" Good comeback, kid. Instead of smacking the wise guy, Roy responds "No, honey...roses!" (We'll assume by "honey," he means his wife. Otherwise this could turn into another *Lisa* or *Wounded Children* tract.) Next, he dumps all of his liquor down the drain, promising that it won't be in their house again (shouldn't the wife have done this earlier? She had plenty of time while he was in the pokey). Roy explains how the preacher led him to Christ. Two months later, the wife and son come around to accepting Jesus, too. The son can finally put the knife away or save it for culinary use.

Twenty-eight years later, Roy Davis dies of a massive heart attack. (It seems that most Christians in Chick tracts die of heart attacks after living many years after their conversion.) Roy meets the Faceless One on His White Throne of Judgment and gets a free pass into paradise. Back on earth, Mrs. Davis calls Roy a "perfect husband. I can't wait to see him in heaven." One wonders what became of the kid, who by now is either playing in a Boy Band or threatening to burn down Bible colleges (see **The Crusaders** volume 11, *Sabotage?*). Maybe he'll need that knife after all. Grade "**B**" for Battered! Recently retired: **$1.50.**

THE SECRET OF PRAYER

CHRISTIAN GROWTH SERIES   By J.T.C

TRUE STORY

YOU HAVE MY WORD, I'LL PAY YOU BACK

YOU SAVED MY NECK!

A FRIEND OF MINE (A CHRISTIAN) LOANED $3,000 TO A MAN IN SERIOUS TROUBLE.

6 MONTHS LATER

KISS YOUR MONEY GOODBYE *BABY*—BECAUSE I'LL *NEVER* PAY YOU BACK!

©1972 Jack T. Chick.

It's hard to give such a tract a poor grade when it has stuff like this in it. For one thing, the story is a delicious tale of twisted cause and effect, making the tract well worthwhile in and of itself. Another reason is I don't want to wind up being incorporated in a similar tract anytime soon: "True story. After criticizing Chick tracts, a writer lost control of his motorcycle and plowed **head-on** into—" So give it a **B** for *Better safe than sorry.* **Value: $25.**

Top Secret
CONFIDENTIAL

THE SECRET WEAPON

By J.T.C.

"What you couldn't do in 100 years with church buildings, mission stations, schools, etc.

We did in ten years... **with literature!**"

Someday, thanks to our secret weapon, we will drive you missionaries out of our country!

©1994 Jack T. Chick.

THE SECRET OF PRAYER Review: (Art by Chick ©1972.) This is companion tract to **Don't Read That Book** (DRTB). Whereas DRTB tells Christians how to read the Bible, this tract tells them how to pray. It shares a variety of other characteristics with DRTB. First, it's part of the "Christian Growth Series" and was probably given away free. Second, it's one of the toughest tracts to find. Third, it's reprinted in **The Next Step** (Chapter 3). Fourth, it's bland compared to other Chick tracts.

There are plenty of 'toons in this tract. (Many more than DRTB.) There are a few panels replaced with different cartoons in *The Next Step* version, as well as one cartoon that is replaced entirely with text. But for the most part, the tract is faithfully reprinted in the book. Its basic premise is that you should pray 5, maybe 6 times a day. (Like Chick points out, Daniel prayed three times a day, and he had three different high-ranking jobs. So what's **your** excuse?) Your prayers will be answered, but there's a catch: "Whatsoever we ask, we receive of him, because we keep his commandments and do those things that are pleasing in his sight" (John 3:22).

In other words, you have to follow all the rules in order to get the goodies. (Which no doubt takes some of the fun out of the equation.) God will also protect you and punish your enemies, so be sure to pray for them or they may wind up dead. Favorite Panel Award goes to just such a story told in three serial panels. It says, "True story. A friend of mine (a Christian) loaned $3,000 to a man in serious trouble. Six months later..." It shows the guy smoking a cigar and taunting the Christian over the phone, "Kiss your money goodbye baby—because I'll NEVER pay you back!" The last panel shows a car going over a cliff, "That man and his girlfriend plunged to a Christless grave." Yikes! And here's the best part— the Christian is to blame! Chick quotes Matthew 18:6 "But whoso shall offend one of these little ones that believe in me, it were better for him that a millstone were hanged about his neck, and that he were drowned in the depth of the sea." Then adds, ominously, "My friend forgot to pray for that man to protect him from God's judgment."

THE SECRET WEAPON Review: (Art by Chick ©1994 and 1974???.) The mysteries surrounding this tract are as interesting as the tract itself. This is one tough title to find, even though it's relatively new (©1994). It looks to have been a promo and given away, and therefore, it wasn't listed in catalogs. Many collectors didn't even know it existed until it was already gone. What's more, it *might have* first appeared in 1974 under a different title, *You Missionaries Are Fools*. Although no copies have yet been discovered, the evidence is more than just rumor. A source at Chick recalls that it was an early tract with that title, but can't find a copy. He may be thinking of an issue of *Battle Cry* that featured a reproduction of a strip with that title. However, it's so condensed that half of the panels are missing. The copyright date of that strip is 1974, even though *Battle Cry* didn't start until 1983. Why would Chick copyright something a decade before publishing it in his paper? One answer is that he might have used it in a catalog earlier, and copyrighted it at that time.

But there's more. A reprinted version of this story was recently published by the *Bible & Literature Missionary Foundation* in tract form. It's released with Chick's permission but not by Chick Publications. And it contains the 1974 copyright! Their title only says *Missionaries are Fools* (with no "You" at the front). Although it is only 20 pages long (4 pages shorter than most Chick tracts) it has several panels not found in *The Secret Weapon*. Unless Chick drew these specifically for the Missionary Foundation, it would seem to indicate the artwork was from a completed tract story that was slated for publishing in the mid-1970s. So keep your eyes open for it! Maybe you can be the one to find a copy and solve this mystery once and for all.

The story line of this tract is rather hard to swallow. A missionary in China preaches to the masses, and is then approached by a communist official. He assumes it's because the man wants to learn about Jesus. He's mistaken. In true Chick style, the officer is a sadistic Commie Atheist whose only purpose is to *mentally torture* the missionary by advising him how he blew his sermon. The really bizarre thing is, his advice is good advice! Why he's so certain the Christian won't follow it is anyone's guess. His suggestion is a simple one: don't just preach, pass out Gospel literature (like say, Chick tracts) so your message will linger long after your speech is forgotten. He confides that this technique is the "Secret Weapon" that the communists used to convert the Chinese before coming to power. You find yourself wanting to shout at the cartoon, "Hey you red rat, get a clue! It won't be a SECRET anymore if you tell your enemy what it is and how it works!" The whole thing is reminiscent of the campy *Batman* show from the 1960s, with villains taking the time and effort to reveal their schemes to the one person who can ruin everything if he manages to act on that information. Like Batman, you get the feeling the hero of this tract will somehow manage to escape and return to fight another day. Only next time, he'll be well equipped with tracts!

Some of the changes between the 1974 reprint from the Bible & Literature Missionary Foundation and the 1994 version are pretty amusing. In the 1974 version, the commie approaches the missionary with the greeting, "You missionaries are fools!" By 1994, he's toned it down to "You just missed a **great** opportunity!" The '74 reprint makes it very obvious the commie is not doing anyone any favors; he's just there to torment the poor Christian. Chick spells it out with the narration, "The Tormentor bowed stiffly and walked away. The Missionary groaned with regret. His feelings of satisfaction had fled." This scene is completely gone in the 1994 version. What's missing in the reprint that's odd is the opening date. The 1994 version starts out with the statement: "**Summer 1947,** The missionary brings his message to an end." The 1974 reprint only says, "The missionary brings his wonderful message to an end." This is strange because both versions have the officer bragging, "We Communists have been in China for less than ten years and EVERY Chinese person knows of Stalin and Communism!" This statement only makes sense if the story takes place in 1947. (By 1974, the Communists had been in China for several decades.)

My personal theory is that this promo originally came out in 1974 as *You Missionaries are Fools,* and is basically identical to the Missionary Foundation's reprint, except the other four pages were filled with Chick tract titles and catalog information. This is in keeping with other Chick promos (e.g., *The Secret Weapon* is padded this way at the end). Chick condensed it for reprinting in *Battle Cry* as filler to push his tract sales. Then he brought it back in the 1990s as another promo tract with a different title, *The Secret Weapon*. Along with the modern copyright date (1994), they replaced the hand drawn dialogue with computer text and inserted "Secret Weapon" into the conversation to tie it into the title. (They probably got negative feedback from missionaries about the earlier title calling them fools. Everyone's a critic!) Meanwhile, Chick had long since given the Missionary Foundation permission to reprint his earlier version to their heart's content, because they drum up business for him. (If missionaries complain about the old title to the Foundation, that's not Chick's problem anymore.) But I emphasize, this is only a theory.

Favorite Panel Award goes to page 12, where the discouraged missionary clenches his fist and looks skyward to whine, "Oh, God...it's true! Why, oh why, couldn't we have had literature?" In the '74 reprint version, he continues with, "Who failed us Lord?—Who?" Well, don't blame Chick! The guilty party is probably the schmuck reading the tract who didn't dig deep and send enough money to the Missionary Foundation to buy more tracts. Why, oh why, do I find the melodramatic tone so hilarious? Grade: **B+** for Bible Blockade! **Value: $90.**

©1991 Jack T. Chick.

SIN BUSTERS Guest review by Ryan Hill: (Art by Carter ©1991.) Jack Chick does his best to counteract the separation of church and state. Like *Doom Town,* this tract has a short modern story as parenthesis to a tale out of the Old Testament. The best panels come from this modern story, which makes me wish he had granted it more time.

One student learns that a teacher was arrested for putting the 10 Commandments on a bulletin board. "The 10 what?" he asks. Another student then explains to him about the story of Moses, and how he received the 10 commandments. This includes some good parts where Chick depicts people ignoring each commandment. Fans of the 8th, 9th, and 10th commandments, however, may be disappointed when those are skimmed over in half a page.

The story then pulls back to present day, as the one student expresses wonder at why this knowledge has been hidden from him. The other student explains that it is the fault of "the evil world system that now controls most schools." The younger student then promptly prays to Jesus to forgive him, with tears streaming from the outside corners of his eyes. The best panel is probably the first, where police lay the boots into the teacher while onlookers cheer and drug dealers operate ten feet away. Another few points for the references to an anti-Christian conspiracy, and some of the portrayals of the commandments are good. All in all, I'd give it a **B+** for Boot Bashing the teacher!

[Interesting trivia: page 3 features the two school kids walking beneath the U.S. flag. This same image is used in the revised reprint of *The Gay Blade,* except the two boys are holding hands!] **Still in print.**

©2001 Jack T. Chick.

©1978 Jack T. Chick.

SIN CITY Review: (Art by Chick ©2001.) This is tract #3 in the series of 25 featuring Bob Bob Williams. In it, Chick slams the gays in his classic "no holds barred" style. It begins with a gay pride parade complete with homosexuals in full drag. A black fundamentalist protests in the center of the street with a sign reading, "Homosexuality is an Abomination." Two cops descend on him with batons and beat him black and blue. (Well, blue, anyway.) The crowd eggs them on, cheering, "kill him!" No encouragement is necessary however, as one cop yells, "Damn straight!", and the other wears mascara and an ear ring. The Christian winds up in the hospital connected to machines and wrapped like a mummy. The PC politicians and policemen show up and threaten to send him to jail for hate crimes (if he recovers) unless he listens to a pro-gay Bible scholar. A balding guy in rainbow robes declares, "I'm Reverend Ray and I'm gay! Jesus *loves* me!" A demon behind Ray says, "I'm Zanah and I hate your guts!" Meanwhile, the black dude's wife calls Bob, the recurring character from the last two tracts. Bob races to the rescue and barges in seconds before Ray convinces the patient that the real reason God destroyed Sodom was because they didn't help the poor. Bob points his finger at Ray and admonishes, "You're perverting the word of God. You forgot about Jude, verse 7. I'm going to pray *right now!*" That sends the demon fleeing the scene. As it exits, it says, "Bye Ray! As a team, we sure ruined a lot of kids!" Ray's stunned. "What happened? Everything's brighter!" (Bob has lifted the dark cloud of perversion from your shoulders, Ray.) Bob relates the tale of Sodom and rattles off a list of anti-gay bible references. Then Bob goes in for the kill: "Tell me, Ray, of all the sins, lying, adultery, stealing, etc., can you think of any other sin where God Himself wiped out entire cities to remove that sin?" Ray can't. Ray finally admits defeat. "I'm not going to fight God anymore. What should I do?" Bob orders him to assume the position and repent like there's no tomorrow. Ray does so and is overjoyed at being saved. It's a happy ending for everyone. Except perhaps, the battered patient who began it all and is still hooked up to life support. But at least if he croaks, Bob's found a replacement. Grade **A** for Activist. **Still in print.**

THE SISSY Review: (Art by Carter ©1978.) Here's a tract that turns up a lot, especially at truck stops. It starts with a big hairy truck driver bragging to a scrawny sidekick while hauling a big load. Duke boasts, "then I knocked the 3rd guy right though a plate glass window into the street... It's a man's world, Billy Joe, Ya gotta be tough to survive." The odd couple pulls into the *Texxon* gas station and Duke sees a "Jesus Saves" bumper sticker. Duke sneers, "Only a gutless idiot would have that up there! Cuz Jesus was a sissy!" When a *bigger* trucker owns up for the sticker, Duke literally eats his words. (He's invited to lunch by the Christian and accepts.) The big but clean cut Christian says grace for everyone and wastes no time waiting to witness. "Duke, what makes you think Jesus was a sissy?" Duke responds with his mouth full, "In my book, any man that turns the other cheek is a chump!" The Christian offers some bait that Duke can't resist. "Duke, if God almighty could turn himself into a man, like us, with all that power still inside him and some dude asked him to fight, who would win?" Duke exclaims, "Hey! That wouldn't be a fair fight... The God-man would KILL him!" The Christian sets the hook: "Let me shake you up, Duke...Jesus IS the God-man!" Duke is dumbfounded.

Then the Christian uses another clever approach. He asks Duke if his house were on fire with his wife and kids inside asleep, and the Christian drove by without waking anyone because he didn't want to upset anyone, how would Duke feel about that? Duke erupts angrily, "Man, I'd hate you. I'd curse you forever!! I'd **NEVER** forgive you! You'd be the WORST kind of murderer!" Now the Christian has Duke right where he wants him. He goes in for the kill: "Then listen good, Duke. You're house IS on fire! You're going to hell on a greased pole and Satan is laughing his head off!" Duke offers to stop cheating on his old woman and go to Church, but the Christian says it won't do him any good. He explains how Jesus was cut to ribbons before being nailed to the cross, and that he'll come back again to fight evil armies at the battle of Armageddon. Billy Joe seems impressed. Jesus is beginning to sound like a man's man! But only those who repent will avoid sliding down the greased pole into Satan's lap. All three men decide to bow down and pray at the table, including the waitress, who seems to have forgotten that it's rude to eavesdrop on other's conversations. The last panel has the odd couple back in their rig driving off into the sunset with a "Jesus Saves" sticker on their bumper too. Duke sighs, "Jesus had more guts than any man that ever lived, and I love him for that." The trucker is a changed man, and so is Billy Joe. (Now if they would just stop speeding and running the rest of us off the road!)

Favorite Panel Award goes to page 21. The chef is looking for his waitress and spots her praying at the table with the other three. "Where's Martha? Am I going bananas or is that a prayer meeting I see?" The answer is both. Grade **A** for Amazing Martha, I mean, Grace. **Still in print.**

©1998 Jack T. Chick.

THE SLUGGER (and *Superstar*) Guest review by T. Alford: (Art by Chick ©1998.) We see Frank Stone (who resembles Tom Selleck from *Mr. Baseball* on the cover) winning the World Series in a predictable grand-slam-with-two-outs-in-the-bottom-of-the-ninth-of-game-seven! "But wait! Something's wrong with The Slugger!" Don't panic. It's nothing that a new $150 million contract won't cover, and a $50 million shoe deal to boot!

In all the excitement, The Slugger doesn't realize how blessed he is to have a "real friend" like his gardener, Oscar Smiley. Oscar is the only one who has the guts to tell him that he is a sinner on the way to hell! (This hits really hard for me because I was 23 before a "real friend" told me how to avoid hell; I had already attempted suicide twice.) When Oscar tries to explain salvation to The Slugger, Frank gets angry and doesn't want to hear about it until...a grim-faced doctor bluntly tells Frank that he has terminal cancer and only a few weeks to live. This results in a conversation that could have been lifted from an ABC After-School Special:

"Oscar, I know you'll tell me the truth. Am I going to hell?" "Yes...but you don't have to." And then, by the grace of God, Frank Stone's name is written in the Book of Life! "I'm not afraid to die anymore!"

Some powerful scriptures from First Timothy are in the margins... Also, Oscar sings that grand old hymn, "There's Room At The Cross For You." (Remember the same song in *Holy Joe*?)

Other than the identical note written by Frank's soccer-playing twin in *The Superstar*, I believe this is the only Chick tract which has a letter from the grave of the deceased! (In *The Letter* tract, it's only a dream.) A lawyer arrives to read Frank's will to his greedy, drooling heirs. (One of them looks like the drummer from the Gorillaz!) Unfortunately for them, The Slugger has left it all to Oscar..."because he's the only one who will use it wisely." I guess he'll splurge on an electric hedge clipper or something.

If you think the story of *The Slugger* is a little bit farfetched, you might prefer the American Tract Society's true story of *Mickey Mantle: His Final Inning* (www.gospelcom.net/ats). Both are excellent reminders of the grace of God.

Favorite Panel Award goes to page 19, where an assortment of blood sucking relatives eagerly await to hear the reading of the will. Grade: **A** for Astronomical $alarie$! **Still in print.**

©1972 Jack T. Chick.

SOMEBODY GOOFED Review: (Art by Chick ©1969, 1972, and 2002.) Classic Chick story of a kid who has a "cool" older friend who gives lots of unsolicited advice. As they watch a guy die, a nearby Christian seizes the opportunity to witness. He wonders aloud if the dead guy will wind up in heaven or hell (a great way to comfort the victim's loved ones). The kid wants to know more, but his partner drags him away from "the fanatic." He also rips up the old man's religious tract and says, "I don't want you to read this propaganda kid—It'll make you mentally sick! Look—let *me* straighten you out—I've got **all** of the answers!" The two drive off and the friend explains that there really isn't such a thing as sin. All one has to do is follow the ten commandments and believe the golden rule. A train approaches the railroad crossing. The friend urges the kid to step on the gas. The train wins the race and the two wind up in Hades. The kid denounces his friend for the bad advice on salvation, but the friend is unapologetic. He pulls off his mask to reveal he's a demon!

Favorite Panel Award goes to the last panel where the big revelation is made. Early versions of this tract feature a red splash on the demon's face after he yanks off his mask (similar to *Angels.*) A fun plot with even funnier pictures. It utilizes lots of full page spreads for the best action shots, including the failed medical rescue, the Christian getting knocked down, the train wreck, and all the Hades scenes. An essential addition to your Chick collection. Grade: **B+** for Bad advice. **Still in print.**

©1973 Jack T. Chick.

SOMEBODY LOVES ME Review: (Art by Chick ©1969, 1972, and 1973.) It's some of the crudest art of any Chick tract. A big-eyed boy gets abused by his elder (dad?) and used to beg for drinking money. Since he fails to bring home enough $, the older man beats him and tosses him out in a storm. He finds a box to curl up in and waits to die, when a "God Loves You" pamphlet blows by him. (Amazingly, Chick didn't make the pamphlet a Chick Tract—this must have been early in his career before he learned to promote his business at every opportunity.) The boy can't read it but a passing Christian reads it for him. She then leaves the boy to die, but thanks to this last minute "love letter from God", he's ushered into the kingdom of heaven. A real tearjerker but not one of my favorites on account of the crude artwork, but many like it for that exact reason. It's also short on dialog and tries to relay the message with pictures only. This tract is often seen and often parodied. I'd give it a **B+** for Basic But Brilliant. (The more recent version has the Christian girl say "I'll go get help", probably in response to readers complaining that she left the kid there to die!) Original no help offered (page 19) version, $10. Recent "I'll go get help" (page 19) version **still in print.**

©1977 Jack T. Chick.

SOUL STORY Review: (Art by Carter ©1977.) Sometimes Chick really seems determined to offend EVERYONE. Just when you thought the blacks would receive a free pass, you discover *Soul Story*. You gotta hand it to Jack: Either he's the one person in American who never heard of "politically correct" or he's the only one in publishing who dares to defy it. The best way to describe this tract is "Blacksploitation!" All the 1970s Superfly clichés are here. The 'fros, the mirror sunglasses, the machine guns, the bell-bottoms...you name it! Only the "main man" in this story gets SAVED in the end. It's kinda like, *Shaft* meets *Pulp Fiction*. (Come to think of it, the bad-ass black mo-fo gets saved in *Pulp Fiction* too!) Even the title is classic: "SOUL Story" (Get it? Black "Soul" vs. your eternal soul? Haw-haw-haw! Good one, Jack.)

The basic plot follows Leroy Brown as he's paroled from prison because he was "denied his rights." (Leroy Brown is also the name of a character in a famous Jimmy Croce song who was one bad dude!) Leroy confronts the thug who took over his old gang and girlfriend. The new leader tells Leroy to beat it. Leroy calls him a *stupid jive turkey* and beats him to a bloody tooth-spitting pulp. The gang business is good and Leroy's back in the black (so to speak). His Christian grandmother dies but witnesses to Leroy before she expires. Leroy takes his main squeeze to the funeral. Rival gang members shoot and kill her in a drive-by situation. Leroy is so torn up by his loss that he hits on his dead girlfriend's sister at the morgue! She goes on the date, but won't give him any sugar unless he becomes Christian. (The old "dogma or the door" ploy.) Leroy says he'll think about it, but wants to murder his rival gang members first. They meet in a church for a truce, when both sides attack each other. The machine gun barks "Budda budda budda!" (So at least they're not Islamic.) Leroy unleashes his grenades: "KAVOOM!" Leroy stumbles from the ruins bleeding. He goes to the Christian girl's home and dies in her arms...but not before repenting. She kisses him, fulfilling her part of the bargain. Leroy snaps back alive and beds the broad—no wait, that last part didn't happen, but you get the picture.

Favorite Panel Award goes to page 9 for the fight and bloody aftermath scenes. They're right on! Grade: **A** for Afro. Original (not divided) cover **$11.50**. Regular cover (with right side in black) reprinted but retired again: **$4.50.**

THE
STORY
TELLER

By J.T.C.

Follow me in prayer: Dear Lord Jesus ... You are our only true prophet. We believe You died on the cross for our sins and rose again to justify us.

"For whosoever shall call upon the name of the Lord shall be saved." (Rom. 10:13)

YOU FILTHY INFIDELS! YOU'LL DIE FOR THIS!

I'll tell *everybody* what you've done!

©1985 Jack T. Chick.

THE STORY TELLER Review: (Art by Carter ©1985.) Any tract that starts with the sentence, "My deepest appreciation to Dr. Alberto Rivera for the information used in this book" is bound to be controversial, and *The Story Teller* is no exception. Ironically, many people claim that Alberto is a storyteller, making up false tales of Catholic treachery. Yet they lack the same proof that they criticize Alberto for lacking. (It's hard to prove that something doesn't exist.) Back to the tract: It takes place in an Arabic country. A man called Yuseff returns home and his elderly father welcomes him. Yuseff has been gone a long time and urges his dad to gather all their friends so he can tell them an important story. But first he makes them all swear by Allah that they won't interrupt or comment until he's finished the entire tale. (He may not be SMART, but he sure ain't STUPID!) It doesn't take long for the digs at the Vatican to start. He begins by reminding his audience how he "fought in the Spanish Civil War under Franco for the Holy Man in Rome." (Rome supported the fascists in the Spanish Civil War.) "Years later, in 1953, while still stationed in Spain, I met a young Jesuit seminarian studying the Messo-Arabic Mass. Just recently I met him again, but he was no longer a Jesuit. He claimed he was now a Christian. He told me of the top secret briefings he heard in the Vatican about Islam." It takes Yuseff another four pages to get around to mentioning this turncoat by name. Can you guess who it is? Why *RIVERA* of course! (The Chick Universe is very small and loves to cross-pollinate. When it comes to Catholic conspiracies, all roads lead to Riveraville.)

One thing you gotta hand Alberto, he sticks to his story. This is the same conspiracy revealed in other critical Catholic tracts like *The Deceived* and *Allah Had No Son*. It claims the Vatican set up Islam to lead Arabs to Catholicism and win Jerusalem for the Pope. Even though we've all heard it a hundred times before, it's still fun to hear the conspiracy explained to a new audience. Then we wait in anticipation to see if the listener(s) will believe the theory and instantly convert, or turn on the narrator and tear him to pieces.

In this case, it's both. A handful fall to their knees and repent before the village hag points a bony finger at Yuseff and screams, "INFIDEL!" Daddy Dearest whacks sonny-boy on the head with his shoe and exiles him from his sight. The crowd eggs him on to continue the beating, but a few secretly wonder if the conspiracy is true. Yuseff walks off in the night

praying loudly for the Lord to forgive them and show them the true path. A footnote reveals the best way for us to learn the truth is to read the full-length comic book, *The Prophet*. Naturally, Chick Publications prints the comic, but if you plan to read it to your Catholic friends, you'll have to supply your own shoes. (I suggest slippers. They can sting a little, but the chance of permanent brain damage is somewhat reduced.)

Favorite Panel Award goes to page 21 where The Hag yells at Yuseff. If you couldn't read, you would assume she was a witch casting a spell on him. Grade: **B** for Bashing the infidel. **Value: $12.**

The Story of Samson

SUPERMAN
?

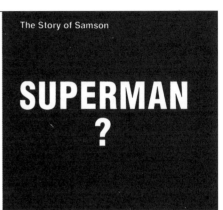

The Story of Samson

SUPERMAN
?

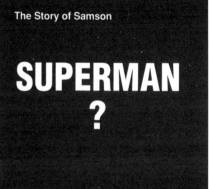

Samson pushed the pillars, and the temple collapsed. Over 3,000 Philistines died and went to hell.

*John 1:3, 10; Col. 1:16-17

Samson had repented of his sins before his death. He died for his people. The One who gave him this strength was the Creator of the universe, the Lord Jesus Christ.*

©1990 Jack T. Chick.

SUPERMAN? Review: (Art by the third artist ©1990.) This is the famous Old Testament story of Samson. After reading this tale, you can't help but wonder how this ruthless madman was ever considered a hero. As Chick puts it, "Samson had a few problems, but sometimes God uses strange people to accomplish great things." A *few* problems is putting it mildly. By modern medical standards, Samson is a raging psychopath. He challenges some wedding guests to a riddle where the winner wins 30 changes of clothing. When he loses, Chick makes it sound like Samson had no choice but to resort to murder: "The only way Samson could pay his debt was to kill 30 Philistines and take their clothing." The **only** way to pay was to kill? Why couldn't he **work** off the debt? He certainly had the strength! Samson can also be pretty cruel to animals. He catches 300 foxes, ties their tails together, sets them ablaze and turns them loose to burn the fields of the Philistines. (Where's the SPCA when you need them?) Another theme of this story is that God doesn't like Jews to marry outside their race. By implication, the opposite must also be true. *Oy!* Chalk up another point for Political Incorrectness! But Samson likes the Philistine girls better than his own race. He marries one and after she's murdered, he beds another. For his **broad** mindedness, he gets his eyes gouged out and turned into a slave. You can guess what happens when his hair grows back: 3,000 more lives lost. (Whatever happened to an eye for an eye? Here's a blatant overdraft of 5,998 Eye-O.U.s.) This tract really makes you wonder if the Old Testament God can possibly be related to the New Testament God. They both have the same Faceless Face and identical White Thrones of Judgment, but they don't seem to act the same.

Favorite Panel Award goes to page 19b. It's a beautiful image of a terrifying situation as the temple collapses and kills 3,000 Philistines. But what the heck, they were pagans so they deserved to die. *Hail Samson! The Pagan Punisher!* Grade: **B** for Better off dead. Original cover with Samson flexing muscles, **$18.** Samsom between column cover, **$2.50**

©1999 Jack T. Chick.

THE SUPERSTAR Review: (Art by Chick ©1999.) This is the same story as *The Slugger* (see above), but the main character is shown playing Soccer instead of Baseball. Only two of the inside panels are changed. Chick realized that South Americans and Europeans identify with Soccer much more than America's favorite pastime. Fundamentalists often pass these sports related tracts out to people as they leave the stadium. They see the cover and assume it has something to do with the game. It's a clever bit of marketing. **Still in print.**

©1976 Jack T. Chick.

SUPPORT YOUR LOCAL JEW (Art by Carter ©1976. **A.k.a. *Jeopardy*, see *Love The Jewish People*.) Value: $20**

©1986 Jack T. Chick.

THE TERMINATOR Review: (Art by Carter ©1986.) This tells the Old Testament tale of David and Goliath. It shows the Philistine king meeting a young Goliath as he pulls up trees with his bare hands. "I'm impressed with his strength and his size," the king observes, "But why do you believe he will be the ultimate weapon?" His Lieutenant replies, "Because, your highness, he's only 9 years old." A decade or so later, Goliath has grown into an 11-1/2-foot giant. Meanwhile, in Israel, devout David tends his sheep herds. A prophet named Samuel anoints David as Israel's future king. The current king is Saul, who suffers from occasional demonic possession. (It's an occupational hazard of powerful leaders.) Page 6 shows a ghost terrorizing Saul while David strums the harp to soothe his nerves. "David was skillful with the harp and was asked to play it for the king. When David did, the evil spirit would depart from Saul."

The Philistines declare war on Israel. The Jews gather to face the Philistines and are shocked to see the giant Goliath. "Choose you a man of you, and let him come down to me," the monster shouts, "If he be able to fight me and kills me, then we will be your servants. But if I prevail against him and kill him, then shall ye be our servants and serve us." The Jews tremble as he yells this challenge every morning and night. One wonders how long the Philistines were prepared to wait for someone to answer the challenge. This goes on for 40 days and they're still waiting for takers. David shows up on day 41 to deliver supplies. He hears the challenge and accepts it. He uses his slingshot to nail the giant in the forehead with a rock. The Philistines watch their champion fall in defeat. They flee in terror, apparently forgetting their promise to stick around and serve as butlers. David becomes the next king of Israel and future ancestor of Jesus. Several panels highlight Christ, one quoting him, "But I say onto you which hear, love your enemies, do good to them which you hate." (The opposite of what David did to Goliath.)

Favorite Panel Award goes to Page 17 for a scene depicting the triumphant David holding a dripping head above the rest of Goliath's dead body. Grade **B+** for Beheaded Bad guy. Original victim held over-head cover: **$30.** Goliath face cover: **$22.**

©1992 Jack T. Chick.

THAT CRAZY GUY Review: (Art by Carter ©1980, 1992.) This isn't just one of Jack's best tracts, it's two of 'em! The reason is because Jack makes major plot revisions that turn the same exact tract into a completely different story. Different, and yet, the same. Both tracks tell the story of Suzi's first "romance" (one night stand). Not surprisingly, she gets Herpes the very first time. (The later version gives her Gonorrhea **AND** AIDS despite using a condom). Of course, Suzi is devastated, but that doesn't stop the doctor from using the opportunity to launch into a lecture about immorality and homosexuals, etc. etc. Suzi withers as Doc tells her that Jesus loves her, but sometimes we must suffer throughout our life for something we've done. In the AIDS version, she gets saved, but only after some aggressive bedside manner. Suzi says "So now that I've got AIDS, all I've got to look forward to is death, right?" and the doctor responds, "**Wrong Susan!** You'll soon face something **far worse**

than AIDS!" Then he proceeds to tell Suzi how sinners get "their scream-ing souls taken and thrown into...that dark, horrible, unspeakable place." (Thanks for the pep talk, Doc!)

Both versions are classic, but the earlier version is probably out of print forever. Why scare 'em with Herpes when you can TERRORIZE them with AIDS? The irony of course is that in the Herpes version, the doctor says "No Suzi, it isn't Gonorrhea or Syphilis, and thank God it isn't AIDS." Yet in a later version, it *is* AIDS! (I guess Suzi didn't thank God enough the first time around.) Grade: **A** for Awful After-glow. Original Herpes version, **$6.** AIDS version recently retired: **$2.50.**

Here's what Satanists truly believe, especially the higher-ups.

Satan teaches them *the lie* that, after the crucifixion, Jesus (the wimp) was chained to a rock in hell.

My God, my God, why hast thou forsaken me?

THE BIG LIE

All He can do is say it over and over.

Satan says that up in heaven, God. the Father and the Holy Spirit plan to res-cue Jesus at the Battle of Armageddon.

Supposedly, they will get on a white horse and lead an army of Christians from heaven to attack Satan.

©1989 Jack T. Chick.

THAT OLD DEVIL Review: (Art by Chick ©1989.) This tract at-tempts to explain Satan's history. Most folks are familiar with the first part of the story but not the last. Lucifer was God's most honored angel. He guards the throne of the Holy Trinity (God the Father, God the Son, and God the Holy Ghost). But then, Lucifer becomes filled with pride and raises an army of angels to help him take over Heaven. He must have forgotten that God is omniscient, because God quickly discovers the plot and the revolution is crushed (but only after "a multitude" of angels orga-nize against God, so things must not have been perfect in paradise). Luci-fer is renamed Satan and sent to Earth along with the other unfaithful angels. "Satan and his fallen angels ended up in the atmosphere surround-ing the planet. One of Satan's titles is the prince of the Power of the air. He believed the planet Earth was his." Boy, is Satan pissed when God creates Adam and sticks him on the EXACT SAME PLANET! We're never told why, *out of all the planets in the universe*, man had to wind up living with Satan, but the Lord works in mysterious ways. As you might expect, Sa-tan does his damnedest to tempt Adam away from God. He succeeds. "Satan became his master. Satan's new title was 'The God of this world'." Satan and his exiled angels destroy mankind through wars, famine, and disease. "But God has limited Satan's activities. Even today, Satan can only go as far as God allows him." This means, in a round about way, that

God is a silent partner when Satan schemes against man. Chick doesn't say that, but what other interpretation is there? God can veto any of Satan's actions he chooses, but lets most of them occur.

The good news is that God sent his son to die as a sacrifice for sinful man. "When Jesus Christ was born in Bethlehem, Satan freaked out." (page 10.) Jesus is eventually crucified. "What took place the next three days *blew Satan away.* Satan and his forces suffered great losses... For had they known it, they would not have crucified the Lord of glory."

Jesus' spirit descends into hell and "preached unto the spirits in prison; which sometime were disobedient." He then snatches the keys of Hell from Satan. "Jesus crossed over to paradise, the place in the lower parts of the Earth where the spirits of those who had trusted in God rested, awaiting Christ's crucifixion. He took captivity captive, and emptied Paradise taking with Him into heaven all those who died trusting in God prior to crucifixion." Jesus then becomes resurrected on Earth.

In response, Satan promotes false religions in order to divert people from God's salvation. Reincarnation through Hinduism, Buddhism, Shintoism, and the New Age are labeled lies that send believers to hell. Then the dangers of believing in good works is also addressed. "Want a shocker? Look at Satan's respectable religions that push good works and ignore the Word of God: Roman Catholicism, Islam, Mormonism, Masonry, Jehovah's Witnesses, and many others."

Chick makes an amusing swipe at Oral Roberts. He shows a preacher pleading on TV to "Send money or I'll die." (Roberts used this tactic to emotionally blackmail viewers to send millions for his medical missionaries. Needless to say, he lived.)

Chick alerts readers to watch for warning signs of the last days. "Visions of Jesus and Mary. (Actually demonic apparitions or sophisticated holograms that make the image speak.) Watch the religions merge into the New Age Movement with the pope as its leader. Watch true Bible-believing Christianity almost become extinct, the target of persecution." Chick explains how Satanists think Jesus never escaped from hell or rose again. They mistakenly think he's chained to a rock and is being punished by demons. Satan says God will try to rescue Jesus at the Battle of Armageddon, but will lose. Satanists are taught a big lie that they will then rule the Earth and hell. Chick shows some *Motley Crue* and *KISS* clones, and says, "Satan's Pied Pipers, in these closing hours, are the heavy metal bands turning our kids into witches and warlocks." But Armageddon is coming soon and will cast Satan and his followers into the Lake of Fire. "When the devil bows before Christ, the Satanists will go insane. They will realize they were betrayed and throughout eternity they will gnash their teeth in pain and curse Satan in the flames of hell."

Chick covers a lot of territory in this cluttered tract. Most of it is epic in proportion and deserves a full-sized comic book. You will certainly feel you got your entire 14 cents worth with this tract. Favorite panel award goes to page 9, where Jesus is getting spanked by demons. You don't see that often! Grade **A-** for Angry Angel. Recently, permanently retired: **$12.**

© 1993 Jack T. Chick.

THE THIEF Review: (Art by Chick © 1993.) The *Home Alone* movie meets *Death Wish!* An incompetent burglar breaks into the home of a Christian and is surprised when the owner becomes overjoyed by the prospect of being murdered! The bad guy warns, "You should have stayed asleep, fool! Now I gotta kill ya! I never let a witness live!" The Christian responds, "Oh... That's WONDERFUL!" The hostage then offers to cook his killer some breakfast. The robber agrees, "Make my eggs over easy!" Somewhere between the non-kosher bacon and aborted chicken baby, the robber gets suspicious about all the generosity. "No, Joey, I WANT my new body, so pull the trigger and *make my day!"* (Make my day? If Clint Eastwood were dead, he's be rolling in his grave!) All the optimism makes the robber curious, so the Christian narrates scenes of paradise (drawn beautifully by Carter). Once the five picture tour is over, Joey declares, "That does it. *It's time to die!"* The Christian thanks him and kneels down on the floor to welcome a bullet in the base of his skull. (Luckily, he's already bald. So no fuss, no muss.) The robber counts, "one... two..." And the Christian shouts "Three!" (No, this isn't a Polish joke. He really shouts it!) The robber chickens out. The disappointed Christian asks, "What's wrong, Joey?" His would-be executor responds, "I... (sniff) I wanna go with you!" Life can be so unfair!

The robber whines that being a thief makes him ineligible for heaven. (He forgets to mention all the witnesses he said he murdered earlier.) The Christian tells him not to sweat it, because God doesn't discriminate as long as you ask for his forgiveness. Soon, Joey is on all fours saying the Sinner's prayer. The Christian grabs the gun and blows a hole in the robbers head, sending him straight to hell and reducing overcrowded jails here on Earth. (Okay, maybe that last sentence was wishful thinking on my part—but the tract ends during the prayer so readers can always add their own ending.)

The unintentional subtext to this "I wanna die and go to heaven" tract is that it presents Christians as pseudo-suicidal! They really *want* to die, and anything that facilitates that outcome is not bad but *good.* It conjures up disturbing images of the Egyptian co-pilot that plunged his jetliner to destruction while repeating over and over on the cockpit recorder, "I rely on God! I rely on God!" (Thank goodness he was Islamic and no Chick tracts were found in the wreckage.) Not being afraid of death is one thing, but wanting it early defies common sense. Eternity will be there tomorrow, so what's the big hurry? Still, it makes for a fun tract. Grade **B+** for Bungling Burglar. **Still in print.**

©1971 Jack T. Chick.

©1969 Jack T. Chick.

THE THING Review: (Art by Chick ©1971.) If you're a horror buff, this will be one of your faves. It's basically *The Exorcist* Chick style. A young Mexican girl (Maria) becomes possessed with a demon named "Verono". The parents tried the Catholic priest, but he was unable to do anything. (In fact, the medal of the blessed Virgin he placed around her neck was immediately bent out of shape—not a good sign.) They find a Protestant "man of God" with more experience in such matters. He muses aloud, "So you ladies believe this girl, Maria, has a demon?" They say yes. The wise Christian explains that Maria must have made herself susceptible to demons when she played with Ouija boards, astrology, and fortune telling. He takes another Christian with him since "there is more strength in numbers—this is very serious business!". A slimy cousin named John hears about the upcoming exorcism and wants to get in on the fun. He promises the two experts he's also a man of God, but he doesn't fool Verono: The demon child attacks the moment she sees him and claws up his face. She also screams that he's making love to his neighbor's wife! His cover blown, John has to leave the festivities. The two true Christians rebuke Satan and evoke the spirit of Jesus. After various Linda Blair impersonations, Maria returns to normal and becomes saved. In a classic 1950s horror homage, someone wonders aloud where Verono went. "He's out looking for a new home," explains the true Christian. Sure enough, the next panel shows Cousin John shaking and howling under the moon, "my name is Verono!" Grade: **A** for Apparition. **Value: $76.**

THIS BOOK HAS BEEN BANNED (Art by Chick ©1969. Same story and most of the same artwork as **Who Me?)** Value: $80

©1972 Jack T. Chick.

THIS WAS YOUR LIFE Guest review by Rev. Rich Lee: (Art by Chick ©1964, 1969, 1972, and 2002.) Although this is not Chick's first tract to be published, it's definitely his most well known tract. Over 80 million copies of this title have been published in several languages since 1972. In fact, this is the first tract I ever read as a child. Undoubtedly, it's the most famous religious tract to be published in the world.

According to Chick himself, *This Was Your Life* was originally a placard presentation given to prisoners. Chick drew it after work at his kitchen table with help from his wife (who provided scripture passages). Eventually he published it in booklet form.

The story begins with an unnamed man who seems smug and self-satisfied. With a new model car in the driveway, a beautiful home with a Spanish-style roof, and a television with a violent program playing, he

seems set for life. The tract is mostly Scripture verses in place of dialogue. The reader is referred to Luke 12:19-20 to show that God has other plans with this guy's life. He is visited by the grim reaper and dies of a heart attack. At his funeral, the preacher intones that "he was a **good** man!" In Chickdom, we know otherwise! Isaiah 64:4 declares that our righteousness are as filthy rags. Incidentally, the man is buried already during the funeral! (The burial usually occurs later.)

While still fresh in the grave, the man is called forth to face judgment: "Marvel not at this: for the hour is coming, in which all that are in the graves shall hear his voice," John 5:28. However, we have a theological dilemma here! Does the soul stay in the body until the end of time, or does the soul immediately face God? Apparently, Chick either hadn't figured out his theology on this yet, or he took shortcuts to make the story flow better.

To his surprise, the man thinks he's still dead and shouldn't be aware of what is going on. "Judgment?—" he exclaims. "But you don't understand, heaven and hell are here on earth! I've always said that!" The tall blond angel responds with "Come, you have an appointment!" He takes the man to a heavenly waiting room, where the man continues with his protest: "Now look! I've lived a REAL GOOD LIFE! I was no different than anyone else!" Boy, is he in for a surprise!

The next page shows us what probably is the first ever scene of the now famous FACELESS GOD of Chickdom. He occupies his throne while issuing the command to review the man's life. A large movie screen with "THIS WAS YOUR LIFE!" (the same basic scene on the tract's cover) is shown. However, this isn't going to be a joyful reunion with former schoolteachers or past girlfriends. This guy has ticked off the Faceless One and now, it's payback time! The angel tells him where in time his life will be reviewed, and it's the seedier side of his life. As a teenager, he told the dirtiest story he ever heard, and later lusts after a hot babe who didn't know that he was fawning over her. His litany of sins is paraded for all to see: Lies, theft, disobedience to parents, pride, being unmerciful, a hater of God, false accuser, whisperer, whoremonger, envy, backbiter, deceit, and hypocrisy—all with dates and facial expressions provided. He shouts, "Why didn't someone warn me about all this?"

The man is relieved when some scenes of him in church are also included. But the relief soon turns to horror. It shows the man ignoring the sermon and daydreaming about the ball game! He couldn't care less, and says aloud "Bunk, I don't need Christ! There's nothing wrong with me! I'll make it my way!" He blows his only chance to clean up his act, and now it's too late. "I must have been insane," he cries," I'm lost! Without hope, without Christ! I'm guilty—guilty!" The Faceless God is unimpressed and thunders, "Open the Book of Life!" The angel responds, "His name does not appear, Lord!" Pointing to the right, the Faceless One quotes Matthew 25:41, "Depart from me, ye cursed into everlasting fire, prepared for the devil and his angels." It's lava lake time, as the man makes Chick history as the first in a tract to be tossed into the Lake of Fire.

This tract doesn't end it here. An alternative "happy ending" is also provided: "THIS CAN BE YOUR LIFE!" The next pages show the man repenting and listening to the preacher this time around. His life now consists of prayer, Bible reading, visiting hospital patients, being a productive worker, and reading Bible stories to his daughter (yet this same dark haired daughter is missing from the dinner table, replaced by a blond girl!) Contrast the earlier funeral scene on page 4 where the man's presumed wife and child are present. The child is a boy! (Either the daughter is boycotting the funeral or underwent a sex change.)

When the grim reaper shows up the second time, the Christian is prepared to see God welcome him into "the joy of thy Lord!" The final inside page directs the readers to commit their lives to Christ. Although this tract is free of sensational conspiracy theories, it is an entertaining tract that takes the reader through a man's life journey in only a few pages. No doubt many became Christians through this world famous tract. There is something wholesome and clean about this tract that makes the Christian life appealing as it was to me the first time I read it back in the 1970s.

Grade **A** for Alternative ending. Giant oversized 38 page version (5 1/2 x 8") **$200**. Medium oversized version (5 1/4 x 3 1/2") **$78**. Regular size (2 3/4 x 5") **still in print**.

©1989 Jack T. Chick.

***TINY SHOES* Review:** (Art by Chick ©1989.) I know a guy who used to drive his family nuts by asking them the following question. "Do you want to hear a sad, sad story?" They knew it was going to be some really depressing tale about how somebody did someone else wrong, but they couldn't help but listen to it. When you pass by a car accident, you HAVE to look. Part of you doesn't want to see the pain and suffering of others, but another part of you does. Let's face it: *Tragedy sells!* Such is the case with the following tract.

Somewhere in Mexico a father is holding his five year old son. He's making him big promises to buy the kid all sorts of things. Little Juanito says, "Papa, all I want is **tiny shoes** to keep my little feet warm." His father promises to buy them, but when payday arrives, his co-workers get him drunk and he gambles all his cash away. He goes home drunk and broke. The following day, Juanito wants his **tiny shoes,** (always italicized to remind us the title of the tract) but daddy has a headache and tells him to get lost. Juanito figures what Papa really wants is a lecture about religion. "You said I could trust you, Papa. **You lied!** And God won't let liars into heaven!" Papa shakes his fist at the brat and tells him to shut up. Juanito runs off and prays for his daddy to get into heaven.

The next payday, co-workers nag Papa into drinking and gambling with them again. He goes home drunk and broke. Meanwhile, Juanito cuts his little foot on some glass. (It was probably one of Papa's broken whiskey bottles.) He asks if his father bought the **tiny shoes.** Papa promises before God that he will next time. (But we know better.)

The next payday, Papa promises he'll return with the money and shoes. His wife warns him that a storm is coming. Juanito's little foot gets infected. (Bet you can't guess where this is heading.) Daddy's buddies get him to join them for one little drink. Mama prays for God to prevent her husband from going to the saloon. A footnote reveals that a sincere prayer of a righteous woman achieves results. (Too bad she didn't pray to heal her son instead.) A lightening bolt suddenly blows up the saloon.

Papa gets the message and goes to buy his son shoes. (Whadayaknow! The shoe store is still open late at night during the storm! Those rural Mexican villages sure keep competitive business hours.) Papa buys the shoes but can't get home because the bridge is washed out. Juanito really wants his **tiny shoes,** so much so that he wanders outside into the cold storm and gets soaking wet. He falls to the mud and hallucinates, "I hear such beautiful music. Are **you** my Jesus?"

The next morning, Papa returns dangling the new shoes in triumph. Alas, Juanito is room temperature. The good doctor tells him Juanito died of pneumonia. Papa sobs that he will never see his son again. The good doctor uses the opportunity to evangelize. Papa goes to the funeral begging forgiveness and wanting to get right with God. He prays over the **tiny grave.** The end.

This story is definitely a downer. But try to look on the bright side: At least Juanito finally got his **tiny shoes**...too bad they won't fit his skeleton feet. Another sad aspect is the fact this all takes place in Mexico where the inhabitants are predominantly Catholic. If Chick is right about the Vatican, Juanito is warming his little feet dancing on hot coals by now. But let's not dwell too much on that.

The good news is that this neat tract is still in print and available at **tiny prices.** You can buy lots of them to pass out and brighten someone else's day. Favorite Panel Award goes to the next to last panel on page 22. As the dark silhouette of the father prays aloud how terrible a father and husband he was, the wife walks behind him with a large SOB above her. It looks like she's calling him an S.O.B.! Grade: **B+** for Busted Bridges. **Still in print.**

© 1983 Jack T. Chick.

TITANIC Review: (Art by Carter ©1983.) You can tell Fred carefully researched the period piece costumes, uniforms, and machinery of the era because the details really go overboard (pardon the pun). This is one topic where everyone knows the tragic ending long before reaching it, so each reader is watching the characters go about their meaningless lives while waiting for the iceberg to hit. The impending doom adds tension throughout the story. This tract revolves around the selfish efforts of

upwardly mobile Chester. He takes his wife on the Titanic's maiden voyage so he can network with well-healed Aristocrats. His biggest frustration is finding notes in his baggage from Aunt Sophie urging him to repent to Jesus so his name will be in the Book of Life. These subtle witnessing tactics drive Chester bonkers. He rips up the notes and screams, "THAT OLD HEN! *!%$ She never leaves me alone! I hate her and her Jesus! I wish she were DEAD-DEAD-DEAD!" (Sophie should have used Chick tracts. If she had used the *Titanic* tract, it could have saved Chester and warned the captain about the iceberg.) Chester's wife tells him to calm down, that it's just "her way of caring about you." Chester responds, "Maybe so, but I NEVER want to see her again!" (A wish God grants.)

Chester woos a rich patron into inviting him to dinner in order to meet an influential business contact and help him "break the ice." (Haw-haw-haw!) While Chester is working his way up the social ladder, the ship's crew is worried about reported icebergs. Meanwhile, the dinner meeting goes well and Chester goes to bed thinking, "In a few months, I'll be rolling in money." (Actually, Chester, you'll be rolling in the surf.) Up topside, a crew member notices that the white mountain approaching their bow is an iceberg. The First Mate orders, "Hard to port! Full speed ahead!" Perhaps he thinks by increasing the speed, he'll also increase the friction and help melt the ice if they scrape against it. *BUZZZZ!* (Wrong answer.) The hull is ripped "like a tin of nuts" and the captain orders transmission of the C.Q.D. The observant radio operator replies, "C.Q.D., sir? That's full distress!" How the captain resists shouting "DUH!" is unknown.

The passengers are awakened and ordered to the deck. Life jackets are passed out but lifeboats are in short supply. The captain orders that only the women and children be allowed to evacuate. That would probably not happen today. All the feminists would demand equal treatment and give up half the seats to the men. (Yeah, right.) Back then, however, the Gloria Steinem types obediently comply with the patriarchal orders and are lowered away to safety. Chester starts to get a little concerned. He asks his rich friend if it's serious. The response is classic British understatement. "Yes, Chester. I'm afraid we'll be eating sand for breakfast." Chester shouts heavenward how pissed he is while the band plays *Nearer My God To Thee*. "You can't do this to me. It's not fair! Just when I had it made! I hate You for this, God!" (Helpful hint to atheists out there: If you don't believe in God, cursing him as your ship sinks won't help your situation.)

Sure enough, Chester drowns in the icy waters but gets a *very hot* reception when he goes before God. The Faceless One shouts, "OPEN THE BOOK OF LIFE!" (Why does God need a Book of Life anyway? Doesn't he have a perfect memory and already know who's in it? He must like watching the accused squirm while the angel flips pages searching for the name.) Big surprise, Chester's name does not appear in The Book. He's sent to dry out in the everlasting fire. (Aunt Sophie gets to say she told him so.)

Favorite Panel Award goes to the angry image of Chester ripping up his Aunt's note (page 5). He's so furious that his eyes bulge, his head shakes, and sweat pours down his face. In fact, his teeth grind so hard that they appear to melt into one solid calcium plate with no space between any teeth whatsoever. (At least he saves on flossing.) Grade: **A-** for *Abandon Ship!* **Still in print.**

©1990 Jack T. Chick.

THE TRAITOR Review: (Art by Carter ©1990.) The plot of this tract is similar to *Satan's Master,* only instead of witches, the devil worshipers are Indians praying to Kali. Like *Satan's Master,* this tract starts off with the bold assertion that, "This is a true story."

A child is sacrificed to Kali. When the police show up to investigate, the high priest warns the inspector to back off or else face reprisals from Kali. The Inspector agrees, but not fast enough. He's killed in an avalanche and Kali gets the credit. The high priest warns the village that Kali will go on a rampage that night. Sure enough, the six-armed Goddess rides her tiger into town and cuts off the head of a villager. The high priest earns new respect. The unseen narrator states, "Villagers, shaking with fear, bring gifts to Kali's high priest. With Kali's help and by astral projection, he knows what's going on in nearby villages at all times... No one dares look into his eyes, including his terrified wife."

Meanwhile, in Bombay, a rich man ignores extortion demands by the Thuggees (the followers of Kali.) A teenager is sent to murder his son in retaliation. The high priest blesses the killer before the assassination by sacrificing a black goat. "With the help of Kali's demons, the thug slays his victim. The rich father is powerless against Kali."

Unlike tracts like *Allah Had No Son,* this story doesn't present Kali as a false god, but as a very real and *evil* god. It states, "The power of Kali is stronger than any god in India, including Shiva, Ganesh, and Hanuman. When Kali actually appeared behind her idol, she stood over 12 feet high." Everyone feared Kali and her high priest...everyone except a joyful Christian. The angry high priest calls forth demons to kill the Christian. Big mistake. We're told, "The demons manifested and started towards their victim. When they hesitated, Kali instantly appeared. In a frenzy, she pushed them on, but a powerful force stopped them just a few feet from the stranger. They all turned slowly and glared at the terrified priest. In a rage, they started toward him. Striking full force, the demons choked, bit, and tore at him from inside his body. After the beating, the priest could barely crawl. What had he done wrong?" (Answer: He didn't read *Satan's Master,* where he would have seen the same thing happen to the witch after she conjured demons against the Christian. It pays to read Chick tracts!)

The high priest is to be shunned by his followers unless he kills the Christian. He tries twice, but the machete never seems to swing close enough to behead the victim. (And the Christian fails to notice the cold draft of the blade narrowly missing his neck.) He finally decides if he can't beat 'em, he should join 'em! He becomes saved. "Instantly, all Ramu's demons departed, setting him free."

On what basis did Chick decide this was a true story? According to his March 1990 issue of *Battle Cry,* an eyewitness walked into his office and told him about it personally. Chick says that he and Randy Chapman had been praying for a tract to reach the Hindus, and within weeks, in walks a former cult member who tells how he was converted to Christ. He's the high priest in the story who conjured up the demons to kill the Christian, but they came back and attacked him instead.

In addition to the action-packed adventure of the story, this tract is stuffed with wonderful imagery. But it also leaves the reader with some disturbing questions. Why does Jesus protect certain Christians from harm while leaving others wide open to die terrible deaths? What about the countless Christians tortured and killed during the Roman persecutions and Catholic Inquisitions? Were they not true Christians? What does it take to get the invincible shield of God put in place? (Can we install it instead of the Strategic Defense System and save some taxes?) Unfortunately, none of these questions are addressed. The Chickster works in mysterious ways...

The historical background on the followers of Kali is quite interesting. It was a death cult that terrorized India until the occupying British crushed it in the early 1800s. The cult's followers were masters of murder and assassination. (The term "thugs" is derived from their name "Thuggees.") It took the British 20 years of ruthless campaigning to succeed; yet followers still exist to this day.

This is a must-have tract. Since it is still in print, it's a bargain at regular retail price. Favorite Panel Award goes to page 6, where Kali rides her tiger down from the moon for some heavenly head action. Grade: **A** for Astral projection. **Still in print.**

©1988 Jack T. Chick.

THE TRAP Review: (Art by Chick ©1988.) This story takes place in a rich mansion during a lavish party where "only the rich and famous are invited. "The hostess is introduced to Robert, a spirit medium. Robert explains that he channels an entity named Seth. He says, "Seth is a *highly evolved soul* who is not currently in a human body... He is extremely wise." A footnote, however, warns the reader that Seth is actually a demon.

Robert then meets Charlie, the rich host. Robert explains that Seth "can tell you about your past lives. The cycle of reincarnations never ends. You chose to be born into this life to solve problems from your past life." Charlie is somewhat skeptical. He asks how Robert knows Seth isn't an evil spirit in disguise. Robert answers, "Oh, but Seth only teaches about love, just as Jesus did. *In fact,* he is an ascended master, just like Jesus."

Unfortunately for the spirit medium, Charlie's Christian brother is there to butt in and call Robert a liar. He starts quoting scripture and Robert beats a hasty retreat. Max then tells his brother Charlie about the New Testament story about the rich man and the beggar, Lazarus. The story includes graphic details, including how the dogs licked Lazarus' open sores. The rich man passes the pathetic beggar in the street with scorn. Time passes and both men eventually die. The rich man winds up in fiery torment, but Lazarus is comfortable in Abraham's bosom, which is conveniently located within earshot of hell. The rich man calls out to Abraham to send Lazarus over with a wet finger to cool his dry tongue, but Abraham refuses. The rich man then shouts over the lava lake a request to dispatch Lazarus back to the land of the living, so that he can warn his brothers to repent. Abraham yells back, "If they hear not Moses and the prophets, neither will they be persuaded, though one rose from the dead." (Better hope Jesus didn't hear that.)

Charlie is really impressed by the story. He decides he wants to repent and bypass hell. Max smiles and sheds the obligatory Chick patented teardrop to prove he's really moved by the experience.

One wonders why Max waited so long to witness to his brother. Maybe he was left off the party list too often. Whatever the cause, the host won't toast, thanks to Max and his debate with the spiritualist. It's a shame that good deeds won't help mediums get into heaven—this could have been Robert's only redeeming moment: The so-called soul that Seth let slip away. He'll probably have better luck channeling for other guests though. After all, "only the rich and famous are invited."

Favorite Panel Award goes to page 8. It's a full page showing Lazarus munching on a piece of bread while the dogs chow down on his open sores. (Umm, yummy flavor! But it tastes man-made!) Grade **B** for Bosom of Abraham. Recently retired: **$2.**

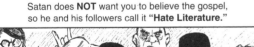

"For they that are such serve not our Lord Jesus Christ, but their own belly; and by good words and fair speeches deceive the hearts of the simple." Rom. 16:18

©1996 Jack T. Chick.

THE TRIAL Review: (Art by Chick ©1996.) This tract follows the uproar that occurs when little Anna tells her friend Debbie that Jesus loves her. The mother of Debbie runs to the ACLQ and demands a lawsuit. (Perhaps Chick was afraid he would also get sued if he used the real name of the ACLU.) A short lawyer with a big nose and diamond earring

is happy to file the $10 million dollar case. (He looks a lot like a bald version of Boris from *Bullwinkle*.) A liberal journalist stokes the flames of controversy with vitriolic hyperbole. She corners little Anna and yells, "You have been charged with a *major hate crime!* Your *hateful* words have *inflamed* the ENTIRE community." When Anna says she only repeated God's words, the glaring blond reporter responds, *"Humph!* How DARE you speak for God?"

In court, the lawyer presents exhibit A: "Jesus said, 'I am the way, the truth, and the life: no man cometh unto the Father, but by me.'" The courtroom explodes in anguish. A villainous gang from Central Casting steps forward to testify against Anna. The jewel encrusted Catholic Bishop Danny O'Tool leads the assault. "There is NO salvation outside the Church of Rome," he declares. Then a rabid Islamic cleric claims, "ISLAM IS OUTRAGED! That statement *destroys* our religion." Rabbi Ginsburg (complete with Orthodox hat, thick beard, and ridiculous looking locks of hair) makes similar complaints. An ivory tower academic with an obvious toupee blathers on about how his Biblical research confirms there are many ways to heaven. "This little FANATIC is guilty of *insulting* all of us!" he snaps. The lynch mob appears heading for success, until the ACLQ calls "the victim" (little Debbie) to the stand. She surprises everyone by announcing that she's been saved. A $10 million dollar bag of loot materializes above her shocked mother and flies away.

But the real fun occurs "many years later (when) the mother and four accusers have passed into eternity. All five rise from their graves. *Oooops!* They thought the trial was over... but it wasn't!" The culturally diverse crowd stands before the Great White Throne of Judgment and it turns out heaven doesn't operate under affirmative action quotas. The gang gets a stern lecture from the Faceless God before having Matthew 25:41 shouted at them and being tossed into hell (the ultimate melting pot).

Favorite Panel Award goes to page 21 which shows Chick's various targets lined up against the wall and ready for rapid-fire lampooning. In the top left, there's Janet Reno, and below her, the Jewish-looking lawyer. A satanic rock & roll punk stands next to the liberal media reporter. The Islamic cleric, the Catholic Bishop, and the Orthodox Jew unite against the Gospel. A bespectacled academic stooge defiantly stands in the front row wearing his silly bow tie. A flaming queer leans in from the side. (It's too bad there wasn't enough room for a witch, Mason, and Mormon. The reunion could have been complete.) It's tracts like these that make you realize how persecuted many Christians in America feel. (And to be fair, all the frivolous law suits against the mere mention of God in school is ripe for satire.) Chick must have enjoyed doing this tract. If nothing else, it provided the fantasy of evening up the score with his detractors. Grade: **B** for Bailiff. Recently retired: **$2.**

© 1986 Jack T. Chick.

THE TRICK **Guest review by Ben:** (Art by Chick © 1986.) J.T.C is back to debunk the widely held but sadly inaccurate theory that Halloween is a harmless, secular holiday. As in his other Halloween tracts, Mr. Chick is eager to illustrate how secret covens of Satan-worshipping witches are out to get your kids to inadvertently swallow razors, needles, and PCP cookies along with their candy apples.

The tract immediately kicks into high gear with the coven convening at their non-descript mansion complex. We step in at just the time when the leaders are giving the low down on their nefarious plans. Halloween is always the busiest season for satanic cults and this year is no exception as that taskmaster Satan has once again upped his soul quota.

Meanwhile, Johnny, Susie, and Jerry are dressed as a devil, witch, and ghost. They are making the Halloween rounds in search for some sweets. The children end up with some tainted goods (courtesy of the coven) and after biting the candy, Johnny bites the dust. Even though Susie and Jerry survived the ordeal, something has changed in their demeanors as their parents note that they are acting much friskier than before. The parents discuss this newfound rebelliousness over a cup of tea and are quite perplexed at what could be the cause. One of the parents is the evil witch Brenda, a member of the coven who poisoned Johnny. (Small world!) Brenda proposes a theory that the children may be going through a phase called "puberty." Fortunately ex-witch (but now serving Jesus) Becky is there to make the save.

Becky quickly strikes down that puberty tomfoolery and uses some deductive logic. She determines that it is the cursed candy that is the source of their problems. Becky then segues into a detailed history lesson about the druidic mayhem that has eventually evolved (?!) into Halloween. Brenda realizes that some potential souls are slipping away so she puts on her best "aw shucks" grin (she also puts on the exact same smile while shedding alligator tears over Johnny) in a final effort to win the mothers over. Needless to say, Becky wins the argument and converts the room shortly after a despondent Brenda flees the scene. Happiness is thus restored back to suburbia as the kids convert and get back to their complacent, non-possessed, old selves.

Pretty standard fare, eh? But what would a J.T.C. tract be without a cameo from the faceless man upstairs or the Prince of Darkness mocking an incorrect religious choice? As usual, Jack delivers with the chief witch Charity suffering a heart attack while enjoying a fine glass of *vino* in self-congratulation for her demonic success. Sister Charity is shocked to find herself standing in flames before a big, black, athletic, and very naked Satan. (But alas, Charity is too distracted by her skin burning off to get aroused.) She begs the "holy father" why he would treat an ex-disciple in this manner. Satan brutally dashes Charity's hopes for a party hearty after-life by proclaiming: "Haw haw haw! You stupid little fool! You're getting what you deserve! My TRICK was getting you to serve me! Now your TREAT is to burn for eternity." I guess since he is the master of all things evil we should expect him to gloat a little bit but *wow,* he really lets the hammer fall hard. For anyone concerned about Lucifer getting the last laugh, Chick has a footnote affirming that "Satan shall also be tormented in hell." (Whew! I was beginning to worry!)

This is my personal favorite of the Halloween tracts since it features druidic shenanigans, a fairly attractive witch in Brenda, and talk of "children who are mutilated and murdered every Halloween." (Huh?...well if the information is provided by everyone's favorite ex-vampire William Schnoebelen, it has to be true!) Grade: **B+** for Burning Babes! Recently retired: **$2.50.**

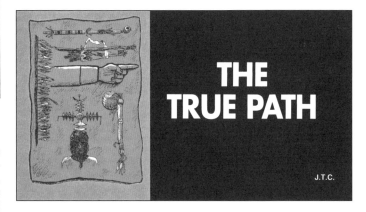

© 2000 Jack T. Chick.

THE TRUE PATH (A Native American version of *One Way.)* **Still in print.**

© 1994 Jack T. Chick.

J.T.C.

These FOOLS believe in sin.

Sin is only an obstacle of ignorance.

Throw it out!

With pleasure!

Only ten more minutes, Mr. Survarnin.

Stop! *STOP!*

The bridge is out!

© 1993 Jack T. Chick.

TRUST ME Review: (Art by Chick © 1994.) This gritty tract is similar to *Somebody Loves Me?*, both in style and that it contains very little dialogue. Most of the story is told in pictures, and what a story it is! A kid walking down the street ignores a drive-by shooting but notices someone inviting him inside an abandoned construction site. A big bald brute operates a drug gang there and gives the kid some free pills. The kid gets so high that he seems to fly through space. Three days later, he's told he has to steal for his next fix. He robs a house and sells the TV to a pawnbroker. His bald boss pats him on the back and gives him "a present" (a drug-filled syringe). He flies even higher than before, but now his boss says he has to sell drugs to get more. One swastika-tattooed customer begs him to "trust me." He turns out to be an undercover cop and arrests the kid after the sale. The judge and jury all give him the thumbs down. The kid is dragged past other Federal inmates who reach out of their cages to touch the fresh meat. During an exercise break, a giant homosexual nabs the newcomer and carts him off as a guard smirks and other disease-ridden inmates look on in approval. The large tattooed assailant declares, "This sweet thing is MINE tonight!" Sure enough, the kid screams from his cell all night, "You're hurting me! Guards, help me! Stop!" But alas, no one intervenes.

The next day, the badly beaten youngster is at the doctor's office with a temperature. Three months later, the doctor determines "It's AIDS!" Six months later, another tattooed prisoner hands him a tract. Although the cover is not one of Chick's titles, the inside is a direct Chick reprint. The sickly prisoner weeps and falls to the floor to pray. As he repents, a heavenly light shines on him, and a ghostly angel looks on in approval. Two days later, he's dead. His corpse is hauled off to the morgue. The last panel shows him flying over the jail walls with the help of an angel who carries him to heaven. (He must be invisible, because the guards don't shoot at him.)

Although this tract is depressing in all but the very last scene, the cynicism and sarcasm are so over the top it's enjoyable to read. Little comic details keep the otherwise dark mood mellow: Characters on various TV screens look on in shock as the pawnbroker buys the stolen TV (on page 8). The crooked shop owner has a "support your local police" bumper sticker on his desk. On page 9, a cat runs by in the background with a rat attacking his tail. People peep out from under trash can lids in page 11. Etc., etc.

The overall lack of dialogue makes this story even more visual than usual. This is clearly a "scared straight" type tract designed for ghetto areas awash in drugs. In a rare nod to political correctness, Chick avoids making the kid or the drug-dealer black. Of course, in so doing, he leaves himself open to charges that he doesn't feature enough African Americans. *Sometimes, you just can't win!*

Favorite Panel Award goes to the kid's walk past all the sex-starved homos on page 14. Their expressions and drooling desire for the scared little fella make it hard to forget. This tract is a fast but fun read. Grade: **A+** for AIDS Ambulance. **Still in print.**

THE TYCOON Review: (Art by Carter © 1993.) Just when you thought Chick was being soft on Asians, in charges *The Tycoon!* It follows the life (and death) of Yut, a millionaire who is considered saintly by the Buddhist monks. A Christian hands Yut a Chick tract, and is quickly given the bum's rush. Yut makes the fatal mistake of not only refusing to believe in the tract, but tossing it out of his limousine as it snakes around a dangerous mountain road. Naturally, the limo skids and plunges to its fiery destruction. Yut is shocked to face judgment. "Impossible!" he says, "I'm supposed to be reincarnated." (Make that incinerated.) Yut is hauled before the Great Throne of Judgment. For some reason, the Faceless God isn't faceless this time. It's a bearded Jesus and he doesn't take too kindly to litterbugs who pollute our scenic roadways with Chick tracts. (Littering bus stations and bathrooms with Chick tracts is a good thing, but not the great outdoors.) God is also miffed that Yut bowed to idols, all because, "you wouldn't offend your family or friends. It was also good for business." The panel showing Yut being tossed into the lake of fire is pretty graphic. Even the most ardent PC type will enjoy seeing a millionaire burn in flames, even if he happens to be a minority. Another nice touch is the high number of prescription sunglasses featured in this tract. Not the cheap dark sunglasses, but the ones that are slightly shaded at the top with yellow (for the yellow race?). Yut wears them, so does his wife, and so do the monks. Why are these glasses so sinister? (It must be the shifty little eyes darting back and forth from behind them.) Grade: **B+** for Buddha Bashing. **Still in print.**

THE
VISITORS

J.T.C.

You poor Mormons have been betrayed by your own false* prophets!

Elder Tanner, wouldn't you like to cut through all this unscriptural nonsense and get to know the real Jesus of the Bible…

Who loved you enough to die for your sins?

Uh,… yes.

No, you don't! C'mon, we're leaving!

*"But there were false prophets also among the people, even as there shall be false teachers among you, who privily shall bring in damnable heresies, even denying the Lord that bought them, and bring upon themselves swift destruction." (2 Peter 2:1, also 2 Cor. 11:13-14)

©1984 Jack T. Chick.

THE VISITORS Guest review by Rev. Richard Lee: (Art by Carter ©1984.) This is the only tract to date that deals with the Church of Jesus Christ of Latter Day Saints, popularly known as the Mormons. Janice, who is going to be a medical missionary to Africa, is spending a quiet evening with her Aunt Fran Palmer. Aunt Fran tells Janice that she has met the most wonderful people. So wonderful in fact that they cared for poor Aunt Fran when no one else did. The doorbell sounds, and who could this be? The cover of the tract is a dead giveaway: *The Mormons* have arrived! "This is going to be a piece of cake," the earlier version reads. The softened version, ostensibly reworked to sound less insidious, says "I'll bet she'll be ready for a baptism commitment tonight."

"They're right on time. They **always** keep their promises," says Aunt Fran. Upon opening the door, she greets them accordingly. "Hello, Bruce and Randy," in the earlier version. The revised version more appropriately has Aunt Fran greeting with "Hello, Elders," since this is the title given to Mormon missionaries.

Janice immediately recognizes them as (gasp!) Mormons! After some small chit-chat, we learn that Bruce and Randy gave her a copy of the Book of Mormon during their last invasion, er, visit. The Mormon Church encourages the testing of the Book of Mormon's claims to divine revelation by having the recipient "pray" about the Book, and seek a burning in the bosom. Truth is determined by heartburn. Lucky for Aunt Fran, Janice is prepared with the antidote. She proceeds to ask the Mormon missionaries about the more peculiar doctrines of the Latter Day Saints such as the belief that God was once a man who was exalted to godhood. The missionaries affirm that this teaching is from Mormon sources. The Mormon god also is quite the swinger, with multiple wives, who occupies a planet near the star Kolob. Joseph Smith, the founder of the Latter Day Saints, parallels science fiction writer L. Ron Hubbard who founded the Church of Scientology. How do we know this spiritual truth? Simply because the "living prophets" of the Mormon Church say so. Aunt Fran, with sweat blowing in all directions, exclaims, "You've got to be kidding!" This doesn't faze either Elder. "It's true," they affirm.

Janice continues her line of questioning, and both Elders are candid. The Elders are quite articulate for teenagers. They proceed to volunteer information that many Mormons may wish was forgotten: in the heavenly battle that resulted in Lucifer's expulsion from heaven, two-thirds who fought valiantly ended up being born as children with white skin. As for the remaining one-third, they ended up as current members of the NAACP. You read it right, they were born as black babies! Dark skin was punishment for the misdeeds of their pre-incarnate existence. Mormons backpedaled in 1978 and allowed blacks to hold priesthoods (but uppity Jesse Jacksons need not apply).

As the Elders continue, they disclose that they hope to become gods with a planet to rule as their own. In this life, they plan to have large families to provide bodies to house the pre-incarnate spirits that currently exist near Kolob right now.

Jesus was promoted to godhood since he was married, we are told. This information is all that the Elders reveal, but Janice discloses more. Mormon founder Joseph Smith was arrested in 1826 for an occult practice known as "glass looking," when he claimed that he could find buried treasure by looking through his magic "peepstone." He and his brother Hyram were both Masons, thus explaining how Masonic symbols are conveniently on the walls of Mormon temples. Janice charges that Mormonism is just a modern form of Baal worship that resembles Catholic tradition. In Chick fashion, we are told that Mormonism is "another daughter of the Mother of Abominations" in Revelation 17:5.

Janice declares, "Joseph Smith says you are both imposters! [sic]" Why? Because anyone who teaches doctrine contrary to the Book of Mormon is to be marked as an impostor, and the doctrine of the Almighty once being a man who progressed onto godhood is absent from the Book of Mormon. Janice further says, "You poor Mormons have been betrayed by your own false prophets! Elder Tanner, wouldn't you like to cut through all this unscriptural nonsense and get to know the **real** Jesus of the Bible…?" He is all too eager to be converted when the other Elder cuts off this discussion. After storming outside, Elder Randy asks his partner how he could be so stupid. Elder Bruce admits, "I think she was right! Nothing makes sense anymore. God help me." After chewing Elder Bruce out, Elder Randy thinks to himself, "I'll get revenge on Janice for interfering. I'll have the workers in the temple put a curse on her." The softened version replaces this remark with "I'd better report this guy before he goes to the mission president himself." (Most folks enjoy the earlier version better.)

Back inside, Aunt Fran admits she almost made a horrible decision in becoming one of *them*…condemned to marry a man with multiple wives and forced to have sons who spend two years as traveling cult salesmen. She would have had to give up caffeine, too. She prays the "Sinner's prayer" and gets saved.

This is a popular tract that was no doubt passed out during the 2002 Olympic Winter Games in Salt Lake City. Grade **B+** for Black Babies. Original "put curse on her" (page 20) version **$12.** Revamped "I better report this guy" (page 20) version **still in print.**

THE
WARNING

J.T.C.

©2000 Jack T. Chick.

THE WARNING Review: (Art by Chick ©2000.) It looks like the cast from Four Brothers was reassembled to perform this tale about four boys who go swimming where they're not supposed to. The signs warn "Danger—Keep Out", but of course, the kids ignore the warnings completely. Only one boy is held back from the dark lake when his clothes snag on the barbed wire fence. The other three dive straight in. "Oops," would be an understatement. In a scene taken straight from Urban Legends, the lake suddenly teams with poisonous snakes that bite and kill all three boys. Fastforward a couple of weeks as the local preacher exploits the tragedy with a sermon about the garden of Eden. "About 6,000 years ago the worst snake attack in history took place." The snake he's referring to is the devil that tempted Eve. Oddly enough, when Chick draws the Satan snake, he forgets to include the legs! (God made him crawl on his belly AFTER tossing the humans out of Eden.) One might question the timing of such a sermon while the parents of the dead children are still in mourning, but from a tract standpoint, it all makes fun reading.

Favorite Panel Award goes to page 12, which shows the bubble thrashing bottom half of a kid swimming as the snakes rise up from the bottom to attack. *Ew!* The grim anticipation is too much! Grade **A-** for Admonition. **Still in print.**

©2000 Jack T. Chick.

WAR ZONE Review: (Art by Chick ©2000.) This tract features some of Chick's best detailed work to date. It's free-for-all time at the local high school, as gang members terrify milquetoast bureaucrats and the rest of the student body. That is, until Chick tracts appear on the scene and cure all the problems. Exposure to the comics convert "Moose", the gang leader of "The Snakes". (That's "Ekans" in Pokemon gang-speak.) Moose first encounters the tracts after throwing a pencil-necked geek against the lockers: "Out of my way, scumbag!" he shouts. The tracts spill to the floor and Moose steals them. Then he meets Scumbag the next day and wants to talk to him. "Last night, Justin read all those tracts to me, I can't get them out of my head. For the first time in my life, I'm *SCARED! What's going on?* When I saw this picture, I could see *me* in it!" That picture is the recurring Chick image of a sinner being tossed in the Lake of Fire. Any tract that plugs tracts is usually fun, but this one goes way overboard. The tracts not only convert Moose, they turn Horrible High into an overnight Utopia. The clouds part and sunshine pours in on the otherwise dark and dingy schoolyard. Moose pays his teacher to replace the tires he vandalized, parents are thrilled, and teachers from around the district want to transfer to the school. Why spend millions when all we really need to fix education is 14 cent tracts? Grade: A straight **A**! **Still in print.**

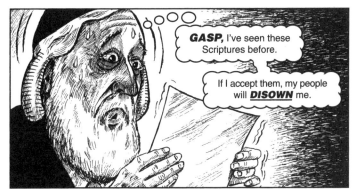

©1996 Jack T. Chick.

WHERE'S RABBI WAXMAN Review: (Art by Chick ©1996.) Chick sure has a way a collecting influential enemies. As if mobilizing the combined resources of the Catholics, Masons, Jehovah's Witnesses, Mormons, and Muslims against him were not enough, Chick goes on to alienate the Jews too! But, to be fair, this isn't really an anti-Semitic tract. It just repeats Chick's strong belief that anyone who doesn't accept Jesus is fuel for Satan's furnace. And of course, that includes The Chosen. (Hey, cut Jack some slack! If he excluded the Jews, that would be discrimination.) This tale chronicles an Orthodox Jew's effort to find out from Rabbi Waxman why Jesus was not the Messiah. Waxman can't answer the question, especially after being confronted with the actual scripture from the Torah. He basically throws the student out of his home. Bad move:

Waxman dies soon thereafter and is shocked to discover there aren't any Waxmans listed in The Book Of Life. Before tossing the old Rabbi into the Lake O' Fire, God (that's pronounced "Jesus", not "Jehovah") takes time out of his busy schedule to list all the prophecies that his Earth visit fulfilled. Two pages of Old Testament scripture are provided. A few panels later, John 1:11 is quoted: "He (Jesus) came unto his own, but his own received him not." Waxman complains and cries, but Jesus has seen that act before and sends the Rabbi down to the blast-furnace basement to join the rest of his Kosher congregation. Just when you think the Jewish Defense League is about to burst in and shoot everyone at Chick Publications, the Jewish student shows up again and converts to Christ. (Did I mention he's blond? Go figure.) Not surprisingly, the Messianic Jew goes straight to heaven. Chick reminds everyone that Jesus made more than just furniture (like say, the universe) and everything is right again. An all-around fun read. Jews naturally resent this tract, but just because they don't actively recruit folks from other races doesn't mean other groups won't try to siphon off their numbers. Remember, all's fair in Love and War, and like they say, "Jesus is Love." Interesting trivia: Chick suffered a stroke after drawing this tract, and while being carted off in the ambulance, he laughed at Satan and swore his stroke wouldn't stop him. Sure enough, it didn't. Grade: **A** for Assimilation. Recently retired: **$2**.

©1987 Jack T. Chick.

WHO ARE THEY GONNA REMEMBER? Review: (Art by Chick ©1987.) This tract is really directed at pastors who are looking for ways to increase membership of their churches. Three guesses what Chick suggests the Church should buy and distribute? That's right, Chick tracts. Some of the art looks rather rushed, especially on pages 5, 14, and 15. Perhaps the limited audience reduced the effort? One would think if ANY tract should be spectacular and full of lights, bells, and whistles, it would be the tract targeting the big buyers. (I would have put Fred Carter on this project, but Chick is probably too honest to use someone who only draws a minority of the tracts.) Nevertheless, the tract makes a compel-

ling argument to invest $600 for 10 thousand tracts with custom ads on the back pushing your church and location. Oddly enough, it's been discontinued for some time and is rather scarce.

On page 11, Chick shows he knows how to manipulate the masses, literally! He suggests the Pastor ask for someone in the congregation to foot the $600 custom-printing job, so it doesn't come out of the Church budget. In case you missed it the first time, Chick repeats the ploy on page 18. He also shows how good old *religious guilt* prevents readers from being able to throw away the merchandise. On page 12, a woman holding a tract thinks, "I can't throw this away. It's sort of holy 'cuz it's quoting the Bible." Chick then reiterates that concept twice as well: He states, "The readers will see enough of God's Word in these little booklets that they will be reluctant to throw them away." It's a pretty crafty technique! First you get someone else to pay for them, plus someone else to distribute them, and then you leave the recipients feeling too guilty to get rid of them!

Chick makes an interesting remark on page 20 where he says, "These tracts are non-controversial, and are proven soul-winners." It shows several of the Bible tracts and the ever popular *This Was Your Life*. Conspicuously missing are such in-your-face classics as *The Death Cookie, The Gay Blade,* and *The Visitors*. Chick appears to be trying to distance himself from his own reputation here.

Favorite Panel Award goes to page 21, where a depressed man considers blowing his brains out while reading a Chick tract. Presumably, the tract prevents him from doing it, although it's possible it's the other way around. He has the gun, the suicide note, and the tract...perhaps he decided to end it all BECAUSE of the tract! Could he be a Catholic who just discovered he's been dieting on death cookies all his life? Find this tract and decide for yourself. Grade: **B** for Blast away! Red title cover **$27**. Other color titles (green or blue) on cover **$7.50**.

©2002 Jack T. Chick.

WHO CARES? Review: (Art by Chick ©2002.) This is tract #20 in a series of 25 featuring Bob Williams. You know this tract is going to be inflammatory before you even open it, because the cover shows a jet liner flying into the World Trade Center. The first page shows the towers in flames. A Muslim woman watching TV is terrified by the live news coverage of the terrorist attacks. She urges her son to stay home from work. Omar doesn't listen to his mother and opens his Jiffy Mart anyway. Big mistake. Three rednecks show up to avenge Uncle Sam. One snares, **"Get** the lousy camel Jockey!" And they do!

Meanwhile, Bob Williams pulls up outside to get some batteries. He notices the telltale pickup truck parked outside. As he enters the scene of the crime, the rednecks (with even redder knuckles) take off, celebrating their symbolic victory over Al Queda. "I feel **better!**" one snorts. The same cannot be said for Omar. He's polishing the floor with his squirming, bleeding body. Bob hauls him to the emergency room, explaining he'll pay for it since Omar has no money. (Maybe he'll get a discount on the batteries.)

Two hours later, Omar is patched up. The doctor reflects aloud that it was lucky Omar was brought in quickly, because he would have otherwise bled to death. Omar thinks, "What kind of infidels **are** these?" Bob explains he's a Christian, and that's what Christians do. Omar fires back that the thugs who beat him up were also Christians. Bob insists that real Christians would never do such a thing, because Jesus taught them to love their enemies. He tells Omar the story of the Good Samaritan. He then tells Omar he has a message from Jesus. He gets Omar to admit that Islam recognizes Jesus as a prophet, and that nowhere in the Koran does it say that Jesus lied. He recites John 9:35, where Jesus reveals he is the Son of God. He explains how Jesus (not Allah) loves Omar so much, that he sent his son to die for Omar's sins. Omar is stunned. He never heard such a thing! (He must have gone to our public schools.)

Omar tries to formulate a counter argument, but Bob's too quick for him. He interrupts Omar and mid-sentence and says, "Did Muhammad **die** for you? Did he **rise** from the dead? **Jesus** did, proving that He is **God**." Omar caves. He falls to the ground and recites the Sinner's Prayer. It's a historic day. Osama and Satan may have each won a tower, but Jesus won a convert, and the fact he was a Muslim must have really thrown salt in the wound. He who laughs last, laughs best, so don't be too surprised if Omar's Jiffy Mart starts stocking a new product: Chick tracts! *Haw-haw-haw!* Grade: B for Bin Laden loses in the long run. **Still in print.**

WHO, ME? Review: (Art by Chick ©1969, 1973, 1998.) This tract has been given away since 1969 as an advertisement for the effectiveness of Chick tracts. Originally, it was called *This Book Has Been Banned* and featured a completely different cover. Some pretty amusing comic images are included within. Page 3 shows a giant thug confronting a Christian, "Are you calling *ME* a sinner?" Another page shows a Christian passing out tracts and turning into ice when a businessman angrily approaches and shoots daggers from his eyes after spotting him. There's also a funny office scene where everyone is fighting over who gets to read the newest Chick tract. Chick's encounter with Bob Hammond is recreated, where he's told, "that communists in China developed a powerful way to reach the multitudes...and they stole the technique from us!" Red Army agents are shown spying on American kids as they read comic books, then they print up commie comics and pass them out to the masses back home. "The Communists spent millions of dollars printing their propaganda in cartoon format. The results were extremely successful." The praises of Gospel tracts are sung. Ideas on where to leave tracts are also provided. We're told that three tracts a day reaches over 1,000 people a year. Testimonies from those who were saved by Chick tracts are plastered on several pages. The back of the tract is a coupon that can be mailed in for a free sample and more information.

Interesting trivia: An Asian version of this tract also exists. You wonder what the Communist Central Planning Committee thought when they realized Red-baiter Chick stole back the technique that they originally stole from our kids reading comics. All's fair in love and spiritual warfare.

Favorite Panel Award goes to page 11 for the picture of the commie spy peering over comic racks and snapping pictures of kids reading cartoons. Talk about dated... Today the spies are busy working in our Top Secret weapons labs and use the office Xerox to run off copies of our designs for Beijing. We've come a long way baby! Grade: **B** for Brazen! Original white cover version: $12. Recently retired green cover version: $1. Red cover version: **still in print.**

Years ago their agents watched our children spend hours reading comic books.

©1973 Jack T. Chick.

There was no funeral or gravesite. Beautiful Clarice was gone.

The crime was shrugged off and forgotten because nobody cared.

Unknown to the participants, someone was watching…

His eyes were like flames. Only He could hear Clarice's silent screams.

©2000 Jack T. Chick.

WHO MURDERED CLARICE? **Review:** (Art by Chick ©2000.) This is a hard-hitting anti-abortion tract that is apparently inspired by Chick's pseudo-recent discovery that "someone" in his family had an abortion without his prior knowledge. Chick stated in the same public letter that his own mother had wanted to abort him as well. So the issue is obviously one of deep personal importance. This tract doesn't focus so much on the "silent scream" type tactics of showing dead baby fetuses, but relies more on showing abortion supporters being sentenced to hell by a Faceless God. One panel states "Jesus Christ can be your most loving friend...or the most *frightening* enemy in the universe." The enthroned deity in this tale is clearly an example of the latter case. He convicts anyone associated with abortion to the Lake of Fire, be they the women who had the abortion, the doctors who performed them, or the Supreme Court Justices who legalized them. But Chick reminds the reader that God will forgive the murderer if (and only if) they sincerely repent and become saved. Other panels provide a brief history of how Satan LOVES to murder babies. Examples include King Herod's "slaughter of the Innocents," the Nazi Holocaust, and the occult's ritual of sacrificing babies and drinking their blood. The main emphasis returns to the modern day Holocaust of 45 million abortions per year. There is very little humor in this tract, either in cartoon style or satire (unlike *Baby Talk*, another anti-abortion Chick tract that is rife with sarcasm).

Favorite Panel Award goes to page 4 where Chick casually mentions that the abortion doctor eventually dies "a VERY wealthy man" and is sent to meet his maker. Instead of the usual Chick treatment showing a rich playboy getting killed in an unexpected jet or limo crash, Chick shows the depressed doctor blowing his highly educated brains out with a .45 caliber Beretta. Apparently, EVERYONE who is involved with abortion is racked with guilt despite outward appearances to the contrary. If they aren't, they probably will be after reading this tract! Grade: **B** for Babyless. **Still in print.**

©2003 Jack T. Chick.

WHO'S MISSING? **Review:** (Art by Chick © 2003.) This is tract #24 of 25 with Bob Williams. The fun all starts with a birthday party for Dr. Ngaba, the head of the U.N. delegation of peacekeeping forces. Hey doc, who's that present from? Urah Goner? That's odd, I don't know anyone named **KA-BOOM!** The explosion kills everyone.

Later, an expert hooded in a chemical protective outfit surveys the damage and confirms they all died of sarin gas. The news media goes into feeding frenzy mode. A talking head reports, "Negotiations are collapsing... Many military leaders fear this could lead to Armageddon." Meanwhile, Bob Williams gets a call from Damien. (The Catholic priest that Bob converted in tract #23.) It seems Damien's sister is freaking out over all the sensational news reports. "She believes we're heading for an all-out war and she's **terrified!**" Damien pleads, "Can you speak with her?" Damien not only left his church, he apparently forgot how to counsel panicked parishioners.

Bob arrives with his wife in tow. Mrs. Williams cajoles Mary Anne that everything is going to be okay. Then Bob throws fuel on the fire by saying, "This is **not** the end. Jesus spoke of wars, earthquakes, famines, and plagues—and He said that this is only the **'beginning** of sorrows'!" Thanks Bob, that should really help calm her down. He offers more counter productive words of encouragement: "Those living through it will wish they had never been **born**... Murder, plagues, witchcraft, cannibalism, Satan will be in **complete** control. So terrible that we can't describe it!"

Bob goes on to explain about "the great falling away." That's where pastors no longer preach from the King James Bible and begin to compromise with Satan. It becomes politically incorrect to condemn sins like "sodomy, divorce, Masonry, Islam or the Whore of Babylon." A scene shows Billy Graham admitting to a reporter that he no longer believes in a literal hell. *(GASP!)* There's even a footnote to prove it.

The second sign of the end times is "the man of sin must be revealed." This is where Bob explains to the despondent Catholic that she's a member of a Satanic cult. "These satanically controlled popes are antichrists, pretending to hold the position of Christ on earth." Mary Ann blinks in disbelief. She responds, "The Holy Father?" Bob admonishes her, "Calling the pope that name is **blasphemy** against God," but she takes no offense. (Not yet.)

Now for the *bad* news: A small remnant will escape all the terrors. They'll be whisked up in the great Rapture. Why is this bad news? Because Mary Ann is a Catholic, and she'll be left behind! All of a sudden, Mary Ann is offended. **"No!** I don't believe **any** of this craziness! My faith is in Mother Church, **not** the Bible. So get out! You too, **Damien!"**

The "ejects" drive off but remain in good spirits. After all, they succeeded in getting Mary Ann's mind off the end of the world. It's a pity they also turned Damien into a homeless bum. But fate—and Mrs. Williams—soon smile upon him. She tells Damien to move in with her and her husband. Bob doesn't seem to mind the new male roommate. He's certainly not in a position to complain. It's his fault Damien was kicked out. Instead of acting jealous, he invites Damien to join them at church.

Pastor Malcolm is fully recovered from the attack at the hands of the queer loving cops who thrashed him in tract #3 (*Sin City*). The pews are filled with characters from previous tracts: Ex-whores, ex-homos, ex-Muslims... The gang's all here. One of them, the skate boarding punk from *Framed* and *God With Us,* shouts "Hallelujah!" Bob smiles in approval. The End.

Granted, it ends a bit abruptly. It's also a little hard to swallow some of the character motivation. Why would Mary Ann tolerate all the Vatican bashing, then suddenly go ballistic after she learns she isn't invited to the Rapture unless she switches teams? And how is it that Bob could sit next to that little brat in church and not ask him to at least remove his hat and shades? (Remember, this is the same Bob who is so respectful, he can't even refer to God without capitalizing 'Him.') But this tract still gets high marks for the militant message and a (literally) dynamite opening scene. Grade: B for Billy Graham Burning in a non-existent hell. **Still in print.**

WHY IS MARY CRYING?

J.T.C.

In these last days, the key to pulling all the religions together is the worship of the satanic mother goddess.

Almost a billion Muslims will join because the Virgin Mary was carefully placed in their holy book, the Koran. Even the "New Agers" refer to a Mother/Father god.

Satanic posers will impersonate Mary in future apparitions of the "virgin" worldwide, including communist countries, to bring the world under Satan's antichrist.

Semiramis, I couldn't have done it without you!

Thank you, Master!

The devil knows his time is running out. Jesus is coming soon, and Satan is desperate.

© 1987 Jack T. Chick.

WHY IS MARY CRYING? Guest review by Rev. Richard Lee: (Art by Chick © 1987.) This is another tract intended for Roman Catholic reading. It begins with a seemingly traditional looking depiction of the Virgin Mary, only with tears. The caption reads "Poor Mary. Her heart is broken...by the very ones who love her." In spite of her veneration by the Catholic faithful worldwide, the tract claims that they haven't done what she wanted them to do.

The tract uses the biblical account of the Magnificat (announcement of Gabriel to the Virgin Mary that she would bear the Christ child, and her response to the news) from the Gospel of Luke. After the miraculous birth of Jesus, Chick faithfully records that the Virgin Mary brought an offering for sin to the temple, as was the custom in those days (Luke 2:21-24). Thus, Chick underscores the fact that Mary was a sinner who needed to offer a sacrifice as all the population did. This undercuts the Roman Catholic doctrine of Mary's sinlessness.

After the crucifixion of her son (the first one, Jesus), the Virgin Mary's tears of anguish should have ended there, but they didn't. We are told: "Little did she know her heart would be broken again in a way she never expected." How? Because people are bowing down to idols of her. She is shown standing before the Faceless God and saying, "My Lord, I never asked them to do this. They should be bowing to **you**!" This is why she cries. Men are calling her "The Mother of God." Yet she insists (in the tract), "When Christ created the universe, I was not there...I was the chosen vessel to bring him forth in the form of a man. But Christ was God long before I was born."

We are also told that she weeps because men teach that she was born sinless and look to her as a mediatrix and pray to her. Mary obviously jettisoned her Jewish birth and became Christian, because she quotes the New Testament many times to prove her point.

The tract shifts gears to show that Mary's veneration began with someone else. It didn't originate with God, because He doesn't "play tricks on people." We are then told: **"Please read carefully the following pages. Where you will spend eternity hinges on it."**

Satan, the unseen force behind all that is wicked, knew that Jesus would be born of a virgin. He had to create his counterfeit virgin named Semiramis whom he used to "put untold millions into hell." Semiramis married her own son, Nimrod, thus making him the "husband of his mother." We are told that Satan used both of them to create a powerful satanic cult that caused multitudes to look to their goddess mother, Semiramis. Nimrod and Semiramis are credited with creating confessionals and celibacy for the priesthood (and you thought satanic cults *encouraged* sex, silly you!).

An interesting overview is presented showing many variations of the Mother/child theme as held in different cultures. Areas as diverse as China, India, Ephesus in Asia Minor, Egypt, Greece, Scandinavia, Rome, and Israel had a mother figure with infant who were venerated. As Catholicism gained influence, it utilized this mother/infant theme and replaced the names with Mary and Jesus. "Little by little," the tract says, "the worship of the pagan goddess was transferred to Mary." The Babylonian religion supposedly had the goddess mother as the only one who could control her son. Indeed, in Catholic circles, this type of logic abounds. If one wants something from Jesus, doesn't it make sense to approach his mother first, so she can ask him for us? Jesus isn't likely to say "no" to his mother, is he? But Protestants like Chick claim it isn't an accurate depiction of the biblical Jesus, who said, "Come unto me, all ye that labor and are heavy laden, and I will give you rest," (Matthew 11:28).

Roman Catholicism teaches that Mary never died, but floated up into heaven. She returns to Earth in this tract to make an appearance on behalf of Chick and say that his concerns about Catholicism are correct. The Scripture is quoted "Neither is there salvation in any other: for there is none other name under heaven given among men, whereby we must be saved," (Acts 4:12). Her parting words are "If I didn't believe that, I would be calling God's Word a lie. And I wouldn't do a thing like that."

Favorite Panel Award goes to the frame showing Satan congratulating Semiramis in hell, "Semiramis, I couldn't have done it without you!" She replies, "Thank you, Master!" You can bet that makes the *Legion of Mary* club members' blood boil!

Although this tract is short on illustrations and is crammed with text, its message overshadows the pictures. It 's sure to provoke your Catholic friends, or at the very least, liven up your relationship with them. Grade **A** for Ave Maria. **Still in print.**

"THE GLORY IS DEPARTED" 1 Samuel 4:21

WHY NO REVIVAL?

J.T.C.

Christians of yesterday!

Are you a follower of Jesus also?

Yes! *He* is my Lord and my Saviour!

Christians of today!

What's this I hear about you being *very* religious?

Oh, uh — it's my *wife* that's so religious. I *only* go to church to keep her off my back! (gulp)

Forgive me, Lord!

"Ye have not yet resisted unto blood, striving against sin." -Heb. 12:4

© 1986 Jack T. Chick.

***WHY NO REVIVAL* Guest review by Rev. Richard Lee:** (Art by Chick ©1970 and 1986.) This tract is the very first tract that Jack T. Chick ever wrote. He obtained a loan for about $2000 to print this booklet, and it has undergone a few revisions. This review concerns the 1986 incarnation of *Why No Revival?*, which is the most recent.

The inner page starts off with "Many pastors are unable or unwilling to say the things that appear in this book." Furthermore, this tract is intended "for Christians only-not the unsaved." Indeed, this book shows some Christian hypocrisy laid bare for all to see. Chick even admits that some of the characters in the story resembled members of his church, and after it's publication, the Lutherans condemned it for being sacrilegious! He begins contrasting the Christians of yesterday with those of today. The former Christians faced martyrdom for their faith, while modern Christians tend to deny their affiliation with anything religious. The family "altar" is composed of a cobweb and dust covered Bible, while *Playboy* and the *TV Guide* magazines are standard reading fare. Self-righteousness plagues the church while Christians have misplaced priorities. Christians neglect the starving neighbors next door, and call them "trash" because they don't go to church. Lack of spiritual fervor is reflected at the dinner table, when the children play around when the father is praying.

My favorite panel depicts an obviously rich man with a diamond ring that would choke a mule, criticize his pastor. He doesn't deserve to earn a cost of living increase, because he's supposed to remain poor. He already earns $300 a month, and preachers aren't supposed to earn big money! However, pastors are not let off the hook, either. One lazy pastor decides to preach a sermon from last year since no one would be able to tell the difference anyway.

A new panel (it didn't exist in earlier versions) shows spiritual decline in the form of a church permitting a Christian heavy metal band (God forbid). This new innovation, a contemporary fad in modern churches, is viewed as apostasy by Chick. Thanks to shenanigans like these, Chick asks, "Why No Revival?" If the church were spiritually sensitive, it would avoid such fads and sing those classic hymns instead. A terrific panel shows a Christian on the job, one who others view with contempt because of his shoddy testimony. In classic cartoon style, several co-workers castigate a Christian because he likes off-color stories, lies, and is a big flirt with the office secretary. The boss looks upon him with an angry scowl. One of the more interesting panels shows witches who have infiltrated the church worldwide, and that the pastors of the world are lulled into complacency.

Also, the contemporary teaching known as "positive confession" popular in Pentecostal/charismatic churches comes under fire from Chick. The Apostle Paul is shown in prison, and he's there because he lacks faith. (A teaching of the positive confession movement is that if one has enough faith, he/she can avoid calamity and always have success). Another sign of apostasy is throwing out the King James Bible in favor of modern versions, thus resulting in a lack of revivalistic spiritual fervor. The signs of judgment are starting to appear on all sides, and no other place is this more evident than on the famed Trinity Broadcasting Network (TBN) founded by Paul and Jan Crouch. In fact, Chick does a fair rendition of Paul and Jan (who founded TBN with Jim and Tammy Bakker back in the 1970s) along with the Pope. Chick warns that compromising with Roman Catholicism is a mark of apostasy. The result will be burning churches and a return of the Inquisitions!!! The tract claims this is what WILL happen unless we REPENT! Upon receiving God's forgiveness, people will be concerned for their souls for a change. Spiritual fervor would break out, and REVIVAL will result.

No Chick tract would be complete without a last panel depicting Jack Chick's favorite judgment spot, the Lake of Fire, with accompanying footnotes of Scripture references. Not bad for a first effort, which would lead to a career spanning over 40 years. Grade **A** for Amen!" Original yellow cover version: **$25.** Green cover version recently retired: **$1.**

©1961 Jack T. Chick.

***WHY NO REVIVAL* Super oversized variations review:** (Art by Chick ©1961.) This was Chick's original version of his very first tract. The 28 page booklet was distributed by Rusthoi Publications. It was very large, about 8-inches high and 10-inches wide. I've only seen one of them, and that was tucked away at Chick Publications. Eventually, the tract was reduced in size to 5 1/2" x 7 1/2". (I've only seen one of those as well.)

The story is very similar to the modern version, but the artwork is completely different. Chick redrew it after members of his church recognized themselves in the cartoons and were not flattered. The characterizations of phony Christians are rather scathing. Ministers are told what they can and can't preach about, while others flip coins deciding which recycled sermon to recite on Sunday. One preacher screams and pounds on the pulpit while his terrified congregation listens to him rave about wide spread crime, shattered morals, communism, modernism, alcoholism, corruption, juvenile delinquency, and The Beast. (All topics that Chick himself would later preach against.) It's the only congregation in the tract that doesn't have someone yawning or sleeping somewhere in the background. The artwork is very rich and detailed. It's a shame so few exist, because it's another classic Chick masterpiece. **Value: speculative.**

©2000 Jack T. Chick.

©1984 Jack T. Chick.

THE WICKED MAGISTRATE Review: (Art by Carter ©1989, ©2000.) This tract is unusual for several reasons. The all-Korean cast is dressed in 500 year old Oriental costumes. It is a custom tract made especially for a Korean audience and was originally printed only in that language. (An English version was printed in 2000 exclusively for the *Chick Tract Fan Club*). It's a very rare tract despite being relatively recent. It tells the story of an Asian King who loves his people, and those who live near him love him in return. But those who live far away under a wicked Governor fear for their lives. The king sends a servant to go to the province and encourage everyone to obey his laws (which were written to protect them) but the messenger is killed by the Governor. Several other servants are dispatched but meet similar fates (beheading). The King is sad because he hears how lost his people are and he wants to help them. The King's son insists that he be allowed to go. Reluctantly, the King gives his permission. His son dresses as a poor farmer and makes the long trip. Once there, he cures a blind person and also a lame girl (which is rather unexpected, because no hint of supernatural powers had been mentioned before.) One of the Governor's spies sees the miracles and tells the Governor, who in turn, has the Prince arrested. He executes the Prince, thinking he's killed the only heir of the king and will now control the region forever. But three days later, the king's son RETURNS FROM THE DEAD! (Bet you didn't see *that* one coming!) Sure enough, this strange tale is really about Jesus, his Father Almighty, and Satan. Grade: **A-** for Asian on Asian violence. **Value: $15.**

THE WORD BECAME FLESH Review: (Art by Carter ©1984.) The catalog promotes this tract as the perfect introduction to Jesus. It tells the story of Mary, Joseph, Jesus, and the prophets predicting his birth, upbringing, teaching, and, of course, his execution. (What Chick tract would be complete without a crucifixion scene?) It's basically the biography of Jesus. The goal seems to be to prove to the reader that Jesus actually existed and that there were lots of witnesses to his miracles and resurrection, and therefore, he must be God. What it doesn't do is cover much of what he said and what the New Testament was all about. The other shortcoming for beginners is that everyone is speaking in King James English, and that can be tough to follow for those unfamiliar with it. How many street punks are going to understand the following text from page 12: "Prepare ye the way of the Lord. Make his paths straight. O generation of vipers, who hath warned you to flee from the wrath to come? Bring forth therefore fruits worthy of repentance." If you study it, it makes sense, but if you pick it up and glance at it on the subway...probably not.

Realistically though, not every tract should be designed for the lowest common denominator. This tract would be a great comic to use in Sunday school to provide beautiful artwork to go along with the text of the Bible. The images are vivid, but sometimes crowded by too much text. One image is puzzling though. On page 15, Jesus is under a tree teaching the multitudes. His face and shoulders are black from the shade of the tree. It looks rather sinister, like something you would expect to see in *The Beast*. Ironically, he's saying, "Ye are the light of the world." Yet he's completely black... How odd.

Another funny image is page 6, where a Shepherd and lamb are in the foreground and a prophet is in the distant background preaching. His word balloon happens to line up with the snout of the lamb, making it look like the lamb is the one doing the talking. *Haw-haw-haw!* This is an interesting but not particularly inspiring tract. Grade: **B** for Biography. **Still in print.**

©1973 Jack T. Chick.

©1987 Jack T. Chick.

WORDLESS GOSPEL (and *Picture Gospel*) Review: (Haitian version art by Carter ©1973. New Guinea version art by Chick ©1971, 1972, 1987. See also African *Picture Gospel* version art by Chick ©1997.) Did you know that Jesus was black? Neither did I, until I saw this tract. Made especially for the uneducated, these tracts contain all pictures and little or no text. Perhaps Chick assumes the darker races don't read? If so, it won't stop him from fulfilling the "White man's burden" and showing them the light. It's the basic tale of a missionary explaining the "God in three persons" theory to clueless natives. (Not an easy task—especially since the third person of God is represented as a bird.) But the natives seem to buy it and that's all that counts. All except one, that is. He dies in his sins and gets carried down to the lake of fire by an angel (who also happens to be black). The good natives all go to heaven. Even Mary is a Negro! (One wonders how this tract goes over in Israel.) Each version features natives who wear whatever clothes or tribal outfits are most common to that country. All three versions contain generous helpings of red to accent the blood spilled by Jesus for man. Grade: **B+** Because Black is Beautiful, Baby! Medium oversized New Guinea versions ©1971 (5 1/4" x 3 5/8") **value is speculative**, ©1972 medium oversized version (5 1/4 x 3 5/8") **$50.** Regular size versions of all three (5 x 2 3/4") are **$3 each.** (Reprinting of these titles seems likely.)

By J.T.C.

WOUNDED CHILDREN Review: (Art by Carter ©1983.) A very popular and very scarce tract: It's a "compassionate" attack on homosexuality, complete with background flashbacks on how the main character became gay in the first place. The best part is the invisible demon that stands beside David as he spirals further into the homosexual hole. The "guardian demon" is always reassuring David with soothing demonic advice. Favorite Panel Award goes to one such scene. Ten-year-old David lies in bed contemplating masturbation and sexual fantasy. The Demon says, "David, think about all those pictures in your Daddy's book...of all those people doing all those strange things... I wonder if..." The footnote goes on to say, "Little David is now facing Demonic forces coming at him using subliminal mind control through the power of suggestion." Another panel shows daddy catching David playing with dolls. The demon urges the father, "What would your friends say if they knew your son was playing with a doll? HIT HIM!" The next page states, "One day his mother discovers him putting on eye make-up, and she takes him to a psychiatrist." But Doc only makes matters worse! He tells the parents that David is gay and that they must learn to accept him as he is. Dad's response is the show stopper, "They should put you on the island with all the rest of the queers and blow it up!" (Meanwhile, the demon laughs hysterically in the background.) David tries to straighten himself out, "but the homosexual tendency is too strong to resist." He takes a girl to dinner and she says she really likes him because he understands what she's going through. David's thought balloon responds, "Oh, honey, you just don't know. I'm really your sister." Needless to say, he doesn't get any.

David moves to the city, gets passed around by various one night stands, and finally moves in with a regular boyfriend. But like most of the queers in Chick's tracts, the boyfriend can't keep it in his pants. David finds out and breaks up with him. Meanwhile, a pickup truck full of rednecks with baseball bats is out cruising (not for sex, just violence). One brags, "We're going to clean up the community." A bystander (that's by, not bi) asks if that means they're going queer hunting. "You got it!" he responds, "We're gonna find us some fags to play baseball with, and bust their !@#&**! heads!" The head they bust belongs to David's ex-partner, and they smash it seven ways to Sunday. David happens to walk by during the piñata practice, but keeps on walking to avoid any trouble. Then he reads in the paper his ex-boyfriend has ex-pired. David feels guilty and contemplates suicide.

DAVID TRIES TO GO STRAIGHT. HE DATES GIRLS, BUT THE HOMOSEXUAL TENDENCY IS TOO STRONG TO RESIST.

I REALLY LIKE YOU, DAVID. YOU'RE DIFFERENT. YOU SEEM TO UNDERSTAND WHAT I'M REALLY GOING THROUGH.

OH, HONEY, YOU JUST DON'T KNOW. I'M REALLY YOUR SISTER.

LATER THAT SAME NIGHT

WHY CAN'T I JUST DIE?
WHY WAS I EVER BORN?
WHY CAN'T I CHANGE?

YOU'RE LONELY AND DEPRESSED, GET IT INTO YOUR HEAD, YOU'RE GAY! SO FACE IT.

©1983 Jack T. Chick.

Time passes and David searches for meaning in his life. He drowns his woes at the local gay bar (which sports the original title of "Gay Bar") when a born again Christian walks in looking for vulnerable queers. He swoops down on David like a vulture. It turns out that it takes one to know one. The preacher is actually an ex-homo himself. He sure looks the part, complete with a perm and turtle neck shirt! In typical Chick fashion, he converts David instantly. The two then save a third homosexual who was just about to kill himself. The guardian demons fly away screaming and the mortals are freed from their evil influence. One never sees any of the homosexuals smile in this tract. They all look tired and sad. Chick's version of being gay doesn't seem very gay at all, at least not in the emotional sense.

The footnote states this tract was written with help from pastor Perry Roberts, a converted homosexual delivered by Jesus. His reference was eventually replaced with a plug for Rebecca Brown's books. Now the tract is permanently discontinued. If you're lucky enough to find one, it's a grand addition to your collection. Grade **A+++** for Abstinence And Atonement! Permanently retired: **$100**

The Mystery Men

Not only is information on Jack Chick limited, but so are details about his other artists. We know Fred Carter is responsible for *The Crusader* comics, the realistic style tracts, and the vast majority of paintings in the Bible movie. (Erik Hollander and Keith Goodson were supposedly commissioned for a few movie paintings as well.) Chick credits Carter at the beginning of the illustrated books *A Solution To The Marriage Mess* and *Going Bananas,* but his name doesn't appear too many other places. Chick once wrote, "Fred is rather shy and declines to put his name on the art." (Chick 1980, 29) Carter also shuns interviews, just like his boss. A local newspaper did a two page spread on Chick Publications and was only able to come up with two paragraphs about Carter. It indicated he was born in 1938 and was living in Chicago when he sent art samples to Chick in 1972. He was soon hired and has worked for Chick ever since. (Cicchese 1997)

The second paragraph was little more than a quote from Chick that said Carter was one of the most "Christ-like men" he's ever known.

A few other details are known from people who have met Carter. He's black, handsome, and resembles the Jim Carter character he draws in *The Crusaders.* He was born about 1938, so he is in his mid-60s. He's very private. Others have tried to interview him on the phone and the response was always the same. He was appreciative of their compliments, but didn't do interviews.

Although I assumed I would get a similar reaction, I felt I should at least give him an opportunity to answer for himself. I called after work hours and Carter answered. He sounded like a nice older man. I told him who I was and that I admired his artwork. He thanked me for my interest in his work, but when I asked if he would say anything about his art training, he politely refused, saying he preferred not to share any information about himself. He said anything the office wanted to reveal was fine, but he didn't want to add anything.

I told him that I had seen some of his upcoming movie paintings, and thought they were marvelous. I asked him if they were painted with acrylics. He said he mainly used marker pens. "There's some acrylic on some of it, but most of it was done with little brush tipped markers." I was stunned. The detail and colors are amazing. Yet it was obvious that he didn't want to go into detail so I respected his wishes and concluded the call.

It was also obvious that Chick liked Carter on a personal as well as professional level. Chick indicated Carter was a devout Christian and a minister. He said those who worked with him all loved him. He also said Carter always wanted to draw for the Lord since he was a boy (Chick 2001).

That's not very much information for such an accomplished artist, but it will have to suffice. At least we have basic information on Carter, and that's a lot more than what was publicly revealed about a possible *third* artist. The prospect of another artist has been long debated among Chick fans and critics. Underground artist Dan Clowes (of *Ghost World* fame) wrote in *Heinous* magazine in 1995 that he believed the other artist at Chick Publications was a Filipino named Jesus Jodloman. He wrote others that he believed references to Fred Carter were "red herrings" (Clowes 1996).

Fantagraphics writer Eric Reynolds decided to find out. He started calling Fred Carters, who lived near Chick Publications, until he reached the actual artist. Carter told Reynolds that he and Chick were the only artists except for one who had helped in the early 1990s and didn't work out. Carter was very tight lipped in that interview as well and gave no specifics. He said he couldn't remember the other artist's name. The only new information he revealed about himself was that he had just finished a one year art school when he went to work for Chick in 1972 and he attributed all his growth as an artist to God (Raeburn 1998).

Dan Raeburn, author of *The Holy War of Jack Thomas Chick,* read the interview and assumed that the third artist Carter referred to was the one who ruined the ink job on *The Prophet* comic in 1988. He didn't think there was another tract artist. And why should he? Carter had already demonstrated he could master almost any style. Other collectors have called to ask the operators at Chick Publications who drew what, and were assured that only Chick and Carter did the art for the tracts. He believed them and repeated their sentiments in his book as well. Unfortunately, the operators are not always accurate. In this particular case, they were downright wrong.

Artist Fred Carter is said to look like one of the two Crusaders, James Carter. *Operation Bucharest* ©1974 Jack T. Chick.

Facing page: There are many mysteries presented in Chick tracts and comics. One of the biggest mysteries is finding out more about who draws them. *Chaos* ©1976 Jack T. Chick.

Greg's original version of *Doom Town*. Notice the exaggerated facial features. ©1989 Jack T. Chick.

Fred Carter's revamped version of *Doom Town*. Notice that the faces are more realistic, in spite of all the added ear rings, wigs, and false eye lashes! ©1999 Jack T. Chick.

There *was* a third artist who worked for Chick from 1989 to the beginning of 1992, and he drew *several* tracts. A source at Chick Publications said the easiest way to distinguish his work was that, "the faces didn't look quite right." Sure enough, if you examine the tracts listed in this section, you'll notice different facial characteristics. They appear longer and skinnier, more plain and less attractive, more cartoonish and not as realistic. The noses tend to be long and skinny at top and knobby at the bottom. Many of these tracts have since received a "face lift" by Fred Carter, who literally pasted on new faces or replaced entire panels.

Who was this mysterious third artist? I was told it was a guy named Greg Hildebrandt, but my source had no idea how big and famous Greg Hildebrandt was as a commercial artist. Hilderbrandt painted the first *Star Wars* movie poster, did wonderful J.R.R. Tolkein *Hobbit* paintings for *The Lord of the Rings* calendars, and had released several non-sports fantasy trading card sets. I had a hard time imagining that such a famous artist drew religious tracts for Chick. So I emailed Jean L. Scrocco, curator of the Hildebrandt's *Spiderwebart* website, to see what he said. He replied:

"Greg Hildebrandt never did any work with Chick Publications.

Thank you,
Jean L. Scrocco
Curator"

I followed up with another email, asking Jean to check again, and to also ask Greg's twin brother, Tim (an equally talented artist). I said I was pretty sure about my source and the Hildebrandt name was tough to confuse. Jean's terse reply was:

"I asked him and he has no idea what a tract even is."

At that point, I was pretty convinced I was mistaken, so I decided to double check at Chick. I contacted my source and asked if they would dig through their records to see who the other artist was for tracts drawn during 1990-1991. There shouldn't be a privacy issue, because Greg Hildebrandt is a public figure. I figured the worse thing that could happen was that I would get no reply. Months passed, but I eventually received word back that his name was indeed Greg Hildebrandt. Not only that, but I received art samples from two more tracts that Greg was working on that were never produced (since the Bible Stories series were losing money and Greg was let go). The two titles were *That Cursed Thing* and *The Test*. What a pity those titles were never published. (The entire Bible tract series was slated for 25 titles, but canceled after the 21st installment, due to slumping sales. Chick later revived the idea for 25 Bible story tracts after adding a modern day character named Bob Williams.)

For a second opinion, I decided to send some samples to Bill Fogg for his analysis. Bill is an art instructor in the San Francisco bay area and is pretty good about identifying artists based on their work. I sent him *Superman?* and the original *Doom Town* tracts, then directed him to Hildebrant's work at spiderwebart.com and asked what he thought. He wrote back:

Unpublished art for *That Cursed Thing*, one of the unfinished four tracts from the 1990s Bible series drawn by the mysterious third artist.

"I've been comparing the art in the tracts you sent with other Hildebrandt work. I would say that they could certainly be a match. The handling of faces, clothing, composition, and value, seem very similar. If I had to bet one way or the other, I would bet that he did the tracts, but of course there is the possibility that I'd lose. Slim possibility, though."

To be fair, it's possible there's another Greg Hildebrandt out there who just happens to do similar style art. There are only 12 other Greg Hildebrandts publicly listed in the USA, and the chances that there would also be a commercial artist with a compatible art style seems unlikely, but not impossible. It's also possible Hildebrandt was embarrassed by being let go by Chick, or that he didn't want to get mixed up in any of the controversy over Chick's religious views.

Another possibility is that the name Hildebrandt was spelled incorrectly. One folder was casually hand labeled "Greg Hildabrand's Art" (with an "a" in the middle and no "t" on the end). Unfortunately, there are only three phone listings for anyone named Hildabrand who's first name starts with the letter "G", and none of those names are variations on Greg. Perhaps it was spelled "Hildabrandt" (with "a" and "t")? There are two listings for that name in the USA, but neither of them have first names starting with "G".

So some of the mystery remains, but at least we can be certain there was a third artist who worked on the tracts around 1990. Here's a list of what, based on my *opinion,* are the tracts drawn by Greg Hildebrandt (whether it's spelled that way or not). Check them out and decide for yourself:

The Brat-The Story of The Prodigal Son. (©1992). This is likely the very last tract Hildebrandt ever drew for Chick. It only contains one drawing from Hildebrandt's artwork, the image of the man wiping his tears away on page 20. (There's also a chance the bloody crucifixion image on page 21 is recycled Hildebrandt art.) However, I've never seen the "A" version of this tract, so it's quite possible more of Hildebrandt's art appeared in the original version and was revised by the time the "B" version was published.

Burn Baby Burn-The story of Shadrach, Meschach, and Abednego (©1991): Unchanged except for page 19 (somewhere between "A" version and 6.6).

The city was under the control of Satan because they worshipped idols (pagan gods, or demons).

There was NO law and order. People did only evil ALL the time. The population was so completely involved in sexual perversions that its very name. "Sodom," now depicts an act of homosexuality.

Greg's original idol worship scene. When Carter redrew it, the "ferry" idol was replaced with a more sinister statue from *The Exorcist.* ©1989 Jack T. Chick.

Doom Town- The story of Sodom (©1989 and again in 1991): Original cover featured a crumbling city on the cover. Then it was changed to a skull and cross bones floating over the horizon of a city skyline. Sometime after the "E" version (1991), the story was completely redrawn by Carter and encapsulated within the modern context of a gay rally.

The Dreamer- The story of Joseph (©1990 and again in 1991): After the original "A" version, many of the faces were redrawn. Joseph now looks more handsome and similar to Michael Landon. The weird part is that the original "A" version was copyrighted 1991, and the newer revamped version was copyrighted 1990!

Earthman-The story of Adam and Eve (©1990): Sometime between the "A" and "F" version, much of the tract was redrawn by Carter (especially the faces).

Empty Tomb-The Resurrection of Christ (©1990): Sometime after the "C" version, the tract was modified by Carter (redrawing most of the faces.)

Going To The Dogs- The story of Ahab and Jezebel (©1992): This tract is especially interesting for two reasons. First, it's probably the next to last tract Hildebrandt worked on for Chick. Only a few of his images can be found in this tract, and two of them are lackluster profiles which get upgraded with more interesting celebrity cameos drawn by Carter.

Remember Peter Lorre? The bulging-eyed, sleazy, short guy from classic film noire flicks like *The Maltese Falcon* and *Casablanca*? His twin appears on page 11. In fact, the other guy on the same panel looks like Sydney Greenstreet, the overweight fat guy who also starred in the same two films. If that's not enough, Ernest Borgnine and Edward G. Robinson clones appear on page 17. All four of these twins were added after the original version. (Code "A" versions have generic Jews in their place.) The 3rd artist may have been let go soon after doing this tract. Carter either finished the tract, or replaced most of it with better art. Eventually, Carter and Chick had some fun with two new revisions—the celebrity guest spots. It's only a theory, but it seems to make sense. After 1992, it's Chick or Carter art only.

Killer Storm-The story of Noah (©1991): All the art appears to be that of the 3rd artist with no revisions. (Some of the ancient ark images looks like Carter's art from the 1976 comic book, but if you look really close, you'll see they don't quite match.)

The Outsider-The story of Ruth (©1991): This one is tough to judge. Some of the faces look like Carter's in the original "A" version, while others don't. It's possible this one was modified from the very start (it was released in 1991, near the end of the third artist's term.) Other minor changes appeared in the "C" version.

Plagues-The story of Moses, part 1 (©1991): Sometime after the "B" version, several panels were redrawn by Carter, especially ones of Pharaoh.

Royal Affair-The story of David and Bathsheba (©1990 and again 1993): The original artwork was completely redrawn by Carter after the "B" version (in 1993). The story was given a more modern opening scene with a courtroom trial for sexual harassment. Chick reissued this tract during the impeachment of President Bill Clinton. Coincidence?

Superman-The story of Samson (©1990): The art remains unchanged from the original, although Carter apparently redrew the Charles Atlas silhouette and replaced it with a detailed image of Samson pulling down the temple walls.

THE STORY OF THE PRODIGAL SON

THE BRAT

"THE BRAT"   COVER - PAGE 1

"THE BRAT"   PAGE 10

Original artwork (never published) for *The Brat* by the mysterious third artist. Carter redrew almost all the art that appeared in the published version.

Public Comments and Criticism

Everyone who has seen Chick's tracts tends to have strong memories and/or opinions about them. Here are some edited reader comments submitted to our fan site, (Chickcomics.com) along with some expanded commentary from other guest writers. As you can see, Chick's supporters and critics span a wide variety of people, special interest groups, and foreign countries. This is a representative sample of reader remarks. No censorship or special quotas were applied in the selection process.

I've been acquainted with Chick tracts since I was about 11 years old. The mother of a school chum used to keep them on her coffee table. Though I did not pray "The Sinner's Prayer" as a result of the tracts I read (actually, I recall that at the time, they kind of creeped me out) it was not long afterward that I first "received Christ" when I attended a local Baptist church. This was in the early 1970s, and things were far less paranoid then; they used to send a bus around to pick up neighborhood children.

And yet...those little tracts hold a peculiar fascination, don't they? I mean, even when one *knows* that Mr. Chick is way out there in "left field," those tracts still manage to catch and hold one's attention. If nothing else, they are a valuable piece of American culture.

-Elaine

I have been viewing Jack's pamphlets with horrified fascination even since I first encountered them in Northern Ireland (a really responsible place to be spreading documents "proving" that all Catholics are bedfellows of Satan)...
-A.C.P., Hong Kong

As a kid growing up in N.C., I was exposed to Chick tracts regularly from a very young age. I still have very distinct memories of having the shit scared out of me by one of those tracts when I was maybe 5 or 6. It was one of the Early Period, crudely drawn numbers, something like *Tiny Shoes*.

-Dave

I was not saved through Chick tracts but they have been influential in my life in many ways. I think Jack taught many of us an important lesson about "directness of method."

One memory of mine goes back to about 1979. I was in high school in Patagonia, Arizona, and one of the school janitors decided to put a Chick tract in EVERY SINGLE LOCKER. (It was a small school—about 150 kids.) Well, needless to say, the entire campus was abuzz all next day. There were all sorts of reactions—rage, laughter, disgust. What I shall never forget is that for about a week the topics of campus conversation were almost entirely SPIRITUAL, no lie!

Well, it was a public school, and the janitor, an ex-hippie Jesus freak type—beard and everything—was fired.

-Al

Some Christians are SHOCKED to learn...

how easy witnessing is with Chick tracts.

I have never placed a Jack Chick tract, but my boyfriend and I (both Bisexual) screen printed images from the *Gay Blade* onto t-shirts. We think the artwork's so cool! It certainly gets people talking. Of course, Jack would rip the shirts off our backs if he saw them...
-Jayelle (one of those evil Witches)

I began to hand out Chick tracts in 1972 when I got saved. I met a street preacher named Red Edward Gay who helped Jack put together the *Gay Blade*. We traveled the streets of Pomona, California, handing out tracts we got from Jack. I will never forget the night Red went into a "Gay Bar" and started preaching, I stood outside handing out *Gay Blades* to all those who were running out the door to avoid Red's preaching. I praise God for all I learned in those days. I have lost contact with Red and pray I see him again. I now am a preacher and minister to those in prison with HIV/Aids.

-Phil

I have enjoyed JTC's tracts for many years and feel they were instrumental in my finding Jesus as my savior (*This Was Your Life*); sent *Hi There* to my dad (he was an iron worker then)—he eventually got saved also. I guess we'll all find out on Judgment Day if all of JTC's opinions are true — If only one tenth of those millions of tracts resulted in someone getting saved I think JTC will be pretty well off in Heaven.

-Freed

Facing page: Chick believes that Christians shouldn't keep their faith to themselves, even though aggressive recruitment often results in criticism. *A Solution to the Marriage Mess*. Art by Carter © 1978 Jack T. Chick.

Evolutionists hate one man more than any others... and they **don't** want you to know about him.

Who brought this lie to school?

This book could soon be banned in public schools... so read it **now!**

The Earthman ©1990 Jack T. Chick.

I must admit that I am a hard-core fan of Chick's work, even though I am not a Christian. I got introduced to my first one a few years ago during the *Titanic* movie mania. One Saturday a zombiotic jeezo nut left some Kooky Kristian literature on my front door. One of them was a Chick track called (lo and behold) *Titanic!* My high suspicions at high alert I glanced through the illustrated toilet paper and found it to be a laugh a minute. Since then I started my hunt for as many Chick tracts as I can.

-Apostate

I'm a born again Jew. I used one track called *Holocaust* and left it on the window sill of a bus. I saw Jewish couples read it. From where I was sitting in the back of the bus, the Jewish couple left and became discouraged. Apparently, they seemed shocked. I do not know them but I can tell you the Lord opened their eyes.

-Gerstein

Jack Chick seems to be more interested in money and his own name than Jesus' teachings. *Death Cookie?* Jesus is not a cookie...He is the Bread of Life! He is God! And God is All-Powerful. What Jesus says is true!

"Unless you eat the flesh of the son of Man and drink His blood, you have no life within you!" Gospel of John Chapter 6.

Jesus says it, I believe it! Case closed!

A saved Catholic Christian, Viva Christo Rey!

-GMC

It was 1982 and I was 8 years old. My sister, her boyfriend, his brother and myself were driving back home to Beaumont, Texas, from a day at Galveston beach. I remember sitting in the back seat of that '78 dark green Catalina with my sister's boyfriends brother. Antsy like most kids are at that age I began to dig my little fingers in the cracks of the seat when out I pulled *THIS WAS YOUR LIFE* by J.T.C. Yesterday by the Beatles was playing on the radio as I read the story, which even at a young age I remember it having some sort of future self-prophesy revelation relevance. The sheer terror that I felt reading that *&%$ has yet to be paralleled. It was like a dirty secret that I couldn't tell anyone in the car.

-CRABCAKES, Houston

Back in 1976 we moved from Massachusetts to Maine. My dad joined Word of Christ Ministries. The Pastor gave me a stack of Chick tracts and boy I loved them. The whole collection. In the mid-1980s, I started to collect the tracts I cherished. (I received Christ through Chick tracts.) I got really excited when others were searching these tracts.

-Michael

I was hired at a beauty salon were the owner was a born-again Christian. She had all of Jack's tracts displayed on her cash register and counter.

I was saved at 9 in a Baptist church, but my life was not fruitful because of many bad life experiences. I am now 35 years old. I was reading some of the tracts during a slow time at the shop when I picked up a tract titled *One Way.* I began leafing through it and decided I wanted to read it from the beginning to the end. So I did, and as I did, it was like a joyful light came on in my head and I rejoiced in my spirit for the gift God gave me!!! Ever since then I have dedicated my life to Christ. I have tried to witness to friends, but it was hard for me to convey the message, since I am very shy and not very well at speaking. So I decided to purchase Jack's tracts. And now I leave them in all the places I visit.

-Lisa

I'm another of those wonderful Chicklets, an addict to Jack's weird world view. Unfortunately, I don't have any of the [rare] titles in my own collection, though I have read many of them! There was this quite deranged evangelical Christian with rabid predatory gay proclivities I knew a few years ago who had collected a mess of 'em - but that's another quite peculiar story.

The only real problem here is that Canada, where I reside, has made some real efforts to suppress the import of Jack's work, so it's often tricky to order directly from The Man. Oh well. I just hope a few more of the street crazies will take care of that minor complication... Happy hunting!

-Donald, Canada

This got me thinking about my own first Chick tract. I think I was 5 or 6 when I got *The Fool* (I think. The one about a jester.) from a creepy old guy running a booth at the swap meet. My father used to take me out junk shopping on the weekends, and as I also was keeping a series of scrapbooks at the time, no brochure or piece of random paper was safe.

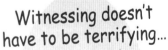

Witnessing doesn't have to be terrifying...

Chick tracts make it EASY!

This was my first real encounter with Christianity. I was scared by the scenario in the tract, but only in the same way I was scared by the box of ratty old *Weird Tales* comic books my father had given me. Being damned to an eternity in Hell became one of my wake-up-in-terror dreams for a while, joining the zombie dream and the one where a ventriloquist's dummy trades bodies with me.

-Anna

The Little Princess ©1998 Jack T. Chick.

The first Chick Publication I ever read was *This Was Your Life*. I have fallen in love with them and try to find new ones everywhere I go. I do a lot of traveling across the country, and I always look for them when I go into Christian bookstores. I have read probably every Chick ever published including his books and magazines.

-Rev. Chara

I actually like Chick's style more than Carter's. Carter undoubtedly has more skill, but Chick is a cartoonist's cartoonist. He draws in a cartoon style with no pretension about being a "real" artist. His aim is to get a point across, and he does it, not eloquently, but clearly. Chick's caricatures are so vicious, both in form and in the language they use.

I have an extract from some book on cartoonists where they deal with Carter's other work. Apparently he did some radical things in Sunday School books way back when, depicting black and white kids playing together etc.

-Jeremy, Australia

I have always (and still do) look forward to uncovering "accidentally" a Jack Chick tract, from behind a video cover box at the video store I work at, underneath a napkin dispenser at a restaurant, or the slickest way yet, from inside the inner pocket of a sport jacket I bought at J.C. Penney, and it was the *Bad Bob* story... That was probably my favorite one. I wonder if it was shipped from the factory with the tract in the pocket, if a customer put it there, or an employee of the store? Sunday comics aren't very comical anymore, comic books are too serious...the only comic style reading that still has me laughing until tears are streaming are Jack Chick Tracts. I think they're hilarious.

-Chuck K.

Chick tracts are alive and well in the penal systems. I was once "a guest of the county of Los Angeles" for driving on a suspended license (10 days) And that is where I came upon my first Chick tract and made my decision to accept the Lord. During "my stay" I encountered a rather large and mean looking Black inmate who I saw was reading a tract, I

approached him and offered him the one I had been reading over and over (*Big Daddy*). He reached in his pocket and handed me three of his to read, but insisted that I return them to him. We became friends over the next couple of days and he saw to it that no harm came my way. So I know they're out there doing some good.

-Johnny G.

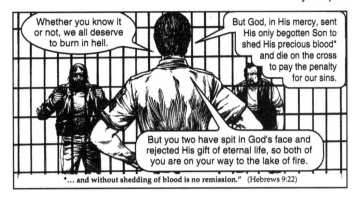

Bad Bob ©1983 Jack T. Chick.

I'm a Catholic and I love Chick Tracts, just because they are so stupid. Haw Haw! What is Karl Keating so bent out of shape about? *Last Rites* is laughable and about as persuasive as Clinton's "I didn't inhale." The way I see it, if Jack's against my religion, I must be doing something right!

-N.Mag

I reread *Dark Dungeons* ... it brought back memories. That tract scared the hell out of me when I was eight or nine and had just begun playing D&D. (I guess I was exactly the target audience: Christian, young, and impressionable). Thankfully, my mom talked me down after I got really worried, and I've been a happy little gamer ever since.

-F.Bush

I've been intrigued with a weird fascination of Chick for years, ever since I first stumbled upon references to *Dark Dungeons* in a role-playing magazine.

-Theo, Sweden

I am a Roman Catholic myself, and while I won't advocate my faith, I will say that a great portion of the tracts seem (to me) a bit lacking in substance. The first thing I noticed was that the antagonist, after having heard the word or God, is so willing to convert. This occurs in many tracts, i.e. in the tract *Allah has No Son*, a Muslim seems quite ready to give up a religion that he has been devoted to for what appears to be more than 40 years, after a mere 40 seconds of preaching. In the evolution vs. religion (*Big Daddy*) a scientist is massively over-zealous for science at first, then after a kid (whose arguments are, while factual, greatly outweighed by other facts — he even admits evolution exists himself when he claims "5 of the 6 evolution theories have not been observed" i.e. one has) talks to the class, the teacher immediately takes the opposite extreme.

You don't need a seminary degree to witness...

You only need Chick tracts.

-WW

I buy all-tract assortments once every couple of months not only to distribute duplicates around town, but also to sort through in search of any unannounced modified tracts that belong in my growing collection. This is much more exciting and less expensive a hobby for me, and one far less contradictory to my beliefs, than the secular comic collecting, from both mainstream and independent publishers, that I spent 15 years pursuing. These tracts of Chick's deserve the "underground comix" appellation every bit as much as anything by Gilbert Shelton or Robert Crumb (the latter surprisingly agreed), and prove that diversity exists even in this niche market. Chick is truly an American icon, even if this nation won't know what it's missing when he finally does perish and go to heaven. Though it's obviously in God's hands, I hope Chick is still around long enough to squeeze out at least a few more of his unique tracts. He never fails to surprise me.

-Ramon, Texas

I must say, I enjoy Mr. Chick's work, partially for the artwork, partially for his viewpoints, both to critique them in a sarcastic way. Although I don't agree with many of his beliefs, he stands VERY firm behind what he believes in, and is sincere. The writing is witty in a simple way. I also appreciate little finds like the "Joke Cola" (in *Dark Dungeons*) along with other finds like Fang the dog, or spotting places where "Rock for the Rock" is used as a song other then *Angels*, (on page 11 of *Why No Revival?*). One could critique Chick and say he's closed-minded, but I think he has a strong conviction and faith in what he believes and feels is moral. I wish we had more people who had such strong convictions out there, both whom I'd come closer to agreeing with morally, and otherwise. I can respect the man, I may be sarcastic about his work, but I respect him, and mean no attempt to insult him by doing so.

-Evan

I found a Chick tract *(This Was Your Life)* in a parking lot when I was a little girl of about 9. It was my first exposure to a "personal" relationship with God. While I did not accept the Lord at that time, the tract seemed nearly sacred to me. I took it with me every time we moved. I just could not bring myself to get rid of it. I finally lost track of it many years later...but I did receive Jesus Christ as my Lord and Savior when I was 17. I never forgot that tract, and was THRILLED to find a Christian bookstore that sold tracts. I nearly leapt for joy when I found they sold *This Was Your Life*. I bought a pack of them on the spot, and have been distributing Chick tracts ever since (20+ years now.) It's a small but real way to reach many more people than I could otherwise, and I know my Lord Jesus will make them fruitful for His purposes.

-Dewy

Let's forget this witnessing idea...

My boss really HATES it!

I have met Jack personally, although it was some years ago. We worked very close with him for a few years and he wrote *Going Home* especially for the work our ministry was doing in Africa. It was at my encouraging that Jack reissued *The Great Escape*, but in my opinion, the original was better. God Bless.

-Evangelist Stephen M.

I can't say whether I agree on the teachings in all of Chick's material, especially from the '80s, but I feel overall that many have been saved through his ministry.

-Carl

Thirty years ago I read a Chick tract for the first time; it was the old reliable *This Was Your Life* one. As a drug taking hippie who never read the Bible before, the idea of a "final Judgment" and your life being reviewed by God and everyone else, seemed like a big joke. I laughed at the tract. Three months later I became one of those "Jesus Freaks" myself, after being scared into God's kingdom by a very bad LSD trip (whatever works I guess). Then that tract I laughed at made more sense.

-Martha

When I got saved, a pastor of mine gave me some of his tracts. That was 4 years ago. I have been giving them out ever since. One day in our park there were about 8 Catholic college students going through the park and they came to our door. My mom listened to them but didn't really say much to them. I could hear the Lord saying to me that I had to go out there. I said "Lord, this is like David and Goliath! Here I am, a 5 foot 2 inch female and there are about 8 of them!" Well, I looked down at my basket of tracts and what do you think was sitting there? *Are Roman Catholics Christians?* So, needless to say, there I went, little me. They surrounded me and were actually pretty angry at first. By this time my step father (who is an ex-catholic) came out and we witnessed to them for about a half hour. They did not want to believe us, but God's word never returns void. And it was just from me handing them a Chick tract and walking away and they followed me back across the street to talk about it. Thank you for listening to our Lord. Jack, don't water it down, tell it like Jesus would!!!!!!!!

-Tract lady

Reverend Wonderful ©1982 Jack T. Chick.

I have never been a collecting-type person, never into coins or stamps or autographs. But there's something about Jack that just makes me want to gobble up everything he produces. My favorite thing to do is share my collection with people who have never heard of Jack Chick. I keep a big stack of my favorite tracts on my desk at work and the best part of all is the variety of reactions of the people who stop by and spot them. From "Wow! Cool! I LOVE those!" and enthusiastic requests to borrow them to enjoy (which I always grant), to the odd, sideways look, followed by a cool "no thanks" when I offer to loan them out. I'm sure you know where I'm coming from.

-Alvin

A Chick memory... I remember when I was still drinking, I was hanging around the bus station just killing time, trying to walk off yet another hangover. I walked inside the terminal to get warm and have a smoke (this is when you could still smoke indoors in most places). On the chair next to me was, I am almost certain, was the *This is Your Life* tract. I read it. At first it didn't much register but I stuck it in my pocket. Later that night as I was laying in my loser basement apt drinking some vodka and *Hawaiian Punch,* I read it again. As the vodka went down the story began to take on more and more meaning. Made me think. Not right away but about a week later I went to a prayer service at the Salvation Army (run by two Jesus bikers) and wish I could say I got saved right away, but I guess life isn't that simple. However I did start going to AA meetings at the sally and eventually sobered up. So in an indirect way Jack probably led me to sobriety. The Lord works in mysterious ways....

- Dave

I started collecting Chick tracts back in the 1980s along with a friend in junior high school. We also bought all the full size comics (*Crusaders, King of Kings,* and *Alberto* comics) as well. Both of us had been reading Chick tracts during church service ever since we could remember.

-David, Atlanta

Try to imagine slipping a tooth under your pillow as a kid and, the next morning, finding a quarter taped to a copy of *This Was Your Life!* That's about the point where I figured that either the Tooth Fairy was looking for a new line of work or my parents were in the tooth collection business!

-Jeff

I'd just like to say that I'm a Catholic fan of Chick tracts. These things are amusing, from the Satanic origins of Rock and Roll to the horrors of the New Catholic Order. I'd also like to list a few of my favorite Chick quotes/moments: In *The Last Generation,* I love how he shows how in a Catholic-ruled world, divorce would be rampant. Guess he never heard of Franco. I also love *Dark Dungeons.*

-Treki

I have always used these tracts to bring people to the Lord and have had Muslims unable to put these things down at all. I am glad to see there are others who support and appreciate his work like I do.

-Peter, South Africa

Some months ago there was an article in the local newspaper about a man who got in trouble for causing, in a roundabout way, the deaths of his neighbor's two dogs. The paper said the man had a long history of trouble with the law and mental instability. I looked up his address and began mailing him one Chick tract a week for about five months. I had been passing Chick's out for a while, and was becoming discouraged that perhaps my efforts were in vain, and slowed down from my once vigorous Chick distribution. I work for a local utility company, and shortly after becoming discouraged, I was given a maintenance job to do at this man's house. The job required me to enter his house, where I saw every one of the Chick tracts prominently displayed in his living room. I didn't mention to him that I sent them, but I took this as a sign that my efforts were not in vain, and am now passing out more Chicks than ever.

-Doug W

Hey, I was thoroughly entertained by Jack Chick's cartooning. It's a shame that good illustrations were put to such awful, discriminatory content. I think the most offensive cartoons were *Sin City, Holocaust, The Gay Blade,* and *Baby Talk.* Give me a break. First of all they were the most offensive portrayals of stereotypes within society (the white trash pregnant teenager, the limp-wristed, disco dancing gay men, etc.), put into situations that are undoubtedly, and completely unrealistic. For instance, the doctor telling the boy Eric that he was committing murder by demanding an abortion. He is a doctor for goodness sake! How hysterical! And if that makes me an "evil lesbian pervert abortionist with Catholic tendencies" or whatever twisted messages Jack Chick creates, then so be it. I'd rather go to hell in Chick's eyes than be intolerant of someone's very nature. Thanks, Jack for turning me off to God just a little bit more!

-Hod

I have used Chick tracts for a number of years, placing them in various places and leaving them in offices, etc. for people to read. They are a great witnessing tool for us, especially if you're a bit timid as I am! The good thing with these tracts is that many people find them irresistible to read and they will read them on their own time, when they are more acceptable.

Living in Canada it is hard to come across any of the more controversial tracts so one must have connections to get a hold of them. Canada is becoming a bleeding heart communist country, sorry to say! It seems the only freedom we have is to do what the government and minority groups tell us to do!!! The funny thing is that it seems the only people the government has anything against are the true Bible believers! It surely must be a sign of the times.

-D.J., Canada

I am a beginning collector, but after reading a friend's *Wounded Children,* which he found in a gay hang-out in Tennessee, I was so fascinated that I am now hooked and can't wait to find more of the outrageous Mr. Chick.

-Julia

Chick tracts...

A witnessing method you can really sink your teeth into.

Think people don't want to hear the gospel?

Wrong! NOBODY can resist Chick tracts!

I have always loved Chick tracts and just recently started a collection with their nifty sample assortment. Man, it was like Christmas 75+ times over! Hah! I am Christian myself, and I believe in many of the things

Chick has to say, but above all there is something about those little comics that I just can't get enough of. Perhaps it is my journalism/media education. I have been a huge fan of any propaganda and these tracts are the cream of the crop. Full of wonderful exaggerations and never abiding by the ridiculous PC laws that America has adapted over the years, who couldn't love these things?!

-Scott

I have not always been a fan of Chick Publications due to its (sometime) severe anti-catholic stance. However, I must acknowledge that their current tract on Islam *(Allah Had No Son)* which tells the story of a Christian talking with a militant Muslim man, and framing a wonderful witness for Jesus Christ, is outstanding work. I would like to see this tract widely distributed. This is a masterful presentation of apologetics.

-Rev. Austin Miles

The first Chick tract I ever saw was one I found at school: *Big Daddy.* I wasn't even a Christian at the time, but it turned me into an immediate anti-evolutionist. My favorite tracts were fiery ones like *This Was Your Life, Hi There, Somebody Goofed,* and *Bewitched.* I could also appreciate the softer, simpler tracts like *Somebody Loves Me* and *One Way.* My Bible study friends and I ordered large quantities of Chick tracts and distributed them wherever we could.

We got into trouble at the public library for putting Chick tracts inside magazines. We conducted "tract raids" on three "spiritually dead" churches in town (i.e., we stuffed hymnals with tracts on a weekday and slipped tracts into the coats of church attendees while the apostate service was in progress). One of my friends was an engineering student and he created a "tract gun" which shot rolled-up tracts through the air while we passed by in our car.

-J. Taylor, Ph.D.

Angels? ©1986 Jack T. Chick.

As someone who was brought up in a fairly conservative Christian family but has since shifted a fair bit in my thinking, I find Chick comics to be a bit like pornography — they are based on something beautiful and precious, but distort it so greatly that they are downright evil, and yet exert a strangely compelling fascination upon all who fall under their sway!

I started reading Chick booklets in my early teens and continued reading and collecting them on and off until I kind of grew out of them at University. I had (have) a fairly good collection, aided by the fact that I used to work weekends in a Christian bookshop, so until Chick got kicked out of the Christian Booksellers' Association, I had first dibs on all new titles that came through the shop. In the end I think it was the anti-Catholic tracts and comics that turned me off. Not, mind you, because I necessarily disagreed with JTC — probably at that stage I was still in the anti-Catholic camp. But it just strained my credulity to the breaking point to believe that the Catholic Church was responsible for the Nazis, Communism, Islam, the KKK, the IRA, the Masons, the American Civil War, the Illuminati, Club of Rome, World Bankers (?), the Spanish Civil War, and the First World War, and they STILL couldn't manage to create One World Government!

-Linz (England)

As a lapsed Catholic (Chick would be proud) and as an Agnostic for the last eighteen years (Chick would shudder), many family members and friends do not understand my obsession with Chick tracts. However, there are some that do, and they are the ones that "get it." If you lead a secular life, it comes down to this: you either get Jack Chick or you don't. And if you do, he's a hoot. If you don't, well, you probably never will.

It is impossible to dismiss the impact that Chick's crusade has had on our collective pop consciousness. We can see Chick's bearing throughout the world of cartooning: National Lampoon, The Church of the SubGenius, and Dan Clowes have copied his format with great success. You take the standard 3 x 5 inch format and stick in a quasi-obsessive message and you have a Jack Chick parody. It's amazing: so simple, yet so universal.

-Paul Shiple

I was introduced to Jack Chick tracts while studying at the University of Kentucky. Someone was passing them out in the free-speech area on campus and I was at first repulsed by them. (They were copies of *Boo!*, the tract explaining Halloween and Samhain.)

But after I finished it, I was drawn in to the world of Jack T. Chick. Chick's style is stark, almost gothic. What Chick captures in his writings are glimpses of religion's dark side. Chick's comics reflect the shortcomings of man, making the real world seem less immoral. God and Jesus might love everyone, but Chick doesn't pull any punches. If he hates something, he lets you *know* it in his writings. Whether it's Judaism, Catholic Church, homosexuals, or any other group not in line with Chick's thinking, Chick condemns them all to eternal suffering in his masterpieces of comic book art.

To say Jack T. Chick has influenced fundamentalism in America would be a gross understatement. He defines it. His comics are not all sparkles and sunshine. What Chick reflects of human behavior is the gritty realism we all endure every day.

-Randolph Vance,

As a kid, one thing I loved about going over to my friend's house was that he had a whole collection of Chick tracts and comics. We would spend hours reading them from cover to cover, from *Fire Starter* to *Lisa*, from *This Was Your Life* to *The Sissy*, from *The Exorcists* to *Primal Man*, from *Sabotage* to *The Godfather*. I found the artwork spectacular! This was not only my introduction to Chick's publications, but also to comics in general. Being raised Roman Catholic—in an Italian Family mind you—it was also my first introduction to the cons of the religion. Yet my friend was a Baptist. It says something about how in childhood, differences are hardly noticed while the things kids have in common are made the most of.

-John (Australia)

Let's talk about the quality of Chick Comics! The lush illustrations of Fred Carter hold their own against anything *Marvel* or *Classics Illustrated* could come up with. What was the message to a young fundamentalist,

growing up in that world, in the early '70s? The message was: you can be a Christian and not forsake quality! You don't have to be weird and reclusive. You can be an active participant in society.

-Dwayne Walker

Young or old...

EVERYBODY loves Chick tracts!

8

Celebrity Comments

THE SUPERSTAR

J.T.C.

I wrote a diverse list of celebrities to see what they thought about Jack Chick. I sent out 50 letters asking famous folks for their opinions on Chick (pro or con). I assured them their remarks could be as long or brief as they liked and would not be edited when they appeared in print. I included a complimentary *This Was Your Life* tract and a self addressed stamped envelope. I wonder what the mail man thought, seeing all those famous names flow out of my mailbox? (He probably thought I was the next *Unibomber*.)

The results were interesting. Only five of the celebs acknowledged my request (a 10% response). Of those who responded, three of the five were familiar with Chick's work. That isn't to say the others weren't. They may have avoided the subject for fear of alienating fans by publicly commenting on religion. Others were either too busy to bother writing back, or enjoyed stealing my stamps! Whatever the reason, I've included all their names for your amusement. Try imagining what they would have said *if* they had responded. (About 12% of the letters were returned undeliverable. Each of those is indicated.)

Woody Allen (comedian/director—undeliverable);
Tom Arnold (actor/comedian—undeliverable);
Dan Aykroyd (actor/comedian—refused delivery);

Is this man praying? Chick tracts get read!

Alec Baldwin (actor—He returned a signed photograph);
Ray Bradbury (Writer);
Patrick Buchanan (commentator);
Kate Bush (former rock singer);
Jimmy Carter (former President);
Yvonne Craig (former actress);
David Duchovny ("X-files" star);
Rev. Jerry Falwell (minister/ activist);

Facing page: Chick's portrayal of Hollywood is less than flattering. *Primal Man?* ©1976 Jack T. Chick.

Ace Frehley (former KISS rock star);
Jane Fonda (former actress, activist);
Bill Gates (computer executive);
Frank Gorshin (actor/comedian—undeliverable);
Matt Groening (cartoonist);
Buck Henry (humor writer—undeliverable);
Pee Wee Herman (actor/comedian);
Denise Hopper (actor);
Rev. Jesse L. Jackson (activist);
Dr. Jack Kevorkian (activist—still in prison);

Someone who looks a lot like a famous writer is brought to tears by a tract. *The Scam* ©2002 Jack T. Chick.

Steven King (horror writer);
Spike Lee (activist/director);
Monica Lewinsky (former 2nd Lady);
G. Gordon Liddy (radio talk show host);
Martin Mull (actor/comedian);
Bill Murry (actor/comedian);
Robert Novak (commentator);
Don Novello (comedian);
Ted Nugent (former rock star);
Conan O'Brien (talk show host);
Rosie O'Donnel (talk show host);
Ozzy Osbourne (actor/ former rock star);
John Paul II (current Pope);
Ross Perot (Presidential hopeful);
Dan Quayle (former Vice President);
Arnold Schwarzenegger (actor);
Rev. Al Sharpton (activist);
William Shatner (actor/pitch man—undeliverable);
Siegfried & Roy (flamboyant magicians);
Gene Simmons (former KISS rock star);
Jean Simmons (former actress);

Would you pass a tract to a guy with this 'tude?

O.J. Simpson (controversial murder suspect);
Steven Speilberg (director);
Rev. Ivan Stang (Founder, Church of the Subgenius);
Ringo Starr (retired Beatle);
Ken Starr (famous prosecutor);
Ben Stiller (actor—He returned a signed photograph);
Rev. Jimmy Swaggert (TV evangelist);
Mr. T (actor/pitch man)

Here's a sample of the generic letter sent:

Dear Mr. Ringo Starr,
I'm writing a book about Jack Chick, the Christian cartoonist who draws the 3 x 5 inch fundamentalist tracts that appear in bus stations, bars, bathrooms and just about anywhere else. I was hoping you would contribute a few words about what you think of Chick tracts for my book. (I'm not affiliated with Chick Publications in anyway, so I'm including all views, pro or con.) It can be as short as a sentence, or as much as three paragraphs. My publisher is Schiffer Publishing and my deadline is September.

I'm sure I'm not the only one who wants to hear what you have to say about this unique American pop icon. He's printed over 1/2 BILLION of these things in the last 40 years, making him the most published author alive today. I've included a sample of his most common tract, *This Was Your Life*. (He's published over 150 others.)

Please take a moment to jot something down and mail it in the self addressed stamped envelope (enclosed for your convenience). You're one of only a few celebrities to be included in this book.

Thanks!

Here are the five responses:

Yvonne Craig (actress):
Unfortunately I am not one of the 1/2 billion folks who are familiar with Mr. Chick's work. Sorry. My best wishes to you on your book.
Sincerely,
Yvonne Craig, a.k.a. Batgirl

Holy Gospel Tracts!

Patrick Buchanan (news commentator and Presidential candidate):

Dear Mr. Kuersteiner,
I will let Eleanor Clift know of your affection, when next I see her. On Jack Chick's work, however, I simply have not read or seen enough to make an intelligent or thoughtful comment. Good luck with the book.

Lazio Toth (Comedian Don Novello, a.k.a. Father Guido Sarducci from *Saturday Night Live*):
Ink shortage mystery solved! One half BILLION of these [printed]? Finally, now we know where all the ink is going!
P.S. Please send me Party Girl *as soon as possible. I plan to read it on my vacation.*

Rev. Ivan Stang (Sacred Scribe of The Church of the SubGenius and President of The SubGenius Foundation, Inc.):
As a religious tract pamphleteer myself, I owe an enormous debt of gratitude to the great Jack Chick. Without question, his work has been one of the foremost inspirations for my own. Furthermore, his unique approach to publishing has been a model that I only wish my outreach could emulate.

I was not raised in a particularly religious family, so religious matters were only a curiosity to me. The church kids seemed weirder to me than I myself was, and I was pretty weird. In high school I was taught comparative religion, but it all seemed rather dry. What finally got me really interested in religion were the less scholarly but more populist and down-home expressions of religious feeling—

crazy hollering radio evangelists, and lurid little prophecy pamphlets. Especially if they were loaded with great artwork depicting world destruction and titanic cosmic events!

A famous cult celebrity is accosted by a Christian in the crowd. The trespasser is quickly whisked away for daring to pass a gospel tract. *The Tycoon* ©1993 Jack T. Chick.

The Jehovah's Witness publications feature some consistently excellent religious artwork, but for sheer storytelling, none can beat Jack Chick's. Even as an unrepentant mocker, I admired Chick's direct approach to story telling. He goes straight to the point, to the meat of the issue. Eliciting plain and basic emotions, he makes the threat to the soul seem real even to the doubter. (At least for a while.) In this respect I have to compare him to Rev. Jimmy Swaggart, the great televangelist—another expert puppeteer of emotional strings (and another inspiration to me personally).

Recently a friend of mine brought me a gift of 5 copies of the classic Chick tract, "This Was Your Life"—in 5 foreign language versions! Turkish, Farsi, Hindi, Serbian, and Armenian. I had never had the opportunity to compare the various versions of a single tract, and when I did so I was astounded at the attention to detail that Chick must lavish on each translation.

For instance, while the first pages of the Armenian, Serbian and Turkish versions are drawn like the English version, depicting the death of a smug, smiling, clean-shaven square with a pipe, in the Farsi version the hero is mustachioed and swarthy, and his cocktail has been changed to Turkish coffee. And he doesn't smoke. The Hindi version is completely re-drawn, showing the living man surrounded by relatives rather than possessions. When the Hindu man dies, there is no literal Grim Reaper figure shown sneaking up behind him. In the Hindi version alone, he does not rise from a grave when called, but from a bed. In following panels,

where we normally see God as a faceless figure on a Heavenly Throne, the Hindu sees only the Throne. (Possibly there is a Hindu god or demon who is commonly depicted as a faceless human figure, and Chick wanted to avoid confusion.)

But in all versions, The Lake of Fire panel at the end is the same. The Lake of Fire does NOT change according to the potential reader's culture. The Lake of Fire is eternal.

Therein lies the vast, gigantic gulf between religious and secular comic books. In that eternally burning, unchanging Lake of Fire. There's the difference.

When I was a child, the artwork of Jack Kirby lured me into secular comics. But Jack Chick's work was possibly my first exposure to The Bible in written form. I must admit that at the time, I found super heroes of more interest than super deities. But as I grew older, gradually becoming a writer and publisher myself, which direction did I take? I followed Jack off the beaten path, veering off more towards God than Superman.

So, my personal thanks to Jack T. Chick!

Dr. Jack Kevorkian (Activist for Doctor Assisted Suicide. The 74-year-old is currently serving a 10- to 25-year sentence for helping a Lou Gehrig's patient commit suicide):

"Dr. K appreciated your letter. I think we should speak by telephone."

The note was signed by Ruth Holmes, who is currently serving as legal assistant to Dr. Kevorkian's attorney during the appeal of his landmark Right to Die case. I called and we spoke for 20 minutes. She indicated that Kevorkian isn't allowed to receive any bound materials in prison (including the tract I sent). She said that Kevorkian wanted to participate in this project and asked if I could fax her specific questions that she could give him during her upcoming visit in the next 24 hours. She also asked for a faxed (unbound) copy of a tract. I wrote some quick questions as storm clouds darkened the afternoon sun. Before I could send the letter, there was a bright flash and tremendous explosion just outside the window. My fax machine was struck by lightning! So I waited for the storm to pass and mailed the questions via regular post. During the weeks between visits, Kevorkian changed his mind. His next correspondence stated:

"Dr. K has decided he can not participate in this project. He wishes you good luck with it. Many thanks."

Was it divine intervention that nixed the interview? It's hard to say. The computer that contained all the text for this book was miraculously unharmed. So if the Faceless God decided to fry my fax, at least he spared the book...and me, for that matter.

Right after that, the city was wiped out with fire and brimstone from heaven.* Only three people made it out to safety. (A picture of the U.S. in the future?) It is estimated that over 10% of our population are homosexuals… and proud of it! God help us!

*See **Doom Town,** by Chick Publications.

A Letter from Jack Chick

You've heard what others say about Chick. Now hear what Chick says, direct from the horse's mouth. Although Chick may not speak to the press, he does speak *via* the press—as long as that press is his own. In almost every issue of *Battle Cry*, there's *A Message From Jack Chick*. These small articles are written by Chick directly to his audience. This is one of the few places where we can hear the artist speak in the voice of the first person.

Another good source for this information is from Chick's open letters, which are sent out with catalogs and/or samples of new tracts to regular customers. (*Battle Cry* is often included in the same envelope.) While probably the least collectible of Chick's works, these open letters are a great well of information explaining what inspired various tracts, what Chick thinks about current events, and even biographical details about his otherwise guarded personal life.

Here are some selected excerpts from his open letters addressing certain hot-button issues. Some of these letters are over 20 years old. Most of then are signed "Yours for the lost," or "Your brother in Christ," than with Jack's signature.

Prison Ministry
(written March 12, 1982)

"I'm getting reports that the forces of darkness are at work in jails and in the military. Protestant chaplains are bowing to the pressures of the Catholic chaplains and are restricting, and in some cases, forbidding the use of our books. Men in prisons keep begging for these tracts but Rome is attempting to intercept your love gifts to them.

"There is an old military saying...when surrounded on three sides...you attack! And God says the gates of hell shall not prevail against us. We are on the offensive and will <u>stay</u> on the offensive until the Lord calls us home."

Catholics in Hollywood
(written Oct. 13, 1981)

"At the end of the Civil War the Jesuit college for America set forth its long range goal to make America Roman Catholic. For example, in the 1920s and 30's a small minority group calling itself the Legion of Decency gained control over the motion picture studios of Hollywood. This was a Roman Catholic organization determined to use motion pictures to brainwash the American public into believing that the Roman Catholic Institution was the true church of Jesus Christ. This small organization had the power, through boycott, to destroy any studio in Hollywood."

THERE ARE THREE THINGS I HATE... IMMORALITY, WAR AND CHICK TRACTS!

At least he's holding up two other fingers!
August *Battle Cry* ©1995 Jack T. Chick.

"As the years passed by, their influence had become so powerful that the Bible-believing Christians of today believe that Roman Catholics are actually Christians."

Liberation Theology
(written 1982)

"He [Satan] is mixing religion and politics in what is called 'liberation theology.' This makes Jesus a political rebel who hates the rich, and wants the poor to unite, destroy the wealthy, take their lands and share the wealth. And this religious Marxism is spreading. Many college-age young people, growing up in political and economic uncertainty, are seriously considering this ungodly philosophy as a solution to the world's problems. The same thing happened during the Great Depression of 1929-1935, when communism made great in-roads in America."

America First
(written 1983)

"I have a large map on the wall at home, and sometimes I feel so heavy-hearted at the multitudes who will pour into the lake of fire from Africa, India, Southeast Asia, South America, China, Russia, etc., that I almost become ill trying to figure out a way to re-work our books to get the message to those people.

"I told the cry of my heart to Dr. Rivera, and he said, 'Jack, don't expend all your energies overseas. Once the U.S. falls, the world will plunge into a terrible darkness. The main battle before us is to awaken the American Christians to action so we can protect our children from the nightmare of a Roman Catholic take-over.'

"He's right, beloved. World missions are necessary, but we must not ignore America. Darkness is rising in the land. Islam, Roman Catholicism, Mormonism, the occult and lawlessness are gaining ground. If we do not wage all-out spiritual warfare for the souls of America, the light of the gospel will go out here, and with it, the world's greatest missionary effort."

Possible Bankruptcy
(written June 27, 1984)

"We are at war, beloved. We may be despised by the religious world, but I am not worried by my criticizing brethren. If I yet please men, I would not a servant of God. By God's grace, Chick Publications will assault the devil and his crowd until the Lord closes our doors. We will stand against the forces of antichrist, and against any coming Roman Catholic inquisition to block and expose their hellish doctrine and attempts to silence the true gospel of our Lord Jesus. When I go out, I want to go out with honor, and I want to take as many with me to Christ as I possibly can."

Chick is unafraid to share his controversial opinions with readers. *King of Kings* ©1980 Jack T. Chick.

Kids and the New Age
(written August 1987)

You may be surprised to know what your kids are learning in school.
The Last Generation ©1992 Jack T. Chick.

"SOMEBODY'S GOT TO DO SOMETHING! And that somebody is you and me. Our nation's kids are on a slide right into the lake of fire. They don't stand a chance against rock music, MTV, drugs, etc. Their only hope is the Word of God.

"But how many kids do you think ever see the Scriptures? The Bible is outlawed in our public school system. It's okay to have ouiji boards in schools or witches addressing assemblies, but woe to the teacher who dares bring the Word of God into the classroom! Many school children are being taught the chants and exercises of eastern religion as young as first grade. Its supposed to help them 'relax.' Satan has stacked the deck against them."

Rock Music
(written August 1986)

"I recently learned about a public school where the kids were becoming violent and uncontrollable in the cafeteria. No one knew what was going wrong until the principal discovered that it always happened when the song "Shout At The Devil" by the rock group Motley Crue was played over the loudspeaker.

"When he banned the playing of that song, the kids settled down and became more manageable. Later, when a student jumped off the gymnasium roof after the playing of "Go Ahead And Jump" by Van Halen, he banned that song, too.

"Parents everywhere are discovering that the heavy-metal rock their kids are listening to at school and home are making them more rebellious and hostile to the Lord. But when they try to talk to the kids, they get nowhere. They don't have the facts to *prove* to their teenagers that these rock stars are heavily into Satanism and witchcraft, yet they're teaching it through their songs!"

Christian Apathy
(written June 27, 1984)

"Conditions today look hopeless. There is unconcern, apathy and candy-coated gospel without repentance going forth to a dying world. Most Christians haven't even got the guts to mail a tract to their own neighbors."

Juvenile Halls
(written May 3, 1999)

"Years ago a couple of friends took handfuls of our tracts into a juvenile hall and passed them out. The following day the warden was in shock. There were absolutely no fights, stabbings or rapes through the night. He was amazed at the power of gospel tracts. A great peace had descended throughout the facility."

Violence in Schools
(written April 1992 catalog)

May *Battle Cry* ©1995 Jack T. Chick.

"Some time ago, not far away, there was a high school that was covered with a cloud of evil. Kids had to be tough just to survive. many hated the teachers and all authority. It wasn't unusual to hear screams from someone being stabbed or beaten. It was a war zone where many students joined gangs just to survive.

"Then someone decided to do something about it. They found ways to put Chick tracts into that awful place. Not allowed to hand out tracts in the halls, they left open suitcases with signs that said, 'Take One!' Soon the entire school was salted down with tracts of all titles everywhere. Kids traded them like baseball cards.

"A few weeks later my phone rang... it was the principal. He was dumbfounded! The fights had stopped, and no one had been stabbed for weeks. The whole atmosphere of the school was changed!"

Disney Cartoons
(written July 1995)

"Young people are watching new films and videos supposedly telling them children's stories, but in reality they are loaded with New Age material. This includes new animated Disney films which talk about the circle of life, with characters talking to the dead and claiming we are all one spirit. This is why it is so important that gospel tracts fall into the hands of young people. The promotion of these major films cost millions and their videos end up in an untold number of homes. What millions of kids are growing up with is completely false!"

His Stroke
(written March 5, 1996)

"After two years of incredible problems, with Satan attacking almost everyone working in Chick Publications and their families, the Lord gave us 'Where's Rabbi Waxman?' Beloved, Satan did not want this tract made. He did everything he could to stop us. A few days after the art was completed, Satan made his final shot. At 2 a.m. I woke up with my right hand numb and out of control as a result of a slight stroke. I laughed to myself all the way to the hospital and told Satan: 'You lost this battle, Satan. Waxman has already been drawn. This hand will be normal again and will come back to serve the Lord.' The Lord was gracious. May hand is already 90% back to normal. I praise God for this. I have learned to have compassion for those who are handicapped.'"

"Hate Literature"
(written May 23, 1996)

"The term 'Hate Literature' has been used by Satan as far back as the time of Martin Luther. It is supposed to shake the confidence of those proclaiming the gospel. I didn't hear those words used against our tract ministry until we printed the tract *'The Gay Blade'* years ago. We started getting phone calls and threats.

"Beloved, the Lord called us to be soldiers. Satan hates our tracts and so do his children because so many souls are being saved. As we get closer to the end, we know the enemy must increase his attacks, because Chick tracts are moving like little bees, swarming into the Americas, Europe, Africa, and Asia. Our job is to hinder Satan and his systems until the Lord calls us home."

Revolution and Riots
(written March 10, 1995)

Rare Chick 1960s promotion for *Why No Revival*. The Watts race riots were shocking to most Americans.

"Beloved, revolution and race riots are in the air. Unrest and tension are growing. Keep on your toes, and remember, tracts can change attitudes. It is a historical fact that when John Wesley passed out tracts in England, France had already fallen into full-blown revolution. That same spirit of rebellion was in the air in England. But God stopped it with gospel tracts. They have more of an impact than many realize."

Peer Pressure
(written Aug 26, 1996)

"Even as young as age 12, youngsters are killing with absolutely no regrets. Little hearts are becoming very hard because television and movies are creating a brutalizing, numbing effect on the viewers. Death means nothing...it's like a game. So these youngsters give in to the pressure. As

a young soldier in Japan, I was caught up in a situation I couldn't seem to get out of. I was unsaved and had never heard the Gospel. I was trapped by my peers into going into a restricted red light district. When the driver said, 'Count me out. I'm staying clean for my wife,' I jumped up and said, 'Me, too!' even though I wasn't married. That driver's stand gave me the courage to do what was right."

Pre-marital Sex
(written June 1992)

"As these young people see their heroes dying of AIDS, the schools and government teach them that condoms and 'safe sex' will protect them. But that's a lie! Not only do these things often fail, but even if you do manage to avoid fornication's physical result, you must still stand before God and account for your behavior. God doesn't play games!"

Super-hero Cartoons
(written Dec. 23, 1996)

"I see a tragedy in the making in America. If you sweep through the television channels on Saturday morning, you will see one production after another, cartoons, aimed at little kids, pushing the occult and rebellion into their minds. The poor little kids don't know anything about Jesus, or Moses, or anyone else in the Bible, but they can tell you all about Thor, or Spiderman, or some other hero who uses occultic powers to destroy his enemies. Their parents don't care, as long as they are occupied. What we have here is a whole generation growing up in spiritual darkness."

Catholic Pressure Tactics
(written for July 1994 *Battle Cry*)

July *Battle Cry* ©1994 Jack T. Chick.

"...Priests are aware of how many Catholics are getting saved reading Chick materials so they have staged their own version of 'act up.' Faithful Roman Catholics enter a crowded Gospel Bookstore and pretend they are making a large purchase.

"They stack the books at the cash register and then tell the clerk, 'I want to look around for a little more.' Then they head like a torpedo to the Chick tract rack and the curtain goes up. The act is on as screams of 'hate literature' or their new phrase, 'Christian pornography' fills the store embarrassing everyone inside.

"These actors are shameless and well trained. If the bookstore owners realize what they are doing they can withstand their onslaught. Years ago, a national Catholic publication guided their readers on how to pull this off. They know exactly what they are doing... As a Bible believing Christian there is no way I would ever walk into a Roman Catholic bookstore and demand that they pull out anything. That would be shameful."

Political Correctness
(written March 5, 1999)

"We are living in a time when everyone is afraid to say something that the world considers 'politically incorrect'. Tragically, the world's thinking has entered the church. Many are afraid to even mention the blood of Christ. It's not 'positive' enough. I've even learned that many of the great hymns of the past, that honored the blood of Lord Jesus, have quietly been dropped from some hymnals. Pastors, in some cases, even avoid speaking on the subject, and this is to their shame."

Abortion
(written July 3, 2000)

"When my parents got married they were young and without Christ. When I finally came along they had to deal with a very sick baby. The doctor lanced my ears 21 times before I was one year old. It was years later, when I was 40 years old, that my mother admitted she had tried to kill me though an abortion. I was stunned! That was ME in there. Where were my rights? In those days the unborn were called babies, not fetuses. I forgave her and let it go.

"But then Satan deceived one of my family members, persuading her to kill her unborn baby. When I heard about the abortion that had occurred without my knowledge, I wept for the death of that precious little one."

Evolution
(written Nov. 3, 2000)

Teachers may control the classroom, but Chick dominates the underground comics industry. *Big Daddy* ©2000 Jack T. Chick.

"Ask any kid how old dinosaurs are. His answer will nearly always be either 'millions' or 'billions' of years old. In fact, all of us have heard this almost all of our lives. Who pushes this? Major film companies, publishers, school systems worldwide, and TV producers. The brainwashing techniques they use have convinced almost everyone that this is true. **WELL, IT ISN'T!** Not according to they Word of God. And there is plenty of scientific evidence that points to a much younger earth."

Harry Potter
(written Nov. 1, 2001)

"In public schools, teachers are allowed and even encouraged to teach the religion of Wicca to their students through the 'Harry Potter' books. The Ten Commandments teach order and justice, but Wicca (witchcraft) teaches rebellion and treachery.

"Beloved, the Harry Potter books will cause a tidal wave of warlocks and witches covering the land."

Sept 11th
(written Sept 12, 2001)

"We at Chick Publications are praying for the families who have suffered loss of life in the great tragedy that has effected our land. Our lives, our country, and our world will never be the same. In the midst of these perilous times, we as Christians must be steadfast in our purpose to go into all the world and preach the gospel (Mark 16:15).

"But here is a word of caution....politicians are trying to hold this whole mess together by creating some kind of all encompassing, universal 'god', composed of all kinds of 'gods', that doesn't offend anybody including the Muslim god 'Allah.' The Bible says there is only one true God, who did have a Son, and that Son, the Lord Jesus Christ, is the answer for the needs of every human being. Our God is a jealous God and will share His glory with no other."

Hate Mail
(written 1983)

"I routinely ask my secretary if we are getting any hate mail. If she says no, I get upset because then I think I'm doing something wrong. Christ didn't come to bring peace, but a sword. Our lives as Christians aren't supposed to be a bowl of cherries. Christ depicts an active Christian in a life-and-death spiritual war, suffering for Christ, having abuse heaped upon him, cursed and hated by relatives and the world because of his Godly, living witness."

The Christian life is no bowl of cherries. Chick believes real Christians suffer constant abuse.

Recurring Themes

After forty years of drawing tracts, Chick has accumulated a number of recurring themes. Some of these are subtle and can be hidden in the background like little Easter eggs, daring readers to spot them. (See the list about Fang the dog). Another example is recurring expressions. Anyone who collects Chick tracts is aware of Chick's ongoing use of "Haw-haw-haw!" It's a gut busting laugh used by heathen to deride Christians who openly praise God. The devil also uses it when he scores another point against the forces of good. It's scattered throughout so many tracts that it isn't funny...which is one of the reasons it *is* funny ! *Haw-haw-haw!*

On the other emotional extreme is the flood of tears Chick soaks his tracts with. Almost every sinner cries at least one tear when they become saved to demonstrate how sincere they are. If you start to count them, you'll be amazed how many tears flow through Chick's tracts. They're usually located on pages 21 or 22, depending on if the sinners are crying before or after they are saved.

There are also the puns and twisted expressions Chick uses in various titles. *This Is Your Life* was a popular TV show that profiled people's lives before a live audience. Chick's most famous tract, *This Was Your Life* uses a similar premise, but in the afterlife. *Hit Parade* was a popular music program decades ago, but Chick uses the title to refer to the nations that met with disaster after daring to slight the Jews. (He does a similar thing with the another pro-Israel tract, *Jeopardy.*) *Superman* was a famous comic superhero, but Chick added a question mark to the title and slapped it on a tract about Samson. He did the same thing with the title from a popular Steven King movie, *Fire Starter* (only his version was about the prophet Elijah instead of a girl who can start fires.) If that weren't enough, he uses the same trick again with *Terminator?* (which is not about the movie and robots from the future, but rather, a retelling of the ancient David and Goliath story.) *Ivan the Terrible* was a famous Russian warrior, but Chick

uses it to refer to a Russian atheist who discovers the Vatican was responsible for creating Communism. *Going To The Dogs* is a common expression used when something is becoming worthless, but Chick uses it to name a tract about two people who are killed and the dogs lick up their blood. Many of these puns surface in his titles. Some of them are obvious to readers while others go over the heads of many in the average audience. *That Crazy Guy* means a lot to fans of Steve Martin, but when Chick uses it, it refers to a cad who sleeps around and gives his one night stand AIDS.

Then there's the famous Chick version of God. Sometimes God is drawn as Jesus, but more often, he appears as a Faceless God sitting on a Great White Throne of Judgment. (His face is so bright, all we see is the outline.) The sinners appear naked before the giant faceless one while the angels are dressed in robes but lack any sunglasses. This image has become burned into the minds of most collectors, so much so that if they ever see a drawing of someone without facial features, they immediately think of Chick. But then again, they think of Chick anytime someone laughs Haw-haw-haw! (Even though no one actually seems to use that expression in real life.)

Speaking of expressions, Chick uses lots of expressions in his tracts. He tries too hard to achieve some sort of *street cred* when he uses outdated expressions like "heavy man" or "that's far out!" These may have been cutting edge expressions back in the 1970s, but the terms became outdated long before the tracts were retired. Then there's the cussing. Chick uses lots of it but never spells it out for us. We have to use our imaginations and translate it from various symbols like @!!!***!! Sometimes, it can get pretty *far out, man.*

What follows are a few of Chick's recurring themes and the tracts in which they appear. This list will almost certainly expand as he adds additional titles.

Facing page: Characters often pass tracts within tracts. It's one of several recurring themes interwoven throughout Chick's works. *A Solution to the Marriage Mess.* Art by Carter ©1978 Jack T. Chick.

Fang's Alot

Here He Comes ©2003 Jack T. Chick.

Fang is a cartoon dog that Chick sneaks into various tracts in subtle places. Sometimes he's rather obvious. Other times, he can be hard to find even if you know what page he's on. Finding Fang is kind of like playing *Where's Waldo?*, but Fang was invented by Chick long before Waldo ever came along. His first appearance was in *The Mad Machine*, copyright 1975. Here's a list of known Fang sightings. (Expect this list to grow as new tracts are published.) Keep an eye out for him in older titles too, because updated versions of older tracts sometimes sneak him in retroactively. (See *Who Me?*) Fang only appears in Chick's art, not Carter's. This list is current through June 2003.

Man In Black: ©2003: (page 2, walking on sidewalk.)

The Monster ©2002: (page 4) on the back of an employee's t-shirt.

Murph ©1999: (page 4b, back of kid's t-shirt)

The Nervous Witch ©2002: (page 2, stuffed animal on the shelf.)

No Fear ©1997: (page 20)

The Outcast ©2001 (page 4, upside down on the box.)

The Promise ©2001: (page 9, on a t-shirt) Spotted by UK Dave.

Party Girl ©1998 (Page 9, in the crowd) spotted by Chris Zion.

Ransom ©1995 (page 6, in background picture on wall. Has title "Fang")

Real Heat ©2002 (page 12, on arm of orderly)

The Scam ©2002: (page 6b). Reported by MidnightV

Scream! ©2002: (page 2, on the back of a pick-up truck)

The Secret ©1999: (page 9, on tattoo of a prisoner)

Sin City ©2001 (page 2, on a poster on a telephone pole)

The Slugger ©1998: (page 3, on tattoo of fan's arm)

The Trap ©1988: (Some claim he's in there, but I only see regular dogs. Can you find him?)

War Zone ©2000: (page 6, photo on wall)

The Warning ©2000: (page 7)

Who Are They Gonna Remember? ©1987: (page 4)

Who Cares? ©2002: (page 6, being walked with a leash.)

Who's Missing? ©2003: (page 4, a poster on Bob's desk.)

Who Murdered Clarice? ©2000: (page 3 in the paper that the woman is reading)

Who Me? (some of the promos ©1998): Old versions didn't have this, but now Fang appears on page 3 of the red/black cover versions with the FREE TAKE ONE in the top right corner.

Why No Revival ©1970: (page 7, a "civil rights" Fang forerunner, but different on account that he's black.)

Prepare for War (book by Rebecca Brown, with a few Chick cartoons): Page 236—Fang in a family setting.

I Used 2 B 1!

One of Chick's favorite plot twists is to have the main character (the Christian who's trying to convert the sinner) reveal that he was also guilty of the same sin before he saw the light. It's a great debate response to someone who otherwise questions the accuser's credibility. After all, the wise Christian already knows everything the sinner knows. *He used to be one!* But then he wised up after hearing the real truth about Jesus and... well, we all know what happens next. Once he tells the sinner what converted him, the sinner hits the floor on all fours and becomes a Christian too. At least, that's how it happens in Tractville.

Here's a list of tracts where a convert is trying to convert a future convert. (Current through June 2003.)

The Bull — A prison's bully gets saved after reading a tract, then uses his considerable intimidation to convert other cons.

The Crisis — The minister who wants to convert a Jehovah's Witness, just happens to be a former Jehovah's Witness himself.

The Curse of Baphomet — Ed is trying to convert some Masons, and he just happens to have been a Mason as well.

Gomez Is Coming — A killer gets out of prison, then returns to his gang to convert them all to Christ.

Going Home — An AIDS infected doctor spends his last days treating and converting AIDS patients.

The Hit — A Mafia Don gets saved, then leans on his criminal friends to convert.

Macho — A missionary is taken hostage by Communists, and just happens to have been a Communist too...until he found out it was a Vatican plot.

Murph — The Protestant cop who takes a bullet for his Catholic partner just happens to have been a former Catholic too.

The Poor Little Witch — Mandy gets in too deep with witchcraft, but gets saved by Mrs. Grayson, who used to be a former witch.

Satan's Master — The Christian who exposes the witches used to be a witch herself.

The Story Teller — Yuseff extracts a promise from fellow Muslims not to interrupt him until he finishes explaining how the Vatican created Islam.

Where's Rabbi Waxman — A converted Jew goes to his Rabbi to share the news about another former Jew...Jesus!

Who's Missing? — Damien, a former Catholic priest, tries to convert his Catholic sister...with some help from Bob Williams!

Wounded Children — The Christian ministering to queers just happens to have been a homosexual himself...and still wears a turtleneck shirt to prove it.

Comics

And of course, there's *The Crusaders!* Fred Carter is a former villain, turned Christian good guy. John Todd (Lance Collins) was a former Satanist, turned preacher. Alberto was a former Catholic priest, turned Protestant preacher. Now they all fight their ex-chums in colorful, action packed adventures.

Books

There's plenty! But the most notable are by Elaine Moses' (Rebecca Brown's sidekick), who was a former witch before she converted. And Willim Schnoebelen was a former Mason and Satanist before converting to Christianity and exposing his former colleagues.

Mirror Mirror

The Bull ©1986 Jack T. Chick.

Chick is a great self-promoter. Tracts often feature other tracts in the storyline. Almost all the promo tracts do this, but even the regular story tracts do it also. Chick started doing this way back in the 1970s, long before *product placement* became a common advertising technique. Here's a list of his tracts within tracts. This list only includes tracts sneaked into the storyline, not display ads with photos of tracts or images of them circling the globe on the back cover. If you spot more elsewhere, let me know and I'll add it to the list. The title of the tract featured within the story is in parentheses (like this). This list is current as of June 2003.

TRACT COVERS seen within the story lines (the title shown in the parentheses)

Angels (*The Contract*.)

A Solution to the Marriage Mess (The Chick book has *A Love Story* tract in it on pg. 159.)

The Bull (*Somebody Loves Me*.)

Don't Read That Book (*Don't Read That Book*.)

Earthmen (*Earthmen*.)

He Never Told Us (shows *This Was Your Life* and an unknown title (looks like *Fire Starter*) and also mentions *The Assignment* & *One Way*.)

How To Get Rich and Keep It (*How To Get Rich and Keep It*).

The Letter (*Somebody Loves Me*.)

The Little Princes (*Happy Halloween*.)

The Little Princes GERMAN version (*Charlie's Ants*.)

Losing the Old Zippp? (*The Assignment, This Was Your Life, One Way, Escape, Demon's Nightmare*.)

Operation Somebody Cares: (*Somebody Loves Me, This Was Your Life, A Demon's Nightmare, Holy Joe, Somebody Goofed, The Beast*.)

Reverend Wonderful (*The Contract*—visible in early version only.)

The Scam (*This Was Your Life*.)

This Book Has Been Banned (*This Was Your Life*.)

The Tycoon (*This Was Your Life*.)

Who Are they Going To Remember (Looks like *This Was Your Life & Fire Starter*.)

Who Me? (*This Was Your Life*.)

War Zone (*The Choice, No Fear, This Was Your Life, War Zone*.)

TRACT PHOTOS (Ads within tracts that act as catalogs with tract covers on display.)

Are Roman Catholics Christians? (25 tracts.)

The Last Missionary (11 tracts.)

Losing the Old Zippp? (17 tracts.)

The Secret Weapon (Other language tracts of *Greatest Story Ever Told, Earthman, How to get rich and keep it, Back from the Dead, This was Your life*.)

This Book Has Been Banned (*This Was Your Life, Who Me?*)

Who Are They Going To Remember (11 different titles.)

Who Me? (*This Was Your Life, A Love Story, The Long Trip, Somebody Goofed, Best Friend, The Gun Slinger*.)

FAKE TRACT REFERENCES (Non-Chick titled tracts within tracts)

Somebody Goofed (*Ye Must Be Born Again*)

Trust Me (*Jesus Loves You*)

Somebody Loves Me (*Somebody Loves You*)

CRUSADER COMICS

My Name In The Vatican (copies of *Alberto*)

Going Down?

They say that in the old days theologians would busy themselves debating how many angels could dance on the head of a pin. Modern Chick fans, however, seemed burdened with a much more difficult question: Which way is hell?

The novice may think this an easy question. "Hell is down!" they shout. But this is the voice of inexperience. Like those who think the forbidden fruit in Eden was "obviously an apple", they are merely repeating a common misconception. The Bible doesn't say WHAT kind of fruit the forbidden fruit is, nor does it state exactly WHERE Hell is either.

A close reading of Chick tracts seems to add to this confusion. In Chick's most famous tract, *This Was Your Life,* God points to the left while shouting Matthew 25:41. But in other tracts, like *Flight 144,* God points to the right while shouting Matthew 7:23.

So which is it? Exit stage left or right?

Hell is usually assumed to be below heaven, but God never points downward. (Nor does he point upward.) Hell could be below heaven yet still above Earth. Yet God points to only the left or right. Could hell be on either side? Is heaven in orbit around hell, so the direction changes depending on what time of day it is? (The fires of hell are supposed to be intense, perhaps they heat heaven like the sun?) Then again, heaven could be orbiting something else, and hell can be in the distant outer edges. (Hell is supposed to be very dark, so it could be like deep space beyond the heavenly solar system.) The direction of hell would still change depending on what time it was. Or it might SURROUND heaven on either side, like a giant donut with heaven being the hole in the middle. Or is it more like an eclair? Surrounding heaven in EVERY direction, so God could point anywhere and be accurate?

In most tracts, when God points, it's not only left or right, but it's usually a precise direction left or right. He points just a little bit downward. Not much, just about 10 degrees. The angel's arm has the identical slight bend when he points the sinner (from *This Was Your Life*) to The Lake of Fire. We even get a glimpse of the hellish hallway, and it has a gentle decline, like a wheel chair ramp. (God doesn't discriminate against the disabled.) So maybe hell isn't to the left or right, or up or down, but a little downward in one direction or another.

Then again, in *The Tycoon,* he actually points just a little bit UP to the reader's right. And in *Titanic,* God points straight out to the right. So who knows *what* to think?!

The good news is that this is one mystery we will all solve...when we die. Unfortunately, we won't be able to tell anyone once we know the answer. Until then, we have plenty of Chick tracts to help us ponder the question.

This Was Your Life ©1972
Jack T. Chick.

The greatest double-cross in history will be when Satan admits:

JESUS IS LORD!

"Wherefore God also hath highly exalted him, and given him a name which is above every name: that at the name of Jesus every knee should bow, of things in heaven, and things in earth, and things under the earth; and that every tongue should confess that Jesus Christ is Lord, to the glory of God the Father." Phil. 2:9-11

Variations & Revisions

One of the most enjoyable recurring themes of Chick tracts are the unintentional mistakes or revisions made to accommodate new circumstances. The growing list of printing errors and revised tracts creates a new field of interest for jaded collectors who would have otherwise finished their collections. Simply put, a variation is a tract that has been released in more than one form. Different covers, cartoon panels or different dialog are typical variations. (Different type fonts or different back cover designs are too common for most collectors to care about, although some collect those as well.) To compare variations with other collectors, it is important to understand the page numbering system. The outside front cover is page 1, the inside cover is page 2, etc. We call the first panel "A", and the second panel "B", so the second panel on page 2 is page 2B.

It is also helpful to know how Chick labels new printings. On the outside back cover in the bottom right hand corner or middle, he lists a catalog number. In earlier days, he also places a letter (a print code) to show what printing it is. So "74-A" is the first printing of *The Death Cookie*, and "74-B" is the second printing of the same title. "74-AA" means he went through 26 different printings, and is now on the 27th! (The highest known print code is AE, or 30 different printings.) Chick abandoned the print code system in August 1994 and replaced it with date codes in the top right hand corner. 12.8 would mean December of 1998. "5.0" would mean May of 2000. Now Chick adds more to the date code to give the exact day of printing. "0928.1" would mean the 28th day of the 9th month of 2001. "1012.1" would mean October 12th, 2001.

The true king of tracking variations is Bob Fowler (author of *The World of Chick?*). He plans on publishing a complete variations guide with over 600 variations listed. That work is in progress, so you may want to watch for it. Bob would be the first to admitt that his list won't be complete. Some errors are quickly corrected and are quite rare, making them difficult to notice or acquire. If compiling a complete list of all the different variations is such a difficult task, you can imagine how big a challenge obtaining the tracts themselves would be.

Not every art or dialog difference between tracts is noticed or collected by fans—just the most obvious and interesting ones. Some collectors ignore the variations and just want to finish all the different titles. Others want all the titles and some of the really big variations (*Doom Town* and *The Royal Affair* are tyical examples of dramatic variations). The hardcore collectors who want even the minor revisions will never run out of variations to collect.

Fortunately, tract collectors are very generous when it comes to trading information. The list is too vast to print here, but you can find it at Chickcomics.com under the variations section. It has the added benefit of staying current since it is updated whenever new variations are spotted.

The original version of *Allah Had No Son* accuses Muhammad of statutory rape. ©1994 Jack T. Chick.

You claim Muhammad was innocent, yet his third wife, little Aesha, was only 8 years old.

Shame on him!

In my country he'd be jailed for **child abuse.**

See *Islamic Invasion,* by Morey, page 86.

Facing page: *Angel of Light.* ©1978
Collecting variations can be Hell!

THE O.S.C. PROGRAM, LAUNCHED SEVERAL YEARS AGO, PRODUCED STARTLING RESULTS...

Bethany Baptist Church of West Covina, California successfully launches a brand new type of visitation evangelism . . .

by Robert L. Owen

"If I were a Communist, I'd be scared to death of this type of evangelism going into effect," said Jack Chick, creator of "Operation: Somebody Cares," a brand new approach to reach into communities for Christ.

Chick was referring to the concentrated, house-to-house evangelistic outreach effort used by the Bethany Baptist Church of West Covina, California, recently. Basically, the operation consisted of a handful of dedicated laymen who visited 100 homes six times each in a three-week period.

"It was rapid-fire brainwashing with the Gospel," Chick said. "And it paid off."

At the heart of the plan was the set of cartoon-type booklets, written and illustrated by Jack Chick, with such gripping titles as: "Somebody Loves Me," "Holy Joe," "This Was Your Life," "A Demon's Nightmare," "Somebody Goofed," and "The Beast," with a simple set of instructions for their use.

Instructions include such basic information as: how to make the master map of the area; how to divide into teams; how to obtain permission for a religious survey; the mechanics of meeting and talking to prospects, and the keeping of records.

Workers are urged to: "Choose your own schedule, but come — blizzard or flood. Don't stop the program once it starts."

At the outset, Pastor Joe Kirkwood, in charge of Bethany's Outreach Program, contacted Jack Chick. The two of them, with the knowledge and co-operation of Dr. Lloyd T. Anderson, pastor of Bethany, planned the strategy for their program. They announced their need for several laymen who would co-operate in making an all-out attempt to win souls in the community. From the willing volunteers, ten were selected: five men and five women.

ONE HUNDRED HOMES IS YOUR TARGET!

- **6 VISITS ARE REQUIRED.**

- **YOU MAY VISIT 2 TIMES A WEEK OR 6 STRAIGHT DAYS.**

- **INSTRUCTION AND SURVEY MATERIALS ARE SUPPLIED WITH THIS O.S.C. KIT.**

- **THE NUMBER OF DECISIONS WILL VARY WITH THE COMMUNITIES YOU VISIT AND YOU WILL HAVE AN UNFORGETTABLE IMPACT.**

- **IF YOU DON'T REACH THEM FOR CHRIST WHO WILL?**

Imitation Tracts

If imitation is the greatest form of flattery, Chick should feel pretty flattered. He has certainly inspired many competitors. Copycat tracts have different art styles but are usually the same size and format as Chick's. Since the publishers never seem to stay in business long or lack Chick's creative stamina, the title selection from any given manufacturer tends to be rather limited. Copycat tracts are not parodies, but serious attempts to copy the Chick formula and save souls with comic tract propaganda.

There are probably hundreds (maybe *thousands)* of different religious tracts drawn by other artists. Anyone can draw and photocopy their own. How many are distributed and saved can be very limited. Only the ones with a heavy dose of comics are real copycats. Tracts filled with text or fold out pamphlets have been around long before Chick.

Some copycat tracts are very professional while others are not. Yet the best of the best rarely reach the routine quality of Chick's tracts. Collecting and reading samples from his competitors allows new appreciation for the work Chick accomplishes. Presenting clear stories in limited space is no easy task, especially when most of the page is filled with art. Try designing your own tract and you'll see how much time and effort it requires. Only a handful of copycat tracts have illustrations as good as Chick's and none of them match Fred Carter's skill.

Of all the religious comic tracts inspired by Chick, one series in particular deserves special attention: The tracts of "cowboy" Chaplain Dann. Dann is a real person who has known Chick since the 1980s. (He prefers that his last name and address not be published.) He ran a prison ministry for 18 years and passed out tons of Chick tracts. Several facilities forbid him from using Chick tracts because they were considered too controversial. Drawings of Dann can be found in *Reverend Wonderful* and *The Letter* tracts. He plays himself and the likeness is accurate. Even his pickup truck and "Hope-4-U" license plate are accurately portrayed. A character is named after him in the *Sabotage* comic, although the character acts different from Dann. (The image of "Gary" on the inside back cover of *Sabotage* is from Dann's wedding photo.) He says the comic is based on a story he told Chick about how the bible colleges were kicking out students who refused to study anything other than the King James Version of the Bible.

Chaplain Dann was born in 1924, around the time of Chick's birth. Like Chick, Dann served in the Pacific during WWII. After the war, he developed a drinking problem. He wanted to stop and thought religion might help. According to one of his own hand drawn tracts, "I looked in the paper for a church and saw where a man that was an artist, would be at a church in Pamona. His name was Jack T. Chick." Dann attended and was impressed enough that he was later saved.

Years later, Dann met Chick at a Christian Businessman's meeting in Covina, California. The cautious Chick refused to surrender his phone number at first, but the two have since become good friends. Dann's landscaping business did the yard at Chick's house, and Dann has also become a regular customer of Chick's. He goes every week to pick up more tracts, which he turns around and provides to other chaplains who work in prisons. He sometimes has to remove the binding materials, since many prisons don't allow staples. (The prisoners use them to make tattoos.)

Chaplain Dann has also been the subject or author of dozens of articles in *Battle Cry!* Chick has certainly had a major impact on his life. He says once he overheard some Christians complaining about Chick tracts, saying there were better ways to reach the lost. Dann interrupted them to say how delighted he was to hear such wonderful news, since he had been using Chick tracts for years. He couldn't wait to hear the better methods they had discovered. The strangers had no reply.

If you would like to see a list of all known copycat tracts, visit the Chickcomics.com website and go to the copycat section. If you create a new tract, please send me a copy so I can add it to the archives.

Facing page: Very early and rare advertisement for Church sponsored tract passing programs.

Like Chick, Dann suspects the Vatican of conspiring to prevent the true word of God from reaching the masses. During his prison ministry, officials forbid him from dispensing all except 16 Chick titles. The other titles were too controversial. (He suspects Catholics were censoring negative references to the Vatican and good works.) When Dann told Chick about this, Chick was outraged. He personally met with prison officials to settle the matter. Apparently, the meeting didn't go too well. Officials suddenly forbade *any* of Chick's tracts from being allowed in the prison. In fact, they required Dann to remove Chick's name from his own home-made tracts. Chick tracts get read alright—and censored!

Dann draws most of his own tracts. They follow the same 24 page format as Chick's. Dann's art is crudely drawn and the text is handwritten. He often cuts out his own image from *Reverend Wonderful* or *The Letter* and pastes it over his character in his own tracts. This creates a humorous clash of styles by juxtaposing his primitive style with the state-of-the-art style of Fred Carter.

Chaplain Dann was a real life cowboy before joining the Marines in 1942. Some of his tracts are signed "cowboy" Chaplain Dann. One such example is his version of *This Was Your Life*. It's a scene for scene homage of Chick's most famous tract, only the main character is a Native American. Dann appears (cut out of *Rev. Wonderful*) as the minister who lead the Indian to Christ. Dann also cuts out a photo of his pre-war horse and

pastes him in the story. The outside back cover of the tract has Dann's image with the word balloon stating, "I really care about people."

Although Dann has retired from the Prison ministry, he continues to "gather ammunition" for others in the field. He mails all the tracts he gets from Chick Publications to other chaplains at his own expense. It's a weekly job that he volunteers for because he remembers how valuable Chick tracts were in his own ministry. He estimates the total number of tracts he's passed out or given away to be "in the millions."

Regrettably, many of Chaplain Dann's tracts have been lost to the ages. He estimated he produced around twenty different titles. The title's I've seen are **Bikers Weekend, Cowboy's Last Round-up, From Carl to Carla to Christ, Golden Years, Long Way To The Son, Party Time, Rail Roaded, The Revenge Seekers, This Was Your Life**. Two titles that he remembers but doesn't have copies of are *Choice of Execution* and *Get Thee Behind Me Satan*. If you encounter any lost titles, please let me know. I would like either originals or copies for my archives.

Each of Dann's tracts are drawn in a crude style by either him or an inmate named Rob (initials "RLS", a former homosexual that drew *From Carl to Carla to Christ* and tells his own conversion story from inside prision). There is no color in any of the tracts. A printer was used to make copies and Chaplain Dann would assemble them by hand. Most of them look very similar to photocopies.

©1992/1997 Jesse Reklaw

Also fun to collect are the countless Chick tract parodies. Of course, any big cultural phenomenon generates parodies, but Chick tracts seem to attract more than most. Some of the parodies are
in poor taste and are offensive to Christians. Others are genuinely funny. You'll have to decide for
yourself which ones go too far.

Most parody tracts are photo-copied, cut out with scissors, and stapled together at home. Some
are only available on the internet (unless downloaded and printed out). A very few are printed with
off-set printers and professionally assembled.

If you decide to make your own parody, here's an important warning. All of Chick's artwork is
copyrighted. You cannot legally use his art and paste in your own words. Others have tried this short
cut. Chick Publications usually finds out and threatens legal action in order to protect their copyright
and livelihood. The proper method is to draw your own from scratch.

To view the ever expanding list of Chick tract parodies, visit Chickcomics.com and go to the
parody section. There are even links to the ones that are available on-line. If you have a tract parody
not listed there, please send me a copy via *The Tract Museum* at 3202 Enterprise Drive, Tallahassee,
FL 32312. That way it can be added to the archives.

Master Template

The proper layout for photocopying original tracts

LET "WHITE" AREA OF COVER SLIGHTLY EXTEND TO **LEFT** OF FOLD LINE...

Width of Chick Tract → 5"
Height " " " → $2\frac{13}{16}$"

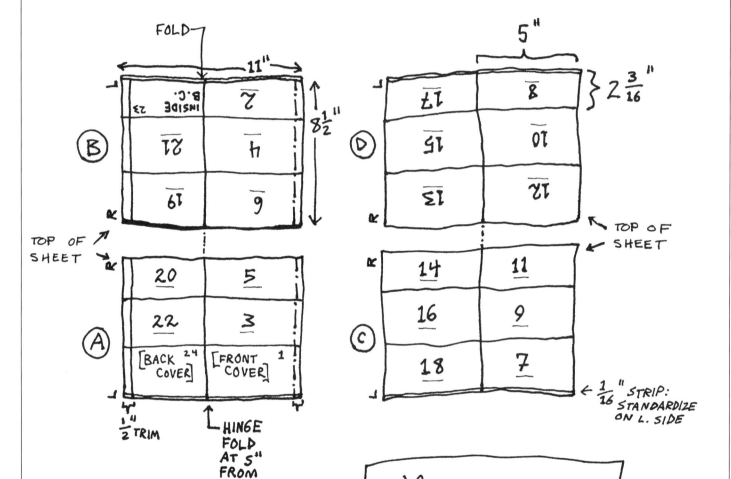

FOLD

11"

$8\frac{1}{2}$"

B
INSIDE B.C. 23
ⵒ (2)
21̄
4̄
19̄
9̄

5"

$2\frac{3}{16}$"

D
17̄
8̄
15̄
10̄
13̄
12̄

TOP OF SHEET

TOP OF SHEET

A
20
5
22
3
[BACK COVER] 24
[FRONT COVER] 1

C
14
11
16
9
18
7

$\frac{1}{2}$" TRIM

HINGE FOLD AT 5" FROM TRIM LINE

$\frac{1}{16}$" STRIP: STANDARDIZE ON L. SIDE

When pasting up, move panels a fraction toward outer edges for better "gutter."

A DIVISION OF A STANDARD $8\frac{1}{2}$" x 11" PAGE INTO 3RDS OF $2\frac{3}{16}$" WILL LEAVE A LEFTOVER STRIP $\frac{1}{16}$" IN HEIGHT.

Make Your Own Tracts!

Anyone can make a tract. Making a *good* tract is another matter completely. That takes good art and good writing. Both of those talents require, well, *talent*. No one can teach talent, but it *is* possible to teach the basic layout of a tract. It also allows a certain amount of insight into why Chick made the choices he did in his own tract formula.

First off, there's the page count. A tract can be any length, but Chick uses 24 pages for a good reason. It's the minimum page count that the US mail considers a book and allows to be mailed at the cheaper book rate. (When mailing hundreds, if not millions of tracts, the postage really adds up.)

Then there's the size. Chick uses pages measuring 2 13/16 inches tall x 5 inches wide. That fits a regular 8 1/2 x 11 inch sheet of paper if laid vertically in three strips (and leaves 1 inch extra at the bottom). When both sides are photocopied, it takes a total of two sheets to make a tract (with printing on four sides). If your copy shop charges a dime per sheet, that will cost you 40 cents per tract (since two double sided sheets counts as four copies.) So Chick's a bargain at just 14 cents per tract retail.

Of course, Chick has economy of scale working on his behalf. He prints four tracts with the same cover color onto a large 30 3/4" x 23" sheet. That's eight rows by six columns (tract pages). So each tract reproduces 12 pages on each side of each sheet. Color is only applied on one side, and then only sparingly. The result is a tract that sells for just 7 cents wholesale. My *Kinkos* charges 8 cents just to photocopy a single side of a single sheet!

For our purposes, we're going to focus on reproducing a *single* tract at a time. That will require four 8 x 10 inch sheets with panels on both sides. There's a trick to the proper layout. One cannot place the panels in chronological order and expect them to reproduce the other side in the proper order as well. Explaining the formula gets complicated. It's much easier to show it.

To demonstrate the process, we commissioned underground artist Harry S. Robins to draw our very own tract. Robins is a big fan of Chick's art and style. Living in San Francisco (the capitol of Political Correctness), he enjoys watching the reactions people provide when they read Chick tracts. Robins collects Chick tracts along with other underground comics from artists like R. Crumb, but he acknowledges that Chick is the king of underground comic publishers.

Robins' previous work includes many of the stickers to the Topps® trading card series, *Dinosaurs Attack!* He also drew *Dinoboy* comics, many of the *Tomb Tales* comic book stories, cartoons for *Salon* on-line magazine, the cover to *The World of Chick?*, and the soon-to-be famous *Chick Tract Club* button.

Robins is also well versed in conspiracy theories. He was the announcer for (and also guest starred on) the TV program, *The Conspiracy Zone* with Kevin Nealon. So he seems the perfect choice to pay homage to Mr. Chick.

What follows is Robins' tract laid out in regular chronological order, then a template which reveals the necessary order required to make a double sided master sheet for easy photocopying. Although page numbers are not usually included in 24 page tracts, they will be provided in the margins here to help keep the order clear for assembling the master (which can otherwise get pretty confusing!)

Page 1 (Outside front cover)

Page 2 (Inside front cover)

Page 3

Page 4

Page 5

Page 6

Page 7

Page 8

Page 9

Page 10

Page 11

Page 12

Page 13

Page 14

Page 15

Page 16

Page 17

Page 18

Page 19

Page 20

Page 21

Page 22

7

Full Color Combat!

The 1970s were years of dramatic change in the United States. The Communists drove America out of Vietnam and raised the red flag in Saigon. At home, the liberals won a less celebrated but far more significant *cultural* war. Abortion was legalized, school prayer was effectively outlawed, and the President resigned in disgrace. Defending God and country was no longer considered fashionable. Jack Chick, however, is not one to concern himself with fashion. While most other conservative Christians were busy retreating, Chick was mobilizing his troops for a counteroffensive.

Fred Carter was Chick's secret weapon. He was brought on board with solid cartooning skills but was quickly developing into a top notch artist. Chick and Carter had become a sort of bi-racial Batman and Robin, defending the faith from the forces of evil. Chick Publications was located in the Los Angeles area not far from Hollywood. Chick envisioned a Christian cartoon series based on two soldiers for Christ, one of them white, the other black. The white hero would be called Tim Clark. Like T. Chick, Tim was a former soldier. Unlike Chick, Clark used to be a Green Beret with the Special Forces. The black hero would be James Carter. Not only do the two share identical last names, James and Fred also look the same. Unlike Fred, James is a former drug dealer. Tim Clark and James Carter become *The Crusaders*. They go on special assignments to fight for Jesus and all that is good.

Equipped with some beautiful storyboards, Chick set out to find a producer for his project. But Hollywood would demand of Chick the one thing he was unwilling to do: compromise. It soon became apparent to Chick that the only way he could produce *The Crusaders* without watering down the message of Jesus was to do it himself. Chick didn't have the resources to make a cartoon TV series on his own, but with Fred Carter's help, he created an exciting line of comic books. The first installment was published in 1974 and called *Operation Bucharest*. The cover was bland, but everything inside was *dyn-o-mite!* Sixteen more issues followed, the last six of which have Clark and Carter meet up with Alberto Rivera. The two sit around and listen while Alberto recounts sensational Catholic conspiracies. All 17 of *Crusader* comics are 32 pages long and are still in print. They retail at only $2.25 each.

Chick also produced three comics without *The Crusaders* team. *King of Kings, The Big Betrayal,* and *Jonah.* Each was 64 pages long, except *Jonah,* which was 32 pages. *King of Kings* and *The Big Betrayal* are still in print and retail for $3.50. *Jonah* went out of print in 2000 and is surprisingly tough to find. I haven't seen it sold on the secondary market, so any value I assigned it would only be a guess. (Expect to pay between $10 and $25 for it.)

In the early 1990s, Chick returned to fulfill his animated series dream. He sidelined comic book production to devote Carter's time to painting beautiful images for a one hour movie. (See *Jonah* review for details.)

Last and least is Chick's publishing of Mary Mitchell's *Overcomers* comic books. The less said about these kiddy comics, the better. They were marginal at best. Four were made and all four are very hard to find. Demand for the four is also scarce, however, so the prices can be rather cheap considering their scarcity. (Expect to pay between $5 and $15 each.)

What follows are reviews of all of Chick's comics in **chronological** order (**not** alphabetical). A special thanks to Rev. Rich Lee for contributing the bulk of these reviews.

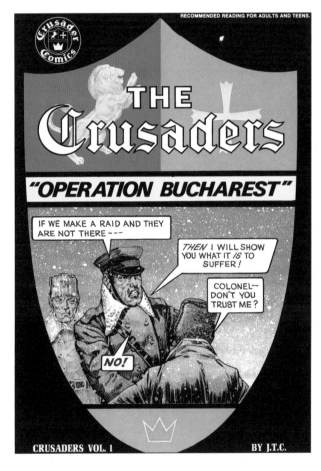

©1974 Jack T. Chick.

Facing page: *Angel of Light*
©1978 Jack T. Chick.

Crusaders vol. 1. **OPERATION BUCHAREST Review:** (©1974.) The very first Crusader comic goes to great lengths to create a dramatic "spy" thriller. Of course, the Crusaders are not spies at all...just Christians out to deliver Bible "micro-film" behind the Iron Curtain! (Insert dramatic music flare here.) But this minor detail is quickly forgotten as the KGB sets out to foil the Crusaders, a former Green Beret Timothy Emerson Clark and ex-drug dealer badass mo-fo James Carter . How does the KGB find out the Crusaders are coming? Gertrude, the Jewish passport clerk, tells them. Meanwhile, on the Politically Correct side of the aisle, Chick seems to support inter-racial sex by condemning Russians who are angry at Carter for appearing to date a white girl. Pretty saucy innuendo for 1974 (the original copyright date). Needless to say, the Crusaders sneak the micro-film to the Christian Underground (by hiding it in a cigarette) and leave a path of converted communists in their wake. Included in the "saved" count is the sex-pot Sofia. She tries to seduce Tim and gets the gift that keeps on giving (born again). She declares to the Crusaders, "I'm ready to lay down my life for Jesus" (they respond "we'll see you in heaven".) She's gets sent to prison in Siberia for her betrayal but manages to run outside in the snow and pray "Dear Lord, thank you for sending Timothy and Jim to tell me about your love and for the beautiful future you have planned for me." (I guess the snow beats the flames of hell.) Hilarious Russian/Spy stereotypes and 32 pages of fantastic color. Grade **A-** for Arrested Agent.

©1974 Jack T. Chick.

Crusaders vol. 2. **THE BROKEN CROSS Review:** (©1974.) This story reads more like a Halloween story than a Christian church tale. There's plenty of foreboding, rain-soaked atmosphere, and subtle detective clues that our two heroes pick up in order to solve the case. Did I forget to mention sex appeal too? The very first panel has a sexy 14 year old girl who is fully developed and is wearing a revealing halter top. (Eat your heart out Britney Spears, you old timer!) She's a hitch hiker and is picked up by a van full of Satanists who grab her and inject her with drugs. Soon she's on the Pagan altar getting sliced to pieces by cloak covered Devil Worshipers. Her body is found without "a drop of blood in her body!" Our biracial God-squad immediately recognizes this as the work of the occult. But a pot-bellied sheriff tells Negro Jim, "Hey BOY, stay out of this if you know what's good for you" in fine Southern style. Do you think they listen? Of course not. They charge straight into the mystery and outsmart all the experts. Naturally, they ruffle a few feathers along the way. For example, there's the sinister Pastor Cooley who reads the watered down Common Bible and doesn't really believe in the resurrection. He calls Tim a religious bigot and proudly proclaims that he's a *liberal* pastor. Once they're gone, he lights his devil candle for revenge.

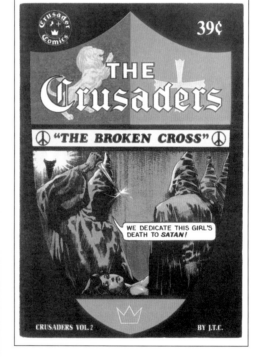

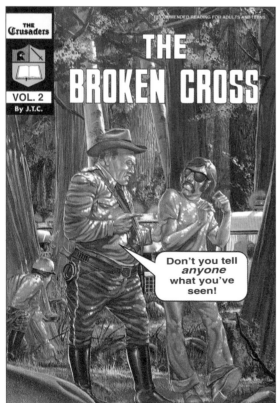

Then there's the little old lady at the library. She seems to know a lot more than what she admits about the missing occult books. And of course, there's the street person they pick up in the road gnawing body parts. (A rather ripe human hand I believe. Which just goes to show that Mom was right all along: Chewing fingernails really is a nasty habit.) They also meet a good person, or at least, a witch that turns into a good person after a quick bible sermon and an impromptu prayer session. Unfortunately, when the other devil worshipers see her on her knees praying with our heroes, they instantly slate her for death. Fast thinking and the power of God save the night in an ending straight out of a *Scooby-Doo* cartoon. All the town's big shots are found hiding beneath the cloaks when the cops arrive. (And they would have gotten away with it too if it hadn't been for those curious Christians!) A friendly neighborhood Book Burning and Ouija Board Bar-B-Q round out this tasty little tale of terror. For sheer action, adventure, mystery, and malevolence, it's hard to imagine a better Chick comic than this. Note the original 39¢ cover. Grade **A+** for Amazing

Atmosphere. (John Todd was the source of information used for this comic, as well as for *Spellbound* and *Angel of Light.)*

Crusaders vol. 3. **SCAR FACE Guest Review by Rev. Rich Lee:** (©1974.) This story begins in 1931 in a British colony in East Africa during the colonial period. An infuriated British outpost agent demands that all blacks salute when they drive through the townships. Higby, a Brit, demands a whip for the front seat so when he drives by, he can use it on anyone who fails to salute. "We're going to teach those @!!*! blacks who their masters are...if we have to kill them doing it!" he intones. Several of the natives salute as the car passes their villages. Meanwhile, little Kruma

©1974 Jack T. Chick.

is sent by his mother to the mission station. The car with the British colonialists is passing when Kruma fails to salute. It's whipping time, as the sergeant cracks the whip and tortures the boy for five panels. A villager takes the boy into his home where he nurses him to recovery. "You'll have to get strong!...to pay them back for what they've done to your face!" "Do I look bad?" Kruma asks. "Is the Pope Catholic?" No, wait, that belongs in the review of *Alberto*.

After screaming to holy hell, little Kruma swears, "I'll do everything I can to destroy them...if it's the last thing I ever do!" Fast forward forty years when Kruma comes to power in Toganda long after the British colonialists leave. His enemies call him Scar Face, hence the name of this issue. Enter Lu Fang, a key member of the Golden Dragon Organization and head of Oriental intelligence (Stereotypes, anyone?). Since Lu Fang's government has financed Kruma's political party, he demands that all missionaries be removed from Toganda.

At a small mission post 25 miles from the capital, a missionary faces a government official who accuses the missionary of being a spy for the CIA and tells him he will be gone in two months. The missionary, Rev. Duncan, prays for wisdom to stop this evil plot. Apparently, God tells him to summon the Crusaders to come to Toganda by letter.

Meanwhile, Lu Fang is secretly financing President Kruma's rival Zuloo. Lu Fang warns his agent Wong that he is to build up Zuloo to the point of toppling Kruma's administration...or face the cost of failure.

Over in the United States, our heroes, Tim Clark and James Carter, are called into Mr. Harris' office at Glenco International. "Gentlemen...I have a letter from Rev. Duncan in Toganda, East Africa...He needs your help! ...you'll need $3,300!" Presumably, this is for the air fare before the days of online travel services. During the Wednesday night prayer meeting, a woman approaches Jim Carter and tells him that she saw Africa and his face. From this, she presumes that God must want him in Africa. Could his being African American have anything to do with her associating his face with Africa? Naw, not in *The Crusaders* world of mixed racial harmony. As expected, the amount she hands him is exactly $3,300.

As the missionary Rev. Duncan picks our heroes up from the airport, a spy reports this development to Lu Fang. "Run a check on Timothy Emerson Clark and James Carter!...I want to know all there is on them....immediately!" Lu Fang barks on a call to Peking, China. Wow, he even has their names quickly!

Kruma's rival Zuloo wants to meet with Carter just because he's a black American. Lu Fang gets his background check finished on the Crusaders. "Hummm...This is worse than I thought...These men are the Crusaders,...who took microfilm into Bucharest...and smashed an occult ring in California! Make sure you keep Zuloo away from them, Wong!"

James Carter and Zuloo meet near the mission station. Jim boldly tells Zuloo that he was sent by God thousands of miles to tell him of the Gospel. "Color means *nothing* to God Almighty...the thing He is concerned with....is your destiny!" "You mean here in Toganda?" Zuloo responds. "No! I mean in eternity!" After receiving the Gospel pitch, Zuloo falls on his knees and accepts Jesus.

During the meal preparation, a native named Ruth is flattered by Jim. Her jealous fiancée, Tonga, in retaliation reports them to the police as missionaries. In turn, President Kruma wants their visas revoked immediately.

The action moves a little faster as Zuloo gives his next political speech. He apologizes for ripping President Kruma a new one during his last political speech. Outside is Kruma himself, waiting to arrest him in the event that Zuloo makes another subversive remark. Not this time. Zuloo says that he repents and that "We are to pray for our president!" Also in the wings is Lu Fang. "Wong...I told you to keep him away from the Crusaders, didn't I?...You are a dead man!"

Lu Fang feeds Wong to a huge snake to make an example of him. "I will never forgive the Crusaders for this!...I *know* our paths will cross again!...And when it does...I will destroy them!" Lu Fang says on his private jet returning to China.

The Crusaders are introduced to President Kruma, who refuses to shake Tim Clark's hand. He still insists that the missionaries leave Toganda and that he won't change his mind. Upon leaving the Presidential suite, a would-be assassin attempts to kill Kruma with a firearm. Tim jumps in front of Kruma to protect him, leaving him a little overwhelmed as to how a white man could risk his life for him. Kruma has a quick change of heart and promises that the missionaries can stay as long as he can do anything about it. He then invites Rev. Duncan and Zuloo to introduce him to Jesus Christ. "Is anything too hard for the Lord?" Jim asks. President Kruma accepts Jesus as his savior and we are told that in heaven, Scar Face will have no scars anymore. Never mind that this means none of his friends will recognize him...

The story moves quickly, and has a little conspiratorial intrigue a la Communist China. The artwork by Fred Carter doesn't get much better and it's obvious he was as accurate as he could be on African clothing and geography. Favorite Panel Award goes to page 29, panel 4, where Wong is swallowed up by the huge snake. Chinese food does a body good! Grade **C+** for Chinese Commies!

Crusaders vol. 4. **EXORCISTS Guest Review by Rev. Rich Lee:** (©1975.) This story may have been inspired by the movie of the same name that came out in 1973. The story begins near Calcutta, India, when two boys, Raj and Santosh, discover an idol. Raj gets bitten by a cobra, while Santosh runs to get help from Rev. Hayes at the mission station. Raj ends up dead, and Rev. Hayes assumes the task of taking his body home. Santosh gets into a theological discussion over the existence of the devil, and he wonders if the devil could have kept Raj from dying. Later, Rev. Hayes breaks his legs while fixing a roof. Santosh surmises that the devil must be stronger than his God.

Meanwhile, in America Tim Clark gets a call from a travel agent claiming that a strange man put $3,000 into an account for him. "Did he give his name?" Tim asks. The agent responds, "No. He said something about God. He sounded like a religious nut. Haw! Haw!" Tim retorts, "Thank you Mr. Kniering. May God richly bless you." While this is going on, Mrs. Hayes summons the Crusaders to come to India.

Santosh, fascinated by the prospects of the devil, gets a friend of his to steal a picture of the devil from a book at the mission station. Upon receiving the picture, Santosh begins praying to him.

Jim Carter and Tim Clark take Flight 217 to Calcutta, India, and send a cable gram to Hayes to confirm. At the same time, a clergyman in Colorado is performing an exorcism. Apparently he is unsuccessful as he is slammed through a front door out into a busy street and killed by a speeding car. The narration states that "a foul smelling wind, filled with voices and laughter, veers to the east. Its destination?...India!"

After arriving, the Crusaders take a tour through Calcutta and are told that there are over 300 million satanic gods in India. Although the Crusaders were summoned to help at the mission station, no one seems to know why. That night, Santosh's mother hears a thumping sound coming from his room as a mysterious cold chill arrives.

The next day, Santosh's father Arjun throws a party for his communist compatriots. Santosh is admonished to behave like a perfect gentleman because what happens will affect his future in the communist party. Santosh vomits all over the spread, while the Commissar loses his appetite and leaves. (What's the matter? Doesn't Lucifer approve of Communism?) Humiliated, Santosh's father doesn't know what to do. Taking a scene from *The Exorcist,* Santosh's bed shakes violently. He undergoes three weeks of tests that leave the doctors baffled. The solution? Find an exorcist—that is, someone who can cast out the demon that could be inside Santosh.

The Crusaders visit Santosh's home and promise to return in a few days after prayer and fasting to expel the demon. Rev. Hayes gives them a crash course on fighting demons. Our heroes reenter the home, and a scream fest a la Linda Blair ensues. Arjun exclaims, "The top communist doctor in Calcutta couldn't help! No one in the party really cares! If these men can help Santosh, I'm willing to become a Christian!" Tim and Jim order the demon to leave, and all is well. Not only that, everyone in the entire village comes to Christ. On the plane trip home, the Crusaders open a present from Santosh—its the missing page of the devil's picture torn to pieces. In the epilogue, Jim Carter warns "Hey, man...don't mess with the occult! All it's gonna give you is fear! Get away from Satan by

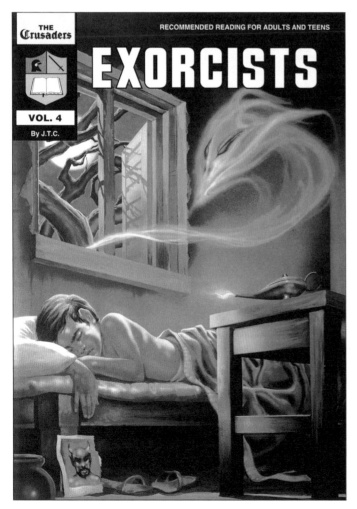

receiving Christ....This may be your last chance!...So don't blow it!" This tale doesn't go as far as *The Exorcist* since we aren't treated to witnessing Santosh doing unholy things to himself with a crucifix (wait until *Double Cross!*) or telling our heroes what their mothers are doing in Hell. We don't actually see the demon except for the cover, and except for a few levitation scenes, we don't really see any demon powers in this adventure. Favorite Panel Award goes to page 18 where Santosh pukes all over the table. This upstages Linda Blair's vomit scene because Santosh contaminates the entire dinner. This kid has good aim! Grade **A+** for Abundant Abdominal fluids!

Crusaders vol. 5. **CHAOS Guest Review by Rev. Rich Lee:** (©1975.) This adventure of Tim Clark and Jim Carter comes a few years after Hal Lindsey's book *The Late, Great Planet Earth* became a bestseller. That book prompted the "end times" prophecy craze in the 1970s much like the *Left Behind* series does in the new millennium.

The story begins when "prophecy expert" Dr. Harry Morse has an attempt made on his life because he led the head of a strange cult to Christ. Sheesh, can't the Crusaders have a normal adventure without someone trying to assassinate anybody or getting run off the road? Apparently not, for Dr. Morse barely misses getting creamed by a Mack truck. He turns to Mr. Harris at Glenco Electronics for help. Harris immediately summons our heroes Tim and Jim to the conference room. Dr. Morse shows them a threatening letter pieced together from various newspapers to spell out "Before you return from Israel you will feel the sting of death!" Morse is scheduled to go to Israel to give a prophecy seminar and the Crusaders tag along.

On board the flight to Israel, Dr. Morse tells Tim and Jim that the most significant event to happen to show that we are in "the last days" is Israel becoming a nation on May 14, 1948. For self-appointed Bible prophecy experts, this date marks the beginning of the final generation on planet Earth before Jesus returns.

Also accompanying them on the flight is an assassin who watches his future targets from behind a magazine. (Or could it be a comic of *The Crusaders?*)

Upon arriving at Ben Gurion Airport, Dr. Morse goes into detail over how the Jews blew it for rejecting Jesus. When the Jews finally learn at the end of time that Jesus is their expected Messiah after all, it will "blow their minds."

They check into a hotel where Dr. Morse has a room all to himself, while the Crusaders share a room. The mysterious stalker manages to check into the room right next door to Dr. Morse.

The next morning, a Jewish taxi driver named Marty chauffeurs Dr. Morse around Jerusalem. We are told that the next battle will trigger World War III only if Russia moves on Israel. What will happen first—the Rapture or WW III? In Morse's opinion, Noah and the incident with Lot in Sodom and Gomorrah were precursors to the Rapture when the righteous were protected before God's wrath fell. The Rapture, for those not in the know, is the instantaneous event when all Christians (and even babies because they are too young to sin) will be seized from the earth before God unleashes famines, ecological devastation, and nuclear war. When planes crash because Christian pilots disappear and when all of the world's babies turn up missing, the world will be turned into *chaos* (hence the title)!

The cult member drills a hole next to Dr. Morse's shower and prepares to slip in a scorpion while Morse is showering. A carefully placed word balloon covers Morse's private parts while the fumbling would-be assassin slips on a bar of soap and gets himself stung to death.

After the Rapture takes place, Morse says that the world leader known as the Antichrist will appear on the scene, solve the Middle-east crisis, betray Israel, and suffer defeat at the hands of Jesus in the end. Included is a picture of the truck with a guillotine on the back for those who refuse the mark of the beast.

After the Jews flee for their lives in the Trans-Jordanian city of Petra, *the beast* (Antichrist) destroys the "apostate church." Funny thing is the "apostate church" is Vatican City, and this comic was published long before *Alberto* came on the scene. Furthermore, in later Chick writings, the Vatican is never referred to as an "apostate church," since this suggests that the Vatican would have been at one time a true Christian church that fell away. So...we see some "evolution" in Chick's views.

Dr. Morse leads Marty to Jesus, with Tim and Jim proudly looking on. "Tim, guess who's joining us at the Marriage Supper of the Lamb?" Jim asks. "A Jewish taxi driver." Tim says. "Right on, baby...right on!" Unfortunately, the plotline involving the assassination attempts on Dr. Morse isn't resolved. Grade **A+** for Absent-minded Assassins!

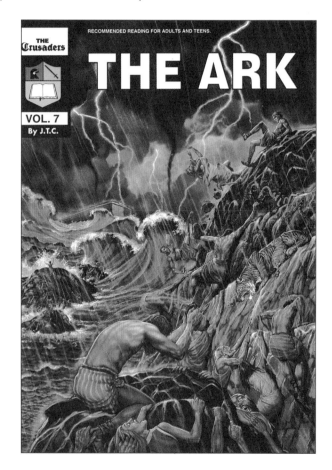

Crusaders Vol. 6. **PRIMAL MAN?** **Review:** (©1976.) The comic starts off with a cave man story. Just when you think Chick is about to reconcile Evolutionism with Creationalism, it turns out it's only a TV show. Then the *real* story begins. A Creationalist anthropologist tries to convince a Hollywood producer that Evolution is bunk. With the Crusaders praying for him on the sidelines, God runs interference, keeping the light-in-the-loafers director and a bitter old evolutionist biologist expert away long enough for the message to "get through" to the producer. After hearing all the holy testimony, he becomes convinced that Evolution is a hoax and contemplates killing the series. He finally tells the Christians, "I'm going to continue making evolution films. Even though it's brainwashing and damaging these kids...many will lose their souls because of these films. You gentlemen serve **your** God...and I in turn will serve mine. His name is '**Money'** and I need **all** I can get!" It's what you might call a "survival of the fittest" ending, and a rare instance where *The Crusaders* fail. Anyone who's ever worked in Hollywood (and I have a long history of never doing so) can tell you this is EXACTLY how it operates! Grade: **A** for Avarice.

Crusaders vol. 7. **THE ARK Review:** (©1976.) Those dirty, low-down commies are up to their old tricks again! This time, the Reds are trying to cover up the truth about Noah's Ark. (No wonder they went bankrupt—they spent too much time fighting Jesus.) A small group of Christians go on an expedition to uncover the remains of Noah's Ark. The aircraft carrier sized vessel sits atop Mt. Ararat, yet no satellite has noticed it yet. (They were probably too busy photographing missile sites.) A Russian pilot first spotted the Ark in 1916, but the messenger sent to deliver the news was caught up in the Bolshevik revolution. "Rumor has it, he was captured and the documents fell into the hands of a Communist leader, Leon Trotsky. The messenger was silenced. He was shot to death." Not mentioned in the comic is the fate of Trotsky, who later winds up with a rather uncomfortable ax in his forehead. (Call it "Russian Retirement".) It turns out the Soviets don't want news of the Ark to leak out because, in the words of one K.G.B. big shot, "There would be renewed interest in the Bible...God forbid!" This same spy explains to his fellow comrades, "In the 1920s we successfully penetrated Christian seminaries in the U.S. And now in the 1970s roughly 75% of their ministers deny the Bible history of the ark... In the U.S. schools, most of the professors and teachers believe and teach evolution and laugh at the Bible. We used these people to destroy the Christian faith of their young people. Also the American press, TV, and motion pictures have been a tremendous help to us." Hey, don't forget the comic books either! (Present company excluded.)

The Reds send Col. Solkov to neutralize the Christian's Ark efforts. He goes to the Turkish Military Intelligence Headquarters and harangues General Kemal to arrest the Christians as spies. A trip into town for supplies prevents Crusader Jim Carter from being arrested along with the rest of his fellow explorers. He quickly calls Crusader Tim Clark in L.A. for assistance. Tim gets a briefing on Noah's Ark by an expert, Dr. Bob Helton. It is rather amusing that any Bible reading Christian would need to have the story of Noah recounted. It's one of the most famous stories in the Bible. What's next? The story of Adam and Eve? But Tim politely listens to *the expert* retell the story one more time.

Tim goes to Turkey and is promptly arrested, along with Jim Carter. The two are thrown in a different jail from the other Christian explorers. A Russian diplomat is also arrested for being drunk and tossed into the same cell. He must be *really drunk,* because any other diplomat would claim diplomatic immunity and get right back out. Perhaps the Lord made him forget that loop-hole so he would have the opportunity to be converted by the Crusaders? After two hours of pressure from the Christian mod-squad, Sergei Malik surrenders to Jesus. (He never really stood a chance against the tag-team approach. They know just which buttons to press.) Sergei says he'll arrange for The Crusaders and their friends to be released once he's let go. Within seconds, he's freed and does as he promised. The Christians all unite and pile into a truck and speed to the nearest border. A convenient windstorm breaks the telephone lines and prevents the border guard from checking the truck. It's another close call for The Crusaders. As usual, they win and the bad guys lose thanks to God tipping the scales in their favor.

On the last page, a fellow Christian wonders if the Ark will always remain hidden from the world. "Who knows? Politics could change and some team may be allowed to find it." WISH GRANTED! Turkey is now our big buddy, allowing us to stage troops there and everything. I wonder what's taking the Crusaders so long to get back and blow this story wide open. They must be too distracted listening to Alberto.

Overall, this is a fun conspiracy filled tale with plenty of cold-war intrigue. Too bad Sergei Malik converted to Christ. After reading the comic, I wanted to nuke ALL of Russia! But alas, we couldn't hurt Sergei... Grade: **A+** for Ark Adventure!

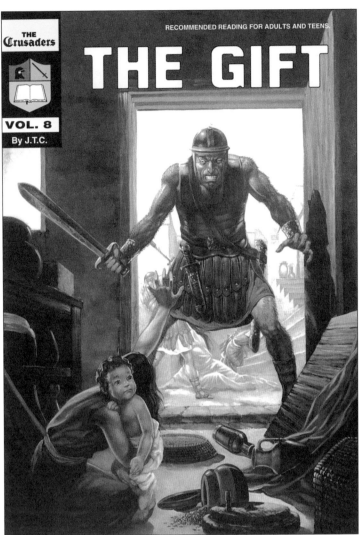

Crusaders vol. 8. **THE GIFT Review by Rev. Rich Lee:** (©1977.) This adventure begins with Marcia Gordon, a young woman who has been dumped by her fiancée, flunked out of school by her professor, and is overall having a bad hair day. She decides to commit suicide.

Meanwhile, our Crusading heroes are finishing dinner with their girlfriends. They leave the restaurant and walk down a pier as Marcia takes a nose-dive into the depths. Jim and Tim jump in to save her, and Tanya, Jim's girlfriend, happens to be a nurse who performs CPR. They take her to Tanya's apartment rather than to a hospital or suicide crisis center.

Upon waking up, Marcia asks who saved her. When she hears that Jim did, she swats his face with her finger nails and screams "Thanks for **nothing!**" When black Tanya brings white Marcia some "good hot soup," she asks, "What's in it, Aunt Jemima? Hog jowls and turnip greens?" Obviously, she took some lessons from Tiger Woods' friend Fuzzy Zeoler!

Undaunted, Tanya says "Marcia, you **can't** get to me...I **love** you!" "Wow!" Marcia replies, "Now I'm stuck with a lesbian!" Tim's girlfriend Lois snaps, "That's cruel, Marsha! We're all Christians here! We're **trying** to help you!" Marcia is unimpressed. "So **that's** it! A bunch of fanatics play hero and **now** you're gonna try and shove a Bible down my throat!" When they sit down for a meal, Jim says grace for the food. Marcia openly adds in her prayer, "O mighty **god of fire**...thank you for lighting this cigarette...and for cooking this meal...and I almost forgot, the **sun god** for growing the coffee bean for this cup of mountain grown coffee!"

Tim asks Marcia what she knows about Jesus. "It's sort of fuzzy...uh...He was a little kid born on Christmas, you know...the Santa Claus bit...And he died on Easter...I **don't** know what the bunny has to do with it...I guess that's about as much as **I** know about it!" Tim then launches into the Gospel story beginning with the Roman occupation of Israel and the angel Gabriel's visit to the virgin Mary. He relates the birth of Jesus, the story of the wise men, the slaughter of the innocents, and finally, the execution of Jesus. The resurrection event is also recounted. At the story's end, Tim asks, "Marsha, **now** do you understand what Jesus did for you?" "I think so," she replies. Tim emphasizes that "God **hates** sin!" "Oh my God...that means I'm going to hell! Right?" Tim assures her that there is a way out. However, she says that she should clean her life up first. "No, Marsha, He wants you just as you are..." Tim says.

After the obligatory tears, she recites the sinner's prayer and suddenly feels better. Tanya even says "Shore nuff?" to round out the earlier Negro jabs. Marcia has the last word. "Yeah!...in fact, now I even like your hog jowls and turnip greens!" Readers nervously laugh at the racially sensitive humor.

This volume lacks controversy and is a straightforward evangelistic comic to win converts. Carter's artwork, even of a kitchen table and living room, is photo realistic. The character of Marcia Gordon must have been modeled on a real person because of her vivid expressions. When she is contrasted with the characters of Lois and Tanya, they're not as lifelike. Vivid portrayals of Hell and underlining conspiracies are noticeably absent. However, the all-time goriest depiction of the crucifixion is included on page 29 with an accompanying medical view of how Jesus suffered during the crucifixion. Not recommended reading at meal time, especially on Spaghetti night. Grade **B** for Bloody!

Crusaders vol. 9. **ANGEL OF LIGHT Guest Review by Rev. Rich Lee:** (©1978) This exciting adventure begins with an unforgettable opening scene. Two men are reading the newspaper about a series of murders. One of the men says, "Isn't that gross? What's the world coming to? Isn't **anyone** safe?" The other reads from the paper, "'The girl was dragged into a black and white car—witnesses heard her screams.' Man that turns me on!" His partner agrees, "Me too, Let's go get another one!"

As the two thugs gun for their next victim, the Crusaders are leaving a restaurant. A woman, whose name we learn is Darlene, is assaulted by the two criminals. James and Tim spring into action, rescuing the hapless damsel in distress. A police chase ensues, only the criminals do not make a clean getaway. They plunge off of a freeway into a Christless eternity. As the Crusaders take Darlene home, they learn that she is shacking up with a guy named Jeff. "My God," Darlene reflects, "I could be dead right now...I wonder what I'd be in the next life...I hope I'd be a better person." "No," Tim interjects. "You'd be in hell right now!...I think this is your place, Darlene."

In Darlene's thought balloon, she wonders, "What kind of creeps are they?" The Crusaders are quick to lift up Jeff and Darlene in prayer upon their return home. Soon, Jeff and Darlene stop by to visit. After introductions, Jeff says, "I'm not the kind of guy that wastes time. Thanks for saving Darlene's life, but I demand an apology for scaring her about going to hell!" Tim replies, "Sorry, Jeff, but Darlene is on her way to hell... And so are you!"

In true Chick fashion, Jeff responds with the trademark **"HAW HAW HAW"** so characteristic of mockers and blasphemers. "Nobody preaches about hell anymore," Jeff sneers, "It's all **love**, man!" Tim sadly agrees, then tells the story of how Lucifer became Satan, and how hell is a place that was made by Jesus for Satan and his fallen angels.

After Adam and Eve were created, Satan tricked them both into sinning and thus obtained dominion over the earth. Tim and James tell how Satan's demons were waiting to plague mankind after Noah's flood. He also explains about the Tower of Babel,

Nimrod and Semiramis, and the story of Exodus. An impatient Jeff snorts, "Let's go home. I'm sick of listening to this garbage!" James warns, "If you walk out that door, Jeff...Satan will laugh his head off." Darlene says, "Shut up, Jeff...I want to hear this." Tim warns, "Jeff, it's this simple...As long as you're going to hell...you might as well know what's ahead for you."

The Crusaders recount how the Dark Ages began, and the world plunged into chaos. Satan stayed busy inspiring the Illuminati, lodges, and the occult, and hatched world wars. In fact, the Illuminati are controlled by the Vatican as "reported by Dr. A.R. Rivera (ex-Jesuit priest)." The earlier printing of *Angel of Light* gives credit to the Rothschilds for being behind the Illuminati, according to John Todd, "(ex-Druid high priest)."

In this short story, the Crusaders take the reader from the gospel accounts of Christ's resurrection to the formation of lodges, all in just 32 pages! We also learn that Satan's spiritual structure consists of a hierarchy with Satan at the top, Beelzebub as his commanding general with several principalities under him (the names of the top demons are withheld, probably to protect the guilty)! Furthermore, the principalities or dukes under Beelzebub are in charge of such categorical sins as, "Addiction & Partying," "Mental Illness," "Murder," which includes the "sub-sin" of "gossip," "The Unspeakable Demon" for hindering Christians only, and "Sexual Lust." Under this interesting category, "Masturbation" is also a "sub-sin." Under the category of "Addiction & Partying," we learn that "Caffeine" and non-hallucinating drugs are also sub-sins. A different archduke demon is responsible for each sin. We are warned that "Satan's spider web covers the whole world...very few escape from him." This means that all of you boys with hairy palms are under the influence of the Horny One.

The only way out is reciting the Sinner's Prayer, with the obligatory "sob" and "sniff." Tim urges Jeff, "Now your job is to tell this good news to others." The next day, Jeff (now sporting a haircut to show how reformed he has become) asks his father, "Dad, uh...er...did you ever think you might be going to hell?" His father becomes outraged. "I'm **what?** Listen, Jeff...don't you **ever** talk to me like that again, **ya hear!** What kind of @!!!**! fanatic are you?"

The epilogue tells the reader in these parting words: "To most of you this story was a big joke and it turned you off. But look at it this way: at least you got a good look at the place you're heading for: Also, when your heart stops beating—as it surely will, you'll look back and remember reading this message a thousand years from now when you're in the lake of fire. It won't be funny then." No, but it sure is funny now, insofar as everyone's over-the-top performances are concerned. This is also the comic where you learn that the Angel of Light (Satan) is the source of both masturbation and caffeine! Better not do both at the same time. If you confused hands, you could scald yourself for life! Grade **A** for Angel of Vice.

Crusaders vol. 10. **SPELLBOUND? Guest Review by Dave:** (©1978.) This is a great comic! Just look at the cover. A row of cassettes surrounding a candle with moths being drawn and consumed by the flame. (The original '70s version featured 8-track tapes forming the circle of Stonehenge.) The story starts out with an exciting car chase. Jim (the black crusader) is almost deliberately run off the road by Bobby Dallas, rock star. The Motive? Just for kicks, man! But Bobby loses control of his car and crashes. Jim ends up saving Bobby's life. Bobby returns the favor by inviting Jim to "a little get together at my pad" complete with food, booze, grass, pills, coke (not the liquid variety), and the usual assortment of Rock artist inspirational substances. The Crusaders and their dates abstain. (The girls cling to their manly dates, terrified by the weirdoes that surround them.) The wholesome foursome find a quiet table to sit down at and say grace. Guests stare at them and one remarks, "It looks like we've got some aliens with us! I don't like this one bit!"

We are also treated to a detailed lecture on the history of various occult objects, all because one dude wears a small piece of Egyptian jewelry. (It doesn't take much to get Chick going!) In case you're worried that having these symbols in your house in comic book form might attract demons, fear not. Chick's footnote assures us: "Witches believe that only occult symbols in 3 dimensional shapes such as jewelry, statues or books pushing the occult can be used for casting spells...so you need not burn this book." (What a relief.)

But inviting the Crusaders to the party proves fatal to Bobby. It seems that one of the characters from a previous adventure is there and recognizes them. Bobby is soon found floating face up in the pool. (Oh well, he would have died anyway if Jim hadn't saved him, so he's really no worse off.) We are then treated to a short history of the Druids, introduced to Penny (a teen with a lot of 'far out' cassettes), and Lance Collins, whose family were witches and Druids FOR OVER 700 years! A lot of the history of the Druids is actually pretty interesting. Did you know the Beatles had a "Druid rock" beat? Or that witches have a language similar to truckers' CB talk? But wait, it gets even better...

We get a short study of the recording industry. Favorite Panel Award goes to an ominous looking Master Tape waiting to be blessed "by an evil force (to a Christian, this means a curse)"! It gets wilder: witches file into the recording studio to perform their demonic ceremonies. (Chick notes: "The witches perform this ceremony skyclad (nude), but we've clothed them for this story". (Bummer.)) A ghost-like blob of blue ectoplasm appears. All this is revealed in Lance's blistering Sermon/ flashback. He shares an anecdote given to him by a missionary in Africa about Rock being the music used to call up demons. Things climax in another exciting car chase and a victorious record burning. I think we see a cameo appearance of the druid cop from the *Broken Cross!* (These comics can be as densely layered as the X-files...I half expected to see the cigarette smoking man appear in the corner.) The story ends with the liberal reporter from "ABS News" giving a big thumbs down to the record burning and equating the Christians with Nazis and Klansmen. Not too far from the liberal media's views on Christians today! Grade: **A** for ABS News. (Note: the cover has recently been redrawn with CDs instead of cassettes.)

Crusaders vol. 11. **SABOTAGE? Guest Review by Rev. Rich Lee:** (©1979.) The burning Bible on the cover says it all! Satan has tried throughout history to destroy God's inspired word, specifically the English translation known as the Authorized King James Version published in 1611. Our heroes James Carter and Timothy Clark are on the road to set another misguided soul straight on this fact.

In this Crusaders volume, we are told that "sabotage" means "to wreck or destroy." This comic defines hard words with an asterisk (*). It is too bad that the trademark swearing symbols (@#%**!) don't get defined in this manner.

Gary Slator is an inmate in Soledad State Prison, a hellhole where the guards want him to rot. When the chaplain* (*a prison pastor for those not in the know) presents a lovely Bible sent from his mother, Slator rips it to shreds. Transition to Tim Clark, who receives a phone call from Slator's mother. She requests that he meet little Gary when he's released from prison. He agrees to meet him when he's released, presumably with five dollars and a bus token.

The warden gives Slator a farewell speech and tells him that he was the biggest troublemaker they've had in prison for a long time. "God help those people you meet on the outside!" he intones. The suckers waiting outsider are, of course, the crusaders.

"You guys were from that church! What the @#%**! are you creeps doing here?" Gary Slator shouts at Jim and Tim. After some angry accusations, Slator reluctantly bums a ride and tells the two what brought him to this lowly state. He tells the Crusaders that he went to a Bible college run by men he could trust. He burned the midnight oil for Christ, won souls for him, preached on street corners, and did well in school until one morning everything blew up. A Greek professor (the New Testament was originally written in Greek) gave a lecture to young, idealistic Gary. The egghead stated that the Word of God only existed in the original manuscripts and those were lost (gasp!). The King James Version of 1611 was not really the Word of God, nor was any other translation. Gary was crushed, since his confidence in the KJV was the reason he became a Christian. "According to you, then, my King James Bible could be just a pile of garbage...it could be full of lies, right?? If that's the case, then this @#*!*! school is based on lies...and that makes you the biggest phony of them all!" The shaking egghead quivers in his shoes, warning Slator to stay away. Slator yells that his faith is destroyed and he is mad enough to kill. "You @#%*#!...This Bible is no good to me anymore, so you might as well eat it! Here!" The Bible is thrust into the face of the professor, his teeth dislodged and blood flowing profusely through the handkerchief. So the Bible is not just food for the soul, but leather bound roughage for the digestive system.

During Slator's rampage, he almost kills the dean and sets the Bible college on fire. The police catch him, but he promises "Okay, pigs...you got me this time, but there'll be another time and other Bible colleges!" In summary, he received two to ten years for *aggravated assault (*this means wild or violent physical attack, kids), attempted murder, and **arson (**to set fire to a building, and you had better not do this at home).

Tim tells Gary that he was set up by the "Alexandrian cult." The trio visit the home of a Dr. Hillman who seems to know that Gary has lost his faith without an introduction (maybe his long hair and the smell of cigarettes gave that away!). According to Hillman (who resembles the real life KJV fundamentalist preacher Peter Ruckman of Pensacola, Florida), the first four words that Satan said is what destroyed Gary's faith: "Yea, hath God said...?" Satan has questioned what God said, but Jesus' words were, "Heaven and earth shall pass away, but my words shall never pass away (Matthew 24:35)." Jesus' words, according to Hillman, are preserved in the King James version of the English Bible, the only Bible Satan has not been able to mess up like other versions.

©1979 Jack T. Chick.

This Crusaders tale gives the reader a historical overview of the Roman persecution of the early Christian church. In spite of fierce opposition, the Christian movement continued to grow. Satan had to destroy the Christian church somehow, so he merged paganism with Christianity, resulting in the dreaded Roman Catholic Institution. Constantine, the emperor, whom history books record as the first Christian emperor, was really a phony politician who pretended to convert to the Christian faith. According to most fundamentalist Christians' understanding, it was Constantine who was the first pope. Under Constantine's leadership, the Bible was translated using bad manuscripts that are the foundation of all modern translations of the Bible into English. Only the King James version is based upon a set of Bible manuscripts that came from Antioch, Syria (where the true Christians were). Unfortunately, the world of higher education swallowed the idea that the rival set of Bible manuscripts that came from Alexandria, Egypt were the best rendition of the original manuscripts. During the Middle Ages, the true Christians (Chickspeak for those who are not Roman Catholics) preserved the Antiochian manuscripts perfectly from generation to generation until the King James version was translated later.

Hillman's diatribe against rival translations is supported with the claim that members of the Church of England, Drs. Hort and Wescott, were really undercover Roman Catholics who despised the manuscripts that the KJV were based upon. Through there influence, the English "update" of the KJV published in 1888 (also known as the Revised Standard Version) was based upon the corrupted Alexandrian manuscripts, NOT the Antiochian manuscripts. Dr. Hillman warns that "soon there will be an ecumenical Bible (one common Bible for all religions) preparing the way for the antichrist. The same game goes on in some Bible colleges today. That's how they got to you, Gary!"

Gary gets saved and returns to the path of Christ. He ends his reconversion experience with an encouraging question: "Do you guys know where I can find a good barber?"

Favorite Panel Award goes to panel 1, page 8, where a ballistic Bible bashing Gary goes berserk, shaking with rage! He totally loses it here! I only wish my days in seminary were so exciting. No one (not even me, known to engage in a little rebellion from time to time) shoved a Bible into the teeth of a theological professor, but there's always a first time.

Grade **B**+ for Burning Bibles!

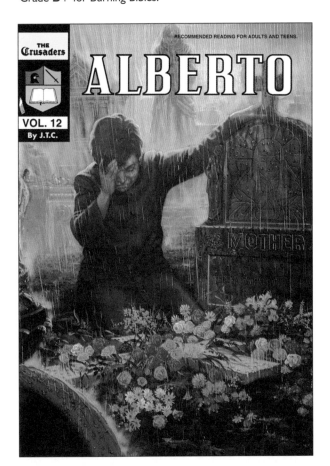

Crusaders vol.12. **ALBERTO Review:** (©1979.) Jack claims he prayed long and hard before printing this comic. The fact that The Lord gave him the go ahead proves that either Alberto is true, or that God has a very broad sense of humor. (Or maybe both.) The comic opens with Alberto being left at a Spanish monastery by his mother. A few years later, she gets sick and dies screaming about demons. Fast forward to San Diego, 1979. Some secret service-looking fellow phones Tim Clark and asks if he'll watch over Alberto for a while. Once in the safe custody of the Crusaders, Alberto reveals he was nearly driven off the road by someone. Who would want to do such a thing? Why, the Vatican, of course. Alberto wastes no time explaining how many feathers he ruffled once he saw the light and broke away from the "Catholic System". Being an ex-Jesuit priest, he knows where all the Vatican bodies are buried...literally! (Baby bodies, no less—page 12.) Other juicy gossip includes homosexuality and promiscuity in the Holy Orders, torture and murder during the Inquisition (complete with graphic images), and predictions of a new holocaust for all heretics once the Vatican's super computer completes the list of Catholic enemies. Several pages explain the ongoing espionage that Jesuits and their operatives conduct against real Bible believing churches. Alberto was one of the undercover agents sent to destroy such churches, and he outlines the clever ploys used to discredit preachers who dared speak out against the Pope. The best dirty tricks seem to involve young women agents. Some of the panels are pretty suggestive! One of the less titillating but unintentionally humorous scenes shows how Alberto "corrupted" the other Bible college students by merely holding hands with a female in public. Old maid teachers look on in outrage and one declares, "well I never!" *Haw-haw-haw!*

But then agent Alberto has doubts about his mission. He starts to read a New Testament without the Official Roman Catholic Seal of Approval (Nihil Obstat, Imprimatur). Sure enough, *the truth* sets him free. He becomes saved and all hell breaks loose! They toss him in an Insane Asylum, give him drugs and electric shock treatment, but eventually give up and let him go. Like most retired insane asylum seekers, he moves to California. Flashback to 1979 and Alberto reminds the Crusaders that Roman Catholics do not go to heaven but to hell, and someone has to warn them. James Carter asks, "who would have the guts to preach that?" Alberto exclaims, "I do! Because I love them." The inside back cover makes the final plea: "THIS IS NO GAME—IT'S WAR FOR YOUR SOUL! Either it's total commitment and submission to Christ or lose everything forever by going on with Satan and Baal worship." (Satan meaning the Pope and Baal worship meaning Catholicism.)

This comic is rather wordy, with several panels devoted entirely to text. But there's some sexy scenes and torturous violence to keep things moving, and, of course, a world class conspiracy theory at the heart of it. This is the first of six *Alberto* comics, and it promises readers they are in for a thrilling (albeit risky) ride with Alberto as he reveals the dirty underbelly of his former masters. Grade **A-** for Alberto!

©1981 Jack T. Chick.

When Maria's cell door was opened, only 60 lbs. of her is left under a blood-soaked habit. Her flesh was rotting away, in spite of a daily feast on "death cookies."

Alberto seized the crucifix from her bony grasp and threw it in the other nuns' direction while he carts her off to safety! Alberto subsequently gets placed on "Rome's death list" thanks to this action. "He is damned forever! The Virgin will take care of this Father Rivera. He is another Judas that has sold out our Holy Father, the Pope," Mother Superior says. Or so we are told, since it's hard to figure out how Alberto could have heard her saying this after he left the building.

Tim and Jim cross-examine Alberto on these facts in the safety of a living room. "Were they concerned about you in the Vatican?" Jim Carter asks. "Oh yes, James," says Alberto. So concerned were Vatican officials that they called an emergency session in Rome to scheme to make Rivera's death look like an accident. Furthermore, they were deeply concerned about help that Alberto could recruit. "Only those that say we are **not** a Christian church will help him," a wine-imbibing, cigar smoking cleric says. "Are there many churches like that, Father?" another asks. "Thank God, no!" the first cleric responds.

What must stroke the egos of the churches that buy *The Crusaders* comics in bulk is the comment from another Vatican crony: "There are not many, but they are **very** strong and **dangerous**. Those who are completely dedicated Bible-believers and totally committed to Christ are the ones we must fear. Unfortunately, Father Rivera has become one of them!"

The secret oath of the Jesuits order is recounted, including all sorts of promises to murder and destroy heretics (true Christians) for the Pope. Only key Jesuits supposedly take this oath before infiltrating governments and assassinating leaders. Alberto also recounts the unsuccessful assassination attempts on his life, including one from a dentist! (I never did trust those guys.) We're told that one of Rome's best agents was the flamboyant healing evangelist of the 1970s, Kathryn Kuhlman, who pushed for ecumenical unity among Jews, Protestants, and Catholics. Worse, the Vatican planned the infamous Jonestown massacre in Guyana in 1978. Jim Jones was a Jesuit under that secret oath with instructions from Rome to commit mass murder in order to discredit Christian camps. According to Alberto, "The cry went up that politicians should pass laws forbidding groups from setting up retreats. This way, Bible-believers would have to hide when the great wave of persecution from Rome begins."

Double Cross ends with a warning in the epilogue: "The government will soon wipe your churches away through new taxes...." If that was impending back in 1981, imagine how close it must be today! We better start building those retreats. Grade **A+** for Assassination Attempt!

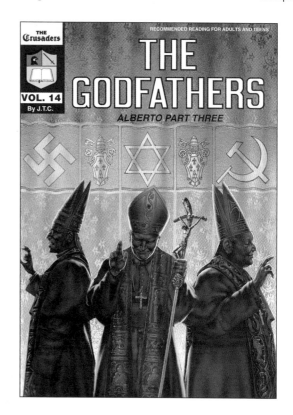

Alberto part 2, *Crusaders* vol. 13. **DOUBLE-CROSS Guest Review by Rev. Richard Lee:** (©1981.) This exciting sequel picks up with Alberto escaping from the "Roman Catholic Institution" with his life. He recounts the adventure to the Crusaders Tim Clark and Jim Carter.

After spending years infiltrating Protestant churches, Alberto was converted to the Protestantism he was sworn to destroy. He had a one-way ticket to Washington, D.C. but missed his flight while phoning his sister. His sister, Maria, was a cloistered nun in a London convent. She is sick, so Alberto flies to London to see her instead.

Upon arrival, Alberto contacts an Anabaptist church to take him to the convent. Sister Maria is held captive by an obese Mother Superior who calls the cops on Alberto. It turns out that one of the police was a "real Bible-believing Christian" who stood with Alberto, and insisted that the Mother Superior let Alberto see Maria.

© 1982 Jack T. Chick.

Alberto part 3, *Crusaders* vol. 14. **THE GODFATHERS Guest Review by Rev. Rich Lee:** (©1982.) Among the most inflammatory Chick comics ever, this installment of "Alberto" promises the reader that "YOU ARE ABOUT TO SEE THE MOTHER OF ABOMINATIONS (REV.17:5) IN ALL HER POLITICAL, ECONOMIC AND MILITARY MIGHT." A rabbi and his nephew stumble upon a neo-Nazi spray painting anti-Semitic comments on a temple. After detaining him for the police, the evening news plays the story up big on television. The neo-Nazi vandal tells the reporter that the Holocaust was "...all a big lie!" Meanwhile, Crusaders Tim Clark and Jim Carter are watching the news with Alberto who says, "What a devil! That man is serving the Vatican and he's lying through his teeth!" He proceeds to tell the Crusaders what he allegedly learned while he was a Jesuit priest.

According to Alberto, both the Nazi and Communist parties were started by the Vatican. The Vatican has supposedly wanted to move to Jerusalem and set up shop there, since that is where Christianity started. However, the Orthodox Jews have stopped her, and that's why they are on "Rome's hit list." During the Crusades in the Middle Ages, children from Jewish and Roman Catholic unions were later recruited to serve as crusaders to capture the Holy Land from Islamic control. Of course, this effort failed. The Vatican had another rival to contend with: the Greek and Russian Orthodox churches. Under Vatican influence, the Communist party was created for the sole purpose of destroying the Czar of Russia since he protected the Russian Orthodox Church.

Later, the Vatican bankrolled the beginning of the Nazi party to destroy the Jews so the Vatican could realize its dream of moving to Jerusalem. In the twentieth century, various popes from Pius X, Benedict XV, and Pius XII supported World Wars I and II to wipe out Jews. Alberto says that Hitler's seminal work *Mein Kampf* was ghost-written by a Jesuit priest named Staempfle. This book served to fuel the Nazi party in Germany, but what history books don't record is that the Holocaust was another Inquisition orchestrated by the Vatican. During World War II, the Jesuits propped up Hitler, Mussolini, and Franco as "The Defenders of the Faith" to conquer the world for the Vatican, since she wasn't satisfied with merely taking over the city of Jerusalem alone. The Vatican wanted to take over the whole world, but Protestants, Jews, and democracy got in their way.

The other rival, the Greek Orthodox churches, were subjugated in Yugoslavia by the Ustachi killing squads made up of Roman Catholic priests. While all of the killing and maiming occurred during the twentieth century, the Vatican also plotted to cover itself in the event that the Nazis lost World War II. This plot included making everybody believe the Vatican had nothing to do with the war, and in time convince the world the Holocaust never happened.

After the obligatory bloody depiction of Christ's crucifixion and calling the reader to salvation through Christ, Alberto continues his anti-Vatican diatribe. Fidel Castro is a Jesuit priest under oath, the Ku Klux Klan was also created by the Jesuits as a masterpiece to make Jews, Catholics, and blacks suspicious of true Protestants, and the Masonic order is controlled by the Jesuit General A.K.A. the "Black Pope." In summary, these revelations from Alberto support the opening page's contention that the Vatican is indeed "THE MOTHER OF HARLOTS AND ABOMINATIONS." The Vatican created competing organizations and masterminded the United States Civil War, both World Wars, and the Shriners' Convention. They sure make our C.I.A. look like a bunch of lazy bones. (They couldn't even make Castro's poison cigar work right. What losers!) Grade **A** for Ardent!

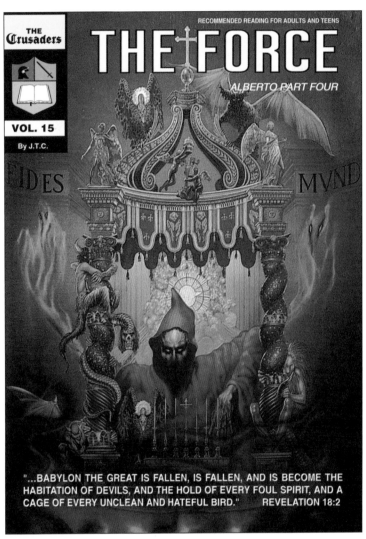

"...BABYLON THE GREAT IS FALLEN, IS FALLEN, AND IS BECOME THE HABITATION OF DEVILS, AND THE HOLD OF EVERY FOUL SPIRIT, AND A CAGE OF EVERY UNCLEAN AND HATEFUL BIRD."　REVELATION 18:2

© 1983 Jack T. Chick.

Alberto part 4, *Crusaders* vol. 15. **THE FORCE Guest Review by Rev. Rich Lee:** (©1983.) This volume reveals the occult side of "Babylon the Great" from Revelation chapter 18. A village has become quiet at night as the residents are in fear. An evil thing had come to their village and even their animals are frightened. Unearthly noises came from the home of a widow named Carmen. In spite of her candles lit to the Virgin Mary, the "thing" came back at sundown! It all began when Carmen dedicated her daughter to the Virgin Mary after the Blessed Virgin healed·the child of seizures. Little Marguerita would become a Carmelite nun in gratitude for the healing miracle. While Marguerita recited the Rosary, objects flew around the house. Alberto Rivera was summoned to perform an exorcism by saying the proper Mass for this occasion. A local priest was to assist Father Alberto, but entered the haunted house before he arrived. When Alberto arrived on the scene, the priest was ripped to shreds and tossed out the front door by an unseen force. Undaunted, Alberto goes inside and performs the exorcism despite being spun like a top and suspended in midair. The laughter of the "souls of the dead" died down after Alberto served the Eucharist to Marguerita.

In after thought, Alberto (now a Protestant) says that these weren't the souls of the dead but demons. The reader is taken down "memory lane" to review various satanic conspiracies, including Babylon, Egyptian transubstaniation, the Apocrypha, and of coruse, the Vatican in general. "Satan's church was off and running. Anything in its way was destroyed.... This religious machine controlled Europe. As it grew, so did witchcraft. The land was filled with hexes, spells, curses, soul travel, black Masses, sacrificial murders, and drinking of human blood. Much of this went on in the convents and monasteries throughout Europe." Joan of Arc was burned to death only because she was a witch who wouldn't serve the Vatican. Otherwise, being a witch alone wasn't that bad...

Alberto purports that any newly formed religious body is visited by Jesuits working undercover to develop it to serve the Vatican. Some of these groups include Jehovah's Witnesses, Mormonism, and Christian Science. Even the Christmas holiday is from Babylon, while Thanksgiving (a Puritan holiday thanking God for their religious freedom in the New World) was tainted by Satan thanks to the infamous Salem witch trials.

Count Dracula puts in a cameo to illustrate the power of the crucifix in warding off weaker demons, since strong demons are behind the crucifix. Crucifixes are tools of the occult since they're charged with dark powers that attract demons. Alberto relates when he was a young seminarian, he and his classmates visited a Salesian monastery that worked with orphans. They stumbled upon seven dead babies with their hearts cut out and crosses cut into their bodies. These babies, says Alberto, were sacrificed to the Virgin Mary, a.k.a. Semiramis from ancient Babylon. One of Alberto's friends who witnessed this made a disastrous mistake in telling his sister, who in turn told her priest about this discovery. She was found dead with her heart cut out, and Alberto's friend disappeared, never to be seen again.

The demonic force that worked through Babylon now works through the Roman Catholic charismatic movement, and Protestants who participate with Catholics in the charismatic renewal are compromising with Satan. Strong stuff. Favorite Panel Award goes to page 29 where we see Count Dracula dance the funky chicken. Grade **B** for Black Mass!

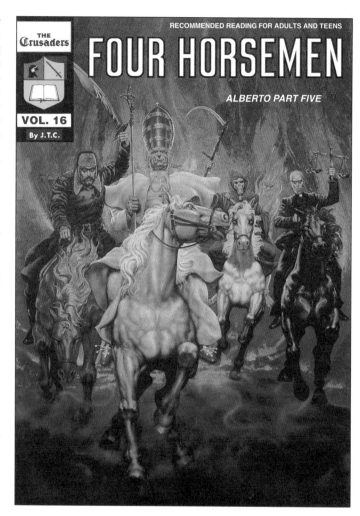

CENTURIES LATER...EVERYTHING WAS STARTING TO FALL APART

Your Holiness... some of the kings and noblemen are not recognizing your authority,

and are refusing to pay tribute.

Some priests have been seen reading the Scriptures in open defiance of Church law.

There have been reports of the heretics spreading their poison among the people.

There was only one solution: set up an Inquisition to cower the people, steal their lands and money, and rule with an iron hand.

©1985 Jack T. Chick.

Alberto part 5, *Crusaders* vol. 16. **FOUR HORSEMEN** Review: (©1985.) What a book! Full of all sorts of Catholic dirty laundry. We're told the Catholics have split their loyalty between the Church and their country of birth (page 7). We're told how the Vatican gets information to store in its secret underground catacombs. "Input from confessionals pours in from even the remotest parts of the world giving the Vatican a constant flow of information on social, religious, military, political, educational and intelligence matters." Vatican II is revealed to be "a big act, a massive cover-up to hide their plans to gain world control... [to] set into operation stage one of the greatest inquisitions of all time under the leadership of the Jesuits." (page 6) The torture of two sisters by Dominicans during the Inquisition is portrayed in graphic detail (page 15). How the Pope tricked King Pepin into rescuing Rome from the Arabs is explained. Other scams are also presented, including how Pope Hadrian I forged a document claiming Constantine had made the popes heir to the entire Roman Empire (page 13). The Jesuits are given credit for creating the Allumbrados, a.k.a. The Illuminati, as a militia of the popes. This militia set out to destroy what was left of Protestantism. More modern conspiracies are also provided, including ties with the Nazi party. Embarrassing photos of various Vatican big shots meeting with Nazis are reproduced, including one with the future Pope Paul VI (page 26). Holocaust photos are shown. "The slaughter of the Jews was perfectly legal according to the laws of the Roman Catholic system. Because according to the Council of Trent they were heretics and considered enemies of God. Nothing has changed! These laws are still in effect today!" (page 27)

The four horsemen of the Apocalypse are presented, especially the antichrist, which turns out to be the Pope (big surprise), and the Black Horseman of Famine, which turns out to be the Jesuit priesthood (page 31). There are other inflammatory images as well, including drawings of Catholic priests leading police raids on a Baptist church, or beheading heretics with a modern guillotine-mobile, or holding public peace demonstrations (the horror!)

In short, this comic is stuffed full of classic material. Conspiracy buffs will certainly savor turning every single paranoid page. Grade **A** for Apocalypse.

29

©1988 Jack T. Chick.

Alberto part 6, *Crusaders* vol. 17. **THE PROPHET Guest Review by Rev. Rich Lee:** (©1988.) For an unknown reason, the inking in this issue is not Fred Carter's, but another unknown artist. The inking appears to only be a tracing over the coloring in order to provide a border. The poor artistic quality is disappointing in light of the vividly detailed inked features in prior issues. This issue ends *The Crusaders* series with no memorable images other than the cover.

The story begins in Beirut, Lebanon in 1983. A reporter named Rosco can't wait to leave because the shelling is driving him nuts. He has one last assignment, which is to do a report in the streets of Beirut. Muslim fanatics accost him and threaten to kill him. After Rosco's return to Los Angeles, he runs into Tim Clark, who knew him back in Vietnam (a clever tie-in to volume 1 of *The Crusaders*). Tim introduces Rosco to Jim Carter and Alberto, who doesn't miss this opportunity to tell this reporter "the truth" about Islam he learned while a Jesuit priest.

In 570 A.D., Muhammad was born in Mecca, Saudi Arabia. He founded Islam after he received his call from Allah. Alberto promises, "What I'm going to tell you is the most incredible story of intrigue you will ever hear." After he gives a brief overview of how Islam supposedly came into existence, Alberto says that the Vatican needed to create a weapon to eliminate "both the Jews and the true Christian believers who refused to accept Roman Catholicism."

Basically, many Arabs who converted to Roman Catholicism were seen by the Vatican as useful tools to report information to Rome. The Vatican wanted to create a "messiah" who would unite the Arabs, and thus eventually create an army to capture Jerusalem for the Vatican. An Arabian widow named Khadijah was a Roman Catholic who retired to a convent. She was commissioned to find a young man who could be used by the Vatican to build up a new religion for the Arabs. She met and married Muhammad. Eventually, Muhammad's religious visions were the basis for the Koran. (They were interpreted by Khadijah's Catholic cousin.) Other unpublished works from Muhammad are in the hands of high ranking Ayatollahs in the Islamic faith that contain information that links the Vatican to the creation of Islam. According to Alberto's recollection of his teacher, Cardinal Augustine Bea, "Both sides have so much information on each other...that if exposed, it would create such a scandal, it would cause a major disaster for both religions." The Vatican created Islam and financed the Arab armies for the purposes of eliminating Jews and "true Christians," protect Roman Catholics, and capture Jerusalem for the Pope. However, the Muslims betrayed the Pope and kept Jerusalem for themselves. Later, the Muslims wanted to capture Europe. The Pope in turn built up the Crusades to fight the Muslims.

Rosco asks Alberto, "Dr. Rivera, wasn't it a Muslim who shot the pope?" Alberto responds, "Oh, yes. The Jesuits planned that very well. A lot was to be gained by that incident." What could be gained? Well, since it was a Muslim who shot the pope, Muslims around the world were humiliated to think that "one of their own shot the one representing the prophet Jesus on this earth...that the Ayatollahs sent condolences and apologies to the pope." Furthermore, the would-be assassin of Pope John Paul II in 1981 was one of Europe's top hit men and an expert marksmen.

"He fired his weapon at a distance of only ten feet. Each bullet hit the pope below the navel. You see, Rosco, he had no intention of killing the pope. He was simply following the instructions of the Jesuits. The upshot was when the world saw the pope forgive Mehmet Ali Agca for shooting him...almost one billion Muslims had nothing but admiration for 'His Holiness.' ...The Whore of Revelation 17 will stop at nothing to gain her ends, including shooting one of her own popes!"

This story of intrigue is captivating, in spite of the shoddy inking and incomplete feel of this volume. The unfinished artwork makes this volume end this series on a down note... but rumor has it Carter will do more once the movie is complete. Grade **C** for Conquering Jerusalem!

KING OF KINGS—THE BIBLE IN PICTURES **Guest Review by Rev. Rich Lee:**(©1980.) This comic is twice the size (64 pages) of *The Crusaders* series, and was the first issue under *The Sword Series*. (*The Big Betrayal* was the second and last.) This is undoubtedly the reason why current printings of both comics are now independent "stand alone" comics which are no longer a part of any series. The emblem *The Sword Series* is removed from the current printings.

Simply put, this is a very abridged version of selected Bible stories adapted in comic book form. The Old Testament portion begins with the creation and fall of Lucifer. Unrecorded in the Bible is the event of fallen angels becoming grotesque demons. The serpent in the Garden of Eden is a weasel who loses his legs after God curses him.

The stories of Cain and Abel, Noah's ark, the fall of Sodom and Gomorrah, and Joseph with his brothers are recounted in several pages. The story of Moses and the plagues of Egypt, the Exodus, and giving of the Ten Commandments is told in the remainder of the Old Testament portion. The New Testament focuses upon the Gospel accounts on the birth of Jesus, his temptation in the wilderness, the Last Supper, the crucifixion and his resurrection. An interesting interlude tells the reader how Satan hatched up the veneration of the Virgin Mary with the advent of the Roman Catholic Institution. "Wars would be fought over this little Jewish maiden, and bloody executions and tortures of Christians and Jews would take place, all in her name." A killer waiving a spike in his upraised hand yells "Die, you dog...for the Blessed Virgin!"

The epistles of Paul are ignored since they don't really convey sequential stories. *King of Kings* concludes with a Dispensationalist fundamentalist interpretation of the book of Revelation. Surprisingly, the antichrist's picture doesn't resemble the pope in the newest version of this comic, unlike the updated version of *The Beast* tract. The last frame shows Jesus submitting to his Father after the 1,000 year reign of Christ on earth.

King of Kings: The Bible in Pictures is Chick's only single volume work that shows a full color chronology of main Bible stories in one volume. This is a precursor to what is promised in *The Light Of The World* movie. Grade **B** for Bible Adaptation!

concede the utter greatness of this comic as effective Protestant propaganda. Chick's goal was to resurrect Chiniquy's old fundy cult favorite (even houses like Revell and Zondervan had published it periodically) and present it in a way that would give it the greatest number of readers possible. On this level, Jack succeeded magnificently. The story is basically that of a priest who rose from humble beginnings in Canada to worldwide fame as a temperance crusader and eventually was converted to Protestantism. (Contrary to what you read sometimes, Chiniquy was very much a real, historical individual: I once saw a detailed bio of him in a very old *ENCYCLOPEDIA BRITANNICA* which gave particular attention to his temperance efforts in Canada.) Jack spends a great deal of time developing Chiniquy's relationship to Abraham Lincoln and his theories about Abe's murder in this adaptation: they actually comprise a much smaller part of Chiniquy's original book. Still, they are very entertaining—at least as much as Oliver Stone's *JFK* and equally as dramatic! Mention must be made of Carter's artwork, which is amazingly precise in its period detail and epic in it scope. I think that the *BIG BETRAYAL* and *TITANIC* are his very best work and truly showcase his awesome power as a sequential artist. My choice for best panel: Carter's depiction of the exact moment of Lincoln's fatal wound! It was so real I thought I HEARD the deadly Derringer go off! If you've never read this one, I actually envy you! You've some great entertainment to look forward to! Grade: **A+** for Alcoholic Jesuits!

©1981 Jack T. Chick.

THE BIG BETRAYAL Guest Review by Steve Trainor: (©1981.) In the early eighties, long before "graphic novels" were the rage, Chick outdid himself in presenting this 64-page blockbuster adaptation of Charles Chiniquy's old anti-Catholic book *Fifty Years In The "Church" Of Rome*. With what is arguably Fred Carter's best art ever, Chick moves Father Chiniquy's long, meandering narrative along at a breakneck pace and proves that he is one of the most underrated ideological propagandists of the entire twentieth century. (Judging from his scant autobiographical references, I think even he would consider that a compliment.) I don't care if you disagree with every page of it—if you are honest, you WILL

At this time, there was a prophet of God, who **hated** the Assyrians.

His name was Jonah.

©1988 Jack T. Chick.

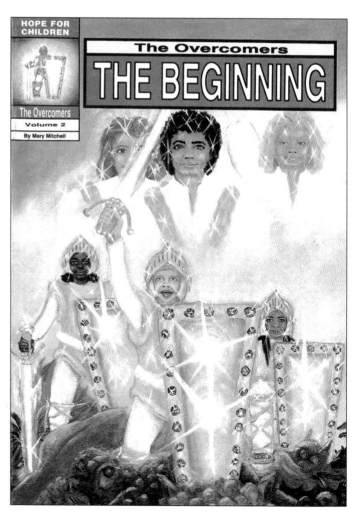

JONAH Review: (©1994.) This comic book is special for several reasons. It's the only Chick comic currently out of print (besides *The Overcomers,* which is an entirely different can of worms). The high cost of producing it on glossy stock made it too expensive. Other Chick comics feature Fred Carter illustrations with color added. *Jonah* features full color Carter *paintings* and the result is colorful indeed. According to those who spoke with Chick about it, *Jonah* was originally slated to be a short movie about the prophet. Fred Carter paintings would relate the story, almost like a slide show with music and narration. But Chick decided to expand the project into a movie about the Bible in general (due out in October of 2003). The paintings from the abandoned *Jonah* movie were used to comprise this comic. So readers can basically get a "sneak preview" of the movie by viewing the comic book.

There are several gross scenes. Jonah getting digested inside the shark, and Jesus getting crucified are both rather graphic. (Jesus is practically sliced to ribbons.) Also of interest are the crossover images used from the tract of the same topic (*First Jaws*). At least ten panels reappear in the comic. Carter probably painted over these illustrations, because they look identical except for small details. The most glaring example is when Jonah is tossed into the sea (comic page 11, tract page 9). In the tract, readers can see Jonah's shipmates in the background tossing him in the ocean, but in the comic, the background is ocean waves only. The tract was ©1985, while the comic was printed in 1994. The early version of the tract cover uses an overhead shot of Jonah as the shark approaches from beneath. Later tract covers (probably after the comic was completed) use a side profile of Jonah being swallowed, the same image used on the comic book cover. This comic is well worth having to compare to both the tract, and other comic books. It gives a good idea what Chick would be producing if unbound by fiscal restraints, plus an exciting glimpse of what's in store in the movie. Grade: **A** for Awesome Artwork. **Out of print.**

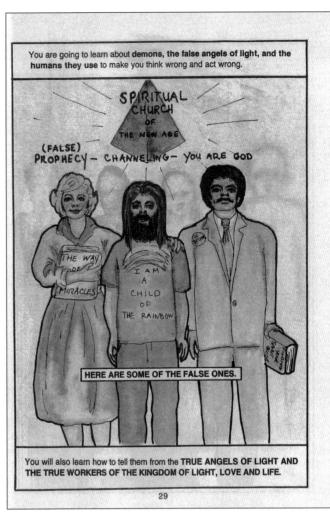

You are going to learn about **demons, the false angels of light, and the humans they use** to make you think wrong and act wrong.

SPIRITUAL CHURCH OF THE NEW AGE

(FALSE) PROPHECY — CHANNELING — YOU ARE GOD

THE WAY OF MIRACLES

I AM A CHILD OF THE RAINBOW

HERE ARE SOME OF THE FALSE ONES.

You will also learn how to tell them from the **TRUE ANGELS OF LIGHT AND THE TRUE WORKERS OF THE KINGDOM OF LIGHT, LOVE AND LIFE.**

29

THE OVERCOMERS Comics Review: (Art by Mary Mitchell ©1987/88.) One of the most odd-ball items Chick ever published was an obscure set of four comics called *The Overcomers*. These full color 32 page comics are universally disdained by Chick fans for their horrible artwork and dumbed-down narration. Mary Mitchell isn't the worst artist ever, but having her follow the incredible Fred Carter is like concluding a Jimi Hendrix concert with Tiny Tim. (If you don't know who Tiny Tim was, I envy you.) All four comics were quietly retired in 1991. They didn't sell very well. They are certainly difficult to find today and extremely rare. However, they are also low demand items, so the prices belie their scarcity. The four titles are *The Escape, The Beginning, Blood of Love,* and *Children of Light*.

Fortunately, there are several redeeming aspects to this series as well. Some feel they are so bad, they are actually good. Could this set be to comics what *Plan Nine From Outer Space* was to film? They certainly match schlock director Ed Wood's standard for dialog. Consider the stilted language uttered on page 25 of volume 1: "Thank God for the children of the Kingdom of Light who fight for their brothers and sisters in the family of God." "Yes, and join us as watchers." What exactly does this *mean?* And what the heck are watchers? When Rebecca Brown talked about watchers, they were demons hiding in pictures, but now, just a few years later, they're suddenly good guys? That's almost as inconsistent as *Plan Nine's* weird camera jumps back and forth to the cemetery, switching from day to night, then back to day again within the same time frame. So much for continuity.

The Overcomers also has its share of monsters (demons). Some of the critters are half way scary too. But like *Plan Nine's* monsters, they never quite make the grade. No matter how good the drawing or make-up, it's difficult to get frightened when the rest of the story is so silly.

Speaking of Rebecca Brown, her spiritual warfare beliefs permeate this series. The central premise is that God sends angels down to protect people from a demon infested world—so long as they evoke his name. "Don't be scared," the deliverance minister-maiden assures the kids, "OUR LORD JESUS, THE TRUE MASTER OF THE UNIVERSE, made it possible for us to have power over them. In the name of Jesus Christ, go!" (The demons scatter on command—page 28, vol. 2.) Guardian angels stand guard around the clock. Jesus summons some on page 13 of vol. 1 by saying, "I have called you to Me because I have chose you to take care of these new children of the Father. You will stay with them always, protecting and watching over them." So apparently, angels spend decades away from Heaven doing sentry duty on Earth. It's a far cry from paradise.

Kids are also told they can get anything if they pray for it right. A youngster explains to his friends, "The BELIEVING ONES said that we have a new Father, the Father of Jesus, and if we ask HIM anything in the Name of Jesus, we'll get what we ask for. IF we BELIEVE that He hears us." (page 15, vol. 1.) Let's hope none of them try to fly like an angel off the roof...

No Chick reader is too young to learn about conspiracies. Page 29 of vol. 2 says, "You are going to learn about demons, the false angels of light, and the humans they use to make you think wrong and act wrong." A pyramid symbol is labeled, "Spiritual Church of the New Age. (False) prophecy—channeling—You are God." A group of New-agers, Jesus People (complete with a "I am a child of the rainbow" T-shirt) and Spirit Guide guru stand above the statement, "Here are some of the false ones."

None of the humans look quite right. Their eyes are too big and the open mouths look like chopped liver. Jesus is always presented with a silver dollar sized hole in his hands. Not a scab, not a scar, but a GIANT GAPING HOLE! No wonder he sees everything; he couldn't cover his eyes if he tried.

The most grotesque cover of all Chickdom is definitely vol. 3, *Blood of Love*. It shows nothing but the arm of Jesus with the large hole punched through the palm and a river of blood pouring out of it. Parents had to have a strong stomach to buy it for their kids.

It's difficult to decide whether to love or hate this series. Many do both. They love to hate it. Yet they still collect it whenever possible. If it isn't as bad as *Plan Nine From Outer Space*, then it's at least as bad as *Bride of the Monster*, and earning second place in **any** contest is nothing to sneer at—except that it happens to be the "worst ever" contest. Grade **D+** for Disastrous Drawings. **Out of print.**

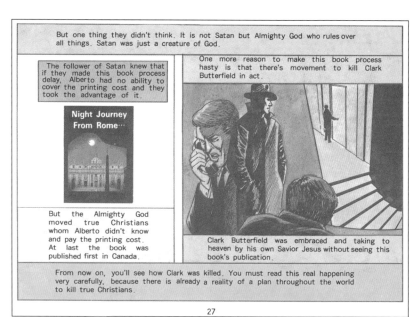

© Alberto Rivera.

Alberto part 7. ***THE GREAT HOLOCAUST I* Review:** (Published by AIC, *not* Chick Publications.) Why include a non-Chick publication in the reviews? Because it's written and published by Alberto, that's why! The cover is really cool, but the rest pales in comparison to the professional quality of Chick's comics. The front shows a montage of what looks like Nazi scientist mixing poisons, secret agents dragging off victims, and Catholics burning heretics. The first two pages are pretty sobering too. They show ancient wood carvings of various tortures used on heretics. Several are particularly graphic with disturbing captions. "Some had their arms cut off"..."A believer and his skin flaked off"..."Some had their mouth slit to their ears"..."Some their bellies burnt till their bowels fell out." Enough already! And this is just the first two pages!

The rest can't possibly top that. It's basically a story of the trials and tribulations of Clark Butterfield after he decides to abandon the Catholic Priesthood and join forces with Alberto...at the expense of his own life (his doctor murdered him). Although he did get his book, *Night Journey From Rome* published, so it wasn't a complete loss. We also get lots of Catholic conspiracies revealed along the way, especially the Jesuits (but you probably guessed that part by now).

Of particular interest in an appearance by Jack Chick (or at least his stand-in). It only *infers* that it is Chick, and of course, it doesn't really look like him. It says, "Chick editor's desk LA...Chick's publisher told me that they couldn't publish Clark's but they didn't tell the exact reason. This still a mistery [sic] to me until this day." Give him a break, Alberto. After all, Chick printed six more of your comics than anyone else did!

The artwork is pedestrian but what is really substandard is all the broken English. (Or maybe that's what makes it worthwhile.) Here's some dialog used as a bus driver sweeps the bus: "Too dirty! What's this? Ah! This is a comic book!" (page 3) Or this narration: "Then he thought he found the worth living and thanked to Mary and his god of Catholic Church." (page 10) Or how about this jewel: "It was shocked to him. Teacher told bad things of many Roman Pope and the church's struggle with the sin." If you have dyslexia, it will be much easier to read this comic, and if you don't have it, you probably will by the time you finish reading. Where was the translator/ proof reader for this project?

There are usually many out-of-register images, making portions of this comic look like they were intended for reading with 3-D glasses. (Maybe I should try some, they may reveal a secret code or something.)

This comic also contains Alberto's strange assertion that "Knights of Columbus was founded by Roman Vatican when Columbus discovered the American continent. In fact, Columbus was also a Jesuits' priest." (page 31). This, despite the fact that the founder of the Jesuits was only one-year-old when Columbus sailed to America. Oh well, perhaps the date-checker was the same person who checked the grammar.

Without boring you with the details, let's just say this comic is quite funny, because of the details—or rather, lack of attention paid to them. **It is still being sold at the time of this writing.** So get one before the Jesuits burn them all as heretic fuel. The back advertises the sequel, *Alberto* part 8: *The Plot of Holocaust,* but AIC never got around to printing this comic. Grade: **B** for Burnt offerings.

Ideas for "soul winners" from Chick's 1986 Winter catalog.

The Other Comics

Chick also produced two graphic novels and several books heavily illustrated with comics. Although they lack the vivid color of his *Crusader* and *Sword* series, they are great reading and fun additions to your Chick collections. Several of these books are out of print, yet inexpensive copies are still available if you are able to locate them. The out of print titles have routinely turned up in auctions for under $15 (except *The Battle*, which is very rare and hasn't turned up for sale recently at all.)

©1972 Jack T. Chick.

Facing page: A small portion of Fred Carter's parody poster of the Rise of Man.
©1973 Jack T. Chick.

THE BATTLE **Review:** A small (4 1/8 x 5") book reprinting seven of Chick's tracts plus a twelve page story called, "The Books That Changed A City." (The "books" are, of course, Chick tracts.) The seven tracts are reprinted two pages per book page. The tracts featured are *This Was Your Life*, *The Passover Plot*, *One Way!*, *Creator or Liar?*, *The Fool!*, *Frame-up*, and *The Assignment*. The twelve page narrative includes a couple of Fred Carter's pictures not found elsewhere. (One has a crook busting into a house and threatening the family inside with a gun. The other has a longhaired hippy leaning against a motorcycle and reading *The Poor Revolutionist*). The story is strong PR about how great tracts are, written by Bob Owen for Bob Garcia (no relation to Jerry, who probably modeled as the freak leaning against the road hog). The cover to this book sports a great color image of demons and angels fighting around a mortal smelling a rose, oblivious to the invisible struggle surrounding him. This book is mostly reprinted material, but is surprisingly rare. No sales have been observed. Grade: **B** for Battling spirits. **Out of print.**

GOING BANANAS? ISN'T EVERYBODY? ...HERE'S HELP! Guest review by Rev. Rich Lee: (Art by Fred Carter ©1979 Jack T. Chick.) This 224 page book is a companion to *A Solution to The Marriage Mess.* It basically is an illustrated novel that acknowledges Fred Carter as the artist. This classic is no longer in print. The book's seven chapters feature the story of Janet and Jerry Roberts who take in extended family members. They are unsaved heathen who drive this Christian family "bananas," resulting in Janet's breakdown.

Janet's niece Cathy had abortions, drinks vodka, is a victim of incest from her good-for-nothing father, and she hates her mother. The nephew Freddy is a foul-mouthed brat who smokes and also hates his parents. Doreen is their dysfunctional mother, who crashes in on poor Janet and Jerry. When Freddy gets saved at church, Doreen goes berserk. She hates Janet and Jerry for "doing this" to her son. Later, Doreen's creepy husband, Chester, comes over to feed mud to little Freddy for daring to become a Christian. "YOU @!!*#! LITTLE FOOL...I WISH YOU WERE BACK SIZZLING YOUR BRAINS ON DRUGS INSTEAD OF HUMILIATING YOUR MOTHER AND ME LIKE THIS," Chester shouts. Nice parents.

In true Chick fashion a la *The Next Step,* Freddy takes his persecution without resisting while the mud oozes down his face. "(**GASP...GASP** HE'S MY LORD AND MY GOD...(**GASP**) AND I LOVE HIM MORE EVERY MINUTE!" Gotta face it, this is more fun than an hour of the Jerry Springer Show!

If this isn't bad enough, Janet's and Doreen's mother imposes on them. She is a dominating hag on the rag who is the source of this family mess. A Christian psychiatrist, Dr. Morgan, gives the sane remedy: get rid of Mom! Now! She is the one responsible for messing up her daughters Janet and Doreen all these years. Janet has to go for treatment, while her mother insists on making herself useful being the codependent, walking incubator she is. Jerry musters up the courage to kick the old battle-ax out on the street while she manipulates the situation in her favor. "YOU UNGRATEFUL LITTLE @!!*#! HOW DARE YOU SAY A THING LIKE THAT TO ME!!...I WILL NOT LEAVE MY BABY!" She eventually caves in and leaves before poor Janet suffers a seizure. "GOODBYE, JANET...I HOPE YOU'RE HAPPY BREAKING MY HEART LIKE THIS...BUT THEN YOU ALWAYS WERE SELFISH." Jeez, enough already. Later, Janet goes for Gestalt therapy and pretends that a chair is her mother. Dr. Morgan tells her to tell her "mother" off. "I'M NOT CRAZY..." says Janet in therapy. "IF THE TRUTH CAME OUT, YOU'D BE THE CRAZY ONE!" Janet is cured and eventually helps others as she was helped. Interestingly enough, many Christians do not believe in telling off their parents no matter how messed up and controlling they are. Jerry didn't even want to kick out Janet's mother in the first place and told Dr. Morgan, "We're trying to show our Christian testimony to her mom." The good Christian doctor says, "What's more important?...Your wife's sanity or your Christian wit-

ness?" This is a surprise, since fundamentalist Christians tend to go for the Christian witness over keeping one's sanity. Being sane is more important than witnessing! And this comes from Chick! Of course, if Mommy dearest had been a Christian, you can bet the good doctor would have insisted she stay, no matter what the consequences. *Haw-haw!*

Another shock is that this book endorses Christian psychology and psychiatry. Most fundamentalist Christians view psychology and psychiatry with suspicion since the founders of these disciplines were atheists and secular humanists like Sigmund Freud, Carl Rogers, and Albert Ellis, who strongly disliked religion. In fact, when this book was published (1979), traditional psychology and psychiatry were openly hostile to religion and blamed it for neurosis. Born-again Christians tend to believe that these disciplines are unscriptural substitutes for repentance and prayer. In fact, if Christians are openly blasted by their mothers, as in Janet's case, they should happily put up with it and not resist lest they be guilty of dishonoring their parents! If the parents want to dominate the household, then they "should" because parental authority never ends over one's life. Hence, the fundamentalist Christian subculture is filled with forty and fifty-year-olds who still live with their dominating parents in trailer parks. Now THAT'S bananas! Grade "**B**" for Bananas! **Out of print.**

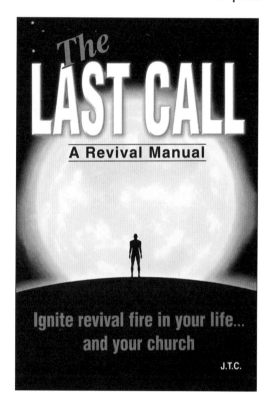

THE LAST CALL Guest review by Ray Ruenes: This book has been around as early as 1963 (but most recently reprinted in standard paperback format since 1978) and is thus among one of the older publications that Chick is still making available. It's full of text and cartoons, and has enough of the latter to fill 3 to 5 tracts. (Though none of the cartoons are reprints from tracts. Most are just a few images in length.) The text is lifted from an old preacher whom Jack obviously was influenced by, Charles G. Finney, who's material I just read prior to starting Chick's tribute. Finney's sermons are, to say the least, very hard hitting, not unlike Chick's tracts. It is strange to see Finney emphasize that churches drive home the message that the Christian fear sin more than the ultimate result of sin (eternal hell), because it seems like Jack is always using hell rather than the reason for it to frighten readers into accepting Jesus as both their Savior and their Lord.

In any case, get the book. The "false Jack Chick portrait" which is provided in *The Imp* (taken from the *Battle Cry* newsletter) is located in this book. (And yes, that bald guy is definitely NOT Jack Chick.) The recent paperback version of *The Last Call* is around $3.50, which should be the same price as *The Next Step*, though this isn't quite as cartoon-heavy as that book. Still, it has many Chick cartoons scattered throughout it in a non-tract and non-sequential format that brilliantly illustrate the concepts presented in Finney's accompanying text. This book was originally sold as a giant tract (8 1/4 x 5 1/2") with over 64 pages before being converted into its current paperback format.

The first four images in the book feature a classic Chick-view of the future. Image one shows a little old lady going door-to-door asking how many Bibles each family owns. Image two shows the cops confiscating the Bibles. Image three has the cops rounding up all the Christians. Image four shows the Christians up against the wall before a firing squad within a concentration camp. That alone is worth the $3.95 retail! Grade **B+** for Busted! **Still in print.**

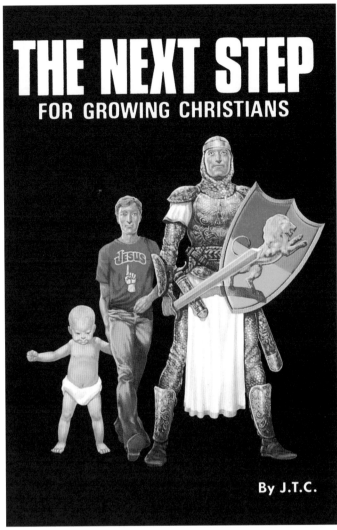

THE NEXT STEP Tract/book review: Is it a tract or is it a book? You decide! From the outside it looks like a 64 page soft cover book. Inside, the cartoons and text are laid out like tracts (3 rows per page). The first one is *The Birth of the Bible*. It is the only chapter with artwork by Fred Carter and focuses on how the early churches determined real scripture from Satan's forgeries. The early editions of *The Next Step* tell this story in twelve tract-sized panels, but the recent edition reduces that number to eleven. Half of the artwork is redrawn as well. The earlier editions tell about Eusebius (Emperor Constantine's chief religious advisor) and how he separated real scripture from false. Current editions leave out the name of Eusebius and one of his four categories, "the 'disputed books:' James, II Peter, Jude, II & III John which, though included in his own bibles, were doubted by some."

Why such details are omitted in the new edition is uncertain. Perhaps it was too confusing. It's more likely that after speaking with Alberto, Chick's views on Constantine soured. (Alberto thought Constantine still worshipped Apollo, died unsaved, and emblazoned ankhs instead of crosses on his roughnecks' shields.)

Chapters 2 and 3 are reprints of *Don't Read That Book* and *The Secret of Prayer*. (You can read their reviews in the tract section.)

Chapter 4 is entitled *Love*. Although it is only 9 tract pages long (16 panels) it's one of the funniest in the book. Some of the humor is intentional, and some not. It starts out with a fat, balding slob putting the moves on Billy's drunk mom in the family room. Billy's friend asks if that's his dad. "No—That's some creep she picked up at the bar!" As the unshaven cigar-chomping loser pulls mom in for a kiss, she cackles, "Haw haw—stop it Harry!" The bum replies, "My name is Ernie!" Billy splits with his longhaired friend because "She makes me sick!" With such loose motherly morals, who can blame poor Billy? Unfortunately, he's a chip off the old block, spending his spare time mugging people.

The two delinquents smash a Christian over the head with a chain and steal his wallet. They're excited to find $28 but the bleeding man begs them to come back... Does he need his medical alert card? Or someone to call an ambulance? Heck no, he wants to give them more money that they overlooked in his other pocket. Billy asks, "Are you crazy?" (Please note: Crazy people never realize they are crazy because they're too crazy to realize what crazy means.) The good Christian insists he's NOT crazy, "but I love you kids with Christ's love!" (So maybe he's crazy for Christ.) Lucky for him, it's contagious because the two hoods immediately sit down and want to convert.

Billy runs home and busts inside declaring he's been saved. Evil Ernie doesn't appreciate the unannounced interruption and punches Billy out. Sleazy mom yells, "Stop it Harry!"—and gets the running gag response, "My name is Ernie!" (We only see her hand, probably because she's naked by now.) The cops arrive and ask Billy if he wants to press charges. In true

45

Chick style, Billy decides to play the martyr and take the abuse without griping. "I don't hate him. All he needs is Jesus in his life." Remember, Chick Christians rarely tattle. They take their muggings, child abuse, and wife abuse with a stiff upper lip... Even though that lip is usually split and bleeding. Billy has a bloody mouth, nose, and black eye, but he quickly heals and sets out to convert mom. Scrubbing the floor for her seems to do the trick. In one panel, she forgets to think using a thought cloud, and instead thinks aloud using a standard word balloon, "I can't stand it. The is kid is driving me nuts—He really does love me!" (Shhh mom! He's right next to you. He can read your balloon!) Two panels later, she's on her knees with Billy. Praise the Lord.

Chapter 5 is called *The Enemy,* and explains Satan's sinister plan for humanity. It's 22 tract pages long (37 panels) and would have fit perfectly in a real tract. But it was never issued as one as far as anyone can tell. More's the pity, because it provides lots of insight into Chick's biblical views. Satan is one bad dude. But he started out as "the most beautiful creature ever made... His beauty was so great that he had built-in pipes for music." Then pride made him rebel and he was exiled along with one-third of the other angels for his trouble. They were "given a new location; the atmospheric heaven is now Satan's domain." (And you thought he was in hell? Silly you.) Satan uses a variety of tricks to attack the weak and disobedient Christian: "Loving the world...taking one's eyes off the Lord...pride." Chick states that Satan does not attack a Christian without permission. (Is this supposed to make us feel better?) The story of Job is recounted where God lets Satan devastate devout Job's life just to see if he'll crack. It brings back memories of the dark comedy *Trading Places,* where two rich guys decide to trade Dan Aykroyd's luxurious life with Eddie Murphy, a down and out street hustler. The motive for ruining Aykroyd's life is to settle a $1 wager. Why would an omniscient God need to test people like that if he already knows the outcome? Chick says, "If he is walking in the Lord, it is always for God's Glory and the Christian's own good." Well, that settles that.

Chick also says "Satan's greatest achievement is that no one believes he exists. A great number of theological graduates do not believe in a personal devil." He then goes on to list 34 satanic religions and gimmicks, including ESP, Ouija Boards, Christian Science, T.M., and of course, the Roman Catholic System. He warns of another sneaky trap: "Satan has liberal pastors scattered throughout the Protestant churches... These are the twentieth century Sadducees." He gives a checklist of 7 litmus test beliefs that liberal pastors pervert or deny. #7 is "Everlasting punishment in the lake of fire for the unsaved... If the pastor denies any of the above, then get out and find a Bible preaching church." Chick paraphrases a few prophecies and asserts "Demon possession is more prevalent today than during the time of Jesus." He winds up on a hopeful note, however, showing Satan praising God while kneeling in the flames of hell. It may be another 1,000 years before this happens, but the important thing is that God gets the last laugh.

Chapter 6 is *Pitfalls.* It's the shortest chapter in the book (only six tract pages or 9 panels long). It shows a boss eavesdropping on his employee, admiring what a fine Christian the man is. He considers becoming saved himself. But then, a **horrible thing** happens. The Christian reaches down and places a box of paper clips in his pocket. "Why that @!!!** thief! I'll get that phony on the next layoff! Christian my foot! It'll be a frosty Friday in H— before I ever become one!" Chick then warns readers that, "Some Christian workers have been laid aside because they failed to have a partner accompany them on a visit to a person of the opposite sex." (Yep, that'll do it all right.) He points out that King David was 50 years old when he saw Bathsheba. Kinda kinky...

Chapter 7 *(Called Out)* is the most bland chapter in the book. It's only 11 pages/panels long and the artwork is pretty basic. It depicts a clean cut guy getting pulled from a group of protesters onto a pedestal by a Christian. He's told what he has to do to stay on the pedestal. The only funny parts are various protest signs in the audience: "boycott garlic" and "kids lib" in particular. A real dud.

Chapter 8 is the last and longest chapter (34 tract pages in length). It's called *Warn Them* and it's a how-to guide for converting the heathen. The first five panels are the best: A Christian stands before a washed out bridge in a storm. A car approaches and he considers warning them. But then he concludes, "I don't want to be branded as a doom merchant. The bad news might upset him. Besides that, he may not want to be my friend because of my fanatical views." The car races off the bridge into the darkness, passengers screaming, "YAAAAAAH!" The rest of the tract is less dramatic. Basic Bible outlining tips are provided, along with ideas on how to prepare for your ambush session with your neighbor. Just such a session is demonstrated.

A Christian approaches his "target" as the unsuspecting neighbor rakes leaves. In a rare endorsement of deception, Chick urges Christians NOT to say what's really on their mind: "Never hit them cold with a question like 'have you been saved?' Talk about the weather or their job for a few minutes." Then Chick suggest that you pop *the question*... "If you were to die tonight, are you sure you would go to heaven? Any reply less than 100% certainty is a sign you must present the Roman Road." Needless to say, the neighbor takes the bait and devours the message. No leaves get raked but another soul is saved. One panel gives some helpful hints, including "Go neatly dressed—you represent the King of Kings," and "Watch your breath—use breath mints." The last third of the story is a shameless pitch for that greatest of all witnessing tools, *Chick Tracts!*

Your Chick tract collection is really not complete without this book. It's only $3.50, so money is no object. Though the quality of the stories within it varies, they go a long way in explaining exactly where Chick is coming from. Grade **B** for Bargain. **Still in print.**

2.95

A SOLUTION TO... **THE MARRIAGE MESS**

By J.T.C.

YOU *CAN'T* BE TALKING ABOUT US!

BECAUSE OUR MARRIAGE IS *PERFECT*... AND SO IS OUR FAMILY!

WE HAVE ONLY ONE LITTLE PROBLEM...

WE CAN'T *STAND* EACH OTHER!

A SOLUTION TO THE MARRIAGE MESS Review: (Art by Fred Carter © 1978 Jack T. Chick.) This is an out of print book containing 224 pages of black and white illustrations with word balloons telling a serial story. There's only one panel per page. It measures a little larger than 8 inches high and 5 inches wide. It allows the reader to really appreciate the detail to Carter's line art. (This is perhaps the only book that publicly acknowledges Carter as the other Chick artist.) The story is about a missionary who returns from Africa and stays with his sister's family for a month. During that time, he tries to convert all of them to hard-core "real" Christians. He's flawless and dedicated in every way, but *they* are phony Christians and basically selfish. The father drinks and watches the babes, the mother is a fat slob, the brat smokes pot, the daughter sleeps around, etc. etc. Of course missionary Mark straightens them all out by the end of the tale. It's funny to see how many times he butts into even the most touchy of topics to dole out his Biblical wisdom, yet they never

turn on him and yell, "This is none of your #%*& business! You're just staying here for free so BUTT OUT!"

A classic example is when the father confronts his daughter about being pregnant. (Of course, Mark already knows.) The daughter doesn't know who the father is, only that it's "one of the boys from Church." Voices rise and tempers flair. It's the perfect time for Mark to stick his nose into their family business: "Excuse me for butting in, Frank. What would it be like if Christ wouldn't forgive us?" Two hours later, everyone is holding hands and hugging. Time for Mark to work his magic again... "I know this is a *very* delicate situation, but I'm *only* trying to help... Let's assume the baby *is* on the way... Are you going to keep it?" Frank says no way, but Mark declares abortion is murder. He then reads a little diary about what it's like to be a baby growing inside the tummy when your mother suddenly aborts you. This makes the daughter declare she is NOT going to have an abortion no matter what. (Too bad Mark is leaving in a month. He won't be around to help raise the child. Oh well, back to Africa to help the foreigners!) In most homes, Mark's suitcases would be outside the door by now, but in THIS house, the family appreciates Mark's unsolicited Godly guidance.

A few chapters later, Mark notices Frank is watching a movie with a kissing scene. Oh-oh! This looks like a job for *Super Christian!* Mark bends a knee and prays, "Lord... Put the right words in my mouth... This is such an explosive and delicate subject..." Then he confronts Frank about his love life. When Frank confesses he hasn't made love to Mark's sister in a month and a half, Mark admonishes Frank: "In the Bible that's a *no, no,* Frank! Outside of illness... The only reason for you not making love is because of prayer and fasting!" A few pages later, Frank is thanking Mark for setting him straight. So Mark asks Frank's permission to give his wife a similar pep talk. Of course, Frank is delighted to give it. Hey, isn't that what in-laws are for???

Another great moment is when Frank is reading the newspaper and complaining about "what that idiot in the White house did today." Mark says, "you mean the Lord's Anointed?" Frank says he isn't talking about King David, but the President. Mark responds, "Frank, King Saul was the Lord's Anointed. So was Hitler and so is the President or any other world leader." Now maybe it's just me, but I can't help but imagine how much kinder and gentler the rhetoric of World War II would have been if all our propaganda posters referred to Hitler that way. "Stop the Lord's Anointed DEAD in his tracks! Buy War Bonds!" I dunno... It just doesn't seem to have the same punch.

But despite its *Leave it to Beaver* run amok premise, this book is a delight to read and probably helpful for new Christian couples. (But I wouldn't stake my guidance practice on it.) Several readers have noted that both the husband and wife look ten years younger by the end of the story. (Amazing what some good old-fashioned Biblical sex can achieve.) If you run across this somewhat obscure Chick book, my suggestion is to nab it. Grade **A** for Advice. **Out of print.**

Battle Cry:
The Bimonthly Newspaper

If you thought the tracts and comics were in-your-face, you ain't seen nothing yet! Battle Cry consisted of a no-holds barred full frontal attack on back-slidden churches, the ecumenical movement, the homosexual brainwashing agenda for schools, persecution of Protestants around the world, underhanded conspiracies, and much, much more!

To cover this unusual and often overlooked aspect of Chick collecting, let's turn over the reins to the Reverend Richard Lee. Rich is not only the President of the Chick Tract Club and an avid tract collector, he also maintains one of the very few complete Battle Cry newspaper archives. His knowledge of the history of Chick Publications and their various products has been an endless source of information and enthusiasm for yours truly. (Thanks Rich!)

Oh, and one other thing. Battle Cry is completely free to regular customers. Chick Publications even pays the postage! Where else can you find a deal like that? For the first couple of years, I collected them but rarely read them. Once I started, though, I was hooked. Read on and find out why!

Headline: "Attack on religious freedom stopped by Canadian Protestant League: Chick comics again flow freely into Canada," blares the front page headline of a newspaper. Chick Publications never garnered such self-promoting headlines in mainstream newspapers, but in Chick Publications' own paper, such headlines were frequent. The fact that Battle Cry began as a newspaper rather than a smaller newsletter (like it is now) is a statement in itself. Newspapers attract more attention! Most secular newspapers ignore the issues that Chick Publications considers important. With Chick Publications' own paper, it could feature banner headlines that dealt with matters fundamentalists were interested in. The headline "Catholic Leaders Pushing 'Perpetual Adoration' of Wafer Idol" would not likely appear in The Washington Post!

During the height of the "Alberto" controversy, Chick Publications lost revenue and credibility among Christian bookstores. Jack T. Chick's own side of the controversy, namely why he chose to attack "the Great Whore of Babylon" remained unheard. The year was 1983, and it seemed time for Chick to take his polemics against "Rome" to new heights. Since Crusader comics took at least a year to produce, it made sense that Chick could continue the campaign against rock music, evolution, Catholicism, and modern translations of the Bible with a newspaper that was published more frequently. Hence, Battle Cry was born!

The target audience for this bold newspaper was Chick's closest fans and supporters. Unlike the tracts that targeted unbelievers, Battle Cry reached an exclusive audience consisting of those who were Chick's mail order customers. Since two-thirds of Christian bookstores stopped carrying any Chick Publications material, Chick was forced to do more business via mail order. A bimonthly newspaper was an effective method to keep his most faithful customers informed and updated on his continuing battles as well as provide advanced previews of his newest tracts. Battle Cry met this need. There was no mistake as for whom it was intended: "A Christian Publication Serving the Bible-believing Protestants of the World" was printed on each issue. For a brief time, Battle Cry was available as a paid subscription, but eventually Chick Publications made it

available to all regular customers at no charge. George A. Collins has been the editor of Battle Cry since its inception and continues as the editor to this day. According to Collins, Battle Cry has a circulation of nearly 30,000 issues every two months.

Battle Cry featured many exclusive cartoons, like this one from the June 1984 issue. ©1984 Jack T. Chick.

Perhaps the most exclusive perk of maintaining a subscription is being treated to a framed religious cartoon by Chick included in almost every issue, a cartoon unavailable anywhere else. The cartoon usually lambasted Roman Catholic leaders, stereotyped hairy cross-dressing homosexuals, ecumenical Protestants, Muslims, rock musicians, and an ever-growing list of sexual deviants. Accompanying the cartoons was usually A Message From Jack Chick, one of the few places Chick spoke directly to the reader in the voice of the first person. The newspaper format also afforded enough room to reproduce new tracts in their entirety for future customers to preview. Almost every tract printed from 1984 through 1994 (when it changed to newsletter format) is first unveiled in Battle Cry.

Each issue always highlighted Roman Catholicism, but other subjects received attention as well. The New Age movement, Hinduism, and all modern English translations of the Bible were fair game. Long before disgraced homosexual/pedophile Catholic priests made national headlines in the mainstream news media, Chick was declaring their sins in Battle Cry such as in the May/June 1986 issue: "Catholic 'Church' fears million dollar losses due to sexual abuse of children by priests." Thus, in some respect, Battle Cry was prophetic!

"For we wrestle not against flesh and blood, but against principalities, against powers, against the rulers of the darkness of this world, against spiritual wickedness in high places."...Ephesians 6:12

This Scripture passage served as a banner across the top of Battle Cry during the years it was a newspaper. A drawing depicting a herald with a horn presumably rallying troops to battle served as the newspaper's icon. Photos accompanied the headlines similar to local city newspapers. Its theme of engaging in spiritual warfare, (enhanced by Dr. Rebecca Brown and Elaine) against the wiles of Satan never changed since its inception to the present time.

Facing page: Part of a three page cartoon by Fred Carter found only in the June issue of Battle Cry ©1984 Jack T. Chick.

"For we wrestle not against flesh and blood, but against principalities, against powers, against the rulers of the darkness of this world, against spiritual wickedness in high places"... *Eph. 6:12*

50¢ per copy

BATTLE CRY

Revised Edition Now Available by Jack T. Chick

THE ROYAL AFFAIR

"Am I therefore become your enemy, because I tell you the truth?" (Gal. 4:16) — March / April, 1993

IN THIS ISSUE

Columbian evangelicals sue to end special treatment of Catholic church in their country. Bishops outraged, claim nation has no right to cancel treaty with Vatican. See page 1 for details.

Human "guard dog" led to Christ by Chaplain Dann. Perhaps you know someone like him. See page 8.

Children taught homosexuality is normal in San Francisco schools. But no one teaches them that homosexuals die early. Will your children be next? See page 3.

Owning Bible can get you killed in Saudi Arabia. See page 4.

Praying to saints keeps Catholic people from ever meeting the true Christ. Here's why. See page 5.

Chick tracts help missionary in field that others consider "impossible." Many of you helped him do it. See page 1.

The path to perversion... the three steps that can destroy a generation. See page 3.

Two Cities Approve Homosexual Recruitment in Public Schools

One School Board objected and got fired

Although homosexuals in the military is disturbing enough, far more dangerous is their invasion of the kindergarten classroom.

Although few school districts nationwide are actually presenting this "alternate lifestyle" in their early childhood curriculum, New York City and San Francisco districts are testing the waters.

A far greater number of elementary and high school students learn about "same sex families" and how to "know if you are gay" in their family life curriculum.

Gary Bower, president of the Family Research Council says, "What is concerning parents is that children are being taught to see *as normal* a life style that for a great majority of people is not normal...." In their efforts to present sodomites as "normal," many schools like the one pictured, are inviting local homosexuals and lesbians into the class rooms.

There they are presented as just normal people who happen to live a little differently.

In the lower grades, books entitled "Heather Has Two Mommies" and "Daddy's Roommate" are used. In one, daddy is shown in bed with his roommate during the child's weekend visit with his father who is divorced from his mother.

Back home, the child questions his mother about what he saw and is reassured by her that it is all okay.

The other describes how two lesbians used artificial insemination by a "special doctor" to become mommies.

In the later grades, students view a 29-minute film called, "What If I'm Gay?" or receive materials such as "The Teenager's Bill of Rights."

These rights include: "...the right to decide whether to have sex and who to have it with" and the "Right to buy and use condoms."

Condoms are then described as "sexy" with glowing specifics about the fun of using them. Other materials laud homosexual conduct too revolting or unsanitary to quote.

In New York, the battle over this "Rainbow Curriculum" is raging

See **Two Cities,** page 3

George Olson/NYT Pictures

A lesbian couple, Terri Massin, left, and Lynn Levey, center, hold their "daughter," Maraya, during a recent visit to the San Francisco kindergarten class of Adeline Aramburo, right, where they read the class a story, "Gloria Goes to Gay Pride."

AIDS Video Educates Whole Congregation

Is it safe to hug someone with AIDS?

Will my baby be safe in the church nursery?

What should my reaction be to the people in our church with HIV?

Plenty of questions and a thoughtful discussion followed the recent viewing of the video *No Second Chance* at Upland (California) Community Foursquare Church.

Assistant Pastor Ron Hernandez, like many pastors, was looking for a Biblical perspective as well as the facts to minister to people that are HIV positive and those dying with AIDS related symptoms.

A member of the church had been diagnosed with HIV that had been contracted through IV drug use years ago.

This incident really brought the issue home and created an opportunity to inform and educate the congregation. But how?

His denomination had an AIDS policy statement that was factual and compassionate, but how does a pastor bring this issue to life for his congregation?

Rev. Hernandez' wife, Denise, knowing his quandary, obtained the video *No Second Chance* from Chick Publications and they viewed it together one evening.

They liked the Biblical perspective and the solid facts it gave on AIDS so well that they shared it with the senior pastor.

They agreed that it should be shown to the adults as well as the youth of their church.

A nurse who was a member of the congregation agreed to discuss the subject and answer questions after the video was shown.

Announcing the subject of the meeting ahead of time guaranteed a good turnout and focused attention during the showing. Afterward the

See **AIDS Video,** page 3

Ron Hernandez, Assistant Pastor, Upland Community Foursquare Church.

Vatican Concordat Challenged By Colombian Evangelicals

When the U.S. established diplomatic relations with the Vatican several years ago, proponents claimed that the relationship contained no religious overtones.

Opponents viewed it as a step toward giving up the precious religious freedom so dearly bought by our founding fathers. They said that the next step would be a concordat with the Vatican.

Few Americans today even know what a "concordat" is.

A struggle currently occurring in Colombia, South America is instructive.

July 4 is an independence day of sorts for Colombia.

On that date in 1991, this South American country of 32 million adopted a new national constitution that guarantees complete freedom and equality before the law to all religions and religious persons.

The first miracle is that such a constitution was even considered in a country where nearly 90 percent claim allegiance to the Roman Catholic Church.

The second miracle will be if it is fully implemented. For over a hundred years the Colombian government has pretty consistently implemented the conditions of the Concordat (agreement or treaty) made with the Vatican in 1887.

The treaty recognized Catholicism as the national religion and "an essential element of the social order."

It also granted judicial immunity to the clergy making it difficult if not impossible to try a Catholic priest in a civil court.

See **Concordat,** page 6

Missionary 'Plants' Nearly a Million Tracts in Taiwan

Using Chick tracts as a foundation, Missionary Ron Powell has developed a thriving outreach on a very difficult missionary field in Taiwan.

He says that some of his state-side associates claim that he "has a tract ministry," but he says that is just the springboard.

Besides handing out over 900,000 tracts since 1986, Powell and his family have put up 15,000 scripture posters in their area, and help translate and type a Bible correspondence course which is mailed to those who respond to the tract ministry.

Powell also mounts loudspeakers on the top of his jeep so that he can preach in the streets.

Two days a week he takes the jeep into the mountains to preach and give tracts to some tribal people where the only other "missionary" is a Jesuit priest who, Powell said, "threatened my life back in 1988!"

He has handed out 80,000 tracts to these mountain tribes.

All this is in addition to regular church services and a Bible school for converts.

In spite of Powell's supreme efforts, his field is hard plowing. Most of the people are Buddhists and the religion has an iron-like hold on the culture and families of the people.

When one gets saved, all the demonic forces of the family and society conspire to pull them back.

Many respond to the tracts and street preaching, only to lose the joy of salvation when the family turns on the pressure. Powell is heart broken when this happens.

One 38-year-old man was an example. He came to church for a while but finally told Powell that the pressure from his wife and family was too much and he never came back.

Powell believes that Chick tracts are an ideal way to penetrate the cultural resistance to the Gospel.

Even though he sees relatively few responses, he

See **Taiwan,** page 7

A CHRISTIAN PUBLICATION SERVING THE BIBLE-BELIEVING PROTESTANTS OF THE WORLD

Battle Cry premiered in October of 1983. In this issue, Jack Chick explained his rationale for printing a newspaper in the following words:

Dear Ones in Christ:

For years now, we have been on the receiving end of all kinds of accusations, name calling, and slander. We've even lost friendships and our reputations simply because we've been obedient to the Lord and kept quiet about the newspaper, magazine, TV and radio attacks. Our enemies have had a field day cutting us to shreds.

Many months ago, we went before the Lord about publishing our own small newspaper, and it was as though the Lord indicated we should be patient. We had appealed to many Christian newspapers to carry our ads promoting new books. But in each case, we were refused, even though many other publishers were given the privilege to do so.

The incredible letters telling of personal battles Christians were facing kept filling up our files, and it came upon our hearts to again go before the Lord to see if it was time for our little newspaper. This time, the answer was yes. And so, we are trying to launch our little paper called *Battle Cry,* which we'll produce about every two or three months, to share the other side of the picture.

You'll see the amazing power of the Vatican in its attempts to silence Chick Publications, and the subtle persecutions going on in the military and prisons against God's people. The big push is on to gag all Bible believing "Protestant" material. But Islamic, Jewish and Catholic material flows without interruption along with pornography. Yet we are blocked. Surely, we must be doing something right for this "great honor."

I sincerely hope you will enjoy reading some of the letters and the great variety of information that has come to us, and you will start seeing things in quite a different light. Keep praying for us as we continue to try publishing the finest quality Christian soulwinning tracts and books possible, to supply you as you serve our coming King.

Your brother in Christ,

Jack T. Chick, President
Chick Publications, Inc.

Why No Revival? ©1986 Jack T. Chick.

In the years that followed, *Battle Cry* never failed to deliver on these promises. The war against Satan's evils was well underway under direct orders from God Himself now that JTC had permission to print his own newspaper. Jack T. Chick was a true underdog without many defenders in the evangelical community. Some of his strongest unlikely allies were Pentecostals, who traditionally are the nemesis of traditional fundamentalists like Chick. Among media ministers, the only ones sympathetic to Chick Publications were Pastor Fred K.C. Price (who openly sells Chick materials in his television ministry bookstore), faith healing Pentecostal revivalist R.W. Schambach, and Pentecostal televangelist Jimmy Swaggart, who lost television outlets for his criticism of Roman Catholic dogma. Chick openly commended Swaggart in the December 1983 *Battle Cry* for preaching against the errors of Roman Catholicism.

Yet Chick basically stood alone. He had few friends and was losing them with greater frequency. The popular Christian radio call-in show, *The Bible Answerman* with famed Southern Baptist and counter-cult ministry *Christian Research Institute* founder Dr. Walter Martin, fielded questions on Chick Publications almost daily. Martin was usually snobbish about Chick tracts, advising listeners to toss them in the trash can or at very least, to take them with a grain of salt. So Chick had a tough time finding well-known Christians who would agree with his controversial views on Roman Catholicism, especially publically. Some *Battle Cry* articles criticized prominent televangelists such as Paul Crouch of the Trinity Broadcasting Network for compromising the true gospel by allowing priests and nuns on their Christian television programs. (Chick even devoted a cartoon panel showing them doing this in his famous tract, *Why No Revival?*)

The ecumenical movement (a movement seeking to unite and urge cooperation among the world's professing Christians of all denominations) in the fundamentalist subculture meant compromising the Bible and pushing for a worldwide super-church. However, Christian media outlets including radio and television ministries, religious publishing, and even the Christian recording industry relies upon revenue from people of all faiths to remain profitable. American fundamentalism of Chick's variety is very small in comparison to more mainstream moderate evangelicalism. Mainstream outlets like *Christianity Today,* founded by ecumenical evangelist Billy Graham, could not be relied upon to promote Chick's materials. Not only was the war against Satan underway, but now Chick's self-promotion through this new medium reached new highs. Incidentally, Graham has been a frequent subject of criticism in *Battle Cry* for his ecumenical activities (and perhaps payback for his magazine's attacks on *Alberto*.)

Avro Manhattan dished out dirt on the Vatican for early issues of *Battle Cry*.

Beginning with the premier issue, Chick Publications used *Battle Cry* to bolster its claims against the evils of Roman Catholicism by enlisting author Avro Manhattan to write a bimonthly column. His visage with bow tie and stern appearance could be found on the front page of the newspaper during its early years. Manhattan's published works focused upon Roman Catholicism's alleged conspiratorial side, with several titles published through Chick Publications. Most other articles in *Battle Cry* were anonymous, and written by in-house staff.

Chick refrained from ever showing his own picture in his paper, yet the one celebrity whose photograph most frequently appeared in *Battle Cry's* two decade publishing history has been none other than Pope John Paul II. The Pontiff usually had front-page coverage almost bimonthly, and thus probably had more front-page coverage than any Roman Catholic periodical. Never strong on tact, the February 1984 issue depicted U.S. President Abraham Lincoln's photo with the caption "Lincoln's Assassins Honored—U.S. to Open Full Diplomatic Ties with Papacy—Billy Graham helps president (Reagan) decide."

Of course, *Battle Cry* did not limit itself to articles on America's diplomatic compromise with the "Great Whore of Babylon." Other news was covered in its pages such as churches picketing adult bookstores and the Salvation Army losing out on New York City contracts because of the charity's refusal to hire gays and lesbians. Photos of punk rockers were tied to articles on Satan worship, although it was never proved that the pictured punk rocker was a Satanist or not.

Yet Chick's fight with Roman Catholic pressure to ban his books dominated *Battle Cry* during the 1980s. Even the Wisconsin State Legislature accused a pastor from the La Crosse, Wisconsin, area of engaging in a "smear campaign" for using the *Alberto Crusader* series comic and other Chick literature. The state of Wisconsin subsequently drafted legislation

to "condemn all efforts to promote religious intolerance, prejudice, and bigotry." Such a story involving Chick literature was too good to pass up, and served as fodder for *Battle Cry* to show yet again that Chick was engaged in a real war against government censorship. As this war progressed, the reader could infer who was winning. The banner headline for the May-June 1985 issue blared, "Catholics Getting Saved: Vatican Studies 'Problem'."

By the mid-1980s, many of the Protestant leaders wouldn't publicly criticize the Catholic church. Instead, they would condemn Rome's critics. November *Battle Cry* ©1995 Jack T. Chick.

As Chick Publications began to shift *Battle Cry's* focus more on Islam, the battle against Rome also shifted. Roman Catholics complained to other Protestants about the promotion of Chick literature, besides using government influence to ban it. In the wake of the distribution of Chick literature during the February 1985 National Religious Broadcasters convention, *Battle Cry* reported that the Catholic League complained to Dr. Ben Armstrong, the president of NRB. The complaint proposed that contracts for booth space at annual conventions preclude "any exhibitor which used the convention as a forum for defaming any religious denomination." Not only were Christian bookstores facing pressure to ban Chick Publications, but prestigious organizations like the NRB, whose membership included Billy Graham, Jerry Falwell, and Pat Robertson were facing the same pressure to exclude Chick's materials from promotion.

Perhaps an embarrassment to the NRB was a *60 Minutes* segment wherein correspondent Morley Safer questioned booth staffers at the NRB convention who sold Chick Publications materials. An incredulous Safer remarked "I thought that all are children of God" when he saw the staffers openly criticize Roman Catholicism with the Chick Publications book *The Secret History of the Jesuits* on sale in open view!

The further adventures of Alberto Rivera from the *Alberto Crusader* series were also chronicled in *Battle Cry*. Oddly, Rivera was never interviewed for any issues, but his scheduled meetings for crusades and church services with accompanied pictures were shown. Alleged ex-Druid priest John Todd was seldom mentioned in any articles.

Immigration, a touchy issue with political liberals and conservatives, was a matter of concern in the pages of *Battle Cry* because of many immigrants' Roman Catholic affiliation. The only way to prevent a collapse of the United States from free flowing immigration is "intense evangelization of North American Hispanics," the August 1984 *Battle Cry* proclaimed. However, a curiosity occurred north of the American border during an intense evangelization campaign for Canadians. Nine members of a controversial charismatic sect called *The Tony and Susan Alamo Christian Foundation of Alma, Arkansas,* were arrested on "hate literature" charges for passing out a pamphlet entitled *The Pope's Secrets* during Pope John Paul II's visit to Canada in 1984. This tract alleged that the Pope was a child molester during his years as a parish priest in Poland, and that the Vatican is planning a new inquisition. According to Alamo, the information in the pamphlet came from "an ex-Jesuit priest," presumably Alberto Rivera. According to the unnamed source, Polish factory workers used to chase off the suspected pedophile by throwing oily rags at him. If this allegation were true, imagine the shock they felt when he was made pope!

Pastor Tony Alamo with his late wife Susan   Photo – 1980

The controversial Tony Alamo with his
(now deceased) first wife.

Although *The Pope's Secrets* was not a Chick Publication product, the October-November 1984 *Battle Cry* gave the resulting controversy front page attention. The headline blared in bold print "Nine Arrested In Canada Over Gospel Literature" with pictures of the defendants. Tony Alamo, long controversial among cult watching organizations, is interviewed in this issue. Not mentioned in the interview is the fact that Tony Alamo's late wife Susan was dead since 1982 and that members of Alamo's church held 24 hour around-the-clock prayer services for two years to raise her from the dead! Now *there's* a story that deserves a headline! But Chick allies were few and precious enough to avoid negative *Battle Cry* coverage. Tony eventually remarried, so let's assume the prayers were not heeded and his first wife remains dead. Then again, Alamo is renowned for his total recall of the Bible, so he could quickly cite every chapter and verse that provided a biblical basis for polygamy if criticized.

One Alamo detail that **did** receive *Battle Cry* attention was an explanation for his trademark sunglasses. Glaucoma eye disease was mentioned, probably in an effort to disassociate Alamo with another religious leader who always wore shades, the infamous Jim Jones. Both men raised eyebrows by surrounding themselves with large numbers of kooky followers (mostly homeless people and former substance abusers) and micro-managed their congregation's lives with mandatory work and religious activities. When Jones went afoul of the law, his members committed mass suicide. Alamo's people were more fortunate: They were eventually freed from Canadian confinement and *Battle Cry* was probably the only publication to applaud their release.

After nearly two years of publication, the printing dates of *Battle Cry* were adjusted to accommodate an even calendar year beginning with the May-June 1985 issue. This reflects the current manner of publication to this date. The themes of religious freedom and Roman Catholic in-

trigue did not abate during these early years. *Battle Cry* continued to report on the effects of the *Alberto* comics series wherever they were significant or new titles were published.

Beginning in the July-August 1985 issue, Islam finally received attention with the reproduction of the tract *The Story Teller* in this issue. Eventually, articles emerged showing the link between Islam and Roman Catholicism with their mutual admiration for the Virgin Mary. However, despite the new Islamic focus, *Battle Cry* still covered stories of religious bookstores on the receiving end of boycotts and picketing for selling Chick Publications material.

Controversy most often dominated the headlines, but occasionally non-controversial stories highlighted the effectiveness of Chick Publications in revitalizing evangelization campaigns of churches. For instance, the January-February 1986 headline depicted "Church Seeds City with 30,000 Tracts, Reaps Harvest for Years." The story was about a pastor who successfully used Chick tracts in a community in West Virginia. In an unrelated story on the same front page, Pope John Paul II was pictured with the late Princess Diana dressed in black because, the reader is told, that "Vatican protocol requires that visiting royalty wear black (the color of mourning and humiliation) if they are not Roman Catholic."

This photo shows actual members of KISS rock group reading the *Somebody Goofed* tract. It appeared in the December 1983 issue of *Battle Cry*.

Again, the might of the Vatican was shown as the real power behind world events. The ouster of President Ferdinand Marcos in the Philippines was attributed to the influence of Cardinal Jaime Sin. The Vatican's influence did not seem to include the power to seduce teenagers as did rock music, a popular fundamentalist Christian target. *Battle Cry* also highlighted rock music's Satanic effects on the younger population in various articles. Chick Publications promoted the view that Satan's work is multifaceted. The Horned One seduces teenagers through rock-and-roll and entire governments through religious empires.

Battle Cry articles were not always consistent over the years. In the March/April 1987 issue, guest editorialist Larry Roundtree wrote an article entitled "Rise of the Cults and Demise of America" wherein he called for "Biblical Reconstruction." This teaching also goes under the name of "Dominion Theology" which calls for the Christian takeover of all institutions in society in order for the Bible to become the law of the land, the occurrence of which will usher in the return of Jesus Christ. Less than a year later in the January/February 1988 issue, Jack Chick condemned this teaching as "heresies like Dominion and Reconstruction theologies are confusing believers in Christ."

The occult was also a popular topic for articles. Jack Chick in one editorial declared that there would be "One Giant Coven in the Last Days." Each Halloween, *Battle Cry* articles would encourage the purchase of tracts like *The Trick* and *The Poor Little Witch* to distribute during Trick or Treat. Sensational articles linking Satanic Ritual Abuse with murder and Satanism abounded, injecting *Battle Cry* with plenty of excitement and more than a few similarities with the "if it bleeds, it leads" tabloids. Probably the most classic example of such sensationalism was the November/December 1993 issue with a headline that screamed:

"Vampires: Hollywood is Pushing Them...But Are They Real?" The writer was William Schnoebelen A.K.A. Christopher P. Syn, a purported ex-Satanist, ex-Wiccan, ex-Mormon, ex-Mason, and ex-vampire who authored *Lucifer Dethroned* published through Chick Publications. The most interesting feature about this article is that it is accompanied by a large cartoon of a vampire done by Chick. The creature of the night resembled the classic Bram Stoker character of Count Dracula dressed in a daper tuxedo and sporting the trademark fangs. This issue was unusual in that the lead article did not have a photograph. However, vampires probably would not show up on film if a picture were taken.

In the article, Schnoebelen asserted "Many people today, even Christians, balk at the idea of vampires walking the earth. They relegate them to the category of horror films,... As one who is a former 'vampire,' now set free by the power of the Cross of Christ, I have a certain vested interest in this issue which goes beyond the academic... Vampires are NOT undead corpses who turn into mist or become bats. If there are such beings, we have never seen them. That is not to discount their possibility, but only to say that they are beyond our experience."

In May of 1994, Chick Publications decided to change *Battle Cry* from a newspaper to a newsletter. Undoubtedly, this was to save on paper and postage expenses. However, newsletters do not have the visual and propaganda impact that newspapers have. By 1994, the controversy with the *Alberto* comic series had died down, and the picketing of Christian bookstores that sold Chick materials ostensibly subsided. Dr. Walter Martin of the Christian Research Institute had died in 1989, and questions about Chick to Martin's radio program *The Bible Answerman* (which subsequently featured a new host) also seemed to subside. Alberto Rivera himself also died in 1997, and *Battle Cry* gave him a tribute in the July/August 1997 issue. *Battle Cry* did not reduce the number of articles on Roman Catholicism, Satanism, or Islam in its new format. If anything, the fight has intensified over censorship in Canada, but this time around the forum featured headlines over the censorship of *other* Christians and their literature not involving Chick Publications. Offended Roman Catholics continue to try to block Chick materials or prosecute retailers under the hate literature laws of Canada, but they are not alone. Muslims have also entered the arena. *Battle Cry* headlined the article "Muslims Using Hate Laws to Stamp Out Religious Freedom in Canada," showing how censorship actions threatened other Christian publishers as well.

Beginning in March/April 2000, Chick Publications further saved on publishing and shipping costs by shrinking *Battle Cry* newsletters by over an inch, yet the newsletter remained at eight pages an issue. *Battle Cry* has not avoided charged allegations, such as in the September/October issue article proclaiming "Homosexual Teachers 8 Times More Likely to Molest Students." Although the publication is conservative in moral orientation, it does not endorse political parties or the "Religious Right" political agenda.

Battle Cry ©2001 Jack T. Chick.

The most prophetic instances to date from Jack Chick and *Battle Cry* occurred before the terrorist events of September 11, 2001. The July/August 2001 issue showed a Chick cartoon depicting images of terrorism, wars, and the United Nations attempting to attack the world while the hand of God holds them back, thus allowing an elderly woman time to give a child a Chick tract. (Perhaps if more folks had passed out more tracts, 9/11 could have been postponed!) Even more prescient is the September/October 2001 issue printed before the September 11 terror attacks. Its headline read "Muslim Countries Becoming Bolder in Persecuting Christians" while the political cartoon in this issue shows Muslims killing Christians while 'a camera crew is attempting to tape the event. One sword-bearing Muslim yells "Stop that camera! We're doing this for Allah!" The other says "This is our religious freedom! Why are you persecuting us?"

In spite of Islam becoming more prominent in American awareness, *Battle Cry* continues to focus on Roman Catholicism and the Pope's role in positioning himself as the moral leader of the world and mediator of all the world's religious traditions. Since Islam has become a fast growing religion in the United States, that is now of concern to fundamentalist Christians. *Battle Cry* will undoubtedly feature more articles on Islam in upcoming years.

In its 20-year run to the present, *Battle Cry* has been a showcase of exclusive Chick cartoons and candid personal comments. It has also been a treasure trove of articles featuring topics that reflect many concerns to fundamentalist Christians that have been sensational, prophetic, and out of the mainstream. For Chick supporters, *Battle Cry* is a refreshing politically incorrect alternative to Christian ecumenism run amok. *Battle Cry* promotes an unashamed enthusiasm for aggressive evangelizing of fundamentalist principals seldom seen anywhere else. However, this tough approach is not meant to produce enemies, but expose The Enemy of Christ in ways secular newspapers would find shocking. The biblical passage at the bottom of each *Battle Cry* is taken from Galatians 4:16 written by the Apostle Paul: "Am I therefore become your enemy, because I tell you the truth?" Jack Chick would answer that question with a resounding "no!"

Web surfers can view an index of old Battle Cry *issues at Chickcomics.com*

GOING HOME... "This mortal shall have put on immortality." I Cor. 15:54-55

A Visit To
Chick Publications

As a rule, Chick avoids getting photographed or interviewed. Of course, that didn't stop Fox TV's The Reporters from surprising him on the street and shouting questions at him. Nor did it prevent a reporter from Our Sunday Visitor from confronting him in his office under false pretenses. Both interviews were short and hostile. The only press Chick gets from the media tends to be negative. So it's not surprising he avoids it. Several death threats have also made him concerned for his safety. These reasons, along with the fact that I live on the opposite side of the country, led me to believe meeting Chick was out of the question.

Imagine my surprise when Reverend Rich Lee, a friend I had spoken on the phone with many times, invited me to meet both him and another of his friends for a casual visit... the reclusive Jack Chick!

What follows is a recounting of that remarkable encounter. It's based on journal entries I made in the evening of July 17th and 18th, 2001.

I survived the flight to L.A. without causing any disasters. I believe this is because I was careful not to discuss with any passengers the purpose of my trip, for fear that the very mention of the word "Chick tracts" might provoke a religious debate. If there was one thing Flight 144 and The Pilgrimage tracts taught me, it was to never debate religion on an airplane.

At the airport, I waited to meet Rich Lee outside the baggage claim area. Then I realized I had a problem: although I knew what Richard looked like, he had never seen a photo of me. How would he recognize me? I had a cell phone number and tried it. It didn't work, and the public pay phone that I dialed from stole my change. I began to worry. Then I remembered I could always start passing out Chick tracts to make my identity more obvious. Fortunately, Rich happened to walk past me and I collared him. We hit it off with pleasant conversation and lots of laughter. We swung by a McDonalds for a late night Big Mac, then crashed at his apartment.

The following day we drove nearly an hour to get to Chick Publications. The anticipation was eerie. If we did meet up with Chick, how would he react? What would we talk about? I had been warned not to pepper him with tract questions. Rich and I passed the time laughing about Phil Henry (the AM radio prankster) and joked about other things. We had a fairly serious discussion about the power of political correctness. The discussion came back to Chick and how bold he was with his unpopular views.

Author (L) argues the merits of *The Gay Blade* with a stranger outside a Los Angeles area McDonalds.

Chick's bullet resistant glass is scarred but still intact.

We drove over some railroad tracts and Richard mentioned that this was probably the location where Alberto was shot at in Chick's presence. We were getting close! Finally, the big moment arrived. The small and unassuming *Chick Publications* sign came into view. It was a modest building to be sure. If I hadn't seen a photo of it before, I would have easily missed it. As we approached the glass doors, I noticed a couple of small holes in the windows. Were these the infamous gun blasts from the drive-by shooter? There was also a big crack in the same glass. I would later learn that although the front door was regular glass, the side windows (including the one damaged) were bullet resistant and shatter proof.

We entered the main lobby. It was a small, rather dim room with shelves lining the wall and packed with books published by Chick. It was a far cry from the roomy lobby I was expecting. Crowded along the other wall were three racks of tracts (one English, another foreign, and

---

Facing page: Fred Carter's original painting of *Going Home* is just one of the stunning works that line the back office halls of Chick Publications. ©1976 Jack T. Chick.

the third Spanish.) A receptionist greeted us through a small opening in the wall, which was about the size of a confessional window. *(Haw-haw-haw!)* Rich gave his name and asked if Jack was in. The receptionist disappeared and a minute later, an elderly man with a weathered face, white hair and dark eyebrows came though the door. With a giant smile and warm words, he embraced Richard. To my surprise, he did the same to me. Far from being paranoid or rabid, Chick looked and acted like the proverbial grandfather, happy to see his grandchildren. He seemed skinnier than I expected. He hair was thinning, but complete. He seemed both healthy and in good humor.

He led us through a short, dim hallway to his office on the right. As we passed, I noticed large framed images that had been burned into my mind from various Chick works. A smiling Pope John Paul sitting atop his large mound of gold as beggars dropped coins in his cup (from *Smokescreens*.) Jesus holding planet Earth in his hands (reproduced in various tracts.) A long poster-sized portrait of an angel taking the soul of an older lady from her deathbed, as the crying family, dog, and doctor looked on in grief *(Going Home)*. All the color and intricate detail was lost in the darkness. The regular passersby had become acclimated and probably ignored their beauty. At least they were safe.

Original story board art for *The Bull*. The composition and dialog are worked out before the final art is drafted by Chick or Carter.

Chick's office was rather humble. We pushed past the "war room" label on the door and faced an L-shaped desk with a computer on it. There were two bullet-proof windows covered with mirror film. He could see out, but visitors in the front or side parking lots could not see in. A clean but inexpensive sofa sat facing his desk. In the cramped walk space between the desk and sofa was a bulletin board which had tract covers sketched on pieces of paper and tacked to the board. All 25 of the Bible tracts were there in five rows of five. The first six titles were photocopied from the actual tracts. These were the completed tracts, including *Framed. Framed* was familiar to me, because I had stumbled across its secret location on Chick's website months before it was announced. Some of the other titles jumped out at me. *The Monster* and *Man In Black* were eye-grabbers. A sketch of a building covered the very last title. I kept hoping a draft from the air conditioning might peel the sketch back so I could see underneath. I tried not to stare and make it look like I was memorizing future titles.

Across the top of the bulletin board were small icons representing a dozen images from the movie. The last one was numbered 358. Only five or so boxes had yet to be checked off. The painting phase of the movie was nearly complete. This project had been going on for twelve years, and kept Fred Carter from doing any more *Crusader* comics or many tracts. How Chick managed to remain patient and move so steadily toward his distant goal was impressive. He must have underestimated how long it would take when he started. Although the paintings were almost finished, I thought that their estimates that the film would be done this year (in 2001) were overly optimistic. The music and post-production would probably take another year. Chick was in his mid-70s, an age when most men die. However, it was a good bet that he intended to see his project through to the end.

On the wall next to the entrance was a large "white board", the kind one writes on with a magic marker. This had just a few lines written on it about Mormons. Below it was a framed plaque with scripture from Jeremiah 48:10 inscribed on it. Something about cursed are those who don't bloody their swords fighting for Christ. It seemed a very apt motto for the author of *Battle Cry!* Above the white board was a shelf full of videos. Next to the shelf in the corner in the room was a video player.

On Chick's desk was another motivational message, much milder than the Jeremiah passage. A small framed note that read, "Most of the things done on Earth are done by tired people." It was facing the sofa, and I wondered whom he was addressing this message to. Was it himself or the staff person sitting on his sofa and helping him? Or perhaps it was meant as a subtle message to any visitors that Chick may look old and tired, but he was a man that got things done.

Chick pulled out some of the movie artwork that he knew would excite us. There was a beautiful painting by Erik Hollander depicting an angel forcing back a demon from an older lady on a park bench. The demon was great, but the angel wasn't as colorful as Chick wanted him. He also thought the demon looked like he was giving up without much of a fight. Chick indicated that this painting would NOT be used in the movie, and that he wanted Fred Carter to replace it with something else. I held back from suggesting that he let me dispose of this "inferior" work for him. How much money Chick had spent commissioning the large two foot wide painting that he never planned to use wasn't specified, but he did indicate he still planned on paying for it. How many other beautiful paintings had met the same fate was also uncertain. Chick apparently owned everything he commissioned, and unlike many other publishing houses, did not "rent" the images, but kept the original artwork stashed away in the vault, never to be seen for sale to the public or auctioned in such crude places as eBay. (At least, not while Chick is in charge.)

He showed us a few other pieces as well, including a heavenly mansion piece and several images of various Bible characters. But the show stopper was a large image of a man drowning in lava as a dragon breathed fire on him from the side and a pair of sinister eyes watched from the horizon. Chick mused that this image had scared some punk with green hair who he had shown it to. It was exactly the kind of reaction he wanted.

Chick asked Richard for an update on his life. As the two talked, we took the sofa and Chick took the recliner chair in the corner next to the white board. I shot a glance at the two photos facing his desk before I sat down. One was of an elderly woman with big white hair and smooth skin. It was a picture of his (now deceased) first wife. I remember reading that they had met way back in acting school at the Pasadena Playhouse in the 1940s. The other photo was of his recent bride. She was an Asian immigrant who appeared to be in her mid-thirties. It showed her in a beautiful white wedding dress being embraced by a smiling Chick wearing a handsome tux. The two made a charming couple, despite their disparate age.

Chick turned his attention to me and thanked me for the work I had done promoting his Gospel tracts. I was always under the impression that he had never read our website, but had received second hand reports from others. I still think this. Whether he's too busy to read it or too embarrassed (or both) I don't know, but basking in the glory of self-adulation is definitely not Chick's style. Even so, I was concerned he would eventually sign on and discover our site wasn't all pro-Chick. In fairness to him, I took the opportunity to clarify that our goal was not to endorse his tracts, but to encourage the reading and collecting of them. Our site visitors were split between those who were Christian and those who weren't. The upside was that we were introducing his work to a wider audience. He agreed. He said he had to get the message out and keep *pounding it in.* "It's just like that Nazi Goebbels said. If you tell something over and over again, people will believe it. But you have to constantly *emphasize* it!" I knew what he was trying to say, but comparing Nazi propaganda to the use of Gospel tracts was a PR guy's nightmare. A newspaper reporter would jump on such a statement and crucify him. Chick's refusal to see reporters was probably a wise move.

Jesus is Chick's primary subject, but Satan comes in a close second. He appears in the movie, countless tracts, and this July *Battle Cry* cartoon promoting Chick products. ©1996 Jack T. Chick.

David Daniels (L) and Rich Lee (R) sit in Chick's office with his giant map of the world behind them.

A disheveled David Daniels burst in carrying his computer and overstuffed brief case. I had spoken to him on the phone but never met him in person. David is a lanky fellow with brown wavy hair and a scruffy beard. He looks like a perpetual student, and considering his love of Biblical research, he basically is one. He hugged both of us and referred to everyone as "brother." David had been involved in the occult, Mormonism, drugs—all the things Chick continuously preaches against. He had read Chick tracts long ago, and says they were instrumental in saving him. Chick seemed proud of him. David has a Masters of Divinity from a right-of-center Evangelical graduate school (Fuller Theological Seminary), as does Rich. But David is more conservative and fundamentalist than Rich. Like Chick, he believes the King James Bible is the only English translation that's divinely inspired, and all others are satanic corruptions. Having experimented and failed with just about everything else before finding Jesus, David isn't one to mince words or go soft on criticizing his former "cults." That's probably another reason why Chick liked him so much.

Chick worries about the Genocide Act and other censorship threats. Canada's 1980s ban of *Alberto* and *Double-Cross* was recently immortalized in a card set depicting global acts of repression. *Don't Let It Happen Here* ©2003.

There was no awkwardness or uncomfortable silence within the group. Indeed, finding an opening to say something was the tough part, especially once the subject of conspiracies came up. The relentless and clever tactics of the Mormons were discussed. "Those guys are slick!" laughed Chick, "They say everyone who follows them will become gods and have eternal sex. Little wonder they're growing so fast." David complained how they change their dogma whenever anyone exposes their weird beliefs. I volunteered how they did a quick 180 degree reversal regarding blacks once *60 Minutes* confronted them about their claim that blacks were marked by the devil. Richard said that another cult to watch was the Scientologists and that someone should do a tract on them. That "someone" agreed they were terrible, but didn't seem as interested in L. Ron Hubbard's conspiracies as he was in the Vatican's. Once we started talking about Alberto, the war stories poured out. Chick explained how the Catholics had engineered the "Genocide Act" for the UN., making it illegal to try to convert anyone to Christianity. "Once that becomes law, we're going to be shut down," Chick exclaimed, "They sneaked that language in there to stop folks like us."

I asked for details about the proposed law and it sounded like P.C. policing run amok. I knew Chick's interpretation of the law was a worst case scenario, but I couldn't imagine how our courts could ever reconcile such an act with the First Amendment. I made a comment about how the names of these laws are always designed to make it impossible for politicians to vote against them. No one would want to be described as not caring about genocide. Chick laughed in agreement.

Alberto was a recurring topic. Chick was clearly impressed with Alberto's prophetic predictions and how so many of them came true. (The prophecies that failed were merely works in progress.) He said that once the movie was done, he wanted to do another *Crusader* comic about how Alberto was murdered. He talked about how he was going to talk with Alberto's widow soon, and how another discussion with an ex-IRA guy confirmed they had a poison that caused cancer (which was the disease that killed Alberto.) He said that Alberto had told him about an old friend who'd suddenly visited him from Spain. Alberto had let the man prepare a meal for him, but then Alberto became violently ill after eating it and had to go to the emergency room for treatment. When he came back home that evening, the man had disappeared without any explanation or note. Alberto soon developed cancer after the incident.

Although the last thing I wanted was to get into a debate about Alberto, I did volunteer one criticism. I said that if they did another *Alberto* comic, then Chick should be very careful to let David research any allegations for obvious flaws. I pointed out that in Alberto's self-published comic, *The Great Holocaust* (which Chick didn't print), Alberto claimed Christopher Columbus was a Jesuit even though Columbus died before the Jesuits were established. Chick rolled his eyes and agreed, "Alberto thought *everyone* was a Jesuit." It was an amusing moment, realizing that Chick himself recognized how overboard one of his gurus could go.

I went on to say what a pity it was that Chick never did a comic on Rebecca Brown, because all the demon battle claims would have made dynamite comic book images. He didn't express any interest in doing that, but he agreed that Rebecca had been great for business. She had generated lots of revenue for herself and Chick Publications. Chick had used his share to branch out into all the different language tracts. "Once Whitaker saw all the money she was making, they started courting her, and at the same time, the Lord just told me those two books were the limit. We parted friends and I wish her the best." I wanted to ask whatever happened to Elaine, but found myself asking about John Todd instead.

Author (L) and David Daniels (R) hold one of 363 original paintings for the new Chick movie, *The Light of The World*. Chick's desk is in the background to the left.

Chick's eyes widened. "I don't know *what* happened to that guy. He seems to have fallen off the face of the planet. I even heard that someone took him over the Pacific and dropped him out of a helicopter. I haven't a clue!"

Chick wanted to show us some scenes from the movie video. He slid in the tape and we watched the beautiful images flash across the screen. The narrator was capable, but there was no music, something which Chick apologized for over and over again. The folks who were editing the movie knew what they were doing. They had a good grasp of timing and when to pan, zoom in, and fade. I asked Chick if he was also going to publish the artwork in a full color coffee table book. He said he wanted to do just that. What a beautiful book that will be!

He cut the video presentation short once he realized the tape he was playing wasn't the most recent version of the project. Chick is a perfectionist and doesn't like to show anything but the latest and greatest. He asked if we would like to see the plant. I was tempted to answer, "Does the Pope have a big nose?" but I held back the urge. Instead, we jumped to our feet and answered with our body language.

Down the paneled hall we went in single file. We made a right turn (toward the rear of the building) and passed the phone room with the label "Front Lines" on the door. Chick said, "This is where all the phone orders come in. You can see we have the walls padded because everyone who works in here has to be nuts." The lady closest to the door chuckled. It was Karen Rockney, with whom I had spoken with on the phone many times and who had always been helpful. However, she was on the phone, so we silently waved. I looked past her and saw four other tables, only one of which was manned with another operator. There were no windows and I thought it must be a bit claustrophobic, yet the operators always seemed in good cheer whenever I called.

As we continued down the hall, we passed numerous Fred Carter masterpieces. On the left side was an entire assortment of *Crusader* comic covers in large frames (about 2' x 3') lined the walls. There was *The Broken Cross, King of Kings, Primal Man, The Four Horsemen,* and the very first *Alberto.* The detail was stunning, but once again, the lighting was dim. An office on the other side of the hall contained Randall Chapman, the fellow in charge of all the translations. He was on the phone too, so I made a mental note to catch up with him later.

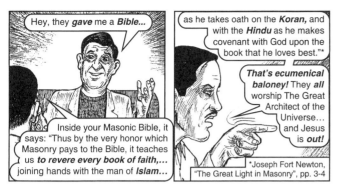

Due to the demands of a constant workload, many unique Chick items are thrown away. Here's an early draft of *Good Ol' Boys* that escaped destruction. Much of the dialog is different from the version that was eventually printed.

Into the warehouse we went. The printing fumes were strong and the atmosphere looked busy. There were about six or eight people running machines or sorting products. The very first one we met was Jim Franklin, a bald black gentleman who looked similar to Scatman Crothers. Chick said that Jim's the fellow who gave him the strength to follow his convictions fighting Rome. "He quoted just the right scripture at just the right time. A wonderful man." We exchanged hellos. My eyes panned down the room. It was a large building, about half the size of a basketball court. The ceilings were high and the number of printing presses was amazing. They all appeared to be running at once. It's appropriate that his logo shows a planet being circled with Chick tracts because he has the printing power to do it! We passed a couple of aisles with college age girls sorting packs of tracts. All the covers were familiar to me, but I couldn't begin to identify all the languages. I saw one wall with various tract covers pasted on it. Some of the covers were quite old and rare, like *Big Spender*. I couldn't help but think, "VANDALS! You destroyed a valuable tract!" But of course, they produced so many, that it must have been like throwing away used tissues at the time.

We walked by a large walk-in vault. "This is were we stash all the original film and older material, just in case we get fire bombed." Chick explained. I noted he said "fire bombed," making it clear that any fire which might occur at Chick Publications would be considered arson as far as Chick was concerned. Though less inclined to believe in conspiracies, I felt myself somewhat relieved to know precautions were being taken. (Against accidents *or* arson.) The door to the vault was as thick as any bank vault. It was the Fort Knox of Chick tracts!

We passed a loading dock and then entered another, larger warehouse that was almost twice the size of the first. This one was devoted solely (no pun intended) to product storage. If you add up all the books, videos, comics, and various tracts in multiple languages, it becomes apparent why they need so much room. Several aisles crisscrossed the large room, each with slots for materials and a bar code for easy computer tracking.

Chick waved at the surroundings and said, "When Rome hit us and two thirds of the bookstores stopped carrying us, we were losing about $23,000 a month. It looked real bad, but the Lord told me it would get better. So when the owner of the property said the next building was available and asked if I wanted it, I said 'yes'." I thought to myself how unwise a business decision that was at the time, given the circumstances, but in retrospect, it was very fortunate. Chick had it all under one roof: talent, production, and storage. The only thing he lacked was a paper mill.

Then another thought dawned on me. Chick's anti-business sense always seemed to boomerang around and produce positive results. Clearly, no MBA would ever attack the Catholic Church, which is the richest organized religion in the world. But Chick did, and despite initial setbacks, it put him on the map. In fact, shutting down many of the retail book outlets forced him into direct mail-order, effectively doubling his profits as he cut out the middleman. It also pushed him onto the Internet ahead of the crowd, allowing him to snatch the "Chick.com" domain name long before the porn folks could.

Then there was the Rebecca Brown story: nobody would touch that story except Chick, and he turned it into a gold mine. The profitable outcomes seemed too many to just chalk up to plain dumb luck. I was tempted to ask exactly how God spoke to him. Was it a voice or a feeling? I resisted asking, afraid I might offend him, but in retrospect I think he would have answered without any problem.

We turned back toward the main office, where Chick introduced two more employees, Steve and Tim Rockney, the clean cut sons of Karen (Chick's secretary) and Ron Rockney (his Treasurer). While returning inside, Tim showed us a machine which he had built to sort tracts into piles of 25, ready for wrapping. It was an ingenious contraption, put together with spit and wire, and was ideal for sorting 25 different tracts into piles instead of the usual homogenous stack. Chick revealed his plan for the Bible series of 25 tracts he was working on. "With this, we'll be able to sell a complete assortment of all 25 tracts in one package, and they'll tie in directly with the movie. It will be a complete mini-Bible in pictures, perfect for getting the word of Jesus out in places of poverty." Once again, Chick avoids contracting out something that he can do under his own roof.

We went back through the building to the parking lot and Chick insisted that he take us out for lunch. Despite the risk of being poisoned by Jesuits by eating at his table, we eagerly agreed. All four of us piled into Chick's Cadillac. I was told to ride shotgun, a term that takes on new meaning when crossing the railroad tracks where Alberto was almost shot. We drove toward Black Angus. Chick seemed a little defensive about owning a nice luxury car. He talked about how old his last Cadillac was and how he eventually had to replace it. This one was quite nice, but I probably wouldn't have thought twice about it unless he had downplayed it so much. David called our attention to the remote microphone above the drivers seat. "In the event of an accident, they automatically call you and confirm you're all right. Otherwise they lock-on to your location and call the paramedics." I joked about the Cadillac company being owned by the Vatican, and that they might be spying on us. We all laughed, and then there was a long pause. Chick asked if I was kidding. I said I was and we laughed again.

The wait at the empty restaurant table was casual and comfortable. There was rarely a silence searching for subjects to discuss. Chick never came on heavy about his religion, or challenged me about my beliefs. Like many of the Christians in his tracts, he's not confrontational, but will tell you exactly what he thinks if you ask him.

The waitress swooped down on us like a vulture. She was the type who gives you her entire life story in a few minutes. She asked if she had seen Chick at the country club, but he said he wasn't a member. She then went on about how she used to work there and that the tips were great. Somewhere in the conversation, Chick asked if she took drama, and she said she did. Being in L.A., it wasn't much of a long shot.

Chick said he couldn't partake in the watermelon lemonade because he was diabetic. It was none of my business, but two red flags immediately shot up, one of which I spoke about. I said doctors urged my mother to see an eye specialist every year for the same problem, because diabetes often robs the elderly of their sight when left unchecked. That could bring his drawing to a screeching halt. Chick acknowledged that he had to be careful. The other note was one to myself. I knew that Chick had published 147 different tracts at that point (combining all the different titles with the same plot, and not counting variations on the same story.) I had planned on sending Chick a giant "Death Cookie" to celebrate his 150th tract when the time came. (It would be a big 12-inch super-cookie with a skull & crossbones design, just like on his famous anti-Vatican tract cover.) This news however, made that idea seem inappropriate.

The Sissy ©1978 Jack T. Chick.

When the food came, Richard gave the blessing. He kept it short, which was good under the circumstances. I have to admit that I was a little worried that the waitress might come and join the prayer like one does in *The Sissy* tract. Anything's possible with Chick.

When lunch was adjourned, a straw drawing of sorts was held, only instead of straws, we pulled a tract out of a stack to leave with the tip. Of the handful that David had to select from, I chose *Sin City*. I figured by leaving that tract, the waitress would know that the three young guys who let the older man buy them dinner weren't looking for a *sugar daddy*. This was, after all, L.A.

We returned to Chick Publications. Rich and David got out of the car to continue their conversations, leaving me alone in the front seat with Chick. We talked about family matters that we had in common. The details were personal and shall remain so. I will say that there was nothing that reflected poorly on him. On the contrary, it made me realize that, unlike most artists, Chick had worked even harder as a husband and father. I left the car with renewed respect, not only for the artist, but also for the man.

As we entered the building again, I figured our audience with Chick was over. Although he had already been more than generous with his time and attention, he invited us back into his office for more conversation. I took the opportunity to ask him about the 25 covers of various Bible tracts that were running across the edge of the ceiling above his desk. The first several were the new series that he was working on; the rest were older Fred Carter tracts, some which were quite rare, including *Terminator*. He said they were essentially replacing all the Bible tracts with new tracts. He said the first series did poorly for him, and he thought the reason was because there was nothing contemporary about them. This new series featured modern characters who relate ancient Biblical events with the present. His theory made sense. Still, I was surprised that the original Bible series didn't do well. One would think Sunday School classes would love them for showing kids what they were studying. The artwork was fantastic and the images hard to forget. I mentioned that they often helped me remember specific stories because the pictures were so vivid.

Then I asked Chick the question that I was dying to ask him and which I had come prepared to pop on him. It was about the third artist, the man David said did a couple of tracts but didn't work out and was let go. Chick's style was so well defined, it wasn't likely to be the cartoony tracts. That meant it had to be an artist who was closer to Fred Carter's style, whose tracts had mistakenly been previously attributed to Fred. I pulled out the only ones that I thought could meet that standard, ones that were good but not as great as others Fred had done in the same time period. Another clue was found by examining tracts that had undergone extensive revisions of artwork, like the original *Doom Town*, *Royal Affair*, and *Earthman*. Chick confirmed that these tracts were indeed by another artist, and his name was Greg Hildebrandt. Could it be *the* Greg Hildebrandt? One of the famous Hildebrandt brothers? Chick didn't confirm the spelling of Greg's last name or say anything about Greg's work outside of Chick Publications. He wasn't the type to care if someone was famous or not.

But Jehosaphat wasn't convinced, so he asked to hear what Micaiah had to say.

Going To The Dogs ©1992 Jack T. Chick.

The tracts that Chick indicated were Greg's were all of the three above titles, plus *The Dreamer* (in which they later replaced Joseph's face with Carter's rendering) and *Empty Tomb* (with many replaced images). Also, *The Outsider*, *Killer Storm*, *The Scoundrel*, *The Sacrifice*, and *Burn Baby Burn* (among others). All of these titles were printed between 1989 and 1991. Does that mean that every title printed at that time was Hildebrandt's? Probably not. Although Carter was beginning work on the movie paintings at that time, he still had his hand in the tracts, and Hildebrandt was probably brought in to ease up the workload. Some tracts in that period, like *Cats* (©1990), look to be Carter's. Chick didn't seem too positive about the timeline, details, or specifics about any of this. It will probably take the expertise of others to determine exactly which tracts were done by which artist, but at least we know that there was a third guy and we know who he was. [At least we *think* we do. Hildebrant's agent firmly denies Greg worked for Chick Publications. See Chapter Six for details.]

Although this was an exciting revelation to me, and I wanted to gather more details, Chick just wasn't very interested in his older tracts and kept changing the subject. He pointed out Edward G. Robinson and Ernest Borgnine in cameos of *Going to the Dogs*, along with a few other (deceased) celebrities inserted elsewhere. David mentioned other celebrities who had inspired various comic characters, but they avoided obvious copies because they didn't want to invite frivolous lawsuits. Chick said, "We've never been sued. There was one guy in prison who tried to sue us once, claiming emotional distress over *Alberto*, but the judge threw it out."

David pointed out a few other interesting appearances within tracts. "Guess who modeled for the cover of *Gay Blade* and the evolution poster? It was Jack!" Chick blushed. The image of him striking the *Gay Blade* pose was hard to imagine. "He's also in the movie a couple of times as the Devil!" David added. I hadn't see those images yet, but I would keep my eyes open for them. Chick seemed to save himself for the really unpopular roles.

Chick received a phone call. It was Fred Carter on the line, telling him his next painting was ready. I couldn't help but wonder what his voice sounded like, and wish that I could speak to him, but what would I say? "Hey Bro, your *Soul Story* tract is RIGHT ON!" No, it was better to watch in silence. David realized who the caller was and mentioned that the black Crusader, Jim Carter, was a mixture of the names Jim Franklin (whom we met earlier) and Fred Carter. Without seeing Fred, it was easy to imagine what he looked like since he modeled for the comic. Then he also mentioned that Fred had had some serious health problems, requiring dialysis, but that he had received a transplant and that it worked. Even so, he wasn't out of the woods yet, I thought, as I remembered that anti-rejection drugs used by recipients often cause complications. Thank goodness he seemed to be an exception.

Chick concluded the call and took us to meet the other staff members. Unfortunately, George Collins, Vice President of Chick Publications, was out for the day. We saw Ron Rockney and Randall Chapmen. Both gentlemen had been with Chick a long time. Rockney was Chick's treasurer. He was a tall man who appeared to be in his mid-50s, wore a suit, and had an easy smile. It was Rockney who went after folks infringing on Chick's copyright, an ever growing list of agitators. Rich, being the lawyer, joked with him about how he had cornered a few notable culprits. Psycho Dave, the web master who threatened to move all his bastardized Chick art to Norway where they don't respect copyright laws, was mentioned. "He thought he devised a plan to avoid honoring our copyright," Rockney quipped, "but then I found out he had temporarily moved his site to his employer's server for storage. I called him up and asked what he thought his boss would think of such a move. He said, 'That's cold!' But it sure resolved the matter." Psycho Dave had written a scathing version of the same story on his site, but in between the lines, it still looked as if Chick Publications was firm but fair.

How To Get Rich ©1978 Jack T. Chick.

Adjacent Rockney's office was Randall's. Randall was in his 40s, wore khaki clothes, and had a smaller and more cluttered office. Randall oversaw translations and had helped me publish the English version of *The Wicked Magistrate* for the Chick Tract Club. I ended up spending time with him while Rich hung out with Dave and Chick left to deal with other matters. Randall knew that I was interested in archiving older tracts and let me go through what he had. He took me out through the press room and into the walk-in vault where all the original art and one-of-a-kind stuff is kept. Chick employees affectionately refer to this vault as "the Cave." It has 3 foot thick walls all around and would probably survive an atomic blast. Randall pulled out from under the art racks a couple of boxes filled with old tracts. We both flipped through them. There were several bootlegs, especially of *This Was Your Life*. He explained that everyone thought Chick wouldn't mind if they copied his material in order to spread the Gospel, but Chick couldn't allow everything to become public domain. "We'll print them up in any language, and we'll do it really cheap. What more do they want?" It was a rhetorical question, so I didn't bother answering that what they wanted was everything for free.

There were several copy-cat tracts, featuring original (and inferior) art and stories by other groups who were imitating Chick's tract formula. Three such tracts were by Chaplain Dann, the man Chick immortalized in *Reverend Wonderful* and *The Letter*. I noted the address and thought I'd try to contact Dann later.

The real heart stopper came as we discovered not one, not two, but *three* unknown tracts. *Breakthrough!*, *Kiss India Goodbye*, and *Operation Somebody Cares*. All of them were circa 1970, and contained forgotten Chick art. "This is incredible!" I blurted out, "Doesn't anyone around here keep complete archives?" Randall sighed. "They're too busy working on new things to worry about any of this stuff. I saved most of this from the trash can."

I shook my head in disbelief. That brought the total number of new titles that Randall had revealed to me to five, since he had unearthed *Psssssssst!* and *Losing The Old Zippp?* a few months earlier. How many forgotten titles had he *not* managed to save from the trash? Randall began work at Chick sometime in the 1980s, so there was plenty of early stuff that probably slipped through his fingers. I was excited and demoralized at the same time.

I didn't want to leave the infamous vault behind, but Randall had work to do. I asked where the photocopy machine was and he led me to another cubicle inside. As I stood before the machine, I turned around and what should I see on the wall? A framed uncut sheet of *Demon's Nightmare* with an all black cast! "Somebody wake me up," I muttered, "I must to be dreaming!" I ran and found Rich. Here was one of Chick's most famous tracts, completely re-drawn with Negro characters, and sitting there on the wall for every employee to see, yet nobody seemed to notice it. We were both stunned.

"Oh that," said David, unfazed, "They tried to form a company just for African-American tracts, sometime in the '80s I think, but the black churches wouldn't buy them. The project eventually floundered. I think they also did *Who Me?* [with a black cast] like that."

Think? You *think*? I had to find out more while I was still at ground zero. Did anyone have copies that I could photocopy? Karen Rockney volunteered, "I believe I have one in here. African-American Gospel version of *Demon's Nightmare*?" She thumbed through a pile of tracts she kept in an address box on her desk. "No, afraid not. The only black version I have is *This Is Your Life*."

WHAT?!? They made a black version of *This Was Your Life* drawn by Chick too? I flipped through it. This was definitely Chick's work, not to be confused with Carter's version for an African audience. I was amazed. If there was also a black version of *Who Me?*, that would mean three previously unknown variations, plus the three unknown new titles, all uncovered in the span of 20 minutes (and practically discovered by accident.) We never did find a copy of the black *Who Me?*, but it's probably there, somewhere, buried beneath a box of forgotten tracts.

Rich Lee (L), author (M), and David Daniels exit Chick Publications after a very busy day.

As the office became deserted, we knew that folks were leaving and so should we. I left Chick Publications with more questions than I had when I arrived. We were both grateful for the generosity and graciousness that Chick had afforded us. Chick turned out to be the exact opposite of the rabid image that his detractors had painted. I was favorably impressed with both him and his staff.

That night, Rich and I took stock of what we had seen. We both agreed that there was no way to be certain that we knew all the various titles that Chick had produced. We probably would never know for sure. But based on what we had seen, it now meant that Chick's latest tract, *The Big Deal*, was actually his 150th new tract. With the giant death cookie idea nixed, we made up a special certificate to commemorate the occasion. It read, "In recognition of *The Big Deal*, Chick Publications' 150th new tract. This certificate is presented on July 18th, 2001, on behalf of readers and collectors of Chick tracts, to the President and employees of Chick Publications, in appreciation of 40 years of service producing over 500,000,000 Gospel tracts in over 100 different languages." (It then listed all 150 tracts.)

The following day, we had it framed and dropped it off at Chick Publications. Chick's car was not there so we figured that he was gone, as is often the case (according to Rich.) But when we entered the building to give it to the receptionist, Chick popped his head in and said, "My goodness, they're back!" He lead us back to his office once more. We told him we weren't going to take up another one of his valuable work days, but wanted to present him with the certificate in recognition of his 150th tract milestone. He was amused that we kept track of all the titles, and said he planned on placing it on his wall at home. I asked if we could take a private (not for publication) photograph of Rich presenting him the award. He apologized but declined. "I've received so many threats and have too many people depending on me these days. I really hate to refuse you, but I hope you understand."

We thanked him again for the visit and returned to the lobby to buy some tracts. While going through the racks, another customer came in to buy tracts as well. The receptionist was gone for some reason and Chick appeared at the window to take the money. Neither man seemed to recognize the other. Chick asked, "Did you hear the President is meeting with the Pope today?" The blue collar, middle-aged stranger's response indicated that he was probably a long time tract reader. "Yep. The end can't be far off now, when the leader of the free world is conferring with the antichrist." Chick shook his head and replied, "Isn't that the truth?!"

That was the last image I had of Chick, him personally selling a handful of his 1/2 billion tracts to a walk-in customer and striking up a conversation on Rome. It seemed a fitting conclusion to a remarkable two days. Chick's success was built on mass production of inexpensive apocalyptic Gospel comics, always keeping his message simple and directed to the common man. He's never afraid to say what was on his mind, even to a stranger who had walked in off the street. If the prophecies that Chick believed were true, then he was destined to fail in his efforts to stop the world from going to hell in a hand basket. Yet despite the doomed nature of his task, he continues his struggle providing endless "ammunition" to fight the spiritual enemy. It's a war he will probably wage to his last breath. Until that fateful day, *praise God and pass the Chick tracts!*

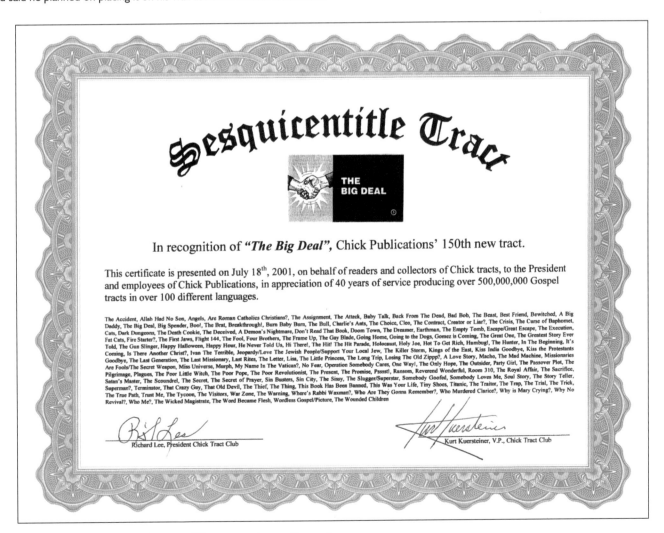

The Big Deal was Chick's 150th tract. We presented a certificate of appreciation to Chick on behalf of tract collectors everywhere.

11

The Broken Cross ©1974 Jack T. Chick.

Additional Collector Resources

THE HUNTER

By J.T.C.

Yes, they're addictive. Yes, they're politically incorrect. Yes, they are "low brow." But let's face it, despite what any of the critics may say, Chick tracts are fun. They're not only enjoyable to read, they're also enjoyable to read *about*. If you are like many others who stumbled across this intriguing artist and thought it would be interesting to collect more of his work, you'll want to know where to find Chick tracts and additional information about them. Here's a list of additional Chick resources. But please remember, being listed here does not mean we endorse the company or their products, or promise that they are still in business when you read this, or that your money won't be lost or stolen in the mail if you order something. (That's why check or money order is always safer.) This section is only provided to aid those who might otherwise have difficulty locating these sources on their own.

The most important source is Chick Publications itself. You can order the tracts and comics over the phone or through the internet using your credit card. The prices are cheap, the delivery is prompt, and they only charge what the postmaster charges them to deliver it. Plus, they'll probably put you on the mailing list for several months and you'll receive free *Battle Cry* newspapers and new samples of tracts. (They'll drop you after several months if you don't order anything else, but it's still quite a deal.)

Chick Publications
P.O. Box 3500
Ontario, CA 91761-1100
www.chick.com
Phone (909) 987-0771

Collectors can join the *Chick Tract Club*, which is completely independent of Chick Publications and open to all individuals regardless of their beliefs. The one-time fee provides a lifetime *and* after-lifetime membership! (Haw-haw-haw!) The club kit includes a fancy certificate, a membership card, a current checklist of tract titles, a club button, a current list of out-of-print titles for sale (supplies and prices subject to change), and an exclusive tract of *The Wicked Magistrate* (an English version that is only available to Club members). Include your email address and get a free subscription to the club's email newsletter as well, *The Chick Stalker*. Send check or money order for $14.95 plus 80 cents postage to *Monsterwax*. (Orders from outside the USA require $3 postage.)

Monsterwax
3202 Enterprise Drive
Tallahassee, FL 32312
members.aol.com/chickclub
email: monsterwax@aol.com

You can also order an audio overview about Chick and his tracts on cassette tape. It's a copy of a special 90 minute call-in talk show all about Chick tracts and their controversies. It's called, *Talking Chick* and features Rev. Richard Lee as a live guest, your author as the host, and a broad cross-section of callers with their various opinions about Chick tracts. Send check or money order for $7.95 plus $1 postage to *Monsterwax* at the same address listed above. (Orders from outside the USA require $3 postage.)

If you want to read another book on Chick tracts, with an emphasis on the technical differences in formats, variations, print codes, etc., you cannot find a more detailed and precise guide than Bob Fowler's book, *The World of Chick*. It's about 275 pages long and is available from the publisher for about $17 plus postage from:

Last Gasp of San Francisco
777 Florida Street
San Francisco, CA 94110
www.lastgasp.com
phone (415) 824-6636

Another book on Chick tracts is by Dan Raeburn. It's called *The Imp #2*. It's more like an extended essay about Chick with a dictionary-concordance in the back. This 63 page book was originally $5 postpaid, but is currently out of print. Dan writes books on his favorite comic artists, and his latest *Imp* release (#4) is on Mexican comics. You may be able to find the earlier *Imp #2* somewhere on the secondary market.

Alberto's ministry is still operating under the leadership of his widow, Nury. They sell several Chick tracts titles, but the out-of-print reissues are not printed at Chick Publications and are technically not Chick tracts. A.I.C.'s service can be slow and unreliable. They request customers send check or money order since they are convinced that Jesuit agents at the post office are opening their mail and stealing the cash. Their website announced in October 2002 that the Jesuits had burgled their mobile home headquarters as well.

A.I.C. (Originally the *Antichrist Information Center*, but now called *Assurance In Christ*)
P.O. Box 690897
Tulsa, OK 74169
www.albertoaic.com

There's also our giant collector website at **www.chickcomics.com**. This site is independent of Chick Publications (www.chick.com), although it links to Chick's site in order to provide on-line viewing of most of the tracts. **Chickcomics.com** has hundreds of pages of chick-related information and references. (It was the original basis of this book.) Especially interesting is the section on Chick's books and tapes. I wanted to include selected excerpts of Chick's rare radio interviews and the *Closet Witches* tapes here, but unfortunately, space restrictions prevented it. Luckily, it's all on-line at chickcomics.com. And best of all, it's completely *free*.

Bibliography

AIC 1998-99 video catalog. Tulsa, Oklahoma: AIC International Ministries, 1998.

Brown, Rebecca. *He Came To Set The Captives Free.* Chino, California: Chick Publications, 1986.

_____. *Prepare For War.* Chino, California: Chick Publications, 1987.

Carter, Fred. Phone interview with author, Tallahassee, Florida, 2002, 30 December.

Chick, Jack. "A Message From Jack Chick." *Battle Cry,* Ontario, California: Chick Publications, August 1999.

_____. "A Message From Jack Chick." *Battle Cry,* Ontario, California: Chick Publications, 2000, July/August.

_____. Biography from company site. http://www.chick.com/information/authors/chick.asp, 2002, 29 Dec.

_____. *Closet Witches* (audio tape) Chino, California: Chick Publications, 1986

_____. *Let's Make A Stand* (audio tape) Chino, California: Chick Publications, 1981

_____. Letter to the *Comics Journal.* Seattle, Washington, Fantagraphics, 1980, March.

_____. Letter to Stan Madrak, reprinted at http://www.demonbuster.com/rebeccab.html, 2000, August 25

_____. Open letter to the customers. Ontario, California: Chick Publications, 1981, 25 March.

_____. Open letter to customers. Ontario, California: Chick Publications, 1984, 27 June.

_____. Open letter to customers. Ontario, California: Chick Publications, 2000, 9 May.

_____. Open letter to customers. Ontario, California: Chick Publications, 2001, 5 March.

_____. Open letter to customers. Ontario, California: Chick Publications, 2002, 15 February.

_____. *Smokescreens* (audio tape) Chino, California: Chick Publications, 1982

_____. *Spellbound?; The Crusaders* Vol. 10. Chino, California: Chick Publications, 1978

_____. Personal meeting at Chick Publications with author and Rev. Rich Lee, Chino, California, 2001, 27 July.

Cicchese, Michael. Living Love or Harboring Hate? *Inland Valley Daily Bulletin.* Ontario, California: 1997, 21 December.

Clowes, Daniel, letter to Bob Fowler; [R50], 1996. *The World of Chick?* San Francisco: Last Gasp, 2001.

Colton, Michael. Cartooning For Christ. *Brill's Content.* New York, New York: 1999, November.

Dann, Chaplain (last name withheld by request). Phone interview with author. 2002, 21 December.

Fisher, Richard G., Paul R. Blizard, M. Kurt Goedelman. "Drugs, Demons & Delusions; The "Amazing" Saga of Rebecca and Elaine." *The Quarterly Journal.* Saint Louis, Missouri: Personal Freedom Outreach, 1989, October.

Fisher, Richard G., M. Kurt Goedelman, *The Curse of Curse Theology; The Return of Rebecca Brown, M.D.* Saint Louis, Missouri: Personal Freedom Outreach, 1996

Fowler, Bob. *The World of Chick?* San Francisco: Last Gasp, 2001.

Hicks, Darryl E., David A. Lewis. *The Todd Phenomenon.* Harrison, Arkansas: New Leaf Press, 1979.

Ito, Robert. "Fear Factor. Fear Factor, Jack Chick is the World's most published author—and one of the strangest." *Los Angeles Magazine* May 2003. Los Angeles. Emmis Publishing LP. May, 2003.

Lee, Richard. Phone conversation with the author. 2002, 9 June.

Metz, Gary. *The Alberto Story.* Chicago: Jesus People USA Productions, 1981.

_____. "Conspiracy or Conspirator? The John Todd Story." *Cornerstone Magazine* Vol. 8 #48. Chicago: Jesus People USA, 1979.

_____. Email to author. 2003, 23 July.

Netizen website, 2002, 7 June. http://www.newnetizen.com/globalelite/bloodlines/collinsbloodline.htm

Plowman, Edward. "The Legend(s) of John Todd." *Christianity Today.* Carol Stream, Illinois. February, 1979.

Raeburn, Daniel K. "The Holy War of Jack Thomas Chick." *The Imp #2.* Chicago: Self published, 1998.

Tiansay, Eric. "Charismatics Have Highest Levels of 'Biblical Accuracy'." *Charisma Magazine.* 2001, 26 June. The survey was conducted by the Barma Research Group. It stated "a majority of Mormons and Assemblies of God attendees firmly believe Satan is real, while only 20 percent of Catholics, Episcopalians, and Methodists hold this view." The researchers went on to summarize, "Overall, charismatics have lower levels of education but higher levels of biblical accuracy, while individuals attending mainline churches are generally better educated but are more likely to have theological perspectives that conflict with the Bible."

Yronwode, Cat. "Blackhawks for Christ." *The Comics Journal,* Seattle, Washington. Fantagraphics, 1979, October.